LATIN AMERICAN EXTRACTIVISM

LATIN AMERICAN EXTRACTIVISM

Dependency, Resource Nationalism, and Resistance in Broad Perspective

Edited by
Steve Ellner

ROWMAN & LITTLEFIELD
Lanham • Boulder • New York • London

Published by Rowman & Littlefield
An imprint of The Rowman & Littlefield Publishing Group, Inc.
4501 Forbes Boulevard, Suite 200, Lanham, Maryland 20706
www.rowman.com

6 Tinworth Street, London SE11 5AL, United Kingdom

British Library Cataloguing in Publication Information Available

Library of Congress Control Number: 2020946242

ISBN 978-1-5381-4155-7 (cloth)
ISBN 978-1-5381-4156-4 (pbk.)
ISBN 978-1-5381-4157-1 (electronic)

Contents

Foreword

THE BRAZILIAN PRESIDENT LULA DA SILVA, who belonged to the so-called Pink Tide of progressive governments in twenty-first-century Latin America, once asked fellow Pink Tide president Pepe Mujica of Uruguay how he got arrested under the military regime that ruled his country in the 1970s and 1980s. Mujica, a former guerrilla and member of the Movimiento de Liberación Nacional Tupamaros, had been wounded by six bullets in different encounters, captured several times, and served thirteen years in prison under extremely harsh conditions. "Why were they able to trap me?" he answered: "Because they ran faster than I did." Mujica, like Nelson Mandela, was condemned as a terrorist but became a hero in his country and internationally acclaimed.

The Pink Tide governments represented a response to the neoliberal model that was born not with the election of Margaret Thatcher in 1979 but with the coup against Salvador Allende in 1973. General Augusto Pinochet assembled a team of economists trained at the University of Chicago under Milton Friedman. The neoliberal experiment's first laboratory was Chile, which was converted into the most unequal country in Latin America. In November 2019, following the protests and disturbances in Chile, Argentine president Alberto Fernández was asked why the neoliberal economy under Pinochet was called the "Chilean miracle." He answered, "The miracle is that the Chilean people did not react."

Now, thirty years after Pinochet's exit from power, the big issue is to what extent the Pink Tide governments broke with the neoliberal past. The discussion centers in large part on government policies in extractive industries. Some writers at both ends of the political spectrum minimize the difference between Pink Tide and conservative governments in strategies toward extractivism. While the contributions to this book recognize that Pink Tide governments did not succeed in eliminating dependence on extractive-sector exports, they do underline important differences.

The Pink Tide benefited from three factors that emerged after the decline of neoliberalism at the turn of the century: the repudiation of the neoliberal model, particularly by excluded sectors of the population; the commodities boom, in which international prices for oil, metals, soybeans, and other extractivist exports sharply increased; and the rise of charismatic leaders promoting ambitious social policies. Although these developments did not alter the economic structure, they did succeed in lifting millions of people out of poverty. The frustration of George Bush at the Mar del Plata Summit of the Americas in 2005, when the Free Trade Area of the Americas was buried, was perhaps the clearest demonstration of the continent's modest transformation. Nevertheless, it has to be recognized, as the contributors to this book do, that governments throughout the region and across the political spectrum were responsible for environmental destruction and violation of indigenous territorial rights while failing to reduce dependence on extractive-sector exports.

At the same time, the challenge of overcoming the extractivist dilemma by reducing dependence on commodities exports cannot be overestimated. The Pink Tide movements won presidential elections and thus gained control of the government but not of power. Neoliberalism penetrated all social structures. In addition, financialization (as discussed in the chapter by Macías Vásquez and García Arias) increasingly took hold of the world economy and was especially relevant to the extractive sectors. These were the obstacles confronted by Hugo Chávez, Lula da Silva and Dilma Rousseff, Rafael Correa, Evo Morales, Néstor Kirchner and Cristina Fernández, Mel Zelaya, Fernando Lugo, and Michelle Bachelet alike, whatever the differences among their countries in history and in the specifics of their current situations. To a greater or lesser extent these leaders fell into the trap created by the commodities boom of the early years of the twenty-first century. The elevated prices of their extractive exports influenced them to prioritize consumer needs across social classes rather than economic development, which in the long run would have paid better dividends from both political and economic standpoints.

The questions that emerge are, first, could those governments have achieved the redistribution of wealth without using the resources derived from extractivism? Second, are such goals as the full recognition of the rights of the indigenous, complete respect for the environment, and economic development compatible in the twenty-first century? Third, does either the national bourgeoisie or a strong state have the capacity and the will to replace international capital and harness resource nationalism to its fullest extent? And, finally, given the fact that privatization, deregulation, and the opening to global markets have sapped the state of its fiscal capacity, are alternative economic policies feasible?

Many members of the popular sectors whose lives improved considerably under the Pink Tide eventually began to distance themselves from those governments, and some of them ended up voting against their own interests. According to the Permanent Household Survey of Argentina, in the first semester of 2019 the government of Mauricio Macri increased the number of poor in the country by 10 percent (to a total of 16 million), while the number of people in extreme poverty in Brazil under the government of Jair Bolsonaro reached its highest level since 2012 (13.5 million). These statistics provide just a glimpse of the contrasts between Pink Tide countries and those governed by the right, which are so stark that, despite certain overlaps with regard to extractivist strategies, these governments cannot be lumped together.

Advancing democracy requires time to balance the different segments of the population and instill a new consciousness. It largely depends on regional unity that will put the brakes on what Boaventura de Sousa Santos calls "financial fascism" and on reactionary governments with the capacity to gain the support of societal majorities. At the same time, it calls for going beyond the neoliberal legacy of the pursuit of increased consumption. Neoliberalism promises the fulfillment of any dream as long as it is converted into merchandise and this leads to the loss of identity, the weakening of the sense of community, increasing inequalities, the loss of rights, and the poisoning of the earth, water, and air.

This book attempts to determine the degree to which extractivism assumed different forms according to the type of government in each country. It is quite possible that the fingerprints that these governments have left are linked with their countries' different responses to the novel coronavirus and their results. These differences as well as those with regard to extractivism among governments and the political parties that inhabit them need to be carefully examined. We need to evaluate all the questions formulated in this book and then ask, as Pepe Mujica did: Are we running faster than those who are pursuing us?

Juan Carlos Monedero
Universidad Complutense de Madrid

Introduction

Rethinking Latin American Extractivism

Steve Ellner

TWO SALIENT FEATURES OF TWENTY-FIRST-CENTURY Latin America are profoundly contradictory. On the one hand, the penetration by foreign capital of local economies has intensified. In the process, the national bourgeoisie in the region has lost the limited independence vis-à-vis foreign capital it previously had. In addition, multinationals have gained control of numerous industries as a result of massive privatization during the neoliberal period of the 1990s, with minimum participation of local capital in the case of countries such as Venezuela, Peru, and Bolivia. Finally, the greater weight of the extractive sector of Latin American economies in comparison with the previous import-substitution stage has heightened dependence on foreign capital and reduced opportunities for local capital.[1] This has occurred because the extractive industries that attract foreign capital tend to be technologically sophisticated and capital-intensive, the more so because of innovations in recent years in such areas as hydraulic fracking, surface mining, and genetically modified agriculture.

On the other hand, the Latin American progressive governments known as the Pink Tide, beginning with Hugo Chávez's election in 1998, implemented policies that improved the terms imposed on foreign capital. Their discourse was characteristic of resource nationalism, based on the idea dating back to Simón Bolívar that the riches in the soil and subsoil belong to the nation and should mainly benefit its people. With the rise of the Pink Tide, Latin America achieved a degree of unity unmatched since independence, a feat that translated into steps toward continental integration aimed at lessening dependence on global capital. Furthermore, the "multipolar world" concept popularized by Chávez became the guiding principle of the foreign policy of Pink Tide governments and was in some cases accepted by conservative ones. The term, in effect, was a euphemism for opposition to U.S. domination, if not anti-imperialism (Cannon, 2009: 178, 190).

Another dimension that challenged the hegemony of multinational capital was the resistance of indigenous and other rural communities to extractivist projects in both Pink Tide and other countries. The chapters in this book by Castriela Hernández Reyes (on Colombia), Amalia Leguizamón (Argentina) and Teresa Velásquez (on Ecuador) focus on the resistance of indigenous groups, women, and Afro-descendants to multinationals in the extractive sector and the neoliberal policies that favored their interests.

This book centers on the dualities with regard to the strengths and vulnerabilities of twenty-first-century Latin American governments and the positive and negative features of their policies with regard to the extractive sector. On the negative side, large-scale extractivist complexes owned and run by multinationals have had a devastating environmental impact throughout the region. In addition, they have encroached on indigenous land and infringed on indigenous rights that are in some cases enshrined in the constitution (the latest example being Brazil under Jair Bolsonaro). On the positive side, the resource nationalism embraced by Pink Tide governments has generated revenue that was used for social programs to alleviate the lot of the poor and in some cases provided them with a sense of empowerment.

This balanced view on extractive industries runs counter to the pessimism of many writers, mainly on the left side of the political spectrum, who focus on the deleterious effects of what they call "neo-extractivism" or twenty-first-century extractivism. Their thesis is that the expansion of the extractivist sector in Latin America over the past several decades has had a highly negative impact on democracy, economic development, the environment, and the indigenous population and has eclipsed any possible positive aspects of the policies of Pink Tide governments. These writers often minimize or deny the importance of differences between Pink Tide governments and conservative ones on grounds that all of them have submitted themselves to the dictates and logic of global capital. Thus while the Pink Tide social programs are generally considered an outstanding achievement, some of these writers argue that they serve to justify and divert attention from neo-extractivism's detrimental effects. Similarly, while some analysts consider China's emergence as an economic powerhouse beneficial for Latin America in that economic ties have been diversified in the framework of "South-South relations," the neo-extractivism writers view this development as replicating satellite/metropolis relationships.

The argument of neo-extractivism writers that twenty-first-century governments failed to achieve industrial and agricultural diversification and lessen the hold of global capital is well taken, partly because the Pink Tide prioritized social goals over economic ones. Indeed, some Pink Tide leaders recognize the seriousness of this shortcoming (García Linera, 2016; Anderson, 2017). Many neo-extractivism writers, however, overstate their thesis in two basic respects. In the first place, they tend to view all the major problems and challenges facing twenty-first-century governments through the lenses of extractivism and global capitalism and downplay the role of reforms that do not directly confront global capital.[2] In the second place, many of them fail to grasp the significance of the dissimilarities among Latin American governments of distinct political orientations. Some writers explicitly deny that Pink Tide governments broke with neoliberalism or that they qualify as leftist, viewing, for instance, the protests in Ecuador against neoliberal president Lenín Moreno as a continuation of the protests against Pink Tide president Rafael Correa (Zibechi, 2019; Acosta, 2020). Others recognize that differences exist (Gudynas, 2012: 11) but tend to minimize their importance and argue that aspects of Pink Tide policies border on neoliberalism. Scholars in this camp point to "the evolution of progressive governments to models of more traditional domination" and their acceptance of the international division of labor (Svampa and Viale, 2014: 360–361, 264; Svampa, 2012: 55).

Nevertheless, on the various issues that concern these writers, from environmental destruction to indigenous rights, different Latin American governments had different records. This was particularly the case with regard to legislation and policies toward foreign capital, which varied significantly from country to country. Differences existed in other areas as well, including environmental policies. Failing to recognize these differences is similar to the advocates of the "Green New Deal" in the United States ignoring or downplaying the differences in position among Democratic Party centrists, the traditional wing of the Republican Party, and climate change deniers like Donald Trump.

The chapters in this book present a broad picture of global capitalism and extractivism in twenty-first-century Latin America.[3] Contributors discuss the severely damaging impact of extractivism and particularly of megaprojects in countries with both Pink Tide and conservative governments. They take note, however, of the differences among governments, particularly with regard to the terms established for foreign investment. This introductory chapter summarizes the main concerns of the neo-extractivism thesis and then attempts to provide a broader analysis of extractivism by examining the implications of, and contextualizing the policies toward, global capital and extractivist industries.

The Neo-Extractivism Thesis and Its Shortcomings

An examination of the neo-extractivism thesis needs to place it in a broad historical context. The stock market crash of 2008 opened the way for the worldwide Great Recession, which undermined job security for workers and much of the middle class and intensified the precarization of work. In the context of these developments, an economistic perspective would have predicted leftist inroads, but instead a rightist trend swept the world. Partly as a result of the slowdown of the Chinese economy, the commodities boom of the first decade of the century gave way to a decline in commodity prices that adversely affected economies throughout Latin America. With a weaker economy, most Pink Tide governments and movements ended up reaching agreements with and making concessions to business interests, which strengthened the hand of extractivist capital (Webber, 2015a: 165). In Brazil, upon her reelection as president in 2014 Dilma Rousseff appointed as finance minister a top executive of the nation's second-largest private bank finance minister; in Bolivia, Evo Morales, reelected in 2009, reached an agreement with the main business organization of the prosperous state of Santa Cruz at the expense of the interests of popular sectors; and in Ecuador (in 2017), Argentina (in 2019), and Uruguay (in 2019) Pink Tide parties selected moderates as presidential candidates. These developments convinced neo-extractivism writers that Pink Tide governments had largely abandoned their commitments to overcoming dependency and tackling environmental and ethnic challenges.

For the neo-extractivism writers, the plans to build a highway through the Territorio Indígena Parque Nacional Isiboro Sécure (Isiboro Sécure Indigenous Territory and National Park—TIPNIS) in Bolivia in 2012 and initiate oil drilling in the Yasuní National Park in Ecuador in 2013, both of which led to indigenous protests and repression, were defining events. In both cases, the decisions to proceed with the projects were designed to offset declining international prices for primary commodities (in the case of the TIPNIS by facilitating exports), but at the same time they threatened to violate constitutional rights and produce severe environmental damage. For these writers, neo-extractivism did not differ in fundamental ways from twentieth-century extractivism but did have "new dimensions" (Svampa, 2019: 12; Gudynas, 2016: 722–724; Lander, 2014: 5–6). Its defining characteristics included extensive economic ties with China, the larger scale of extractivist projects, the existence of an ecological crisis, a greater role for the state, and (in the case of Pink Tide countries) ambitious social programs financed by the revenue derived from extractivism.

In their emphasis on common denominators in the face of global imperatives, neo-extractivism writers maintain that a consensus existed among Latin American governments on the benefits of extractivism as a generator of revenue and foreign exchange and on the lack of feasible alternatives. Maristella Svampa labels this belief the "commodities consensus." Adherence by some Latin American political leaders to the notion that extractivism was inevitable as a matter of "destiny" (Svampa, 2019: 13) and was "irrevocable or irresistible" (Svampa, 2015: 67) recalls earlier thinking regarding globalization and neoliberalism embodied in the Washington Consensus and referred to as "there is no alternative" (Svampa, 2019: 13–14). In line with their adherence to this paradigm, Latin American governments, even progressive ones, allegedly displayed a degree of intolerance toward alternative thinking as they "sought to deny or conceal discussions regarding the implications (impacts, consequences, damage) of the extractive export model" (Svampa, 2019: 1). Furthermore, according to these writers, any positive benefits stemming from the nationalization of extractivist industries and social and developmental programs financed by extractivism were offset by the fact that they were used to divert attention from extractivism's harmful effects (Svampa, 2012: 53–54; Petras and Veltmeyer, 2014: 35–36; López and Vértiz, 2015: 162–165; Webber, 2017: 287–288).

Pink Tide governments, in accordance with their commitment to welfare-statism, justified large-scale extractivist projects on grounds that by increasing public revenue they strengthened the state (Svampa, 2019: 15). Svampa argues that President Cristina Fernández's partial nationalization of the oil company Yacimientos Petrolíferos Fiscales (YPF) reinforced her pledge to "promote the transformation from the 'commodity' paradigm to that of 'strategic resources,' based on state control of hydrocarbons," but in the process it served to "suppress . . . debate on the environmental and social risks of fracking" in Patagonia (Svampa, 2014: 324, 2019: 23). Some writers on the left reduced the Pink Tide governments' justification of extractivism to empty rhetoric. Jeppe Krommes-Ravnsmet (2019: 77–78), for instance, argues that Evo Morales "covered up" his environmentally damaging policies in the extractivist sector "with a revolutionary discourse" at the same time that his government "intensified class collaboration."

The neo-extractivism thesis has both strengths and weaknesses. On the positive side, neo-extractivism writers explore the concrete and harmful ways in which globalization in Latin America has rolled back the breakthroughs of the import-substitution stage. Neo-extractivism writers and others present abundant empirical evidence that extractivism is conducive to violation of indigenous rights, ecological devastation, violence (Toledo et al., 2015: 144–145), consumerism (Svampa and Viale, 2014: 362), corruption (Gudynas, 2018: 43–70; Farthing and Fabricant, 2018: 10–11), violation of the spirit of democracy (Lander, 2014: 11), and gender inequality-patriarchal relationships (for a discussion of the latter, see the chapter in this volume by Amalia Leguizamón). In doing so, they demonstrate the negative impact of global capital, technological innovations, and heightened demand for primary commodities on both leftist and non-leftist Latin American nations. Some of the neo-extractivism writers recognize the harsher repression of the environmental and indigenous movements by right-wing governments in comparison with Pink Tide ones.

The problem is when neo-extractivism scholars compare the "commodities consensus" to the Washington Consensus, and in the process imply that the former is an all-encompassing economic doctrine just like the latter (Svampa, 2019: 12–16). Viewing neo-extractivism as a stage based on a production model whose effects are overriding tends to obscure the factors that differentiate governments of distinct ideological orientations. This viewpoint would be justified if the rhetoric of Pink Tide governments regarding extractivism were empty (as some claim) and if the hostility of powerful economic and political actors were directed only at individual Pink Tide leaders in power (as some also claim) and they were not responsible for the extreme difficulties their nations face (Ellner, 2019: 160–161). The challenges posed by these adversaries, however, limited the options for Pink Tide leaders and forced them to adopt populist strategies to reinforce popular support in the face of destabilizing campaigns. For this reason, the decisions to initiate extractivist projects have to be contextualized, albeit not necessarily justified.

Svampa (2019: 1) overstates her case when she claims that, beyond their ideological differences, "all the Latin American governments . . . sought to deny or conceal discussions regarding the implications (impacts, consequences, damage) of the extractive export model." In fact, a consensus at the level of either strategy or policy formulation regarding developmental models and the need to overcome dependency hardly existed. Paz and Ramírez-Cendrero, for instance, end their chapter in this volume by pointing out that policies favoring economic development under the Evo Morales government (as embodied in the National Development Plan of 2006) such as prioritization of production for Bolivia's internal market were reversed by his right-wing successor Jeanine Añez to the benefit of agribusiness interests.

Neo-extractivism writers also tend to exaggerate the homogeneity of twenty-first-century Latin American politics. Important policies related to extractivism differentiate not only Pink Tide governments from conservative ones but also governments within both categories. Indeed, with the emergence of far-right regimes in Argentina (2015), Colombia (2018), Chile (2018), Brazil (2019), and Bolivia (2019), these differences have become especially pronounced. Moreover, these writers generally bypass or play down the extractivism-related issue that most differentiates governments, namely the conditions imposed on foreign investment, such as taxes and worker rights, and the assertion of greater state control (see, for instance, Svampa and Viale, 2014: 190–195).

The omission regarding policy toward big capital both foreign and domestic is particularly serious considering the fact that Pink Tide adversaries centered their critique of those governments on their excessive requirements and their alleged hostility toward private investment (to be discussed in detail in the following section). In Argentina, for instance, the sharp contrast in policies toward the agribusiness export sector between Pink Tide governments and the conservative one of Mauricio Macri (2015–2019) demonstrates that a consensus on extractivism hardly existed. As Leguizamón notes, diverse legislation favoring agribusiness promoted by the Macri administration favored the interests of large agribusinesses, the same interests that vigorously opposed the tax increases on their exports implemented by the progressive governments that came before and after Macri.

The study of extractivism in the twenty-first century thus needs to place the confrontation between powerful political and corporate actors, on the one hand, and Pink Tide governments, on the other, at the center of its analysis. Again, context is essential.

Finally, one may question the validity of a basic assumption of neo-extractivism writers, namely that the utilization of extractivist revenue to promote economic development is an inherently flawed strategy. The commodities consensus thesis claims that Pink Tide governments failed to address developmental objectives and that "no country in the South has achieved development appealing to the exploitation of mineral resources" (Svampa and Viale, 2014: 194–195; Svampa, 2019: 14–15). In fact, Pink Tide governments prioritized social objectives over economic development not because they necessarily underestimated the importance of the latter, but because of the political imperative of securing active popular support in a hostile political environment (Ellner, 2020: 48–50). Macías Vásquez and García-Arias end their chapter in this volume by attempting to refute this fundamental premise of neo-extractivism writers: "In our opinion, what is problematic is not attempting to overcome an extractivist model through extractivism itself, as postdevelopment writers claim . . ., but trying to achieve structural change in the economy without decisively confronting the influence of" global financial capital.

Extractivism and Resource Nationalism

At the heart of the differences between conservative and Pink Tide governments is the resource nationalism embraced by the latter. The justification for resource nationalism stands in sharp contrast with the critique of Pink Tide governments for being rentier states—states whose revenue comes mostly from rent (from mines, fertile soil, etc.) rather than labor productivity. While the champions of resource nationalism consider the stringent conditions for foreign capital tantamount to "corrective justice" and beneficial for the nation, the rentier analysis employed by neo-extractivism writers focuses on the negative side, namely the dependence on global capital engendered by extractivism.

The resource nationalist policies promoted by Pink Tide governments contrast with those of more conservative ones. Most important, the overriding importance of resource nationalism should not be clouded by the thesis that there was consensus about extractivism's potential to favor national interests. Twenty-first-century Latin Americans may have agreed about the benefits of extractive industry, but there was certainly no consensus regarding how to maximize the revenue derived from extractivism and how to put it to good use.

This section will attempt to demonstrate that resource nationalism went far beyond empty slogans, unlike what some claim, as it was at the center of the confrontations between Pink Tide governments and their political adversaries and with multinational corporations. Intense conflict sometimes leading to attempts at regime change took place not only over the expropriation of extractivist industries and the founding of state companies (in Venezuela, Bolivia, and Argentina) but also over other instances of state intervention in the economy. This occurred both in the case of radical Pink Tide governments and in the case of moderate ones like Brazil's.

Furthermore, many analysts including neo-extractivism writers attribute windfall state revenue in the early twenty-first century to the international commodities boom (which increased both prices and production), without recognizing that resource nationalism also greatly contributed to increased state income (Svampa and Viale, 2014: 194–195). Hydrocarbon legislation in Pink Tide countries, for instance, played a major role in filling state coffers. The additional 32 percent royalty and tax levied on multinational hydrocarbon corporations in Bolivia in May 2006 and even more so (according to the economist Mark Weisbrot) the state's heightened participation in the industry produced a nearly sevenfold increase in revenue derived from that sector (Weisbrot, 2015: 193; Otis, 2014: A-9; see also the chapters by Macías Vásquez and García-Arias and Paz and Ramírez-Cendrero in this volume). In Venezuela, the hydrocarbons law passed in November 2001 had a similar impact, nearly doubling the royalty on oil to 30 percent, far above that of the rest of the region. It also established majority state ownership of mixed companies in the oil sector, a percentage that was increased to 60 percent in 2007.

These terms contrasted with the lenient requirements for multinational oil companies established by conservative governments, such as that of Colombia, which the *Wall Street Journal* lauded for their having "managed their finances prudently" in contrast to Venezuela, Brazil, and Argentina

(Luhnow, 2019: A-2). The international corporate community praised the rightist Colombian president Iván Duque for encouraging offshore exploration and being receptive to fracking (thus reversing his previous opposition to the practice) and promising to "cut corporate tax rates, slash red tape, clamp down on tax evasion and reduce legal uncertainty for foreign investors looking to enter the country's oil and mining sectors." By contrast, Duque's main electoral rival, the left-leaning Gustavo Petro, promised a "rapid move away from hydrocarbons production" in favor of "more environmentally friendly, sustainable policies" (Long, 2018: 6). Teresa Velásquez in her chapter in this volume points to a similar contrast between conservative and Pink Tide governments in the case of Ecuador. Conservative president Lenín Moreno, for instance, rolled back mining tax reforms of the Correa government, including a 70 percent windfall tax on profits in that sector, which he eliminated.

An examination of the historical context of resource nationalism in Latin America sheds light on the importance of its reemergence in the twenty-first century following the period of neoliberal ascendancy. State control of strategic sectors of the economy was originally a leftist banner that hailed the nationalization of oil in Mexico in 1938 and of tin in Bolivia in 1952 and the creation of YPF in Argentina in 1922. By the 1960s, support for the proposition went far beyond the left, as centrist parties, multinational companies, and Washington no longer claimed that it smacked of socialism. This near-consensus, however, lasted until the neoliberal period of the 1990s and subsequent years, when the nationalization of strategic industries and interventionism in general generated sharp conflict that destabilized governments in Venezuela, Bolivia, and Argentina.

The nationalization and "renationalization" of oil in Venezuela exemplified the change in the political environment. Multinational oil companies and Washington put up no resistance to the industry's nationalization in 1976 and actually cooperated closely with the state oil company Petroleos de Venezuela S.A. in facilitating the transition (Hellinger, 2006–2007: 57). This concurrence and collaboration contrasted with the reaction of powerful proestablishment actors to the policies of Hugo Chávez, whose November 2001 law reasserting state control of the oil industry led to an abortive coup five months later. Exxon and ConocoPhillips reacted to Chávez's 2007 decision to increase state ownership of mixed companies in the oil sector to 60 percent by pulling out of the country and taking their case to international court. At the same time Exxon-Mobile's Rex Tillerson called for the seizure of Venezuelan assets in the United States.

The two prongs of resource nationalism—the expropriation of extractivist sectors and maximization of the benefits derived from them—were at the center of the intense conflict that pitted the nonradical Pink Tide governments of Argentina and Brazil against multinational oil interests and their supporters. State control of the oil industry was an historical banner dating back to the creation of YPF in 1922 and Petrobras in 1953 under the slogan "The Oil Is Ours." Presidents Cristina Fernández de Kirchner and Luiz Inácio Lula da Silva reversed the reduction of the state's role in the industry that had occurred under neoliberal governments in the 1990s.

Powerful international actors reacted aggressively to Fernández's decision to assert state majority ownership of YPF in 2012. The former owner, the Spanish company Repsol, took the Argentine government to international court and pressured the Spanish prime minister Mariano Rajoy to respond with economic reprisals and to petition the European Union to impose sanctions on Argentine exports (Burgueño, 2015: 226). At the same time the *Wall Street Journal* called for the expulsion of Argentina from the G20 (as did the *Washington Post*), noting in an editorial that "when its president wants to behave like a real head of state and not a thug, the country can be invited back into the club of serious nations" (*Wall Street Journal*, 2012: A-16). Fernández's supporters treated the takeover as a national holiday as posters and graffiti heralded the move as "taking back what's ours" (Schmall, 2012: 95).

In Brazil, neoliberal governments of the 1990s named mining and steel company executives to Petrobras's board of directors, sold 16 percent of its stock, and opened the oil industry to competition from multinationals, which objected to the nation's environmental legislation. Lula (in his second term) and his successor Dilma Rousseff reversed this "flexibilization" trend as part of a neodevelopmentalist strategy (Schutte, 2013: 58–61). For doing so they were heavily criticized by the international corporate community which considered their subsidized prices for gasoline and other oil derivatives tantamount to the politicization of the industry and commended Michel Temer (who succeeded Rousseff after her impeachment) for revising those policies (Moffett, 2007: A-1; Oddone, 2016: 2). The *Wall Street Journal* editor Mary Anastasia O'Grady heaped special praise on the Brazilian president Jair Bolsonaro, whose election in 2018 represented "a national awakening in which socialism—the alternative to a Bolsonaro presidency—has been put on trial." She added that "Bolsonaro offers much of what those who want to modernize Brazil could only dream of during the PT [Workers' Party] reign" (O'Grady, 2018: A-21). O'Grady applauded the Bolsonaro government's commitment to sell off Petrobras' noncore assets and reduce its debt and its deregulation, some privatization, and creation of an independent central bank.

Divergent Positions on Latin American Integration and Chinese Investment

Initiatives for Latin American integration also reflected fundamental differences between Pink Tide governments, which employed nationalistic rhetoric and championed resource nationalism, and conservative ones. At the heart of the divide was the Pink Tide's rejection of pan-Americanism, which was a continuation of a century-long debate among Latin Americans as to whether unity should be hemisphere-wide or continent-wide. Chávez voiced the latter position at the Summit of the Americas at Quebec City in 2001 when he argued against the U.S.-sponsored Free Trade Area of the Americas (FTAA), at least for the time being, on grounds that Latin America was not in a position to negotiate with the United States as an equal. Chávez, along with Néstor Kirchner and Lula, was instrumental in burying the FTAA proposal in 2005 and went on to help found the Alianza Bolivariana para los Pueblos de Nuestra América (Bolivarian Alliance for the Peoples of Our America—ALBA) in 2004, the Unión de Naciones Suramericanas (Union of South American Nations—UNASUR) in 2008, and the Comunidad de Naciones Latinoamericanos y Caribeños (Community of Latin American and Caribbean States—CELAC) in 2010. The strength of UNASUR and CELAC, whose slogan was "unity in diversity," was that they took in governments of diverse ideological orientations but at the same time stood for Latin American nationalism and rejection of pan-Americanism. The founding of UNASUR represented a reaction to the FTAA and became in the words of two scholars, "a political project to keep the U.S. out of the region in relation to strategic topics," while CELAC may have been "pointed at replacing the OAS" (Quiliconi and Salgado Espinoza, 2017: 30–31, 36). Along the same lines, the Pink Tide leaders who were the driving forces behind the founding of these organizations promoted economic ties with China in order to achieve diversification and lessen dependence on the United States in accordance with the goal of a multipolar world.

A contrasting strategy was embodied by the Pacific Alliance, formed by Mexico, Colombia, Peru, and Chile in 2011 and including the United States, for the purpose of promoting regional arrangements that furthered global liberalization. The alliance was also "created with political aims," namely "to consolidate a group of Latin American countries" that were committed to neoliberal policies (Quiliconi and Salgado Espinoza, 2017: 32). The reasons for Venezuela's withdrawal from the Andean Community in 2006 shed light on the divide between the Pacific Alliance nations and those of the Pink Tide: Peru's and Colombia's signing of a bilateral trade agreement with the United States, U.S. interference in the community's decision-making, the U.S.-promoted drug eradication program, and the military component of Plan Colombia.

During the Pink Tide period, viewpoints regarding the initiatives in favor of Latin American integration varied widely, as those who identified with the left tended to have favorable opinions, unlike in previous years (Deutschmann and Minkus, 2018: 42–43). Some scholars, including the neo-extractivism writers, were skeptical about the concrete benefits derived from the initiatives, while others were relatively optimistic. Svampa (2019: 18) writes of the "failure of Latin American regionalism," which she states appears to be associated with "a new dialectic of dependence." She goes on to point to the lack of concrete results of the ambitious projects that were launched. The governments that were most active in creating ALBA, UNASUR, and CELAC "ended up assuming a belligerently developmentalist discourse in defense of extractivism" with devastating results (Svampa and Viale, 2014: 360; Lander, 2014: 9–10; Lo Brutto et al., 2015: 68). Finally, bilateral commercial agreements with China and the competition to attract Chinese investment went against the spirit of Latin American integration, while China's voracious need for raw materials only intensified extractivism, with all its undesirable consequences.

Political struggle and issues cannot be left out of the discussion—a point made by the "optimists" who wrote favorably with regard to the steps taken by UNASUR and CELAC in favor of "regional governance" encompassing diverse ideological currents (Quiliconi and Salgado Espinoza, 2017: 22). Both organizations lost relevance as a result of the political defeats suffered by the Pink Tide, while the Petrocaribe oil agreement—created in the framework of integration that functioned effectively for over a decade after its founding in 2005—was the victim of the collapse of the Venezuelan oil industry, partly due to international sanctions.

National sovereignty and economic nationalism in the context of globalization are also key political elements with regard to Chinese economic ties (for a balanced analysis of China's economic role in Latin America, see the chapter by Emma To in this volume). Important cleavages emerged along political lines. Pink Tide leaders lauded the Chinese for respecting national sovereignty in contrast to the International Monetary Fund, with its "humiliating" terms and its rigid criteria for loans (Burgeño, 2015: 39; Harris, 2015: 154; Malm, 2019). Chinese contracts came under heavy criticism for avoiding political criteria in cases of flagrant violation of human rights, as in Sudan at the time of the Darfur tragedy and in other "rogue" states. Beijing responded by pointing out that it was guided by the principle of noninterventionism formulated at the Bandung Conference in 1955 (Allard, 2012: 280–281).

Pink Tide leaders viewed the diversification of economic relations (and the investments in infrastructure that the Chinese prioritized) as especially advantageous. They took note of the fact that Chinese investments, official rhetoric notwithstanding, were not free of ideological considerations, being skewed in favor of Pink Tide countries (Harris, 2015: 176). By contrast, during Brazil's presidential elections in 2018, Bolsonaro employed anti-Chinese rhetoric, alleging that the nation was a predator looking to dominate key sectors of his country's economy. Furthermore, the right-wing regime that came to power in

Bolivia in 2019 canceled Evo Morales' plans for joint projects in the framework of China's Belt and Road Initiative.

In short, far from constituting a "consensus," the economic ties and institutional arrangements at the international level promoted mainly by Pink Tide governments were highly polemical. Indeed, they pointed in the direction of significant changes that will be at the center of discussion and debate among policy makers and the public for years to come,

Territoriality, Indigenous Autonomy, and the Environment

A number of complex issues lay behind the controversies involving extractivism and territoriality in Latin America. This complexity presented a special dilemma for Pink Tide leaders because of the glaring contrast between their lofty rhetoric in favor of change and the hard choices they had to make in deciding how to proceed. An objective analysis needs to distinguish between situations in which compromise solutions over the environment and indigenous rights were feasible and ones in which unbending principles were at stake.

Three Problematic Issues

Should the approach to the problem of extractivism vary according to the international context? Should developing nations receive special treatment and be held to different standards from developed ones in conflicts involving extractivism?

Rafael Correa took the position in favor of differentiating between developed and developing nations on the issue of extractivism when he famously said, "We can't be beggars sitting on a sack of gold." The statement was meant to justify extractivist projects that had been questioned by indigenous and environmental activists. Along the same lines, the Argentine leftist sociologist Atilio Borón (2013: 11–12) suggests that neo-extactivism writers fail to consider where Third World countries are going to obtain the "essential resources for improving living conditions" for those most victimized by imperialism, such as the indigenous population.

Borón goes on to argue that the transformation envisioned by neo-extractivism writers, based on a complete break with global capitalism and avoidance of megaprojects, is infeasible for the Third World. If the Soviet Union and China were unable to consolidate socialism in a single country, smaller nations such as Bolivia and Ecuador cannot be expected to achieve even more radical change "within a few short years and in an environment as unfavorable as the one imposed by the aggressive decadence of the imperial power" (Borón, 2012: 141). Bolivia's former vice president Alvaro García

Linera also defended a long-term perspective and in doing so justified his government's ambitious extractivist projects, which were designed to harness natural resources in order to pave the way for an indigenous-based capitalism ("Andean-Amazonian capitalism") that would eventually create the conditions for socialism. Borón (2013: 12) is particularly critical of "extreme versions of the critique of extractivism" that favor zero economic growth, a position associated with Ecuador's former minister of energy and mines, Alberto Acosta (2017: 77, 97), who inveighs against the "religion of economic growth." Borón argues that economic growth for the developing world, especially in nations with substantial population increases, is imperative even in cases where redistribution of wealth favors the popular sectors of the population. At the same time, he takes issue with anti-extractivism defenders of deep ecology who believe that a country like Bolivia "can feed its population . . . by taking up the cultivation techniques of its indigenous population" (Borón, 2012: 129).

One of Latin America's most important and controversial struggles, that of the Yasuní National Park in Ecuador's Amazonian region, which contains about 40 percent of the nation's oil reserves, initially involved the issue of "ecological justice" and North-South relations. Rafael Correa's proposal, presented at the United Nations in 2007, of a US$3.5 billion international fund in defense of Yasuní's fragile ecosystem was a by-product of the global environmental movement and its banner of ecological justice. As far back as the Rio Earth Summit in 1992, the movement demanded that developed nations assume responsibility for the "environmental debt" created by their historic plunder of Third World resources and their disproportionate consumption (this point is persuasively argued by Angosto-Ferrández in his chapter). Correa's proposal also reflected the conviction among environmental activists that the South had to become "a protagonist and a leader in the solution toward climate change" (Martínez Alier, 2007: 4227). The plan, which consisted of compensation to the government in exchange for its pledge not to drill for oil in the area, was formulated by a major Ecuadorian-based nongovernmental organization (NGO) and incorporated into Correa's electoral platform. The proposal raised great expectations and resulted in commitments from various countries including China and Germany.

Correa accepted a mere US$5 a barrel for the oil not produced in the form of funding for programs benefiting the indigenous population and the environment but insisted on the Ecuadorian state's veto power over the fund's allocation. This position was not surprising given the importance Pink Tide governments attached to national sovereignty, but it created distrust among potential donors. Until August 2013, when Correa announced that the money raised at the international level fell far short of what was needed to make the plan viable, the proposal was subject to intense debate within his government

(Martin, 2015: 131), which began to make alternative plans. But the main explanation for the proposal's failure was the lack of commitment on the part of the governments of the developed nations. Some anti-Correa analysts who accuse the Ecuadorian president of "populist developmentalism" leave these theoretical issues as well as the historical context out of the discussion and instead focus on the controversies and clashes that ensued once drilling was undertaken (Eisenstadt and West, 2017: 232).

When are extractivist projects that are questioned on environmental grounds fundamentally flawed, and when can they be redesigned to minimize ecological damage? In the developed world, environmentalists have presented cogent arguments on the need to scrap megaprojects such as the Dakota Access and Keystone XL pipelines and have argued that the term "clean coal" is an oxymoron. Similarly, neo-extractivism writers attempt to demonstrate the all-encompassing "negative social, cultural, and environmental consequences" of Latin American megaprojects (Svampa, 2019: 32; Lander, 2019: 94–98). By contrast, writers more sympathetic toward the Pink Tide experience claim that governments such as Correa's responded to ecological concerns by pledging to limit the areas subject to oil drilling and apply strict environmental controls (Anderson, 2015: 116–117). Svampa (2019: 42) suggests that in regions with a mining tradition, communities are more inclined to accept extractivist projects but call for modifications to improve "working and environmental conditions," whereas in new areas such as those subject to open-pit mining they adopt a more intransigent and "radical" stance.

In the case of the TIPNIS dispute, environmental and indigenous groups claimed that the project was inherently unsound and that there was "no sustainable solution." García Linera, in contrast, called the road an "ecological highway" and asserted that, in accordance with recent legislation, it would be designed with "indigenous participation and in compliance with environmental norms" (Achtenberg, 2017).

Does the stipulation that the state consult indigenous communities over extractivist projects imply they have veto power? The constitutions passed by the Pink Tide in Bolivia and Ecuador require the state to consult indigenous communities about extractivist undertakings—an obligation also acquired elsewhere in the region by national legislation and international agreements (Carrión, 2012: 9–15). The International Labour Organization insists that the state's consultation with the community be conducted "in good faith" and that the prime aim should be to reach an agreement (Svampa, 2019: 30). Svampa examines regional experiences and concludes that "there was no Latin American government that did not attempt to minimize" the right of informed, previous consultation and "to limit it to its weakest version" in order to "establish its nonbinding character" (32). Some conflicts examined by neo-extractivism writers and other Pink Tide critics on the left involve the failure to respect the right of previous consultation (Svampa, 2019: 31; Postero, 2017: 142; Achtenberg, 2013: 6), but most of the cases concern the government's failure to act in good faith. Svampa points out that the issue of consultation involves "an increasingly complex and dynamic field of social and legal disputes" and goes on to accuse presidents Morales and Correa of being "manipulative" in their implementation of "pre-legislative consultation" (2019: 31–33).

Differences among Governments on Extractivism and Territoriality

As I have argued throughout this chapter, differences among Latin American governments over key issues and sharp conflict between governments and domestic actors have characterized the extractivist sector in twenty-first-century Latin America. Although Svampa, Gudynas, and other neo-extractivism writers point to some of these differences, they need to be incorporated into the neo-extractivism model so as to avoid the impression of homogeneity. Labor legislation, for instance, affected extractive industry in major ways and fundamentally distinguished neoliberal from Pink Tide governments. In Argentina, Mauricio Macri, elected president in 2015, rolled back practices and labor laws enacted under the two previous nationalistic Peronist governments (Svampa, 2019: 24; see also this book's chapter by Leguizamón). In Venezuela, the neoliberal-inspired "oil opening" of the 1990s stripped oil workers of historical benefits such as industry-wide bargaining, which Chávez restored with what he called the "nationalization" of the industry in 2007 and then the nation's new labor law of 2012.[4]

Similar distinctions need to be made with regard to environmental issues, even while Pink Tide governments undertook projects with destructive environmental impacts. Svampa (2014: 325–351) documents the ecological damage at the expense of Mapuche communities caused by fracking in Patagonia under the government of Cristina Fernández. Another scholar, however, presents a balanced, if not sympathetic, account of the environmental sensibilities of Fernández and her husband Néstor Kirchner in contrast to their neoliberal predecessor Carlos Menem. Both as politicians in their home state of Santa Cruz and as presidents, the Kirchners promoted green projects and education in the strategic locality of El Chaltén and popular environmental fronts for sustainable development in Patagonia that have "provided the bases of social opposition to transnational mining interests and state-corporate hydropower ventures" (Mendoza, 2018: 182). Similarly, some writers view the Pink Tide governments of Bolivia, Brazil, and El Salvador as more progressive than neoliberal ones from an environmental viewpoint (Fabricant and Gustafson, 2017; Amigo, 2020; see the chapter by Bebbington, Fash, and Rogan in this volume).

The right's rise to power in various Latin American nations in recent years casts in relief fundamental distinctions among governments on issues related to the environment, territoriality, and indigenous rights. Nowhere is the contrast in policies that affect the environment and the indigenous population more evident than in Brazil and Bolivia with Bolsonaro's election in 2018 and the forced resignation of Evo Morales in 2019. A comparison of the reactions of Bolsonaro and Morales to the wildfires that destroyed vast areas of Amazonian rain forest in late 2019 is especially instructive. Morales's critics blamed him for having substantially increased available land for deforestation to the benefit of cattle ranchers and small farmers. That controversy aside, the responses to the fires by the two heads of state demonstrate radically different approaches and sensibilities to ecological challenges. The immediate reaction of Bolsonaro and leading cabinet members was to reject outside aid and to articulate a developmentalist discourse in which European powers were alleged to be using the incident to halt the government's efforts to "rebuild Brazil." At the same time Bolsonaro characterized rain-forest protection as an obstacle to economic development. He also blamed local environmental NGOs and the World Wildlife Fund (which he falsely claimed was financed by Leonardo DiCaprio) for setting the fires in order to receive donations. By contrast, Morales welcomed foreign support to combat the fires and took proactive measures that were recognized by the president of the UN General Assembly, María Fernanda Espinosa.

Similarly, the contrast between Morales and the provisional government of Jeanine Añez that replaced him in 2019 sheds light on the diversity of the actors participating in issues related to indigenous communities. The mass mobilization against the Añez government in the face of fierce repression demonstrated the active and organized support of Morales by popular sectors, including those affected by extractivist projects as well as the indigenous population as a whole. Extractivist undertakings throughout the world invariably have winners and losers and elicit mixed reactions, but in the case of Bolivia support for the government went beyond passive approval in the form of public opinion surveys or votes at the polls. *Cocaleros* (coca growers), who were the most ardent supporters of the construction of the TIPNIS highway, put up the strongest resistance to the Añez government, taking control of the Chapare region where they were concentrated and forcing the police to flee the area.

The only way to interpret the popular opposition to Morales's ouster is to consider the mixed reaction among nonelite sectors to the government's ambitious developmental projects. The TIPNIS conflict did not just pit the cocaleros against the lowland indigenous population; other social and ethnic groups were also involved. Most important, the government's extensive public works projects won over the local peasant population, a fact that many antigovernment indigenous activists recognized. Nancy Postero (2017: 143) quotes one such activist as saying, "Many see Evo as a traitor. I don't see him that way. I see him as who he is, a leader of a campesino union. Where did we get the idea that the campesinos were revolutionary?" Postero goes on to point to "the diversity of interests and strategies we see among local peoples," in which even the lowland Guaranís in the TIPNIS area were split over the issue. The pro-Morales confederation of lowland indigenous peoples received generous funding to administer "production projects in indigenous communities friendly to the government," a practice that was conducive to "new kinds of patronage" (2017: 146, 149).

In addition to the lowland indigenous people, the members of mining cooperatives at one point resisted efforts by the Morales government to strengthen state regulation. In other countries, extractivist projects have also pitted well-organized nonelite groups against each other. Luis Angosto-Ferrández in his chapter in this volume and elsewhere describes a similar complexity, with winners and losers within and outside of indigenous communities in the mineral-rich area south of the Orinoco River known as the Orinoco Mining Arc (Angosto-Ferrández, 2020: 256–260).

Recent events in Bolivia also demonstrate the need to contextualize the controversial issue of territoriality and the complexity of the demands for regional autonomy in Third World nations, where national unity and state building are long-standing goals. The proposed construction of the TIPNIS highway, for instance, was designed to integrate the country's Amazonian and Andean regions, a feat that one scholar, herself a Morales critic on the left, describes as "a dream since Bolivian independence" (Achtenberg, 2017). The highway was also designed to offset the high cost of commercial transportation—estimated at 20 percent above that of neighboring countries—as a result of Bolivia being a landlocked nation. The aspirations of the Morales government clashed, however, with the concept of the plurinational state based on local rule, which the governing Movimiento al Socialismo (Movement toward Socialism—MAS) party defended and incorporated in the 2009 constitution. The issue of territoriality was also behind the government's sharp confrontations with the mining cooperatives (Fabricant and Gustafson, 2017).

At the time of the drafting of the constitution, the banner of regional autonomy was also raised by reactionary elite political and economic groups in the department of Santa Cruz. The control of rich natural resources, particularly hydrocarbons and soy production, was a key issue underlying the controversy over territoriality in Santa Cruz, as it has been in the case of indigenous struggles such as that of TIPNIS and Yasuní. The Santa Cruz elite and the privileged sectors of Potosí that demanded control of lithium exploitation[5] played a key role in the resistance to Morales's presidency and his removal from office in 2019. Once in power, these same elites put forward a new narrative that was blatantly anti-indigenous. The Áñez government refused to honor indigenous autonomy, including indigenous religions. At the same time, its supporters demonized symbols of the indigenous people such as their flag (known as the *wiphala*) in the name of Bolivian nationalism. In short, regional autonomy and nationalism played out in Bolivia in contradictory ways, showing that the issue of territoriality in extractivist conflicts has had different implications depending on time and place.

Resistance

Since the return to democratic rule in the 1980s, rural struggles around extractivism and territoriality and socio-environmental movements in urban areas have been of paramount importance, even more than labor conflicts in some Latin American countries. The indigenous and other rural organizations that have often led these struggles have become major actors in the politics of their respective nations. Women have also been in the forefront of many of the movements, as is shown by the case studies in the chapters by Leguizamón and Hernández Reyes in this volume. Leguizamón argues that gender is basic to understanding twenty-first-century extractivism. In the first place, it exacerbates gender inequality, since employment is skewed in favor of men. In the second place, men are at the helm of the extractivist economy, controlling natural resources and technological innovation. Finally, women play a central role in protesting abuses at the same time that "political and economic elites respond with traditional gendered insults and practices to silence and discipline them" (see also Fabricant and Gustafson, 2014–2015: 42). Leguizamón also argues that the oppression of those groups most victimized by extractivism is structural and that "gender intersects with other structures of inequality, such as race, class, and ethnicity, to create multiple vectors of . . . domination."

State repression under Pink Tide governments in Bolivia and Ecuador was accompanied by a narrative in which protest movements were accused of furthering the interests of the oligarchy and reactionary politicians, engaging in sabotage and terrorism, and being "conservative, anti-modern, and ultimately opposed to twenty-first-century socialism" (Moore and Velásquez, 2013: 141; Becker, 2014: 142). Nevertheless, as Svampa (2019: 39–40) points out, the repression has intensified under the conservative governments that have come to power in the recent past. "The current conservative turn" in Brazil and in Argentina under Macri "deepened the extractivist model in all its versions, accentuating state violence on the most vulnerable populations."

Svampa also notes that Latin America "holds the world record for murders of environmental activists."

In their chapter in this volume, Bebbington, Fash, and Rogan make the same point, specifically with regard to the contrast between the Frente Farabundo Martí de la Liberación Nacional governments in El Salvador and the governments of Honduras that succeeded Pink Tide president Manuel Zelaya in 2009. They point out that Honduran environmental activists in recent years have been subjected to greater danger than even in the years prior to Zelaya's rule. In fact, Honduras has become the most dangerous country in the world for environmentalists. In a similar contrast, Toledo Orozco in her chapter in this volume argues that under Evo Morales "Bolivian communities surrounding mining camps [were] . . . less exposed to state repression and nonstate violence" than was the case with rightist governments in the region.

The two most high-profile assassinations of social movement activists in recent years in Latin America—that of Berta Cáceres of Honduras and that of Marielle Franco of Brazil—reflect these recent trends. Cáceres was a leading environmental and indigenous activist who was murdered undoubtedly because of her opposition to the construction of a hydroelectric dam. Franco was a human rights and LGBT activist whose murder followed her denunciation of police violence. The two cases are significant for what they say about resistance and repression in Latin America. In the first place, gender and ethnicity are central in twenty-first-century social struggles and specifically those in opposition to extractivism. Both victims were women, one an indigenous leader and the other a leader of the LGBT movement. In the second place, the assassinations took place under right-wing governments that had risen to power as a result of "soft coups" against Pink Tide governments (those of Zelaya and Rousseff). In the third place, the state was implicated in the assassinations and coverups. Several of those arrested for Cáceres's murder were linked to United States–trained elite troops, while two of those arrested for Franco's death were former members of the military police and two others were close to Bolsonaro and especially his son Flávio. Human rights groups strongly denounced the governments of both nations for failing to undertake impartial investigations into the crimes.

In short, as poor a record as leftist, moderate, and centrist governments had on issues related to extractivism in specific instances, the policies of governments on the right were more atrocious. Leguizamón illustrates this dissimilarity with regard to Macri, who favored the extractivist soybean export sector in contrast to the policies of the Kirchners before him and those of Alberto Fernández after him. In her chapter on Colombia, Kyla Sankey recognizes the poor record of President Juan Manuel Santos on extractivism issues but compares him favorably with the right-wing presidents Uribe and Duque. She writes: "While the cornerstone of Uribe's mining strategy was a militarized securitization of resource-rich territories, Santos's discourse has focused on institution-building and stability [and] . . . whereas Uribe had closed the Ministry for the Environment, Santos reopened it."

Conclusion

Linda Farthing and Nicole Fabricant (2018), in their introductory essay to *Latin American Perspectives'* issue titled "*Open Veins* Revisited: The New Extractivism in Latin America," clearly state what I also assert in this chapter: governments throughout the region and across the political spectrum are responsible for environmental destruction and violation of indigenous rights and have failed to prioritize diversification of the economy in order to eliminate dependency on commodity exports. Addressing the broad context of twenty-first-century Latin American politics, I have taken issue with neo-extractivism writers, who play down—even though most of them recognize—the differences between Pink Tide, conservative, and right-wing governments. Needless to say, this tendency to deemphasize differences does not apply to all scholars who critically examine the environmental and indigenous policies of progressive governments or their failure to lesson economic dependency.

Neo-extractivism writers, in focusing on the "consensus" among diverse Latin American governments regarding the need to exploit their nation's extractivist potential, fail to give proper weight to policies that clearly differentiate Pink Tide and non-Pink Tide countries. This tendency has caused some activists and writers on the left to condemn progressive and conservative governments more or less equally (declaring "a plague on both your houses" [Ellner, 2020: 53]). Those on the left who defend this position base their argument on the failure of Pink Tide governments to break with the extractivist "model." Indeed, the harmful effects of extractivism are a key issue of concern for leftist detractors of Pink Tide governments.

The recent cases of instability and regime change in Brazil, Bolivia, Venezuela, Ecuador, and other countries point to the unintended consequences of this line of thinking. In each of these nations, political leaders identified with neoliberalism and enjoying U.S. backing have used illicit means and repression in an attempt to roll back reforms initiated by Pink Tide governments. The reaction of Pink Tide critics on the left to these events has been varied. In Bolivia, some of Morales's staunchest intellectual and activist critics thoroughly condemned the soft coup staged in 2019 (Achtenberg, 2020; Fabricant, 2019), but others have remained "disturbingly silent" (Achtenberg, 2020) and still others, such as the former UN ambassador and indigenous movement activist Pablo Salón, have denied that what took place was a coup. Prior to Morales's exit from office, Salón (who had broken with Morales as a result of the TIPNIS conflict) underestimated the determination of the economic elite and the political right to revert to the disruptive tactics of the past and the significance of the nation's ideological divide. He mistakenly believed that the important business organizations of Santa Cruz and elsewhere would be neutral in the 2019 presidential elections. At the same time, he claimed that the "dichotomy between the left and right is not essential," since all parties supported the "extractivist economic model of export" (Salón, 2019). His position, which borrows heavily from neo-extractivism writing, amounts to a "plague on both your houses" with regard to Morales and Bolivia's right-wing opposition.

In Ecuador, the indigenous group Confederación de Nacionalidades Indígenas del Ecuador (Confederation of Indigenous Nationalities of Ecuador—CONAIE), which had led the opposition to the Yasuní project, adopted a similar position with reference to both the neoliberal government of Lenín Moreno and the former Pink Tide president Rafael Correa. The attacks on Correa of CONAIE president Jaime Vargas held back the formation of a united front against the Moreno government's neoliberal policies. In the process, Vargas played into the divisive strategy of Moreno, who claimed that Correa's followers and not CONAIE were responsible for the violence that occurred during the popular anti-neoliberal protests in late 2019.

In Venezuela many of those opposed to the Mining Arc project as inherently destructive of the environment defended the same "plague on both your houses" position. The longtime union leader Stalin Pérez Borges, himself a critic of the Maduro government and the Mining Arc, voiced opposition to certain leftist political organizations and individuals for maintaining a position equidistant between the domestic right and Washington, on the one hand, and the Chavista leadership, on the other. These Maduro opponents, who according to Pérez included various "respected" former Chávez ministers staunchly opposed to the project, called the government a "criminal dictatorship." In doing so, Pérez (2016, 2019) argued, they "coincide with the campaign . . . of the world bourgeois press," whose narrative "serves to call for immediate military intervention" along with economic sanctions against Venezuela.

As various chapters in this volume point out, much of the criticism formulated by the neo-extractivism writers is well substantiated. Beyond the shadow of a doubt, environmentally damaging extractivist projects and violence against those who have protested against them have been carried out by, or occurred under, Pink Tide governments. Nevertheless, the broader picture needs to be thoroughly incorporated into the analysis rather than just mentioned in passing. As I have indicated above, this context includes the full range of policies associated with extractivism, Latin America's historical condition of underdevelopment, and the aggressiveness of the domestic and foreign opposition to progressive governments.

In short, the issues raised by the neo-extractivism writers are complex. Given that topics such as the environment and indigenous rights are emotional and involve matters of principle, differences among analysts of similar ideological orientations are understandable. These differences notwithstanding, a broad analysis of extractivism that gives proper weight to contextual factors is indispensable for achieving a balanced and objective account of the performances of twenty-first-century Latin American governments.

Notes

1. Extractivism, the extraction of natural resources from the earth and their sale on the world market, refers to primary commodities that are for the most part processed outside of the country where they are produced.

2. Pro-Pink Tide leaders and writers such as former Bolivian vice president Álvaro García Linera accuse the neo-extractivist scholars of being "naïve romantics" (Webber, 2015b: 575), but some of them have presented blueprints for achieving material goals along with transition away from extractivism (Acosta, 2017: 89; Weyer, 2017: 131–135).

3. I thank Linda Farthing and Nicole Fabricant, who edited two issues of *Latin American Perspectives* entitled "*Open Veins* Revisited: The New Extractivism in Latin America" (45 [5] and 46 [2]). Eight of the chapters in this book are modified versions of articles that appeared in those two issues.

4. Under Chávez's reorganization of the oil industry in 2007, workers who were not covered by the industry-wide contract were incorporated into the payroll of PDVSA.

5. Gustafson (2019) points out that the "proto-fascist" head of Santa Cruz's civic committee, Luis Fernando Camacho, joined the top leader of Potosí's civic committee —which opposed Morales's plan to set up a national lithium company—in the takeover of the National Palace.

References

Achtenberg, Emily

2013 "Contested development: the geopolitics of Bolivia's TIPNIS conflict." *NACLA: Report on the Americas* 46 (2): 6–11.

2017 "Why is Evo Morales reviving Bolivia's controversial TIPNIS road?" *NACLA: Report on the Americas.* August 21. https://nacla.org/blog/2017/08/22/why-evo-morales-reviving-bolivia's-controversial-tipnis-road.

2020 "MAS party under threat as Bolivia moves towards new elections (without Evo)." *NACLA: Report on the Americas.* January 10. https://nacla.org/blog/2020/01/10/mas-party-under-threat-bolivia-new-elections-without-evo.

Acosta, Alberto

2017 "Post-extractivism: from discourse to practice—reflections for action," pp. 77–101 in Gilles Carbonnier, Humberto Campodónico, and Sergio Tezanos Vázquez (eds.), *Alternative Pathways to Sustainable Development: Lessons from Latin America.* Leiden: Brill.

2020 "Los progresismos demuestran en la práctica que no son gobiernos de izquierda" (interview by Angeles Fernández and J. Marcos). *CTXT* (Madrid) 257 (February). https://www.ctxt.es/es/20200203/Politica/30926/alberto-acosta-politico-ecuador-exministro-evo-morales-entrevista-izquierda-latinoamerica.htm.

Allard, Gayle

2012 "Chinese OFDI in Africa: trends, prospects and threats," pp. 279–299 in Ilan Alon, Marc Fetscherin and Philppe Gugler (eds.), *Chinese International Investments.* London: Palgrave Macmillan.

Amigo, Ignacio

2020 "When will the Amazon hit a tipping point?" *Nature.* February 25. https://www.nature.com/articles/d41586-020-00508-4.

Anderson, Jon Lee

2017 "Nicolás Maduro's accelerating revolution." *The New Yorker* 93 (40). https://www.newyorker.com/magazine/2017/12/11/nicolas-maduros-accelerating-revolution.

Anderson, Tim

2015 "From Havana to Quito: understanding economic reform in Cuba and Ecuador." *Journal of Australian Political Economy* 76: 103–128.

Angosto-Ferrández, Luis

2020 "Neo-extractivism, class formations, and the Pink Tide: considerations of the Venezuelan case," pp. 243–269 in Steve Ellner (ed.), *Latin America's Pink Tide: Breakthroughs and Shortcomings.* Lanham, MD: Rowman and Littlefield.

Becker, Marc

2014 "Rafael Correa and social movements in Ecuador," pp. 127–148 in Steve Ellner (ed.), *Latin America's Radical Left: Challenges and Complexities of Political Power in the Twenty-first Century.* Lanham, MD: Rowman and Littlefield.

Borón, Atilio

2012 *América Latina en la geopolítica del imperialismo.* Buenos Aires: Ediciones Luxemburg.

2013 "Prólogo," pp. 9–14 in José Seoane, Emilio Taddei, and Clara Algranati (eds.), *Extractivismo, despojo y crisis climática: Desafíos para los movimientos sociales y los proyectos emancipatorios de Nuestra América.* Buenos Aires: Editorial El Colectivo.

Burgueño, Carlos

2015 *Las batallas económicas del Kirchnerismo.* Buenos Aires: Edhasa.

Cannon, Barry

2009 *Hugo Chávez and the Bolivarian Revolution: Populism and Democracy in a Globalised Age.* Manchester: Manchester University Press.

Carrión, Patricia
2012 *Análisis de la consulta previa, libre e informada en el Ecuador.* Quito: Centro Ecuatoriano de Derecho Ambiental.
Deutschmann, Emanuel, and Lar Minkus
2018 "Swinging leftward: public opinion on economic and political integration in Latin America, 1997–2010." *Latin American Research Review* 53 (1): 38–56.
Eisenstadt, Todd A., and Karleen Jones West
2017 "Public opinion, vulnerability, and living with extraction on Ecuador's oil frontier: where the debate between development and environmentalism gets personal." *Comparative Politics* 49 (2): 231–251.
Ellner, Steve
2019 "Explanations for the current crisis in Venezuela: a clash of paradigms and narratives." *Global Labour Journal* 10 (2): 159–169.
2020 "Has the Pink Tide cycle come to an end?" pp. 39–58 in Steve Ellner (ed.), *Latin America's Pink Tide: Breakthroughs and Shortcomings.* Lanham, MD: Rowman and Littlefield.
Fabricant, Nicole
2019 "The roots of the right-wing coup in Bolivia." *Dissent.* December 23. https://www.dissentmagazine.org/online_articles/roots-coup-bolivia-morales-anez-camacho.
Fabricant, Nicole, and Bret Gustafson
2014–2015 "Moving beyond the extractivism debate: imagining new social economies." *NACLA: Report on the Americas* 47 (4): 40–45.
2017 "Socialism from below: Bolivia in an age of extractivism." *New Politics* 56 (3). https://newpol.org/issue_post/socialism-below-bolivia-age-extractivism/.
Farthing, Linda and Nicole Fabricant
2018 "Introduction: charting the social, economic, and political contours of the new extractivism in Latin America." *Latin American Perspectives* 45 (5): 4–17.
García Linera, Alvaro
2016 "Discurso completo de Alvaro García Linera." May 29. http://www.cta.org.ar/discurso-completo-de-alvaro-garcia.html.
Gudynas, Eduardo
2012 "Una izquierda marrón en América del Sur." *Ecología Política* 43 (July): 9–12.
2016 "Beyond varieties of development: disputes and alternatives." *Third World Quarterly* 37: 721–732.
2018 *Naturaleza, extractivismos y corrupción: Anatomía de una íntima relación.* Montevideo: CLAES/La Libre.
Gustafson, Bret
2019 "Brazil and Bolivia at the crossroads" (interview by Jeremy Scahill). *The Intercept.* November 13. https://theintercept.com/2019/11/13/bolivia-and-brazil-at-the-crossroads/.
Harris, Richard
2015 "China and Latin America: processes and paradoxes." *Latin American Perspectives* 42 (6): 153–190.

Hellinger, Daniel
2006–2007 "Venezuelan oil: free gift of nature or wealth of a nation?" *International Journal* 62 (1): 55–67.
Krommes-Ravnsmet, Jeppe
2019 "The frustrated nationalization of hydrocarbons and the plunder of Bolivia." *Latin American Perspectives* 46 (2): 65–83.
Lander, Edgardo
2014 *El neoextractivismo como modelo de desarrollo en América Latina y sus contradicciones.* Berlin: Heinrich Böll Stiftung.
2019 *Crisis civilizatoria: Experiencias de los gobiernos progresistas y debates en la izquierda latinoamericana.* Guadalajara: CALAS.
Lo Brutto, Giuseppe, Carlos Otto Vásquez Salazar, and Margot Olavarria
2015 "The strategic integration of Latin America: a disputed project." *Latin American Perspectives* 42 (4): 61–72.
Long, Gideon
2018 "Colombia's young president faces old challenges." *Financial Times.* June 19.
López, Emiliano and Francisco Vértiz
2015 "Extractivism, transnational capital, and subaltern struggles in Latin America." *Latin American Perspectives* 42 (5): 152–168.
Luhnow, David
2019 "The outlook: Latin America's prospects dim, again." *Wall Street Journal.* August 26, p. A-2.
Malm, Johanna
2019 "China's new debt sustainability framework for the BRI." *The China-Africa Research Initiative Blog.* August 27. http://www.chinaafricarealstory.com/.
Martin, Pamela L.
2015 "Leaving oil under the Amazon: The Yasuní-ITT Initiative as a postpetroleum model?" pp. 119–144 in Thomas Princen, Jack P. Manno, and Pamela L. Martin (eds.), *Ending the Fossil Fuel Era.* Cambridge: MIT Press.
Martínez Alier, Joan
2007 "Keep oil in the ground: Yasuní in Ecuador." *Economic and Political Weekly* 42 (42): 4227–4228.
Mendoza, Marcos
2018 *The Patagonian Sublime: The Green Economy and Post-Neoliberal Politics.* New Brunswick, NJ: Rutgers University Press.
Moffett, Matt
2007 "Beyond 'Petrosaurus': how a sleeping oil giant became a world power." *Wall Street Journal.* August, 30 p. A-1.
Moore, Jennifer, and Teresa Velásquez
2013 "Water for gold: confronting state and corporate mining discourses in Azuay, Ecuador," pp. 119–148 in Anthony Bebbington and Jeffrey Bury (eds.), *Subterranean Struggles: New Dynamics of Mining, Oil, and Gas in Latin America.* Austin: University of Texas Press

Oddone, Décio

2016 "The oil and gas sector: a first glance at its changes." *Atlantic Council*. https://publications.atlanticcouncil.org/brazil-oil-gas/.

O'Grady, Mary Anastasia

2018 "Bolsonaro takes Brazil." *Wall Street Journal*. October 29, p. A-21.

Otis, John

2014 "Socialist leader gets lift in Bolivian boom." *Wall Street Journal*. October 10, p. A-9.

Pérez Borges, Stalin

2016 "Entrevista a Stalin Pérez Borges, dirigente de LUCHAS (Venezuela)." *Democracia Socialista*. October 3. http://www.democraciasocialista.org/?p=6278.

2019 "Entrevista a Stalin Pérez Borges: 'Costará mucho doblegarnos.'" *Aporrea*. August 2. https://www.aporrea.org/venezuelaexterior/n338171.html.

Petras, James, and Henry Veltmeyer

2014 "A new model or a new form of imperialism?" pp. 19–48 in James Petras and Henry Veltmeyer (eds.), *Extractive Imperialism in the Americas: Capitalism's New Frontier*. Chicago: Haymarket Books.

Postero, Nancy

2017 *The Indigenous State: Race, Politics, and Performance in Plurinational Bolivia*. Oakland: University of California Press.

Quiliconi, Cintia, and Raúl Salgado Espinoza

2017 "Latin American integration: regionalism à la carte in a multipolar world?" *Colombia International* 92: 15–41.

Salón, Pablo

2019 "Bolivian horizons: an interview with Pablo Salón" (interview by Jeffery R. Webber). *Solidarity*. November 5. https://solidarity-us.org/bolivian-horizons-an-interview-with-pablo-solon/.

Schmall, Emily

2012 "Argentina: back to Peronism." *World Policy Journal* 29 (3): 90–96, 98–99.

Schutte, Giorgio Romano

2013 "Brazil: new developmentalism and the management of offshore oil wealth." *European Review of Latin American and Caribbean Studies* 95 (October): 49–70.

Svampa, Maristella

2012 "Resource extractivism and alternatives: Latin American perspectives on development." *Journal für Entwicklungspolitik* 28: 43–73.

2015 "Commodities consensus: neoextractivism and enclosure of the commons in Latin America." *South Atlantic Quarterly* 114 (1): 65–82.

2019 *Neo-Extractivism in Latin America: Socio-environmental Conflicts, the Territorial Turn, and New Political Narratives*. Cambridge: Cambridge University Press.

Svampa, Maristella, and Enrique Viale

2014 *Maldesarrollo: La Argentina del extractivismo y el despojo*. Buenos Aires: Katz Editores.

Toledo, Víctor, David Garrido, and Narciso Barrera-Bassols
2015 "The struggle for life: socio-environmental conflicts in Mexico." *Latin American Perspectives* 42 (5): 133–147.
Wall Street Journal
2012 "Editorial." April 18, p. A-16.
Webber, Jeffery R.
2015a "Crisis and class, advance and retreat: the political economy of the new Latin American left," pp. 157–168 in Lucia Pradella and Thomas Marois (eds.), *Polarizing Development: Alternatives to Neoliberalism and the Crisis.* London: Pluto Press.
2015b "The indigenous community as 'living organism': José Carlos Mariátegui, romantic Marxism, and extractive capitalism in the Andes." *Theory and Society* 44: 575–598.
2017 *The Last Day of Oppression, and the First Day of the Same: The Politics and Economics of the New Latin American Left.* Chicago: Haymarket Books.
Weisbrot, Mark
2015 *Failed: What the "Experts" Got Wrong about the Global Economy.* New York: Oxford University Press.
Weyer, Frédérique
2017 "Implementing 'vivir bien': results and lessons from the biocultural programme, Bolivia," pp. 128–137 in Gilles Carbonnier, Humberto Campodónico, and Sergio Tezanos Vázquez (eds.), *Alternative Pathways to Sustainable Development: Lessons from Latin America.* Leiden: Brill.
Zibechi, Raúl
2019 "Las vueltas del neoliberalismo." *La Jornada.* September 27. https://www.jornada.com.mx/2019/09/27/opinion/020a1pol.

I

THE GLOBAL FOCUS

MAJOR DEVELOPMENTS IN THE AGE of globalization over the past four decades have thoroughly transformed Latin American extractivism, an activity dating back to the outset of the Spanish conquest. First, the emergence of resource-hungry China as a world economic powerhouse generated a commodity boom that lasted longer and encompassed more products than in the past. Second, sophisticated technological innovation (such as genetically modified organisms and fracking), a salient feature of globalization, gave transnational capital more of an upper hand vis-à-vis developing nations and strengthened dependency in extractive industries. Third, dependency was also reinforced by the new or increased use of financial mechanisms known as financialization (discussed in the chapter by Macías Vásquez and García-Arias), which impeded the ability of Latin American nations to gain greater control of extractive industries and make full use of the revenue they produced. Finally (and in contradiction to the previous two factors), the resource nationalism pursued by Pink Tide governments generated windfall revenue and thus greater maneuverability.

The three chapters in this section examine various key aspects of globalization in order to contextualize the impact of extractivism at the national level. They point to the obstacles facing Pink Tide governments in their effort to break the hold of global forces short of an all-encompassing anticapitalist revolution.

Kyla Sankey, in her article on the Colombian mining industry, reviews different theories on the relationship between the state and the global economy and rejects those that play down the role of Third World states in extractive industry and that view them as weak or "failed." On the one hand, in an "updated version of the theories of Lenin" on imperialism, some writers take an instrumentalist approach by seeing Washington as responding directly to the corporate interests of U.S. capital. In the process, they virtually write off the power of transnational capital and instead highlight "territorial domination" by individual advanced capitalist nations more in tune with the era that Lenin wrote about. On the other hand, she takes issue with globalization theory that has dominated political economy writing on the nation-state for the past several decades. Globalization theory scholars view states as "victims of new global power structures" and national sovereignty as reduced to a minimum, threatened by global capital, especially transnational mining interests. In the process, these writers fail to recognize the "active role of the state in facilitating capital accumulation." In the case of Colombia, which has become a "neoliberal mining country," the state's role as a key agent is expressed through the "realignment of institutes with transnational capital, revision of property law, free-trade agreements, flexibilized labor laws, and state-sponsored repression." The harshness of the policies favoring mining interests has been intensified under the far-right governments of Iván Duque and Álvaro Uribe, whose "mining strategy was based on two main pillars: legal reforms and state-sponsored violence."

The article by Alfredo Macías Vázquez and Jorge García-Arias focuses on financialization, which they claim especially impacts extractive sectors in that it leads to the "predominance of rent over profit," given that "profitability depends less on the sale of raw materials than on the mechanisms external to the extractive activity." In their analysis of Bolivia under the presidency of Evo Morales, they point to the paradoxical situation in which, in spite of the high "level of international reserves . . . in state coffers as a result of the hydrocarbons boom," the government ended up borrowing money. A major explanation, they argue, was the International Monetary Fund's insistence that Bolivia "maintain healthy fiscal accounts." This requirement, however, infringed on the state's capacity to use the revenue from mining and hydrocarbons to "transform the economy and take significant steps forward in the fight against poverty." Nevertheless, "heterodox reforms" under the Morales government, in line with the resource nationalism that it embraced, contrasted with the policies of previous neoliberal presidents and gave it "some room for maneuver in decision making." These measures included the government's takeover of the administration of pension funds in 2011 and a law on financial institutions passed the same year that "prioritized the reduction of lending rates and encouraged productive loans to agricultural and microenterprises." The real dilemma facing nations like Bolivia, according to these contributors, is not the attempt to "overcome an extractivist model through extractivism itself"—as is claimed by writers such as Eduardo Gudynas and

Maristella Svampa. The major challenge is achieving structural economic change "without decisively confronting the influence of financialization on the channeling of fiscal resources" obtained from raw materials.

The chapter by Emma Miriam Yin-Hang To shows the ways that Venezuela's burgeoning Chinese ties, particularly in the petroleum industry, increased the options available to it but in other ways maintained its status as a dependent nation. The two elements of the relationship, one based on South-South cooperation and the other on "rearticulated global political and economic inequalities," are not mutually exclusive. On the one hand, the state-to-state agreements are characterized by cooperation in that the advice offered by the Chinese, particularly in the area of infrastructure, is "difficult to call an imposition," in contrast to "neoliberal prescriptions" tied to World Bank and IMF loans. In addition, To points to technological transfer facilitated by bilateral agreements, specifically in the areas of satellite engineering, military technology, mobile phones, household appliances, and transport. On the other hand, she labels much of the funding "boomerang aid" in that money from the state-owned China Development Bank is "fed back to Chinese companies in the form of Venezuelan government contracts," a "common practice" among donor countries. Nevertheless, she characterizes initiatives originating from the Chinese state as for the most part beneficial for Venezuela, in contrast to the practices of China's private sector, which reinforce "many of the structural problems that Venezuela has long faced."

1

The Political Economy of Mining in Colombia

The New Face of Globalization?

Kyla Sankey

In the past fifteen years, major changes in the international political economy have resulted in the conversion of Colombia into a mining country. The administrations of presidents Álvaro Uribe (2002–2010), Juan Manuel Santos (2010–2018), and Iván Duque (2018–) have played a key role in facilitating this process by orienting national development policy toward natural-resource extraction as the chief "locomotive" of economic growth. The goal laid out in "Mining and Energy Vision 2019" was to turn Colombia into the main mining country in Latin America by attracting foreign direct investment in mining (UPME, 2006). The results were dramatic: by 2014, the mining sector represented 70 percent of Colombia's total exports, a sevenfold increase from 1970 (ECLAC, 2015).

The emergence of Colombia as a mining country is also a manifestation of epoch-defining shifts in the global economy and geopolitical power relations driven by three interrelated processes on the international level: the rise of China as an economic force with a growing demand for natural resources, a commodities boom in the first decade of the 2000s that was then propelled by the 2008 global crisis, and a surge of "resource-seeking" foreign investment in fossil fuels and minerals. This sudden influx of foreign direct investment in natural resources abruptly reversed the trend in world capital flows that had been dominant throughout the twentieth century: until 2000, Latin America had never received more than 10 percent of worldwide foreign investment, but in 2012 this figure rose to 22 percent (ECLAC, 2015). It peaked in the wake of the financial crisis. In 2008, against the background of a 15 percent decline in foreign direct investment worldwide, capital flows toward the extractives sector of Latin America reached an all-time high, with foreign direct investment at US$128 billion (ECLAC, 2015). These changes reflect emergent forms of interdependence in the world economy that have simultaneously deepened uneven geographical development with Colombia's incorporation into the global division of labor as a primary commodities exporter.

In Colombia the mining boom has been particularly predatory, violent, and corrupt. The influx of investment in mining precipitated a land and resource grab driven by multinational corporations, with concessions for exploration or exploitation of natural resources on an estimated 59 percent of Colombia's national territory (Garay, 2013). Dispossession, political violence, and corruption played a central role in facilitating this land grab. As Grajales (2015: 542) has argued, "This country's situation is characterized by a combination of legal and illegal strategies presiding at the distribution of power and resources." As investment poured into the mining sector, violent displacement increasingly became the chief means for gaining access to land and natural resources. One UN investigation reported that "a pattern of displacement has also appeared in relation to the exploration and exploitation of natural resources and the implementation of large-scale development projects, in some cases involving multinational corporations" (ABColombia, 2011). Countless reports have linked the paramilitary forces to mining companies through a range of activities including providing protection from guerrilla forces, forcibly removing local communities, repressing labor unions, and controlling subcontracting agencies and extortion (ABColombia, 2011; Pax, 2014).

The emergence of mining as a driving force behind economic growth in Colombia has a number of implications for contemporary debates on globalization, imperialism, and the role of the state in the global political economy. One common view among scholars and policy analysts is that many of the problems associated with resource extraction are a consequence of a "failed" or "weak" state unable to rein in the power of transnational corporations and violent groups (McLean, 2002; Pizarro and Bejarano, 2003). However, this notion reflects a superficial understanding of the state that overlooks the increasingly state-like functions adopted by paramilitary groups, particularly after the decentralization of the 1990s, and the relation between state power and paramilitary violence in creating the political and territorial conditions for capital accumulation (Ballvé, 2012).

In this chapter I offer an alternative interpretation emphasizing the role of state interventions and parastate violence in facilitating and enforcing Colombia's mining boom. I explore the relationship between the influx of investment in mining and new processes of elite class configuration and the restructuring of the state apparatus and mechanisms of territorial control.

In particular, I explore the way Presidents Uribe and Santos have deployed state power in implementing this new form of capital accumulation by revising property laws, flexibilizing labor markets, implementing new trade and investment policies, and overseeing new mechanisms of social repression. In this sense, rather than suggesting that the "weak" Colombian state has been overshadowed by multinational corporations and nonstate violent actors, my analysis focuses on the variety of ways in which the state has been a key agent in implementing this new form of capital accumulation and guaranteeing the political, economic, and physical conditions necessary for an economy fueled by raw-material extraction. The chapter begins by reviewing the theoretical debates surrounding globalization and then presents my position and its application to the case of mining in Colombia.[1]

Globalization, U.S. Empire, and the State

For at least three decades, political economy research on the nation-state has been dominated by "globalization" theory (Held and McGrew, 2003). Commonly taken to refer to qualitative changes in the world market characterized by the rise of multinational companies, the growing importance of foreign direct investment, and the liberalization of global trade, among other processes, "the retreat of the state" has been a central theme of the discussion. This is understood as a decline in domestic state power and the loss of control over national economies and territorial boundaries. The political conclusion accompanying this theory is that globalization has brought about a new international order based on the rise of multilateral governance. The implication is that the nation-state as an explanatory tool and a political force has become increasingly redundant.

While the surge in foreign direct investment in mining in Colombia and the problems associated with this form of economic development have received much attention among scholars and policy analysts, the most common explanation is that the phenomenon is reflective of the erosion of the power of the state in the face of globalization. As Garay (2013: 8) sees it, the rise of "mining extractivism" in Colombia is related to a new process of "transnational management of public resources . . . operating under a logic that transcends national spaces and the nation-state." This analysis suggests that the rise in mining is evidence that national economies are increasingly dominated by global forces and that emergent transnational power structures are undermining state sovereignty. According to this line of reasoning, states should be seen as *victims* of new global power structures or national sovereignty is threatened by the power of transnational mining corporations and multilateral institutes. The presumption is that a distinction can be made between an uncivilized globalization—the predatory and lawless activities of mining companies—and a civilized one, with a better balance between states and markets achieved through transnational regulatory bodies and a global civil society.

Yet this analysis overlooks the class and elite composition of states, the relation between states and markets, and the active role of the state in facilitating capital accumulation. There is little historical analysis of the sociopolitical power conflicts surrounding the neoliberal restructuring that has taken place since the 1970s. As Weiss (1998: 4) writes, "Rather than counterposing nation-state and global market as antinomies, in certain important respects we find that 'globalisation' is often the by-product of states promoting the internationalisation strategies of their corporations, and sometimes in the process 'internationalising' state capacity." In this sense, the common framing of the globalization debate as a question of finding the right balance between states and markets is misleading. Rather, we must look to the role of states in facilitating capital accumulation and processes of elite class formation.

An alternative interpretation common among Marxist scholars depicts mining in Colombia as an example of U.S. imperialism in an updated version of the theories of Lenin and Bukharin. According to this argument, the expansion of mining in Colombia is related to the strategies adopted by the United States to "ensure access to the world's largest resources" (Leech, 2006: 3; see also Klare, 2012). This paints a picture of the U.S. state carving out spaces in Latin American territories in order to obtain access to natural resources for U.S. corporations and thereby secure their continued profits (Petras, 2012; Villar and Cottle, 2011). These views have stressed the use of U.S. militarism through Plan Colombia and the War on Drugs to defend U.S. territorial control over oil and natural resources.

This interpretation provides an important analysis of the centrality of natural resources in geopolitical power struggles and the role of U.S. imperialism in propelling the Colombian armed conflict. The problem with it is that it tends to take an instrumentalist approach to the actions of imperial states, which are seen as directly intervening to defend the particular interests of their national capital. Such reverberations of the classic theories of imperialism as territorial domination through the export of capital understate the dynamics of the global expansion of capital under neoliberalism. As Kiely (2010: 157) points out, "In the current period, neoliberalism entails increased openness rather than the sealing off of colonized spaces from all but the colonizing power." In other words, to view the development of Colombia's mining economy as the result of a drive by imperialist states to gain control over natural resources or even a "resource war" between imperialist rivals underestimates the fact that no single state is in a position to "control" natural resources, militarily or otherwise (Bieler and Morton, 2015; Bromley, 2006).

The emphasis on competition and rivalry also neglects the dynamics of transnational coordination of capitals and the integration of production, trade, and consumption of raw materials on the world market. In this sense, Avilés (2008: 413) is correct to point out that

> "the economic policies furthered through Plan Colombia, such as a secure and stable business environment, the liberalization of capital markets, and the opening of markets to foreign direct investment, are not simply policies that benefit U.S.-based TNCs [transnational corporations], but represent an economic agenda from which TNCs from around the world can benefit."

Understood in this way, the United States' role in Colombia has not been defined precisely as defending its own corporations so much as defending the system as a whole and "maintaining a stable supply of crucial energy onto the world market" (Stokes, 2005). While contemporary multinational mining corporations are certainly nationally based and depend on the actions of imperial states to facilitate their entry into territories abroad, this does not mean that they are also united along national boundaries, defending national interests against foreign competition. Their operations are spread out all over the world, with degrees of international integration and financialization that, although often exaggerated by globalization theorists, extend far beyond those observed by classical-era Marxists (Bieler and Morton, 2014; Kiely, 2010). This analysis suggests that imperialist interventions in Colombia are best conceived less as strategies for gaining direct control over natural resources in defense of the interests of national capital than as strategies for maintaining territories open for global capital accumulation. Instead of defending national interests abroad against rivals, U.S. imperialism should be seen as promoting the spread of capitalist relations throughout the world.

An alternative position within the Marxist tradition has emphasized the relevance of transnational production and finance to an understanding of the contemporary world political economy. The most influential writer in this line of research is William Robinson (2004, 2008), whose theory of global capitalism has posed an important challenge to the classical Marxist theories of imperialism in the context of the rise of a new global rather than international economy and the formation of a new transnational "historic bloc." For Robinson, "globalization" is a qualitatively new phase of global capitalism linked to neoliberalism that is associated with (1) the rise of a transnational capitalist class "tied to globalized circuits of production, marketing, and finances unbound from particular national territories and identities [whose] interests lie in global over local or national accumulation" (Robinson, 2004:

47) and (2) the transcendence of the nation-state by an emergent transnational state or architecture of multilateral institutions (Robinson, 2004: 85–144).

The implication of this theory is that traditional notions of U.S. imperialism cannot explain the dynamics of an emergent transnational hegemony or the role of the transnational capitalist class in promoting neoliberal expansion across the globe. Under this argument, even if the nation-state does not disappear entirely, it is no longer the necessary or predominant form for securing capital accumulation. The state has been not only transformed but also superseded as an organizing principle of capitalism by a transnational state apparatus. In Robinson's conceptualization, the nation-state is a historically specific form in the development of world capitalism that has been transcended by the forces of global capital. It is not static or immutable but "a specific social relation inserted into larger social structures" (Robinson, 2004: 100). Nor is it "immanent to capitalist development"; it may take different institutional forms at any historical moment (93). This provides the grounds for the argument that a new configuration of global capitalism is giving rise to an incipient transnational state that is coming to supplant the nation-state. "Power . . . shifts from groups with interests in national accumulation to those whose interests lie in the new global circuits of accumulation" (Robinson, 2004: 109). Robinson's proposed alternative for political economy research is a framework that does not regard the nation-state as the chief arena for capitalist development or class formation. In this vein, Avilés (2006: 113) has argued for a framework that sees the Colombian and Latin American states as "components of transnational states." This analysis has guided an important research agenda for exploring new processes of elite class formation as well as reconfiguration of the state in relation to new forms of capital accumulation in Colombia.

However, the problem with this framework is that it tends to view nation-states as "transmission belts" for the interests of global capital and the transnational elite (Robinson, 2004), with capital and the state developing more or less in parallel. The notion is based on a problematic understanding of the historical relation between the nation-state and capitalist development. It presumes that the state is the "institutionalized political form of the capital relation" (Lacher, 2005: 44). If this were so, it would suggest that "the territorial state rises and falls in more or less mechanical response to the movements of capital" (Wood, 2007: 154). This misleadingly implies an incompatibility between global capital and the nation-state, leading to the conclusion that transnational capital must operate primarily through a transnational state. States do not simply respond to the demands arising from capital accumulation but actively develop capacities and mechanisms to promote capital accumulation and manage its contradictions. This would suggest that instead of the nation-state's being eroded under global capitalism "the form of state intervention in the economy and society has changed considerably" (Barrow, 2005: 129).

In this regard, Panitch and Gindin (2003: 35) have criticized the tendency among globalization theorists to see states as "passive victims of globalization" rather than "its authors and enforcers." The increased internationalization of capital that has taken place since the postwar era is not so much about bypassing or eroding states as about being instigated by state activity (Panitch and Gindin, 2012: 4–5):

> It is . . . wrong to assume an irresolvable contradiction between the international space of accumulation and the national space of states. Rather, when looking at the role that states have always played on the international economic stage, we need to ask how far their activities have been consistent with extending capitalist markets internationally—and also consistent with the actions of other states.

Since the postwar era, the establishment of the international world order has depended on the role of nation-states both in "reorganizing and reproducing their respective countries' social relations and institutions of class, property, currency, contract, and markets" and in "promoting the accumulation of capital in a manner that contributed to the U.S.-led management of the international capitalist order."

At issue here is the separation of the political and the economic under capitalism, a historical notion that cannot be straightforwardly characterized as the former's reacting to the needs of the latter. The actions of states may have specific characteristics under capitalism, but they are not dictated by its needs. While states do not play a direct role in the organization of production, there is nonetheless an interdependent relation between capital and the state, with the latter taking responsibility for "maintaining property rights, overseeing contracts, stabilizing currencies, reproducing class relations, and containing crises" (Panitch and Gindin, 2012: 2). As Panitch and Gindin (2003: 35) point out, "Capitalism could not exist unless states did these things; and states are impelled to do them by virtue of their dependence on private accumulation for their own tax resources and the material foundations of their legitimacy." It is because of this particular relation between capital and the state that, as capitalism expands globally, it does not supersede the nation-state but rather "depends more than ever on a system of multiple and more-or-less sovereign national states" (Wood, 2003: 141) for its reproduction.

While the notions of the transnational state and the transnational corporation emphasize that the growing interpenetration of capital renders territorial notions of imperialism redundant, it is unnecessary to conclude that the

United States has lost its leading role in the world order. For Panitch and Gindin (2012: 9) what distinguishes the "U.S. informal empire" from the imperialism of the past is that, rather than simply defending its interests, the United States acts in favor of "the expansion, protection, and reproduction" of the global capitalist system *as a whole*. The distinctive feature of U.S. imperialism is not only promoting the interests of U.S. multinational corporations abroad but taking "responsibility for creating the political and juridical conditions for the general extension and reproduction of capitalism internationally" (6). While promoting the hegemony of U.S. capitalism, the United States creates the conditions for the spread of capitalist relations across the globe. In this sense, it plays a unique leading role in the world order without taking direct territorial control of other states in that order.

Within this United States–led world order, other states such as Canada have assumed the role of secondary or "sub-superpowers" that, despite not having the influence and resources of the United States, nonetheless play an important role in facilitating the entry of capital throughout the world (Gordon, 2010). Canadian imperialism has played a central role in natural-resource extraction in Latin America, as Gordon and Webber (2016: 29) have argued: "The Canadian state is assertively pursuing the conditions amenable to Canadian investors: liberalized markets, weak environmental regulatory regimes, and contained or repressed social movements." A further problem for the transnational state theory is the presumption that global expansion of capitalism merges all states into the world market in similar ways. According to Robinson (2001: 529), "The processes of uneven accumulation are unfolding in accordance with a social and not a national logic." The territorial differentiation of states is being ironed out by the conditions of uneven development. Although Robinson may accept that uneven geographic development takes place both within and across states, he argues that the notions of center and periphery and uneven development should be reconciled through "the point of insertion into global accumulation rather than their relationship to a particular national market or state structure" (2008: 44). However, as Bieler and Morton (2015: 113) emphasize, this leads to "a flattened ontology" removed from "the spatial and territorial logics of capital accumulation" and "the class struggles extant in specific locations." The notion overlooks the point that the internationalization of capital is accompanied by a simultaneous differentiation of capital into nation-states for the reproduction of class power and capital accumulation. As Wood (2007: 155) argues, "There are fundamental characteristics of capitalism that reproduce and benefit from the fragmentation of political space and uneven development, so that the current association of capitalism and the territorial state—with all its attendant contradictions—is not just a historical relic but is reinforced by the essential dynamics of capitalism." Rather than positing the inevitable formation of a transnational state, what is required is historical analysis of the territorial dynamics of capital accumulation, the role of states in making markets, the power struggles between elite factions, and the class struggles from below.

This chapter is based on historical materialist investigation into the role of imperialism and the processes of state and class formation in the making of Colombia as a mining country. Far from representing a neoliberal "withdrawal" of the state, the liberalization of the Colombian economy has been accompanied by considerable deployment of state power in the form of crisis management, institutional reform, security measures, and social repression to create the conditions for this form of capital accumulation. In particular, the growing dependence of the economy on foreign direct investment in mining has led the state to establish new mechanisms for guaranteeing the conditions of territorial security for these investments. This is evidenced in the strengthening of the Colombian state, the increase in military power, and the adoption of state-like functions by paramilitaries that took place between the late 1990s and early 2000s, in large part to attract and protect investments in mining.

The State and Extractive Capital: The Case of Colombia

Colombia's conversion into a neoliberal mining country provides an important illustration of the way nation-states act as the agents of the expansion of global capital. This is demonstrated in the reconfigurations of class relations and the state apparatus that have taken place in order to promote this new form of accumulation. During the postwar era, state policy on mining emphasized the role of this sector in import-substitution industrialization. In line with the developmentalist policy orientation of the time, the hydrocarbons sector was of key strategic importance for industrialization and the diversification of the economy (Hirschman, 1958). The state-owned company Ecopetrol maintained a monopoly on oil and limited foreign participation in oil production. This in turn supported the developmentalist agenda, allowing the government to use profits from high oil prices in the 1970s to modernize infrastructure, subsidize other sectors of national industry, and import capital goods.

A distinctive feature of the industrialization policies implemented in Colombia during this period is that, in contrast to the situation in other Latin American countries, they were not associated with left-leaning "national-populist" regimes. Rather, import-substitution policies from the 1930s on were introduced under conservative hegemony and the National Front power-sharing agreement of the ruling parties (1958–1974). In conjunction with the continued importance of primary commodities exports in the Colombian economy, this meant that rapid economic growth could take place without destabilizing the power of traditional elite forces. During this period, state protection and subsidies allowed for a rapid concentration and centralization of industry and finance, while highly capital-intensive technologies and limited worker rights served to depress wages (Avilés, 2006: 28–35).

The goal of developmentalist policy had been to use oil rents generated by high prices to establish a national industrial base. However, by the 1980s the model was increasingly less sustainable because of the growing inefficiency of state enterprises such as Ecopetrol, associated with its large management bureaucracy, high labor costs, the lack of international competitiveness, and the lack of investment in exploration. The exhaustion of many important oil fields coincided with a slump in oil prices in the late 1980s, which resulted in a major drop in oil production. The rapid growth experienced by Colombia in the postwar period was now giving way to stagnation, low levels of savings and investment, balance-of-payments problems, declining commodity prices, and capital flight. This scenario provided the background for the consolidation of power in socioeconomic blocs and a reorientation of the economic development agenda. The powerful economic groups abandoned their support for state protection and sought to rejuvenate their profits by joining the ranks of the transnational elite, pushing for trade liberalization, deregulation, and privatization (Kalmanovitz, 2003: 466).

Pressure from the United States and multilateral institutions was also mounting. Although Colombia was never subjected to the debt crises and structural adjustment programs that plagued most of Latin America in the 1980s, pressure to liberalize the economy was magnified by an International Monetary Fund (IMF) macroeconomic program and the conditionalities that increasingly accompanied U.S. military aid in this period. Under the principle that internal conflict could be resolved through the expansion of international commerce, accompanied by enhanced access to foreign markets and free-trade agreements that attracted foreign and domestic investment, U.S. military aid was granted on the condition of the implementation of a series of stabilization measures and the privatization of state companies (Leech, 2004).

In response to economic decline, on his 1990 election President César Gaviria introduced the "program for economic opening and modernization of the state," which liberalized trade in a bid to attract new foreign direct investment. The aim was for half of economic growth to come from foreign direct investment during his presidency, and the mining industry was singled out as the most dynamic sector to attract that investment (*Semana*, 1992). By 1998 the level of foreign direct investment had risen to US$3 billion (six times that of 1990), most of which went to the oil, coal, and nickel sectors (Giugale et al., 2003: 314).The surge in investment was a product of reorganization within the state. Connections with multinational mining corporations such as Drummond and Glencore were tightened (Cuervo, 2012), and the result was a new configuration of power involving the prioritization of apparatuses responsible for dealing with international capital. The liquidation of the state mining company, Minercol (along with the national mining union), and the sale of the state coal corporation, Carbocol, to a foreign consortium composed of Exxon Mobil, Anglo American, BHP Billiton, and Glencore International (Ismi, 2000) were reflective of the changing balance of power within the state apparatus, with the eventual subordination of the internal mining policy bodies such as the Industrial Development Institute and the prioritization of the section of Ecopetrol that had aligned its operations with multinational corporations such as Exxon.

By the late 1990s the declining productive base and increasing financial speculation had created a crisis in the economy and a soaring fiscal deficit. Against this backdrop, the state began to intervene with increasing force in an effort to maintain the conditions for global capital accumulation under neoliberalism. The economic crisis and social repression softened political resistance to policy change, and the government initiated a sustained and far-reaching program called the "second wave of reforms" (Estrada, 2006). The acceleration of liberalization measures was a direct response to conditions laid out in agreements with the IMF in 1999 and 2002, and the international financial institutions increasingly directed economic policy as the crisis grew (Estrada, 2006). Policies were designed as a means of crisis management, federal budget deficit reduction, and the restoration of investor and business confidence by increasing exports. They centered on liberalizing trade and attracting foreign capital, largely in the sectors of biofuels, oil and coal mining, and mineral extraction.

The neoliberal consensus on mining policy was enshrined in the adoption of the new mining code, Law 685 of 2001, which involved an agreement between the Colombian Ministry for Mines and Energy and the Canadian Energy Research Institute. The code reconstituted the property and contract law surrounding mining, opening up the titling process on a "first come, first served" basis, with equal access granted to foreign and domestic firms. It removed entry barriers for private investment such as taxes, restrictions, and environmental regulations. State participation in extraction was ruled out, and the role of the state was relegated to regulation and rent collection (Fierro, 2012: 38). With regard to minerals, mining royalty rates were reduced from up to 10 percent to a minimum of 0.4 percent (Pardo, 2012). These developments represented not a withdrawal of the state but its active reorganization and reorientation to create the conditions of reproduction of international capital. As the former minister for mines put it, "The role of the state is . . . to support businessmen, facilitate their work, and guarantee the stability and viability of the large-scale investments that the mining industry demands" (quoted in Fierro, 2012: 39).

The liberalization of mining policy opened the doors to a flood of foreign investment in the sector. While in 1996 the mining sector had represented only 2.2 percent of total foreign investment, by 2001 this had risen to 26 percent (Fernández and Valencia, 2010: 11). In particular, Canadian investment in the mining and petroleum sectors skyrocketed from US$1.4 million in 1999 to US$663.9 million in 2000 (Banco de la República, 2015). One result of the liberalization of mining policy was to make the mining sector a source of export growth that from 2002 on recorded growth rates far above the national average. Between 2002 and 2010 the mining sector's proportion of total exports rose from 13 to 24 percent (Banco de la República, 2015).

By the turn of the century it was increasingly clear that the neoliberal policy orientation had thrown the country into turmoil, marked by a decline in industry and agriculture and a dramatic rise in unemployment, which reached 20 percent in cities by 2001 (Lozano, 2001). Alongside this, the government was facing a legitimacy crisis associated with the rise of illegal armed groups and unprecedented levels of civil conflict. This spurred new processes of elite class formation. The increasingly unstable social climate generated by civil tensions provided the basis for the strengthening of alliances among the far-right sectors of large landlords, rural politicians, narcotraffickers, and paramilitary groups as well as the economic elites and multinational mining companies. This bloc, which Richani (2007) describes as "reactionary class configuration," also underwent major changes in terms of social composition and function during this period. The rural caudillos and private regional armies of the 1940s and 1950s were reconstituted as a reactionary social force of land speculators, agribusiness, multinational corporations, and the narco-bourgeoisie. Fearful of the incremental growth of the guerrilla forces throughout the countryside, other sectors of the industrial-finance elite and the political classes allied themselves with this rural bloc, which they saw as the only bulwark against social revolution.

As the Colombian countryside transitioned to neoliberalism, far-right armed groups were transformed into forces for securing the conditions of global capital accumulation, violently implementing repressive labor practices and dispossessing rural communities from strategic areas. Hristov (2014: 97) describes how this paramilitary activity focused on "forced displacement of populations from areas of strategic economic and/or military importance such as: land high in fertility; territories containing valuable natural resources such as minerals, gold, oil or precious woods." The land grab that ensued displaced an estimated 6 million predominantly rural inhabitants from 10 million hectares of land and initiated antiunion violence that saw the assassination of over 2,800 unionists between 1986 and 2010 (ABColombia, 2011). Through mechanisms of violent displacement and repression of labor, coercive state and parastate forces have been key to securing the conditions for this new form of capital accumulation.

This violence did not take place strictly outside the sphere of the state but was a vital part of its activities. As Hristov (2014: 151) notes, paramilitary violence was often carried out in conjunction with military operations and state control, combining violence with legal mechanisms to ensure social control, surveillance, restrictions on civil liberties, and the criminalization of dissent. She observes: "The relationship between the concentration of wealth and the use of violence has become more important than ever during the epoch of neoliberal restructuring." The increasing interconnection between the political classes and paramilitary groups went beyond corruption to become a systemic part of their operations, which were often formalized through pacts. In this sense, while the armed conflict in Colombia is rooted in the historical trajectory of class conflict, it has also been specifically adapted to new forms of state power in the neoliberal and extractive economy.

The United States played a major role in supporting and facilitating this reorganization of class and state under neoliberalism. In the late 1990s it intervened with the US$7 billion military aid package known as Plan Colombia, which integrated the Colombian conflict into the international War on Drugs by supporting a military (and, indirectly, paramilitary) offensive against peasants in the agrarian frontier zones. The result was the creation of the second-largest military institution in Latin America, with 500,000 soldiers and police officers, at a cost of 6 percent of the gross domestic product (GDP) and seven U.S. military bases (Villar and Cottle, 2011).

The 2002 election of Álvaro Uribe represented the culmination of the rise of the far-right elite from their origins as rural warlords to the capture of hegemonic state power under a repressive authoritarian regime (Hylton, 2014). Uribe embarked on a "scorched earth" strategy for defeating the guerrilla insurgents that enjoyed support from factions of the industrial and finance elite as well as the United States. Uribe's mining strategy was based on two main pillars: legal reforms and state-sponsored violence (Sankey, 2014). Foreign investment was promoted through further privatization of public resources, labor flexibilization, new labor laws including the extension of the workday and flexible dismissal, and incentives for extractive industry. Under the Democratic Security program, the Uribe administration raised the defense budget to 5.6 percent of GDP in 2008, up from 2.2 percent in 1990, increasing the numbers of public forces to around 250,000. The program saw extensive and systematic violation of human rights and sparked constant confrontations with the judicial branch. While coercive state power was justified as a means of containing the guerrilla insurgency, its biggest impact was in securing the conditions for the entry of extractive companies. Two-thirds of the troops were dedicated to protecting oil and mining industry infrastructure, and labor flexibilization was enforced through physical violence. Colombia has the world's largest number of unionists murdered, and the mining sector has been a particular target for violence. Between 2002 and 2011, 401 human rights violations were recorded among workers in the mining and energy sector, including 40 assassinations, 8 disappearances, 21 kidnappings, 5 cases of torture, and 180 death threats (Villamil, 2012). According to research by the unionist and lawyer Francisco Ramírez, 74 percent of human rights violations take place in mining and oil regions (which currently represent 32 percent of the national territory), and 87 percent of the people currently displaced originate from these zones. Between 1995 and 2002 there were 7,500 assassinations in these regions (Ramírez, 2015).

By the mid-2000s, the mounting costs of the military program and the growing fiscal deficit pushed Uribe to expand the mining industry further. Foreign investment and the prospect of new oil discoveries provided life support for a failing war economy, and Uribe desperately sought to attract foreign mining companies to make up for the shortfall. "Colombia will be attractive for investors," he announced at one mining conference in Medellín: "Colombia is ready to be a major mining country" (Harris, 2006). A 2005 report from the national planning agency for mines and energy entitled "Colombia: A Mining Country" aimed to make Colombia's mining sector the third-largest receiver of foreign direct investment (UPME, 2005) through an array of reforms surrounding taxes and investor protections. The regional president of one oil company in Colombia went so far as to observe that "the government is literally desperate to attract companies by presenting all types of concessions to entice them" (*New York Times*, 2004, quoted in Richani, 2010: 133). Uribe also expanded the war apparatus, provisioning a second phase of Plan Colombia entitled the "Social Recovery of Territory." This extended the military presence into fifty-three new regions of strategic importance where major companies such as BP, Repsol, and Harken were operating, and two new battalions were created to protect the mining and energy companies (Ramírez, 2015; Ismi, 2000).

Uribe proceeded to extend free-market policies, implementing labor and pension reforms and public-sector cuts to all areas except the military, and initiating free-trade agreements with the EU, China, the United States, and Canada. Ecopetrol was divided into three companies, and in its place the National Hydrocarbon Agency was made responsible for administering concessions for multinational corporations. What remained of the parastate institute was restricted to provision of infrastructure, pipelines, and transport (Quevedo, 2007). Protesting oil workers were met with fierce repression. The various measures had the expected effect of dramatically increasing foreign direct investment in mining and energy, which expanded tenfold from US$466 million to US$4.5 billion between 2002 and 2010, increasing its share of total foreign direct investment from 42 to 67 percent (Banco de la República, 2015). While during the Andrés Pastrana administration (1998–2002), 221,000 hectares of land were under mining concessions, during the Uribe administration this rose to 7.4 million (ABColombia, 2011).

Under the Santos administration, mining continued to expand as a result of favorable legislation and initially high commodities prices. Within the first year of the Santos administration, the number of mining concessions rose to 8.4 million, and in 2012 Santos opened two "strategic mining districts" covering 20.5 million hectares between them to be auctioned off to international investors (ABColombia, 2012). While Santos shared Uribe's aim of opening the country to untrammeled exploitation of natural resources, there were also differences in the approach. While the cornerstone of Uribe's mining strategy was a militarized securitization of resource-rich territories, Santos's discourse focused on institution-building and stability. Santos's National Development Plans of 2011–2014 and 2014–2018 both aimed at establishing the political and physical conditions that would place Colombia as one of the top destinations for foreign investment in mining in Latin America through mechanisms of juridical stability, institution-building, competitive fiscal policy, combating illegal mining activity, and development of physical infrastructure. Whereas Uribe had closed the Ministry for the Environment, Santos reopened it, providing more scope for an environmental agenda and national park protection.

The peace negotiations between Santos and the FARC-EP that took place between 2012 and 2016 were in part another reflection of Santos's aim to expand mining by creating more stable conditions in FARC-controlled territories. Costs of guerrilla attacks on oil pipelines and coal railroads were mounting up, with losses estimated to amount to US$400 million a year (Sequera, 2012). The treasury minister estimated that if peace negotiations were successful Colombia's GDP could grow by 1 to 2 percentage points annually (Sequera, 2012). Santos's aim, as Hylton and Tauss (2016) summarize, was to "consolidate this most recent period of primitive accumulation and 'stabilize' the country for local and transnational investment." However, the opening of spaces for rural participation such as peasant reserves and citizen participation in investment decisions put rural communities on the frontline of conflict and sparked new confrontations over the open-pit mining mode (Gutiérrez Sanín, 2019)

By the early 2010s, Colombia's extractives-based growth model was facing two existential threats: the exhaustion of oil reserves and a slump in commodities prices beginning in 2013. Increased dependence on the extractives sector had exposed the country to volatile world markets. In 2015 foreign direct investment fell to US$500 million, a quarter the level of 2010–2014, resulting in declining rates of economic growth and an increasing fiscal deficit.

Santos responded by deepening the country's dependency on raw-material extraction. "The mining locomotive is going to run full steam ahead," Santos declared in a meeting with the country's thirteen largest mining companies in 2013, and soon afterward he laid out a strategy of regulatory changes, tax cuts, and tributary benefits for mining corporations with the goal of expanding mining activities (Bermúdez, 2013). By the end of his presidency in 2018, Santos had the lowest approval rating of any Colombian president in a decade, 28 percent, as the economy continued to plummet and successive waves of protest shook the countryside.

Questions of land and resources and the extractives-based growth model were at the center of the 2018 election campaign. The Progressive candidate Gustavo Petro supported the peace deal and called for a move away from extractives-based growth in favor of a "productive economy." Notwithstanding a significant surge in support for the center-left, it was the right-wing candidate Duque who eventually won the election on a platform of opposition to Santos's peace deal and continuation of the extractivist-based growth strategy. His National Mining Plan 2018–2022 sought to extend natural-resource extraction by developing fracking and thermal coal and slashing taxes and royalties on mining. The increasing pressures on land that resulted from the rapid expansion of natural-resource extraction have brought displaced and rural communities into confrontation with mining companies. Duque has responded to emerging social conflicts with fierce repression, stigmatization, and attacks. In 2018 there was a 44 percent rise in attacks on human rights defenders, and in 2019 there was a further 66 percent rise. Around 700 social leaders were killed in the two years following the signing of the peace agreement in November 2016, many of whom were rural victims involved in land disputes (Indepaz, 2019). As rural conflicts proliferate under the extractivist growth model, Duque's regime has been associated with greater repression against frontline communities.

Imperialism and the Transformation of the Colombian State in the Neoliberal Era

Poulantzas (1974: 73) pointed out that "the current internationalization of capital neither suppresses nor bypasses the nation-states" but "deeply affects the politics and institutional forms of these states by including them in a system of interconnections." Multinational mining in Colombia is an example of the way the entrance of foreign capital is promoted by transformations of internal bourgeoisies and state apparatuses, but it would be misleading to view such transformations as the dismantling, bypassing, or weakening of the state. Rather, the Colombian state has taken active initiatives and implemented new forms of social repression to create and maintain the extractive economy. What the neoliberal project involves is not the dismantling of the state but a kind of reconfiguration of it to ensure the conditions for its own continued reproduction (Graf, 1995). This implies a major internal reconfiguration, with the expansion of institutes with functions such as debt management, accumulation, structural adjustment, and surplus extraction, alongside a severe contraction of social rights (Graf, 1995).

The institutional reorganization of the state has involved selectively dismantling or subordinating all or part of the internally oriented institutions and functions of the state, such as the Industrial Development Institute and Minercol, and promoting others that are responsible for the planning and implementation of the internationalization of the economy, including the Advisory Council on Economic Policy, the National Planning Department, the Geological Service, and the Fiscal Policy Institute. Since the economic opening of the 1990s, the Colombian state has exercised a significant degree of power in realigning state apparatuses with transnational capital by reconstituting property and contract law and implementing and enforcing the provisions of international trade and investment agreements. Meanwhile, state and paramilitary forces have increasingly engaged in violent territorial expansion. The Colombian state has not been "weakened" by global forces but has been a principal agent of global capital accumulation.

While the conversion of Colombia into a neoliberal mining country has been closely linked with authoritarian styles of governance and state-sponsored violence, corruption, and dispossession, it would be wrong to conclude that this is the only political form the mining economy could adopt. Under Santos there was a slight retreat from Uribe's authoritarian type of regime toward an emphasis on institution-building and infrastructure paying lip service to peace and democracy. However, the shift in Santos's policy and peace agenda took place in the context of severely limited room for maneuver in economic policy, with the economic development agenda limited to macroeconomic stability, high levels of foreign debt, the destruction of the country's productive base, and dependence on foreign direct investment for economic growth. It is an attempt to establish something akin to what Gills and Rocamora (1992) described as "low intensity democracy," which involves the minimum elements of democratic participation required to maintain stability, reduce class antagonisms, and preempt the struggle for more radical change.

The nation-state has always been a contested terrain between various blocs of capitalist classes. The growing dominance of foreign direct investment and the transnational elite within the economy is not so much a sign that a "transnational capitalist class" has delinked itself from its national territorial boundaries in favor of a transnational state as an indication of new alliances and realignments within elite power blocs. The fact that implementation of neoliberal policies has entailed a rise of social struggles, civil conflict, and a crisis of legitimation has in fact led Colombia's so-called transnational elite to ally itself with the forces of the far right in the exercise of unprecedented levels of state power in the form of social discipline.

The dynamics of the mining economy place severe limitations on the requirements for domestic legitimation. Critics have described this model as "predatory extractivism" because the costs of economic growth are placed on natural resources, precipitating ecological disaster and dispossession of peasant and indigenous communities from their lands by multinational corporations. According to government estimates, the current mining policy is set to come into conflict with 5.3 million rural inhabitants (*El Espectador*, January 25, 2011). Meanwhile, mining provides few jobs, brings no linkages to other sectors of the economy, and poses a threat to the economy's productive base. Thus, despite the peace accords, the transformation of Colombia into a mining country will continue to require strong state authority, since it requires prioritizing the demands of multinational corporations over domestic concerns and popular needs. In this context, the peace and democracy envisaged by Santos can at best be weak and only serve to contain the legitimacy crisis and quell the social conflict surrounding the mining economy.

Conclusion

The rise of neoliberalism and the extractive economy in Colombia are associated with both the restructuring of the state and the realignment of sociopolitical forces, but this does not amount to the retreat or end of the state. The Colombian state should not be seen as defenseless against the immutable forces of the global market, U.S. imperialism, or the power of transnational corporations. It is not that foreign capital has been imposed on the Colombian economy but rather that the state has exerted considerable power and played an active role in providing the political and territorial conditions for an increasingly globalized economy and the penetration of resource-seeking capital. Under changing conditions of the internationalization of capital, neoliberalism, and extractivism, the Colombian state has adopted new mechanisms and developed new capacities to pave the way for this form of accumulation through crisis management, realignment of institutes with transnational capital, revision of property law, free-trade agreements, flexibilized labor laws, and state-sponsored repression to deal with the legitimacy crisis.

Note

1. This chapter is a revised version of an article that appeared in *Latin American Perspectives* in 2018 (45 [5]: 52–70).

References

ABColombia

2011 "Returning land to Colombia's victims." https://www.abcolombia.org.uk/returning-land-colombias-victims-devolviendo-la-tierra-las-victimas-de-colombia/.

Avilés, William

2006 *Global Capitalism, Democracy, and Civil-Military Relations in Colombia.* Albany: SUNY Press.

2008 "US intervention in Colombia: the role of transnational relations." *Bulletin of Latin American Research* 27: 410–429.

Ballvé, Teo

2012 "Everyday state formation: territory, decentralization, and the narco landgrab in Colombia." *Environment and Planning D: Society and Space* 30: 603–622.

Banco de la República

2015 "Series estadísticas." http://www.banrep.gov.co/series-estadisticas/see_s_externo.

Barrow, Clyde

2005 "The return of the state: globalization, state theory, and the new imperialism." *New Political Science* 27 (2): 123–145.

Bermúdez, Andrés

2013 "La locomotora minera: a una velocidad para Santos, a otra para los mineros." http://lasillavacia.com/historia/la-locomotora-minera-una-velocidad-para-santos-otra-para-los-mineros-41593.

Bieler, Andreas, and Adam Morton

2015 "Axis of evil or access to diesel? Spaces of new imperialism and the Iraq War." *Historical Materialism* 23 (2): 94–130.

Bromley, Simon

2006 "Blood for oil?" *New Political Economy* 11: 419–434.

Cuervo Sotelo, Yohanna

2012 "Una aproximación a la megaminería en Colombia." *Theomai* 25: 137–147.

ECLAC (Economic Commission for Latin America and the Caribbean)

2015 "Foreign direct investment in Latin America and the Caribbean." http://repositorio.cepal.org/bitstream/handle/11362/38215S1500534_en.pdf;jsessionid=212071A3A39C58BC8A0363DD22D16A6B?sequence=4.

Estrada Álvarez, Jairo

2006 "Las reformas estructurales y la construcción del orden neoliberal en Colombia," in Ana Esther Ceceña (ed.), *Los desafíos de las emancipaciones en un contexto militarizado.* Buenos Aires: CLACSO.

Fernández, J. P., and M. A. Valencia

2010 *Libre comercio y minería en Colombia: El caso de la Anglogold Ashanti.* Bogotá: RECALCA.

Fierro, Julio

2012 *Políticas mineras en Colombia.* Bogotá: Instituto Latinoamericano para una Sociedad y un Derecho Alternativos.

Garay, Luis
2013 *Minería en Colombia: Fundamentos para superar el modelo extractivista.* Bogotá: Contraloría General de la Nación.
Gills, Barry, and Joel Rocamora
1992 "Low intensity democracy." *Third World Quarterly* 13: 501–523.
Giugale, Marcelo, Olivier Lafourcade, and Connie Luff
2003 *Colombia: The Economic Foundation of Peace.* Washington, DC: World Bank.
Gordon, Todd
2010 *Imperialist Canada.* Winnipeg: Arbeiter Ring Publishing.
Gordon, Todd, and Jeffery R. Webber
2016 *Blood of Extraction: Canadian Imperialism in Latin America.* Blackpoint, NS: Fernwood Publishing.
Graf, William
1995 "The state in the third world." *Socialist Register* 31: 140–162.
Grajales, Jacobo
2015 "Land grabbing, legal contention and institutional change in Colombia." *Journal of Peasant Studies* 42: 541–560.
Gutiérrez Sanín, Francisco.
2019 "The politics of peace: competing agendas in the Colombian agrarian agreement and implementation." *Peacebuilding* 7: 314–328.
Harris, Peter
2006 "Colombia gold again luring miners." *Mines and Communities.* January 4. http:// www.minesandcommunities.org/article.php?a=262.
Held, David, and Anthony McGrew (eds.)
2003 *The Global Transformations Reader: An Introduction to the Globalization Debate.* 2d edition revised. Cambridge: Polity Press.
Hirschman, Albert
1958 *The Strategy of Economic Development.* New Haven: Yale University Press.
Hristov, Jasmin
2014 *Paramilitarism and Neoliberalism: Violent Systems of Capital Accumulation in Colombia and Beyond.* London: Pluto Press.
Hylton, Forrest
2014 "The experience of defeat." *Historical Materialism* 22: 67–104.
Hylton, Forrest, and Aaron Tauss
2016 "Peace in Colombia, a new growth strategy: Colombia's peace deal is a remarkable achievement, but its economic implications are troubling." *NACLA Report on the Americas* 48 (3): 253–259.
Indepaz
2019 "Separata de actualizacion." http://www.indepaz.org.co/wp-content/uploads/2019/05/SEPARATA-DE-ACTUALIZACIO%CC%81N-mayo-Informe-Todas-las-voces-todos-los-rostros.-23-mayo-de-2019-ok.pdf.
Ismi, Asad
2000 "Profiting from repression: Canadian investment in and trade with Colombia." *Americas Update* 72.

Kalmanovitz, Salomon
2003 *Economía y nación: Una breve historia de Colombia*. Bogotá: Norma.
Kiely, Ray
2010 *Rethinking Imperialism*. Basingstoke: Palgrave.
Klare, Michael
2012 *The Race for What's Left: The Global Scramble for the World's Last Resources*. London: Macmillan.
Lacher, Hannes
2005 "International transformation and the persistence of territoriality: toward a new political geography of capitalism." *Review of International Political Economy* 12 (1): 26–52.
Leech, Garry
2004 "Plan petroleum in Putumayo." garryleech.com/2004/05/10/plan-petroleum-in-putumayo/.
2006 *Crude Interventions: The United States, Oil and the New World (Dis)Order*. London: Zed Books.
Lozano, Ignacio
2001 "Colombia's economy at the turn of the century: reforms and results of the free-market paradigm." http://www.yorku.ca/drache/talks/2001/pdf/lozano.pdf.
McLean, Phillip
2002 "Colombia: failed, failing, or just weak?" *Washington Quarterly* 25 (3): 123–134.
Panitch, Leo, and Sam Gindin
2003 "Global capitalism and American empire," in Leo Panitch and Colin Leys (eds.), *Socialist Register 2004: The New Imperial Challenge*. London: Merlin Press.
2012 *The Making of Global Capitalism: The Political Economy of American Empire*. London: Verso.
Pardo, Alvaro
2012 "Minería, renta minera y tributación." http://www.colombiapuntomedio.com/Portals/0/NuestrosDocumentos/Miner%C3%ADa,%20renta%20minera%20y%20tributaci%C3%B3n%202.pdf.
Pax
2014 "The dark side of coal." Pax for Peace. https://www.paxforpeace.nl.Petras, James
2012 "Imperialism and violence in Colombia." Paper presented at the national conference of SINALTRAINAL, "Multinationals, Violence, Trade Union Freedom, and Democracy in Colombia," Bogotá, July 26.
Pizarro, Eduardo, and Ana María Bejarano
2003 "Colombia, a failing state?" *ReVista: Harvard Review of Latin America*, Spring, 1–6.
Poulantzas, Nico
1974 *Classes in Contemporary Capitalism*. London: NLB.
Ramírez Cuellar, Francisco
2015 "Minería, territorio y conflicto en Colombia." *Memoria y Sociedad* 19 (39): 196–202.

Richani, Nazir
2007 "Caudillos and the crisis of the Colombian state: fragmented sovereignty, the war system, and the privatisation of counterinsurgency in Colombia." *Third World Quarterly* 28: 403–417.
2010 "Colombia: predatory state and rentier political economy." *Labour, Capital and Society* 43 (2): 120–141.
Robinson, William
2001 "Transnational processes, development studies and changing social hierarchies in the world system: a Central American case study." *Third World Quarterly* 22: 529–563.
2004 *A Theory of Global Capitalism: Production, Class, and State in a Transnational World*. Baltimore: Johns Hopkins University Press.
2008 *Latin America and Global Capitalism: A Critical Globalization Perspective*. Baltimore: Johns Hopkins University Press.
Sankey, Kyla
2014 "The mining boom: a motor of development or resistance?" in Henry Veltmeyer and James Petras (eds.), *The New Extractivism: A Post-Neoliberal Development Model or Imperialism of the Twenty-first Century?* London: Zed Books.
Semana
1992 "En busca de El Dorado." http://www.semana.com/economia/articulo/en-busca-el-dorado/17737-3.
Sequera, Vincent
2012 "Rebels step up attacks on Colombia energy targets." http://finance.yahoo.com/news/rebels-step-attacks-colombia-energy-targets-181308106.html.
Stokes, Doug
2005 "The heart of empire? Theorising US empire in an era of transnational capitalism." *Third World Quarterly* 26: 217–236.
UPME (Unidad de Planeación Minero Energética)
2005 *Buletín estadística de minas y energía 1999–2005*. Bogotá: UPME.
2006 *Colombia país minero*. Bogotá: UPME.
Villamil Velásquez, Javier Fernando
2012 "Consolidación de la gran minería transnacional en latinoamérica." *Theomai* 25: 46–57.
Villar, Oliver, and Daniel Cottle
2011 *Cocaine, Death Squads, and the War on Terror: US Imperialism and Class Struggle in Colombia*. New York: Monthly Review Press.
Weiss, Linda
1998 *The Myth of the Powerless State: Governing the Economy in a Global Era*. Cambridge: Polity Press.
Wood, Ellen Meiksins
2003 *Empire of Capital*. London: Verso.
2007 "A reply to critics." *Historical Materialism* 15: 143–170.

2

Financialization, Institutional Reform, and Structural Change in the Bolivian Boom (2006–2019)

Alfredo Macías Vásquez and Jorge García-Arias

THE BOLIVIAN ECONOMY HAS UNDERGONE substantial changes since Evo Morales came to power in 2006 (Farthing and Kohl, 2014). The social and economic outcomes of these changes have fostered hope for improvement in human development indicators for the majority of the population. However, a deeper analysis of these changes suggests the need for caution in determining what development strategy is best for the country. In the first place, the changes must be considered in terms of Bolivia's structural conditions in the framework of the international economy and beyond the cyclical fluctuations affecting the relevant macroeconomic variables (ECLAC, 2012). In the second place, the acceleration of international integration since the adoption of neoliberalism in 1985 significantly affects the institutional configuration of the Bolivian economy and conditions its medium- and long-term structural dynamics in both social and economic spheres (Boyer, 2012). To relate the two analytical dimensions, it is important to understand how financialization[1] impacts the socioeconomic structure of developing countries (Arestis and Caner, 2010; Morgan, 2011). In this article we attempt to analyze how the institutional control imposed on hydrocarbon revenue by financialization inhibits structural change in the Bolivian economy and threatens the long-term sustainability of recent improvements in social indicators.

Since Morales came to power a model of natural-resource exploitation has been established that differs significantly from classical extractivism, with more state intervention, more favorable contracts with transnational corporations, and efforts to add value to exports based on natural resources (see Ellner's introductory chapter in this volume). However, as noted by Gudynas (2012), although revenues have increased, altering the country's economic structure has remained enormously difficult. Taking into account the classical debates concerning structural and institutional obstacles to using economic surplus in peripheral economies (Baran, 1957; Diamand, 1972; Prebisch, 1981), we consider why increased resource nationalism has not been sufficient to produce a structural transformation of the Bolivian economy. Specifically, we explain how the conditions imposed by international financial institutions prevent the utilization of hydrocarbon revenues to promote national development, despite the clear political will of the Bolivian government. We first consider the characteristics of financialization in the present-day global economy, paying particular attention to developing countries endowed with natural resources. Second, we summarize the macroeconomic developments in Bolivia as they relate to our analytical discussion. Third, we analyze the policies and institutional reforms imposed on the country by the multinational debt relief initiatives[2] between 1998 and 2019 that specifically prevent the social appropriation of hydrocarbon revenue. Fourth, we consider the development strategy of the Bolivian government under Morales, based on resource nationalism.

Financialization and Economies Based on Natural-Resource Revenue

Financialization is pervasive in the current world economy. It influences the entire economic cycle and is part of the production of all goods and services (Marazzi, 2010). Financialization is no longer understood, as it was in much of the twentieth century, as an attempt to recover from financial markets what capital could not capture in the real economy. Previously, the financial and real economies were presented as antagonistic spheres; the financial economy thrived when the real economy declined. Today this is also the case—the financial economy works as an "artificial respiration" mechanism of the real economy—but financialization implies a new role. To the extent that the immaterial dimension acquires greater weight in the process of economic valorization, the financial economy appears not at the end of the production process but from its early stages. For example, if a pharmaceutical company discovers that an active ingredient in an Amazonian plant can cure COVID-19 (a discovery that represents an immaterial asset, knowledge), the first thing that will happen, before the material production of the drug, is a sharp rise in the stock of the pharmaceutical company, enhancing its capacity to borrow and issue new stock.

Financialization is now recognized as setting in motion new forms of value production that cannot be directly exploited by the elites (as can common natural and cultural resources when they are not their direct property). For example, the pharmaceutical company did not put the jungle and the tribal shaman to work to produce the jungle plant and the knowledge about its active ingredient. This is not a matter of the materials or workers involved in the production process of a factory. A new way of extracting its economic value is needed. First, it is necessary to dispossess the natives of these riches through intangible assets based on the enclosure of natural and cultural resources (especially patents). Secondly, the valuation of these intangible assets is carried out through the financial markets (a factory of salaried shamans is not created in the middle of the Amazon), with futures contracts and the issuance of corporate bonds and stock.

All areas of everyday life, from education to communication, health, and pensions, are part of the process. Any development strategy based on the contradictory relationship between the real and the financial economy that attempts to ignore the role of the financial markets is doomed to failure. Although financialization today, as in the past, involves a paralysis of accumulation (investment) produced by the failure to reinvest increasing profits in production, the sources of these profits have diversified over the past three decades and now transcend classical surplus-value production. For example, today mining and agricultural operations are mainly a financial business. These companies make their production and marketing decisions on the basis of the evolution of the financial markets for raw materials. The successive speculative bubbles associated with raw-material production are clear examples of this increase in nonaccumulated gains, that is, benefits that are not reinvested in the real economy.

Many scholars point out that financialization affects not only the manner in which the economy is regulated financially but also capital accumulation and creates contradictory outcomes such as asset or real estate bubbles (Aglietta and Rebérioux, 2004).[3] Increasingly, the pursuit of profit is based on value appropriation mechanisms operating outside production. Consequently, the only way to maintain the value of the assets is to provoke, through deliberate political actions (privatizations), a scarcity of natural resources, health, or knowledge. The important thing is to limit access to resources through the imposition of property rights, copyrights, trademarks, etc. In these appropriation mechanisms, financial income is transformed into profits (Vercellone, 2010). Benefits are increasingly based on two mechanisms related to unproductive capital appreciation. On the one hand, property rights (shares, patents, royalties) and credit instruments (which include public debt) represent important profit-making mechanisms (Fumagalli, 2007; Chesnais, 2012). On the other hand, while direct control over production depends on hierarchical relationships within the firm (managers impose on workers what they should produce), indirect control over the market depends on mechanisms external to the firm, above all on the establishment of monopolistic or oligopolistic arrangements that guarantee the concentration of profits in the most powerful actors (Boyer, 2012).

Applied to natural resources, financialization means that business is largely based on the rentier management of the income derived from the exploitation of those resources. The predominance of rent over profit is based on the fact that profitability depends less on the sale of raw materials than on the mechanisms external to the extractive activity itself (for example, the privatization of the financial system or pension administration, which becomes another financial business) that are responsible for diverting the surplus generated toward the elites that control the process. For this reason, the institutional configuration of a given economy plays an important role (Acemoglu and Robinson, 2012). Specifically, in the case of Latin American countries, the hierarchical role of international economic relations is critical (Boyer, 2012). In recent decades, international financial organizations have imposed on Latin American economies institutional reforms, such as the liberalization, privatization, and fiscal discipline applied in the context of the Washington Consensus, that are designed to reduce the ability of national and sovereign entities to manage those economies (Ffrench-Davis, 2010).

Structural Challenges Posed by the Bolivian Economy

As of 2006, Bolivia had experienced a historical change in its development and its near-future development opportunities (Farthing and Kohl, 2014; Martínez Erades, 2017; Stefanoni, 2011). Legislative measures on the taxation of hydrocarbons activity beginning in 2006 led to a significant increase in tax and other revenues that were further increased by favorable international prices for hydrocarbon products. Moreover, despite the conditions imposed by the International Monetary Fund and the World Bank on economic policies and institutional reforms (primarily associated with the national financing system), the multilateral debt relief initiatives implemented since 1998 have led to a significant improvement in the financial sustainability of the country. In this context, the Bolivian economy benefited from a period of increased economic growth that enabled the gross domestic product (GDP) to double between 2006 and 2011, largely because of the 2000s commodities boom (IMF, 2012) and the economic nationalism of the Morales government. This led to an increase in per capita income that had been almost unimaginable just a few years before. In the middle of the past decade Bolivia was a low-income

TABLE 2.1
Evolution of the Bolivian Economy, 2006–2015

Year	*GDP Growth (%)*	*Trade Balance (US$ millions)*	*International Reserves (US $ millions)*	*International Reserves (% GDP)*	*Fiscal Deficit (% GDP)*	*Inflation (%)*
2006	4.8	1,243	3,194	28	4.5	4.9
2007	4.6	1,215	5,314	40	1.7	11.7
2008	6.1	1,698	7,720	46	3.2	11.8
2009	3.4	909	8,575	49	0.1	0.3
2010	4.1	1,448	9,730	49	1.7	7.2
2011	5.2	1,280	12,019	50	0.8	6.9
2012	5.1	3,401	13,927	51	1.8	4.5
2013	6.8	2,673	14,430	47	0.6	6.5
2014	5.5	2,360	15,123	46	−3.3	5.2
2015	4.8	−920	13,054	39	−6.9	3.0
2016	4.3	−1,305	10,081	30	−7.2	4.0
2017	4.2	−970	10,261	27	−7.8	2.7
2018	4.2	−981	8,946	22	−8.3	1.5
2019	2.4	–	6,468	16	–	1.5

Source: CBB (2020) and NIS (2020).

country with a per capita income of less than US$1,000; by 2015 it was a lower-middle-income country with a per capita income of US$3,077, and it has remained at this level over the past few years. Public finance, foreign accounts, and net foreign exchange reserves have achieved record highs (table 2.1).

The period from 2006 to the end of high raw-materials prices in 2014 can be considered a genuine boom. However, with the global crisis of 2008 Bolivia experienced three exogenous shocks that, however brief, highlighted its vulnerability to shifts in the global economy. First, the rapid deterioration in the terms of trade driven by the decline in the international prices of gas and minerals was reflected in the development of an unfavorable trade balance and the reduction of economic growth. Second, there was a reduction in emigrant remittances from 7.4 percent of the GDP in 2007 to 3.6 percent in 2015 (CBB, 2016). Third, there was a reduction of international aid associated with the implementation of the multilateral relief initiatives from 2.9 percent of GDP in 2003 to 1.2 percent in 2008. (Since the global economic crisis, international aid has partially recovered, reaching 2.5 percent in 2015.)

With the end of the period of high raw-material prices, structural problems in the Bolivian economy became increasingly evident and worsened (Smith, 2019). For example, there was a sharp deterioration in fiscal and trade deficits between 2014 and 2019, along with a significant increase in external debt (table 2.2).

TABLE 2.2
Evolution of Public Debt (US$ millions) in Bolivia, 2006–2015

	2006	*2007*	*2008*	*2009*	*2010*	*2011*	*2012*	*2013*	*2014*	*2015*	*2016*	*2017*	*2018*
Domestic	3,378	3,433	3,831	4,144	4,456	4,413	4,123	3,903	4,012	3,949	4,150	4,360	5,239
External	3,248	2,208	2,443	2,918	3,235	3,837	4,525	5,584	6,036	6,613	7,268	9,428	10,178

Source: CBB (2020).

However, government policy under Morales has been prudent, as is evidenced by high levels of foreign currency reserves and low levels of inflation.[4] In contrast to what has occurred in Ecuador and Venezuela, the Bolivian economy has maintained a stable macroeconomic policy within very orthodox limits (Macías Vázquez and Alonso González, 2016). Historically, it has followed a primary-export-growth model. The revenue from the export of underground resources (initially tin and now natural gas) has played a key role in financing major macroeconomic imbalances. This revenue has represented the main source of foreign exchange for the import of industrial intermediate and finished goods, especially durable goods, mainly to satisfy the demand of the members of the elite (NIS, 2020). When the foreign exchange obtained from international trade was insufficient, the country was forced to resort to borrowing on the international markets or from official multilateral or bilateral entities. This type of borrowing was typically accompanied by economic and political requirements (cutbacks in public spending, institutional reforms, or liberalization of protected markets), and consequently external constraints on economic growth have served to mortgage the development aspirations of the Bolivian people.

Since the 1952 revolution and especially since the 1970s, political projects aimed at promoting structural change in the economy have failed as a result of financial constraints imposed from abroad.[5] The trigger of these crises has always been the same—deteriorating terms of trade. These projects have been temporarily financed by loans from abroad, which ultimately lead to financial insolvency. Consequently, revenue derived from the export of natural resources has not guaranteed sustained economic growth over time. State ownership of these resources and the levies imposed on the profits generated have increased the feasibility of development strategies based on primary resources but have been insufficient (Kaup, 2010). In fact, beyond the negative effects of sudden fluctuations in the international prices of raw materials, there are other structural limitations inherent in a low-income economy that make it difficult to build long-term alternative development strategies,[6] even when the terms of trade improve and external financial restrictions are relaxed.

Thus the political debates currently taking place in Latin America, particularly within Pink Tide governments and movements, with regard to the possibility of developing alternative strategies for moving beyond extractivism are of central importance to the future of the region. These governments embraced resource nationalism in order to channel rents from extractive industries toward new productive sectors. However, after a decade of boom, the extractivist model of accumulation remained hegemonic in these countries, demonstrating that the problems impeding structural transformations are far deeper (Macías Vázquez and Alonso González, 2016).

The Bolivian economy is structurally heterogeneous, and this greatly impedes the flow of capital from one modern sector to another that is lagging behind. Thus the popular economy characterized by low productivity, especially in rural and low-income urban areas, was responsible in 2005 for nearly 83 percent of employment but only 25 percent of GDP. By contrast, the large corporate economy (including mining and gas companies) was highly productive in capital terms, contributing 65 percent of GDP with only 9 percent of the employed workforce (World Bank, 2005). Although rents derived from mining and hydrocarbons have grown substantially, public investment of these resources in productive activities linked to the economic fabric of the community and the informal economy cannot automatically solve the profitability problems inherent in these sectors as a result of skill shortages, the small size of farms, and the deterioration of communication and transport infrastructure. In addition, deepening the primary-export model in recent years (table 2.3) has not turned foreign trade into an instrument for structurally transforming the productive economy. Between 2015 and 2019, the decline in the share of hydrocarbon exports in foreign trade has mainly been due to falling international prices. However, the decline has been offset by the higher share of mineral exports.

Bolivia is increasingly orienting its foreign trade toward neighboring countries, highlighting that the country's exports are concentrated in the sale of natural gas and certain minerals and reproducing classic center-periphery patterns. This focus on the export of natural resources has been strengthened in recent years by subregional integration initiatives such as Mercosur and the Bolivarian Alliance for the Peoples of Our America (ALBA).

TABLE 2.3
Sectorial Structure of Exports (% of total), 2006–2015

	2006	*2007*	*2008*	*2009*	*2010*	*2011*	*2012*	*2013*	*2014*	*2015*	*2016*	*2017*	*2018*
Mineral resources	24.3	28.4	27.4	33.6	33.9	37.3	31.2	24.9	30.2	32.2	42.3	46.7	44.1
Hydrocarbons	47.9	45.9	49.4	38.5	42.4	44.9	49.0	53.6	50.8	44.7	30.6	32.8	34.6
Nontraditional exports	18.9	19.6	17.2	21.8	19.8	15.0	17.0	19.3	16.7	19.4	25.2	18.8	20.2
Others	9.2	6.1	6.1	6.1	3.9	2.8	2.8	2.3	2.3	3.9	1.9	1.7	1.1

Source: NIS (2020).

Economic and Institutional Obstacles to Mobilizing Domestic Public Resources

The International Monetary Fund (IMF) boldly predicted in 2012 that there would be no financial problems in Bolivia in the coming decades (IMF, 2012). Because of external debt relief, the country's accumulated foreign exchange reserves,[7] and the overall strength of the economy, there does not appear to be a risk of financial insolvency in the near future as there has been in previous crises. Instead, the challenge for the Morales government has been how to finance the structural change anticipated by the five-year national development plan approved in 2007 (Ministry of Development Planning, 2006). This plan was constrained by the institutional reforms and macroeconomic conditions imposed during the course of multilateral debt relief initiatives since 1998.

A single event demonstrates the tensions created by this situation. In the fall of 2009, the Morales government requested a loan of US$10 billion from the World Bank to finance investments for the national development plan, particularly transportation infrastructure. Because it is a landlocked country, transportation costs in Bolivia are on average 20 percent higher than those in Brazil (World Bank, 2005). The amount requested was nearly equivalent to the country's GDP. Among Bolivian commentators (Fundación Jubileo, 2009; *La Clase*, 2009) there was controversy about the purpose of these transportation infrastructure investments. The government argued that infrastructure development was needed to strengthen the domestic market and thus encourage industrialization. Its critics suggested that the investments were designed to strengthen Bolivia's role in creating bioceanic corridors, prolonging its primary-exports approach. The multilateral loan was rejected, and this led to an increase in foreign borrowing by other means to finance new infrastructure investments; in 2016 the Inter-American Development Bank (IADB) replaced the Andean Development Corporation (ADC) as the main creditor of the Bolivian economy, followed by the ADC, the World Bank, and China.[9] The government has also turned to the private market in New York to offer US$1 billion in sovereign bonds. In recent years, with the increase of Bolivia's foreign debt, the IADB and the World Bank have again become the nation's principal creditors.

An analysis of these actions raises the following important question: Despite the growing financial needs associated with infrastructure investment and the development of new productive projects, why must the country borrow so much foreign currency, especially given the level of international reserves and revenue in state coffers as a result of the hydrocarbons boom? There is no simple answer to this question. It might be argued that long-term loans from development financial institutions are better suited to this type of investment than the direct allocation of fiscal resources or reserves. Conversely, others argue that concessional external financing may reduce incentives to increase domestic resources (derived, for instance, from taxes). In fact, however, the government had no choice. The macroeconomic conditions imposed by the IMF forced it to maintain healthy fiscal accounts and high international reserves, preventing the use of revenues generated by the raw-materials boom to achieve the objectives set by the national development strategy. These conditions culminated in the loss of state control over the surplus generated by hydrocarbons activity. In addition, they greatly limited the ability to use the revenue to transform the economy and take significant steps forward in the fight against poverty.

Macroeconomic Conditionality

In recent decades, international financial institutions have imposed low inflation targets on poor countries, although there is no evidence that they necessarily lead to economic growth (Pollin and Zhu, 2006). Among all the possible options, a restrictive monetary policy is likely to be the most damaging to the achievement of structural change in an economy, since inflation may have a structural cause (Pinto, 1973). When agriculture is unable to produce enough to feed the growing population due to urban growth, inflationary tensions arise that cannot be eliminated through restrictive monetary policy.

In Bolivia, as inflation threatened to rise, the countercyclical orientation of economic policy intensified through interest-rate increases and fiscal prudence. Notwithstanding, the Morales government not only maintained its fight against inflation with restrictive policies but also sought alternatives that would generate some political leeway for stimulating economic growth. Because inflationary pressures have been closely associated with rising food prices, measures have been implemented to supply domestic markets (CBB, 2012). In addition to applying these heterodox measures, the monetary policy of the Morales government has been characterized by the defense of the national currency to counter the budding dollarization that had occurred prior to 2006. Although all these measures have proven insufficient to promote the structural change of the economy, they have achieved price and exchange rate stability without going too deep into monetary and fiscal restrictions (Martínez Erades, 2017).

In addition, a rather orthodox exchange rate policy has negatively impacted the economy's competitiveness. The international financial institutions continued to press the government to strengthen the Central Bank beyond the legislative concessions made by the Morales government in 2012 (IMF, 2016). However, in response to the transitory shock represented by the rise in food prices (2007–2008), the monetary authorities overreacted with restrictive measures on the money supply (Arestis et al., 2008). Consequently, the national currency has remained strong in an effort to contain external inflationary pressures due to the rise in international prices mentioned above (CBB, 2012). Despite the intent of industrial policy, this has reduced the possibility of increasing nontraditional exports, again strengthening an economic structure based on extraction. With better development of the national financial system, inflation would have had less of an impact on the foreign currency market, the Central Bank would have been less pressured to design its monetary policy in terms of the risks that international financial crises have for its banks, and the government would have had much greater leeway in decision making (ECLAC, 2012). The Central Bank has to keep the currencies as reserves in the event of banking crises instead of using them as an investment to promote the national economy.

Finally, the conditions imposed by stabilization and structural adjustment programs[9] in the 1980s and 1990s forced Latin American governments to exercise strict fiscal prudence; as a result, fiscal policy has not been used to promote economic growth (Weeks and Patel, 2007). The obsession with combating fiscal deficits may make countercyclical fiscal policy chronic, with significant implications for the country's development prospects (Ffrench-Davis, 2010). Persistent fiscal austerity limits the ability to use fiscal resources for infrastructure investment and productive projects. Moreover, by freezing or reducing public spending on social services, austerity strategy impedes the generation of equality of opportunity through the improvement of education and health (Sen, 1999).

Institutional Reforms

The combination of these macroeconomic policies undoubtedly intensified Bolivia's history of dependence on natural resources, which accelerated with the economic reforms spanning the period from 1985 until Morales's assumption of power (ECLAC, 2012). The problem, however, is not just that macroeconomic policy generated difficulties in channeling domestic resources toward structural change. In addition, institutional reforms, especially those adopted in the pension system and in public finance, diverted resources to other areas. Thus a second question arises: Why is it that we see such significant growth in domestic and external public debt[10] when public accounts have shown a persistent fiscal surplus over the past decade?

There are two reasons a country issues debt: to fund the fiscal deficit generated by the government and to withdraw from the economy the money supply that is cyclically issued by the Central Bank (when the economy grows, it

TABLE 2.4
Pension Fund Participation in Domestic Public Debt (Bs millions), 1998–2011

Year	*Domestic Public Debt*	*Bonds in Pension Funds*
1998	6,538	1,224
1999	8,128	2,239
2000	10,134	3,298
2001	14,009	4,453
2002	16,225	5,879
2003	18,996	7,142
2004	21,962	8,437
2005	23,748	9,658
2006	24,130	10,922
2007	24,522	11,799
2008	27,371	12,147
2009	29,602	12,459
2010	31,831	12,558
2011	31,528	13,082

Source: Ministry of Economy and Public Finance (2012).

issues less; when it declines, it issues more). In Bolivia (after five years of fiscal surplus) it is quite surprising that the debt issued by the National Treasury increased steadily in the remaining years of the Morales government. The largest holder of securities is the Pension Fund Administration (table 2.4). Since the pension reform imposed by international financial institutions in 1996, the government has had to purchase debt owed to the Pension Fund. In principle, these figures might be considered in a positive light. In the first place, it is useful to reduce the risk of financial investments made with the pension savings of Bolivians, and government bonds appear to be a good tool for achieving this goal. In the second place, resorting to public-sector domestic financing by structuring the savings of Bolivian workers in this manner (through issuing bonds to the Pension Fund) may be appropriate provided that it does not replace better investment alternatives.

However, to fully assess the overall impact of pension system reform, we should consider the most contentious issues. The worldwide trend toward privatizing social protection systems in which banks came to play a key role is one of the direct consequences of financialization (Martin, 2002). In Bolivia pension fund management is in the hands of foreign banks[11] and represents a risk to the extent that, despite oversight by national monetary authorities, it is conditioned by the economic performance of these banks on a global scale. In December 2010 a new pensions law was enacted that provided a new method for collecting and distributing contributions and retirement payments. Beginning in January 2011 the Morales government took over the administration of pension funds, thus entering a new period that might be called "pension nationalization." With this reform, foreign private entities were replaced by a state long-term social security management system, and a comprehensive pension fund including solidarity contributions was created.

This kind of state intervention in the economy, which is typical of resource nationalism, was implemented in other spheres, such as the financial and fiscal system. Changes were also made in the financial system with the May 2011 law on banks and financial entities, under which the system's interest-rate regulation prioritized the reduction of lending rates and encouraged productive loans to agricultural and microenterprises. In addition, the Productive Development Bank was assigned a greater role in this endeavor, which was accompanied by a greater emphasis on equity, solidarity, and equality of opportunity. This law was expected to eliminate the institutional barriers to structural change established over the past decade—an indication of the relative independence of the government in the financial arena.

These heterodox reforms demonstrated that the Morales government enjoyed some room for maneuver in decision making, given that it did not require external financing during the boom period (Arauz et al., 2019). In fact, the political influence of international financial institutions in Bolivia was not as strong as it had been in previous years (Kohl and Farthing, 2009; Fernández Terán, 2003). While the IMF and the World Bank lending policies have been relaxed globally following the 2008 market crisis (Macías Vázquez, 2011), the conditionality intended to ensure the solvency of debtor nations continues to be stringent. The government's increased room for maneuver is the result of its greater financial independence. Nevertheless, the possibilities for maneuver were significantly reduced between 2015 and 2019 by greater financial dependence on multilateral agencies, which will most likely increase after the coup d'état against Morales in November 2019.

In the case of the tax reforms, the situation was less positive (Evia et al., 2008). During the boom, Bolivia accumulated significant budget surpluses each year. Indeed, the state had historically never had so much money saved (Ministry of Economy and Public Finance, 2012). With these resources, which exceeded the total annual revenue from hydrocarbons, social and infrastructure investments could have been made without external borrowing. This situation was the result of several factors, but all pointed to the inconsistency between the distribution of resources and the needs of existing departments (states) across the country. For one thing, the richest departments received five times more resources than the poorest (*Correo del Sur*, July 18, 2015). Moreover, the law required that the proceeds of the direct tax on hydrocarbons be invested in infrastructure, particularly in the national road network, but infrastructure needs were not considered when the resources were distributed. As a result, there was increasing reliance on external debt. The increase in tax revenue following the nationalization of

TABLE 2.5
Proportion of Public Sector Income Represented by State Hydrocarbon Revenue (US$ millions)

Year	*State Hydrocarbon Revenue*	*Public Sector Income*	*% Revenue / Income*
2005	1016.3	2895.0	35
2006	1547.3	3721.6	42
2007	1705.2	4273.8	40
2008	2548.6	5422.1	47
2009	2731.3	5653.5	48
2010	2614.0	6001.6	44
2011	3240.9	7793.3	42
2012	4563.2	9224.6	48
2013	5758.2	11181.9	51
2014	5777.2	12363.2	47
2015	4149.1	11827.16	35
2016	2339.4	10538.8	22
2017	2371.5	10906.5	22
2018	2788.5	11217.5	25

Source: Ministry of Economy and Public Finance (2016).

the hydrocarbons industry in 2006 would have had a major impact on the structural transformation of the national economy if territorial distributions were subject to national strategic planning criteria. In large part, the belligerence of departments controlled by the opposition impeded progress in this direction. At the same time, dependence of public finances on hydrocarbons income (table 2.5) was problematic because hydrocarbons are nonrenewable and their prices highly volatile.

Development Strategy during the Boom

According to a 2012 IMF report on the Bolivian economy, it appears that macroeconomic performance has been the reward for social sacrifices. In this study, as in others,[12] the IMF associated advances in macroeconomic performance with the implementation of economic policies it had imposed but ignored the role played by economic policies and institutional reforms applied as a result of government initiatives (Weisbrot et al., 2009). In 2003 the country's fourth general economic and social development plan characterized the structure of the economy as heterogeneous and as having a tendency to concentrate income in the richest sectors of the population (Wanderley, 2009). Thereafter, in the context of national dialogue during those years of intense political and social conflict, a development strategy based on a "broad base" was considered (UNDP, 2005). When Evo Morales came to power in 2006, this alternative vision of development was consolidated and deepened. Specifically, the new government's 2007 development plan represented a milestone in Bolivian economic history in that it sought to overcome the country's historical development pattern and eliminate the poverty and social exclusion suffered by much of the population, particularly indigenous people. From our perspective, the most interesting aspect of the plan was that it aimed to address the country's serious social problems through changes in the productive structure (through diversification) with the goal of achieving a more just society.

In previous decades, the fight against poverty had been conceived of as part of the neoliberal-inspired "trickle-down theory" (Macías Vázquez, 2014). Hopes were placed in economic growth through liberalization that would stimulate productivity. Instead of changes in the country's productive structure what was sought was short-term interventions linked to a continuation of the existing one, which remained weak as a result of the application of successive adjustment programs following the external debt crisis. By contrast, the 2007 plan's economic policy guidelines were based on a structural analysis of the economy rather than on marginal calculations without structural consequences.[13] They were centered on two broad sectors[14]: the surplus-generating (hydrocarbons, mining, electricity, and natural resources) and the employment- and income-generating (agriculture, manufacturing and handicrafts, tourism, and housing). The surplus-generating sector was seen as strategic for economic growth but as requiring significant investment in technology. Accordingly, state intervention was crucial to ensure that public companies maximized surplus and provided reinvestment or transfer to sectors that would generate employment and revenue. The employment- and income-generating sector was essential for articulating development processes that were economically sound and socially equitable. There were, however, difficulties associated with the extreme heterogeneity of this sector, which included companies with very low productivity that made profitable investments in them particularly problematic.

The relationship between the two sectors developed as follows: The surpluses generated (primarily) by the hydrocarbons and mining sectors provided resources to the sectors that generated employment and revenue, contributing to the diversification of the country and improving social conditions. However, at an early stage, a percentage of the surplus was invested in the "above-ground" industrialization of extractive activity to add value to the primary hydrocarbons resources so that the evolution of the surplus was not unduly exposed to cyclical swings in the international prices of raw materials. The main means for achieving these development goals was the nationalization of hydrocarbons announced in May 2006.[15] The objective was to increase the state revenue obtained from the extraction of hydrocarbons in accordance with resource nationalism. Although there is reasonable doubt about the capacity of the government to control the distribution of profits between the state and the transnational corporations (Molero and Paz, 2012), it is clear that tax revenues increased significantly after nationalization, from US$174 million in 2001 to US$1.7 billion in 2010.

The 2010 national development plan (Ministry of Development Planning, 2010) abandoned structural analysis and the objective of channeling rents from extractive industry into the community and the informal economy. In large part this change in orientation was related to the weakening of the social bloc that had brought Morales to power and the political offensive of the elites and the opposition. The main objective of the new plan was to incorporate value added from the exploitation of natural resources, the emblematic project being the industrialization of lithium.[16] As in Ecuador and other Pink Tide countries, there was a strategic turn in development objectives and in the social alliances that supported them (Macías Vázquez and Alonso González, 2016). Investments were once again concentrated around extractive industries and the construction of infrastructure to connect hydrocarbons and mineral deposits more rapidly to global markets (table 2.6). In parallel fashion, productive alliances were formed between business and government technocrats with the financial participation of other governments, such as those of China and Brazil. In these alliances, popular sectors and communities were no longer prioritized.

Following Rodrik (2007), we think that the country correctly identified institutional devices to trigger rapid economic growth. Some of these have

TABLE 2.6
Priority Investments (US$ millions), 2010–2015

Mining	7,294
Hydrocarbons	7,048
Electric power	6,585
Transport	5,597
Industrial production	931
Home building	680
Communication	460
Water and sanitation	386
Eradication of poverty	251
Dams and irrigation	91
Tourism	69
Health	68
Citizen security	58
Science and technology	40
Others	2,435

Source: Ministry of Development Planning (2010).

been noted above, among them the nationalization of hydrocarbons and the pension and financial system reforms. In the fiscal and labor spheres, more ambitious reforms were needed to move toward a less structurally and territorially heterogeneous economy with less revenue concentrated in a few hands. It remained to be seen whether the country could articulate an institutional framework that allowed for the consolidation of long-term growth, deeper structural change, and protection from the inevitable exogenous shocks of the future (Seoane, 2008). The strategic changes carried out under the 2010 development plan did not point in this direction.

Final Thoughts

In contrast with the neo-extractivism thesis, which argues that the policies of the Pink Tide governments represented a return to the neoliberal past (Gudynas, 2012; Swampa, 2019), we propose a more balanced assessment of the actions taken by these governments. Analyzing the Bolivian experience, we consider it important to differentiate two aspects. On the one hand, there is no doubt that the policies pursued by Evo Morales's government were very different from those of previous administrations and that their economic and social objectives were extremely ambitious considering the historical evolution of the country. In fact, the results obtained for certain social and even economic indicators (such as doubling the GDP) have been clearly positive (Arauz et al., 2019). On the other hand, this experience brings to light the limits of the political voluntarism of resource nationalism, especially when the country's structural and institutional imperatives at the international level are taken into account. Certainly, in the context of the commodities boom, these global requirements were practically neutralized. But as the international economic situation worsened during the 2015–2019 period, the structural problems derived from overreliance on raw-material exports were aggravated. Lack of political ambition is not the underlying problem of Pink Tide governments like that of Morales. They adopted a resource nationalist policy that was markedly different from those applied by other Latin American governments. However, although resource nationalism is positive, it does not in itself guarantee that the resources obtained by the state from extractive industries will contribute to the structural economic change necessary to move beyond the extractivist model.

Institutional reforms sponsored by international organizations as a result of debt relief initiatives have conditioned the capacity of the Bolivian government to allocate hydrocarbons revenue toward structural change (Endegnanen and Tessema, 2019). In the financialization of the global economy, these institutional reforms are conceived as value appropriation mechanisms derived from the external exploitation by multinational corporations of natural resources, mainly through the management of public debt (domestic and foreign), trade and financial liberalization, and fiscal decentralization. Macroeconomic policies are conceived as mechanisms for disciplining public and private actors and end up discouraging any national-developmental impulse.

Essentially, stronger state intervention, including radical tax reform to finance revenue redistribution and to make education and health policy more consistent, is required to influence this structural dynamic (Salama, 2006). Obviously, the state intervention cannot be identical to that implemented in recent decades; manufacturing has changed, and so have the integration of countries into the world economy and the structure of domestic consumption. This is not simply a matter of increasing public spending; instead, it will require an intelligently restructured allocation of public resources in each specific case. At the same time, an effective development strategy should distance itself from the political and economic frameworks employed thus far, particularly since multilateral agencies are ready to impose stricter guidelines to ensure the financial sustainability of low-income countries (Macías Vázquez, 2011). Thus the goal should be to continue developing sustainable financing strategies for lower-income countries from the perspective of structural relationships between external financing and economic development, including financial instruments for development cooperation and substantial reforms of the international financial system (García-Arias, 2013).

Bolivia under Morales was well placed to implement structural economic changes and accumulated sufficient capital to start the process. The nationalization of oil and gas and the pension system, along with financial reforms, pointed in the right direction, reducing dependence on multilateral institutions. However, the development process only began to take its first steps (Rodrik, 2007). It was necessary to reconsider the strategic orientation of the development process, recovering the objectives of national productive integration and overcoming the endemic heterogeneity of the socioeconomic structure. In Morales's last development plan, attempts were made to address these problems (Ministry of Development Planning, 2016). Nevertheless, a second generation of institutional reforms and a new political economy that increases long-term growth across a broader social and territorial base were needed to take the next steps.

The Bolivian experience, like those of Venezuela and Ecuador (Macías Vázquez and Alonso González, 2016), contains important lessons. After a decade of launching new development projects, it is time to take stock of their results. In our opinion, what is problematic is not attempting to overcome an extractivist model through extractivism itself, as postdevelopment writers claim (Gudynas, 2012; Svampa, 2019), but trying to achieve structural change in the economy without decisively confronting the influence of financialization on the channeling of fiscal resources obtained from the export of raw materials.

Notes

1. This chapter is a revised version of an article that appeared in *Latin American Perspectives* in 2019 (46 [2]: 47–64). "Financialization," a term widely used since the late 1990s (Lapavitsas, 2013), refers to a systemic transformation in the world economy that combines expansion of the role of finance with strategic changes in the behavior of nonfinancial actors such as the involvement of nonfinancial corporations in the world of finance, the increased indebtedness of individuals who invest their savings in financial markets, and the tendency for states to act as financial agents.

2. These initiatives represent a joint push by the International Monetary Fund (IMF) and the World Bank to address the structural problems of large foreign debt in low-income countries. They aim to ensure that these countries, which have serious deficiencies in their human development indicators, stop allocating scarce financial resources to debt service payments and devote more to social spending. The Heavily Indebted Poor Countries initiative, for example, contemplates the reduction of debt to all creditors, including the multilateral organizations themselves. Countries participating must adopt an adjustment program including strict compliance with the payment schedule established with the creditors and a poverty reduction strategy consisting of institutional reforms that are considered fundamental for improving the effectiveness of social spending.

3. This position was defended by the regulation school, which emerged in France in the 1970s as a theoretical response to the crisis of Fordism and the failure of Keynesian policies. The school argued that institutional forms and the economic system interact to give rise to different regimes of accumulation, such as the Fordist and the Post-Fordist regimes.

4. In addition to being defended by the relevant ministers of the Morales government (such as Minister of Economics Luis Arce Catacora), the prudence shown by the Bolivian monetary authorities under Morales corresponded closely to the guidelines issued by the IMF (2006). These guidelines have also been applied in many other Latin American countries (ECLAC, 2017).

5. In 1971 Hugo Banzer, supported by the Nationalist Revolutionary Movement, led a coup that initiated the last authoritarian development project experienced by the country and ended in dismal failure several years later.

6. Such limitations might include the following: a very low national productive investment rate, the most obvious manifestation of a bourgeoisie with a strong rentier profile; foreign direct investment oriented toward the exploitation and sale of natural resources with little connection to the national productivity framework; and marked technological constraints on a natural-resource exploitation strategy consisting of investment in upstream links to the supply chains of hydrocarbons and other resources.

7. In terms of percentage of GDP, Bolivia maintains higher international reserves than those held by China. However, in addition to taking into account the prevention mechanism involved in accumulating these reserves, maintaining them involves an opportunity cost. For example, a portion of Bolivia's reserves is invested in U.S. Treasury securities, which have very low yields. Returns might be higher if domestic investments were made.

8. Recently, China granted the Bolivian government a loan of US$7 billion (22.8 percent of GDP) for the construction of the interoceanic railroad.

9. Programs applied when there are problems in the payments of credit granted by international financial institutions, which continued with a more social orientation in this century

10. Although public-sector domestic financing eliminates currency risk, domestic debt is more expensive than foreign debt because domestic interest rates are higher than international ones.

11. The two main pension funds are managed by two major foreign financial groups: Previsión AFP, which controls almost 55 percent of the market and belongs to BBVA, and Futuro de Bolivia, which controls 45 percent of the market and belongs to the Zurich Group.

12. Specifically, the IMF praised the Morales government's fiscal policy but considered its successes to be based on the prudent management of revenue, which generated significant surpluses. It also welcomed the government's monetary policy for keeping inflation under control.

13. Marginal analysis, in economics, rejects the use of value judgments for making economic policy decisions, taking into account only decisions that do not affect the distribution of income among different groups.

14. In addition, there are two transverse areas of action. The first area is related to infrastructure (transportation and telecommunications). The second is associated with supporting production and is subdivided into two instruments: financial services for production (the National Productive Development Finance System, including the Productive Development Bank) and services oriented toward technological development (the Bolivian System of Innovation).

15. Presidential Decree 28071, which nationalized oil and gas reserves, establishes that the state will control at least 51 percent of each of the companies privatized in the previous decade, in addition to installed refineries, and receive 82 percent of the revenue from large gas companies.

16. Brazil and Bolivia signed an agreement on cooperation for the scientific and technological development of the lithium industry concentrated in the Salar de Uyuni, where according to the Morales government half of the world's reserves of this mineral lie.

References

Acemoglu, Daron, and James A. Robinson
2012 *Why Nations Fail: The Origins of Power, Prosperity, and Poverty.* New York: Crown Publishing Group.

Aglietta, Michel, and Antoine Rebérioux
2004 *Dérives du capitalisme financier.* Paris: Albin Michel.

Arauz, Andrés, Mark Weisbrot, Andrew Bunker, and Jake Johnston
2019 *Bolivia's Economic Transformation: Macroeconomic Policies, Institutional Changes and Results.* Washington, DC: Center for Economic and Policy Research.

Arestis, Philip, and Asena Caner
2010 "Capital account liberalization and poverty: how close is the link?" *Cambridge Journal of Economics* 34 (2): 295–323.
Arestis, Philip, Luiz Fernando de Paula, and Fernando Ferrari-Filho
2008 *Inflation Targeting in Brazil.* Working Paper 544. New York: Levy Economics Institute of Bard College.
Baran, Paul A.
1957 *The Political Economy of Growth.* New York: Monthly Review Press.
Boyer, Robert
2012 "Diversité et évolution des capitalismes en Amérique Latine: de la régulation économique au politique." *Revue de la Régulation: Capitalisme, Institutions, Pouvoirs* 11 (1). http://regulation.revues.org/10026.
CBB (Central Bank of Bolivia)
2012 *Boletín estadístico.* La Paz: Central Bank of Bolivia.
2016 *Boletín del sector externo.* La Paz: Central Bank of Bolivia.
Chesnais, François
2012 *Las deudas ilegítimas: Cuando los bancos meten mano en las políticas públicas.* Madrid: Clave Intelectual.
Diamand, Marcelo
1972 "La estructura productiva desequilibrada argentina y el tipo de cambio." *Desarrollo Económico* 12 (45): 25–47.
ECLAC (Economic Commision for Latin America and the Caribbean)
2012 *Cambio estructural para la igualdad: Una visión integrada del desarrollo.* Santiago: Economic Commission for Latin America and the Caribbean.
Endegnanew, Yehenew, and Dawit Tessema
2019 *Public Investment in Bolivia: Prospects and Implications.* IMF Working Paper WP/10/151. Washington, DC: International Monetary Fund.
Evia, José Luis, Ximena Coronado, and Markus Steinich
2008 "¿Hacia dónde se encamina la descentralización fiscal en Bolivia?" *Revista Latinoamericana de Desarrollo Económico* 10: 9–58.
Farthing, Linda C., and Benjamin H. Kohl
2014 *Evo's Bolivia: Continuity and Change.* Austin: University of Texas Press.
Fernández Terán, Roberto
2003 *Fondo Monetario Internacional, Banco Mundial y Estado neocolonial: Poder supranacional en Bolivia.* La Paz: Plural Editores.
Ffrench-Davis, Ricardo
2010 "Macroeconomics for development: from 'financierism' to 'productivism.'" *CEPAL Review* 102: 7–26.
Fumagalli, A.
2007 *Bioeconomia e capitalism cognitive: Verso un nuovo paradigma di accumulazione.* Rome: Carocci.
Fundación Jubileo
2009 *¿Continúa la cadena de deuda externa para Bolivia?* Fundación Jubileo, Reporte de Coyuntura 8. La Paz: Fundación Jubileo.

Garcia-Arias, Jorge
2013 "The systemic approach to international financing for development and the need for a world tax and financial organization." *European Journal of Development Research* 25 (1): 60–77.
Gudynas, Eduardo
2012 "Estado compensador y nuevos extractivismos: las ambivalencias del progresismo sudamericano." *Nueva Sociedad* 237, 128–146.
IMF (International Monetary Fund)
2006 *World Economic Outlook: Globalization and Inflation.* Washington, DC: International Monetary Fund.
2012 *Bolivia: 2012 Article IV Consultation.* IMF Country Report 12/149. Washington, DC: International Monetary Fund.
2016 *Bolivia: 2016 Article IV Consultation.* IMF Country Report 16/577. Washington, DC: International Monetary Fund.
Kaup, Brent Z.
2010 "A neoliberal nationalization? The constraints on natural-gas-led development in Bolivia." *Latin American Perspectives* 37 (3): 123–138.
Kohl, B., and L. Farthing
2009 "Less than fully satisfactory development outcomes: international financial institutions and social unrest in Bolivia." *Latin American Perspectives* 36 (3): 56–78.
La Clase
2009 "Bolivia: ¿Es necesario endeudarse con el FMI y Banco Mundial?" October 15.
Lapavitsas, Costas
2013 *Profiting Without Producing: How Finance Exploits Us All.* London: Verso.
Macías Vázquez, Alfredo
2011 "Replanteamiento de la cooperación en los países de bajos ingresos en el contexto de la crisis global." *Revista de Economía Mundial* 29: 121–149.
2014 "Crecimiento, desigualdad y pobreza: estado de la cuestión." *Revista de Economía Institucional* 16 (31): 101–126.
Macías Vázquez, Alfredo, and Pablo Alonso González
2016 "Between 'neodevelopmentalism' and 'postdevelopmentalism': towards a theory of a dispersed knowledge economy in Ecuador." *Canadian Journal of Development Studies* 37 (1): 47–65.
Marazzi, Christian
2010 *The Violence of Financial Capitalism.* Cambridge: MIT Press.
Martin, Randy L.
2002 *Financialization of Daily Life.* Philadelphia: Temple University Press.
Martínez Erades, Coral
2017 "Modelo económico y patrón de desarrollo en Bolivia: tendencia de reproducción y ruptura entre 2005 y 2015." Ph.D. diss., Complutense Universidad de Madrid.
Ministry of Development Planning
2006 *Plan nacional de desarrollo "Bolivia digna, soberana, productiva y democrática para vivir bien": Lineamientos estratégicos 2006–2011.* La Paz: Ministry of Development Planning.

2010 *Plan nacional de desarrollo 2010–2015.* La Paz: Ministry of Development Planning.
2016 *Plan nacional de desarrollo 2016–2020.* La Paz: Ministry of Development Planning.
Ministry of Economy and Public Finance
2012 *Estadísticas fiscales.* La Paz: Ministry of Economy and Public Finance.
2020 *Estadísticas fiscales.* La Paz: Ministry of Economy and Public Finance.
Molero Simarro, Ricardo, and María José Paz Antolín
2012 "Development strategy of the MAS in Bolivia: characterization and an early assessment." *Development and Change* 43: 531–556.
Morgan, G.
2011 "Global financial architecture and national capitalisms." *Socio-Economic Review* 9: 588–596.
NIS (National Institute of Statistics)
2020 *Estadísticas económicas.* La Paz: National Institute of Statistics.
Pinto, Aníbal
1973 *Inflación: Raíces estructurales.* Mexico City: Fondo de Cultura Económica/El Trimestre Económico.
Pollin, Robert, and Andong Zhu
2006 "Inflation and economic growth: a cross-country non-linear analysis." *Journal of Post-Keynesian Economics* 28: 593–614.
Prebisch, Raúl
1981 *Capitalismo periférico: Crisis y transformación.* Mexico City: Fondo de Cultura Económica.
Rodrik, Dani
2007 *One Economics, Many Recipes: Globalization, Institutions, and Economic Growth.* Princeton: Princeton University Press.
Salama, Pierre
2006 *Le défi des inégalités: Amérique latine/Asie, une comparaison économique.* Paris: La Découverte.
Sen, Amartya
1999 *Development as Freedom.* Oxford: Oxford University Press.
Seoane, Alfredo Flores
2008 "La inserción de Bolivia en la economía mundial: una mirada crítica al post-neoliberalismo." *Umbrales* 17: 57–92.
Smith, Noah
2019 "Bolivia's problem is macroeconomics, not socialism." *Bloomberg.* https://www.bloomberg.com/opinion/articles/2019-02-22/bolivia-s-problem-is-macroeconomics-not-socialism.
Stefanoni, Pablo
2011 "Bolivia hoy: rupturas, inercias y desafíos." *Bolivian Studies Journal* 18: 23–48.
Svampa, Maristella
2019 *Las fronteras del neoextractivismo en América Latina: Conflictos socioambientales, giro ecoterritorial y nuevas dependencias.* Bielefeld: Bielefeld University Press.

UNDP (United Nations Development Program)
2005 *Informe temático sobre desarrollo humano 2005: La economía más allá del gas.* La Paz: United Nations Development Program.
Vercellone, Carlo
2010 "The crisis of the law of value and the becoming-rent of profit," pp. 85–118 in A. Fumagalli and S. Mezzadra (eds.), *Crisis in the Global Economy. Financial Markets, Social Struggles, and New Political Scenarios.* Cambridge: MIT Press.
Wanderley, Fernanda
2009 *Crecimiento, empleo y bienestar social: ¿Por qué Bolivia es tan desigual?* La Paz: CIDES/UMSA/Plural Editores.
Weeks, J., and S. Patel
2007 *Fiscal Policy.* Brasilia: Centro Internacional de Políticas para el Crecimiento Inclusivo.
Weisbrot, Mark, Rebecca Ray, and Jake Johnston
2009 *Bolivia: The Economy during the Morales Administration.* Washington, DC: Center for Economic and Policy Research.
World Bank
2005 *Bolivia Poverty Assessment: Establishing the Basis for Pro-poor Growth.* Informe 28068-BO. Washington, DC: World Bank.

3

South-South Cooperation or Dependency with "Chinese Characteristics" in Venezuela?

Emma Miriam Yin-Hang To

CHINA'S INCREASED PARTICIPATION IN THE world market and its resultant demand for energy has contributed to exacerbating the vulnerability of many externally oriented resource-rich countries. As a consequence, since the early 2000s the relationship between China and Venezuela has gone far beyond trade to an "energy cooperation" model with joint ventures and development funds not only in oil but also in nonresource sectors of the Venezuelan economy. Despite massive increases in social expenditure, Latin American theorists arguing from a neo-dependency perspective have questioned the long-term benefits of this so-called cooperation. They have characterized the relationship as "neo-extractivist" in reference to the historically dependent relationship between Latin America and countries in the Global North. I argue that the relationship is contradictorily based on both South-South cooperation and rearticulated global political and economic inequalities; they are not mutually exclusive. The state-state relationship is based on cooperation, but the behavior of the Chinese private sector reflects many of the structural problems that Venezuela has faced since the discovery of oil.[1]

The economic relationship between China and Latin America has grown exponentially since the early 2000s, a period that coincided with the so-called Pink Tide—the electoral victories of left and moderate left governments in much of Latin America. The relationship between China and Venezuela has attracted considerable attention because of the emphasis of the former government of Hugo Chávez on South-South cooperation as a means to ending the dependent relationship between Venezuela and the United States and the Global North. With declassified documents exposing U.S. intervention in Venezuela in the April 2002 coup (Golinger, 2005), Venezuela sought to diversify its export markets with a focus on China.

Despite China's willingness to extend this relationship beyond the oil sector, Latin American neo-dependency theorists such as Alberto Acosta (2009, 2011), Edgardo Guydnas (2010a), and Maristella Svampa (2011) have characterized the relationship between China and Latin American countries like Venezuela as "neo-extractivist," arguing that Chinese capital has simply replaced that of the United States and Europe. One of their key concerns is the irony of consciously anti-neoliberal left-wing Latin American governments' continuing the historical dependency on natural-resource extraction (Gudynas, 2010). They argue that despite government rhetoric against such dependency, the logic of the Washington Consensus has been replaced by the "commodities consensus" led by resource exports to China. To what extent is the relationship between China and Venezuela based on South-South cooperation and to what extent on rearticulated global political and economic inequalities? Does the current context of U.S. sanctions against Venezuela reflect South-South cooperation or rearticulated dependency in the Sino-Venezuelan relationship?

Overview

The Sino-Venezuelan diplomatic relationship was established on June 28, 1974, during the first presidency of Carlos Andrés Pérez (1974–1979), a period characterized by an outward-oriented Venezuelan foreign policy that sought stronger ties with countries of the Global South. This period was also marked by very high oil prices, which contributed to high fiscal spending but also to heavy indebtedness through the mortgaging of future oil profits. Between 1974 and the electoral victory of President Hugo Chávez in 1998, the key event in Sino-Venezuelan relations was the signing of a bilateral agreement for joint oil exploitation in 1996 in the context of the policy known as the "opening" ("Apertura") of the Venezuelan state oil company Petróleos de Venezuela S.A. (PDVSA).

In 1999 Sino-Venezuelan trade amounted to US$200 million, but nine years later, during the Chávez era (1999–2013), it had increased fiftyfold, to US$10 billion (Paz, 2013: 223). By 2014 trade between Venezuela and China had reportedly reached US$169.8 billion (Xinhua, 2015). Between 2004 and 2011, Venezuelan oil exports to China increased from 14,000 to more than 400,000 barrels per day (Crooks and Cancel, 2012), with Venezuela becoming one of China's top 10 sources of oil imports by 2011 (Sun, 2015: 223). Between 2008 and 2012, the China Development Bank (CDB) loaned over US$40 billion to Venezuela's Banco de Desarrollo Económico y Social (Economic and Social Development Bank —BANDES) (Liu Kegu, cited in Sanderson and Forsythe, 2012: 123, 127). By 2016 loans had reportedly expanded to more than US$65 billion (BBC Mundo, 2016), the most that the CDB had ever lent to a Latin American country. China has continued to be a significant trading partner under President Nicolás Maduro (2013–present). In 2015, Venezuela was exporting approximately 700,000 barrels per day to China (*Petroleum Economist*, 2015). China has reportedly invested US$62 billion in developmental projects in Venezuela since 2007 (*Latin American Herald Tribune*, February 14, 2017). In July 2014 the Chinese government elevated the Sino-Venezuelan relationship to the status of a "comprehensive strategic partnership" (Ministry of Foreign Affairs of the People's Republic of China, 2014).

Since the death of President Chávez in March 2013 and the fall in oil prices in the second half of 2014, the Venezuelan economy has been in deep recession and Venezuela has experienced significant political instability. Since 2016, China has ceased extending so-called unconditional loans and instead tied new loans to joint ventures in the Venezuela oil industry (Kaplan, 2016: 659; Kaplan and Penfold, 2019: 5). Following the executive order of 2015 that sanctioned seven Venezuelan officials, the United States began imposing sanctions on the Venezuelan economy in August 2017. These sanctions, which were followed by additional ones, have contributed to the deepening recession in Venezuela.

The sanctions in August 2017 prevented Venezuela from borrowing in the U.S. financial market and prevented the Venezuelan government from restructuring its foreign debt (Weisbrot and Sachs, 2019: 7). This in turn inhibited Venezuela's access to foreign exchange and cash flow for ongoing costs associated with maintaining oil production and the import of basic consumption goods. Sanctions in 2019 cut U.S. imports of Venezuelan crude and pressured third parties to avoid all trade with Venezuela.

Prior to the 2019 sanctions on the Venezuelan oil industry, the majority of Venezuelan crude had been destined for the U.S. and European market, although there had been significant increases in Venezuelan oil exports to Asia, particularly China. The nation's oil exports to the United States declined from over 1,000,000 barrels per day in the late 1990s to under 800,000 barrels per day in 2015 (*Petroleum Economist*, 2015; EIA, 2017). Until the introduction of the 2019 sanctions, the United States had been the top cash buyer of Venezuelan crude (Eaton and Cohen, 2019), notwithstanding the fact that Asia had overtaken the United States as the top destination for Venezuelan oil exports (Buitrago, 2014).

The Sino-Venezuelan relationship is ostensibly based on two complementary characteristics: China's pursuit of energy security and Venezuela's need to "sow the oil" out of oil-dependency.[2] Since the economic reforms of 1978, the Chinese economy has been transformed into the world's manufacturing workshop and has increased demand for raw materials, particularly energy. Despite some oil production by the China National Petroleum Corporation (CNPC) in China, it is highly dependent on external energy sources. This demand led it first to resource-rich East Asian neighbors but then to South America, Africa, and Australia.

During the 2000s, high mineral prices and increased demand from China and elsewhere saw many resource-rich countries around the world escape many of the recessionary effects of the 2008 global financial crisis. In the wake of the global financial crisis, Chinese banks saw a key opportunity to expand as financial sectors in the United States and Britain were contracting (Guo, 2010). Key to this objective was developing Chinese investments in both developed and developing countries. The CDB altered its focus as part of this wider strategy, becoming a major financier of energy deals in the pursuit of the status of a "sound top-ranking international bank" (former governor of CDB Chen Yuan, quoted in Sanderson and Forsythe, 2013: 39). In 2010 alone, it extended to Venezuela a loan of US$20 billion (Ferchen, 2018).

Since the early 2010s, factors such as excess industrial capacity in China and increased production of nonconventional energy in North America and elsewhere have produced a glut of oil on the world market, resulting in falling mineral prices. For many resource-rich countries, the significant increase in extractive activity has undercut the profitability of labor-intensive sectors such as manufacturing (Goodman and Whitworth, 2008: 205). This takes place as a result of the inflationary effects accompanying high resource prices, a phenomenon economists call the "Dutch Disease" (Corden, 1984): a boom in the resource sector that causes incomes to rise in that sector and draws labor from lagging nonresource export and other nontradable sectors. China's increased participation in the world market through its demand for energy has thus contributed to exacerbating the vulnerability of many externally oriented resource-rich countries.

The "Dutch Disease" is often thought of as a purely economic problem in which government intervention can ameliorate the so-called distortions created by a booming resource sector relative to lagging nonresource domestic sectors (Sachs, 2007). Despite the existence of resources and particularly oil in both advanced industrial Northern countries and postcolonial Southern countries, the "Dutch Disease" appears to be an affliction more for the latter. Consequently, this structural imbalance cannot be viewed ahistorically. In addition, it has been reinforced by various foreign institutions and political interventions. Oil-exporting countries have historically been the target of high levels of external intervention, whether from foreign private interests or from foreign national states acting on behalf of those interests (Karl, 2007: 256). In Venezuela this external intervention has shaped the very establishment of Venezuelan state institutions and local cultural attitudes toward oil (Tinker Salas, 2009; Coronil, 1997: 91, 94).

For most of the twentieth century, successive Venezuelan governments have attempted to ameliorate the effects of the "Dutch Disease" by increasing oil income and reinvesting it in nonresource sectors. Despite government investment in agricultural and industrial sectors during boom times, these sectors have continued to lag, causing heavy reliance on imports for basic consumption goods. In 1999 the newly elected Chávez government revamped Venezuela's political institutions after a period of economic recession and the demise of the previous two-party ruling establishment.[3] In doing so, the government claimed that it was trying to ameliorate the booms and busts associated with extreme economic dependence on external demand for oil in a highly unpredictable and volatile market.

Despite investments in many nonresource sectors, the Chávez era actually saw increased dependence on oil rather than diversification in nonresource export industries. Between 1998 and 2014, the proportion of oil in Venezuelan exports increased from 68.7 percent to 96 percent (Lander, 2014; BCV, 2015). Since 2014, the Venezuelan economy has been in severe recession due to an oil bust. However, the current economic downturn has different characteristics from previous ones because of Venezuela's more diverse oil export markets, which now include China, India, and Russia. To what extent are the bilateral agreements between Caracas and Beijing aiding Venezuela's progress toward a more diversified economy and to what extent a continuation of dependence on foreign capital? How is this new relationship between China and Venezuela different from previous relationships with U.S. and European capital?

South-South Cooperation or "Boomerang Aid"?

Sino-Venezuelan cooperation in nonresource activities such as infrastructure, technology, and agriculture is facilitated by three institutions—the China-Venezuela High-Level Mixed Joint Committee (MJC), the China-Venezuela Joint Fund (JF), and PDVSA (Sun, 2015: 170–171). The MJC facilitates bilateral negotiations. The JF provides liquidity through Chinese financial institutions and is the mechanism through which Venezuelan agencies repay Chinese companies. PDVSA underpins the relationship between China and Venezuela, since it is Venezuelan crude oil exports that repay Chinese loans, and it does so by selling to Chinese oil companies.

The agreements established by the MJC have opened up the Venezuelan market to Chinese companies. Chinese companies, financed by generous low-interest loans from the CDB, are guaranteed contracts—though they need to compete among themselves—for infrastructure projects from the Venezuelan government (Kaplan, 2016: 661). These projects have included the Simón Bolívar satellite, worth US$406 million, five metro lines (two in Caracas and one each in Los Teques, Valencia, and Maracaibo), the train line from Cúa to Ecrucijida, and the Gran Mariscal de Ayacucho highway (Barbosa, 2008; PDVSA, 2009: 128). CITIC Construction, a subsidiary of the Chinese government majority-owned CITIC Limited, won the contract to build the Fuerte Tiuna housing project in Caracas, which was worth US$1.57 billion and consists of 116 apartment blocks and 29 public buildings and provided 13,000 residences (CITIC Limited, 2014: 41; 2017: 150). CITIC Construction has also since completed a desalination plant and an air force and navy command headquarters (CITIC Limited, 2017: 148; 2018: 157).

The telecommunications companies Alcatel Shanghai Bell, Huawei Technologies, and ZTE Corporation signed with Venezuelan state-owned CVG Telecom to develop a fiber-optic network in Venezuela (Mather, 2006). In 2009 ZTE collaborated with the VTELCA workers' cooperative in Falcón state to produce the first Venezuelan mobile, the Vergatario (VTELCA, 2017). In August 2011 the first Chinese automotive factory was opened in Aragua state by Chery Auto, producing two cars, the Arauca and the Orinoco, named after Venezuelan rivers (Sanderson and Forsythe, 2012: 138). In February 2017 China and Venezuela signed twenty-two new agreements worth US$2.7 billion to expand investments in heavy machinery production, infrastructure projects, cargo transport, and imports of vehicles, computers, and other consumer goods (Koerner, 2017; *Latin American Herald Tribune*, 2017).

Western financial analysts, using the short-term measures for returns applied by U.S. credit-rating agencies, have questioned the wisdom of China's unprecedented number of loans to Venezuela. From independence until the 1990s, foreign investors have viewed sovereign defaults and hyperinflation as the main reasons for the lack of stable returns in Venezuela (Sanderson and Forsythe, 2012: 126). Is this really a worthwhile risk for China? Following the logic of China's long-term need to secure oil supplies, the oil-for-loans arrangement can be considered a means to reduce risk, since it essentially provides China with a hedge against future fluctuations in the price of oil (Sanderson and Forsythe, 2012: 132–133). Although supply contracts between China and Venezuela have varied over time, after the peak in oil prices in 2008[4] agreements were switched to call-options contracts in which maximum and minimum prices were set. China had the right but not the obligation to buy an agreed-upon quantity of oil from Venezuela within a given time frame at a particular price,[5] which reduced the risk of its having to pay an upward-spiraling price for oil.

The three-year supply contract associated with the CDB's initial US$4 billion loan stipulated that PDVSA would ship 100,000 barrels per day to a subsidiary of the CNPC, the China United National Oil Corporation (PDVSA, 2009: 128). The second such contract, tied to the CDB's second US$4 billion loan in 2009, required PDVSA to ship from 107,000 barrels per day when the price was above US$60 per barrel to 153,000 barrels per day when the price was below US$42. Thus the agreements between China and Venezuela can be characterized as hedges against fluctuations in world oil prices through the use of financial instruments such as futures and options rather than purely as accumulated external debt.

The CDB's loan conditions differ vastly from those tied to loans from the World Bank or the International Monetary Fund (IMF). One of these stipulations is sitting down with the CDB to analyze the country's development needs (Sanderson and Forsythe, 2012: 131, 136). In Venezuela's case, the strategic plan covering the period 2010 to 2030 is outlined in a 600-page book written by the CDB that is full of proposals focused on infrastructure projects such as dams, ports, highways, and railroads. In comparison with the neoliberal prescriptions that triggered so much discontent in Latin America, advice on infrastructure needs is difficult to call an imposition. At the same time, it is no coincidence that this advice for long-term strategic planning requires substantial Chinese financing, a third of which is denominated in renminbi. In turn, the money borrowed by the Venezuelan government through the BANDES from the CDB is fed back to Chinese companies in the form of Venezuelan government contracts. This is essentially "boomerang aid," since profits are repatriated back to China, a historically common practice in aid-donor countries. Between 2008 and 2012, six Chinese companies won a total of US$11.6 billion in government-tied contracts, nearly a quarter of a total of some US$50 billion borrowed from the CDB by the BANDES (Sanderson and Forsythe, 2012: 137–138). The CDB is an active participant in pushing Chinese companies into new markets through generous lines of credit; in Venezuela these have totaled US$96.5 billion, and Chinese companies have made substantial profits. The 2011 annual report of China CAMC Engineering Company showed that two-thirds of its revenue of RMB5 billion (US$794 million) stemmed from agriculture and energy projects in Venezuela.

This partnering has not been without its problems. Relations between Chinese capital and Venezuelan labor have been tense, thus highlighting the need to see the Chinese government and Chinese companies as two intertwined but different actors with contradictory interests. Venezuelan employees of Chinese companies tend to occupy positions of less responsibility. In

September 2011 unionized Venezuelan workers on the Tinaco-Anaco railway line contracted to the China Railway Engineering Corporation (CREC) occupied a segment of the rail line to demand that better positions be given to Venezuelan workers (Luces, 2011). Venezuelan workers have also accused the CREC of not respecting local labor laws (Luces, 2014a). According to the CREC, this project was to employ 600 Venezuelan workers but in Anaco only 20 of the 150 employed in 2010 remain (Luces, 2014b; CCTV, 2015). The project was due to be completed in 2012, but labor disputes have thrown it into disarray. By 2015, CREC had completely abandoned the project due to the Venezuelan government's failure to keep up payments (Niu, 2018: 184). The project was worth US$7.5 billion and was intended to be 462.3 kilometers in length (CREC, 2018). After the project was abandoned by CREC, the Zaraza part of the railway project in Guarico state was ransacked in full view of National Guardsmen and allegedly in collaboration with the local *chavista* mayor.

In June 2012 the Venezuelan Workers' Confederation publicly criticized the authorization granted to 30,000 Chinese workers in addition to the 3,000 already hired by CITIC Construction for the Fuerte Tiuna housing project (Ellis, 2014: 157). Furthermore, in January 2013 it was reported that the 20,000 Chinese workers hired for the housing project worked 14 hours a day when Venezuelan labor law permitted only 4 hours beyond the usual 8 (Rodríguez, 2013). In 2016, the Bolivarian Construction Workers' Union publicly pleaded with President Maduro to urge CITIC Construction to hire Venezuelan workers for the desalination plant but to no avail (Aporrea, 2016).

Despite the portrayal of the Sino-Venezuelan relationship as a "win-win" arrangement, the labor disputes highlight clear supply chain issues in the contracts granted to Chinese companies. With Chinese contractors bringing in Chinese labor to carry out infrastructure projects, Venezuela's economy has missed out on the employment-generating effects of the investments and on Venezuelan workers spending their income locally, thus stimulating the economy. Many projects undertaken by Chinese contractors have been left incomplete for various reasons, but Venezuela's debt to China remains.

The partnering arrangement has also spawned some opportunist profiteering that has reduced the stimulatory effects of Chinese loans. The CAMC rice-processing plant is an important case study in how Venezuelan intermediaries with access to government officials and Chinese contractors have benefited from the oil-for-loans deals despite the failure to complete projects. Construction began in 2010 and is still incomplete. According to a Reuters special report, CAMC paid US$100 million in bribes to Venezuelan intermediaries to secure contracts for the rice-processing plant and at least four other agricultural contracts (Berwick, 2019). The Venezuelan intermediaries and CAMC have been investigated by an Andorran court in Spain for money laundering and tax evasion. In addition to the bribes paid to Venezuelan intermediaries and indirectly to officials, the Andorran prosecutors reported that CAMC had agreed to at least five projects that it never completed and received US$1.4 billion for unfinished works.

Despite the favorable *balance* of trade between the two countries, the *terms* of trade are unfavorable to Venezuela. In quantitative terms, Venezuela has a trade surplus with China in spite of the declining price of oil in recent years. Venezuela exported goods and services worth US$11.32 billion to China in 2014 and US$6.88 billion in 2015, while China exported goods and services worth only US$5.66 billion to Venezuela in 2014 and US$5.31 billion in 2015 (AVEX, 2016). However, the terms of trade are not favorable for Venezuela when the types of goods and services exchanged are taken into account. The overwhelming export from Venezuela to China is oil (95–97 percent), a primary good with wide price fluctuations. The value of Venezuela's exports to China dropped by almost half between 2014 and 2015 because of a dramatic decline in the price of oil (AVEX, 2016), from US$130 per barrel in 2014 to US$30 per barrel in 2015 (Hellinger, 2017: 69). In contrast, the value of Chinese exports to Venezuela, which are almost all industrial goods, decreased only slightly, from US$5.66 billion in 2014 to US$5.31 billion in 2015. The risk burden is more on Venezuela given the unpredictability of the price of oil.

The disparity between the balance of trade and the terms of trade is partly explained by the oligopolistic market structure of firms in the industrial sector compared with primary sectors such as agriculture and mining, where competitive conditions prevail. In the long run, the terms of trade tend to favor industrial sectors such as the cars, telecommunications, computers, and construction materials that Venezuela imports from China over primary sectors. Because of the oligopolistic market structure of industrial firms, increases in productive capacity often lead to increased profit margins and higher wages (Halevi, 2016: 197; Sylos-Labini, 1962: 119, 152, 168). Consequently, prices in the industrial sector do not fall in the same proportion as prices in the primary sector. This pattern confirms the thesis of Latin American structuralists such as Prebisch (1951) and Singer (1950), who identified the deteriorating terms of trade between countries producing primary goods and the producers of industrial goods.

Chinese "Outward-Looking" Capitalism, PDVSA, and External Debt

The contradiction between the behavior of Chinese private companies in Venezuela and the state-state agreements based on cooperation can be better understood by recognizing that China's government and its private companies are two different but intertwined actors. Given their significant overlap through CDB loans and ownership structures (Yu, 2013: 76), Chinese boomerang aid is part of the wider pattern of an outward-looking Chinese government pushing its top companies to become internationally competitive multinationals. Sino-Venezuelan oil cooperation is ostensibly a state-state agreement premised on China's pursuit of energy security and on South-South cooperation, but Chinese oil companies clearly reflect behavior typical of profit-maximizing firms seeking to increase their market share.

An example of this contradiction was the disparity between the quantity of oil that Venezuela exports to China and the number of barrels China actually received. In the first three months of 2011, of 37.7 million barrels shipped, only 21.1 million barrels reached China. Some 44 percent—16.6 million barrels—were sold to the United States by Chinese oil companies (Crooks and Cancel, 2012; Sanderson and Forsythe, 2012: 135). Moreover, the CNPC and Sinopec joint ventures in exploration and development of Venezuelan heavy crude do not correspond to China's supposed energy security premise, since Chinese refineries cannot refine Venezuelan crude but U.S. refineries can. Given the Chinese oil companies' practice of on-selling Venezuelan crude to the U.S. market, the CNPC and its subsidiary PetroChina recently canceled deliveries of Venezuelan crude, since they no longer had access to the U.S. market after Washington's imposition of secondary sanctions in 2019 (Waine, 2019a).

In addition, a tanker from Venezuela takes five days to reach the United States and forty to reach China, so it makes more sense for Chinese companies to take crude oil deliveries closer to home. The oil-for-loans supply contract arrangement has not been as "win-win" as it appears. Although the bilateral agreements are established in the MJC and financed through the JF, ultimately PDVSA has to repay the loans. The "option"-based supply agreements between China and Venezuela should also be viewed as hedges against uncertainty only for China. Venezuela still bears the burden of any downward price movement. While much has been made of the Chinese exposure to Venezuela's economic downturn (Ferchen, 2018; Kaplan and Penfold, 2019), the burden still rests on PDVSA and the Venezuelan people, who are exposed to the vulnerability of an economy dependent on foreign exchange.

Between 2001 and 2011, PDVSA's financial contributions to social programs increased from US$34 *million* to US$ 39.6 *billion*—an astronomical increase of 1,165 percent (PDVSA, 2011: 158). Total expenditure on social programs in this period represented US$123.7 billion in education, health, food, vocational training, housing, infrastructure, agriculture, etc. Between 2007 and 2011 alone, PDVSA (2011: 219) contributed US$69.45 billion to social spending while it spent only US$1 billion on exploration. A key stated reason PDVSA directed so much funding to social programs was to repay the "social debt" incurred during the 1980s and 1990s, when poverty dramatically increased (Riutort, 1999: 4). The political decision to finance social programs has overshadowed the need to sustain PDVSA's long-term reinvestment and meet its financial obligations with the CDB.

The Venezuelan government has used accounting methods to obscure the extent of the state's debt obligations. As discussed earlier, the repayment burden is not directly on the Venezuelan government but on PDVSA. The loans are considered sovereign debt for the Venezuelan government, which means that PDVSA's debt-servicing expenditures are not recorded as part of the national budget (Kaplan and Penfold, 2019: 18).

In the first quarter of 2011, one-sixth of PDVSA's production—419,000 barrels per day—went to servicing its debt to the CDB. An internal memo from the Venezuelan oil minister and PDVSA president Rafael Ramírez to President Chávez stated that this meant that PDVSA was not receiving any revenue from its exports to China (Tovar, 2011a). In November 2011 Ramírez announced a new repayment structure that allowed PDVSA to obtain more than US$7 billion from China for the year (Tovar, 2011b). However, the burden on PDVSA of repaying the government's debt at the expense of reinvestment in the industry has continued. In October 2014, approximately half of PDVSA's production was sold to China to repay the government's sovereign debt (Kaplan, 2016: 662).

Despite seemingly generous loan conditions from the CDB, the repayment structure was such a heavy burden that PDVSA had resorted to borrowing from U.S. creditors at extremely high rates of interest because of Venezuela's poor credit ratings (Crooks and Cancel, 2012). Between 2006 and 2012 its borrowing from non-Chinese sources increased from US$2.6 billion to US$34.9 billion. This included the 2007 sale of a record US$7.5 billion of dollar-denominated bonds. Essentially PDVSA has been compensating for its low cash flow by issuing debt, running arrears with suppliers, and postponing dividend payments to private partners (Jacobs, 2014a). In March 2014 it had arrears of US$577 million with Halliburton, an estimated US$584 million with Schlumberger, and more than US$200 million with Weatherford (all service companies). PDVSA has not released new financial statements since 2016. Notwithstanding some optimism back in 2014 around PDVSA's increased infrastructure investments and restructuring of debt repayments with U.S. creditors and China (Jacobs, 2014a, 2014b), the Venezuelan oil-dependent economy is threatened with declines in oil production and possible default (Jacobs, 2017). PDVSA financial statements (2014: 2, 2016) show that its net income was US$15.8 billion in 2013, US$9.07 billion in 2014, and a mere US$828 million in 2016. The course of 2017 saw a steep decline in oil production output to 1.7 million barrels per day (Jacobs, 2018a, 2018b). This is a level not seen since the late 1980s and below the current OPEC quota of

1.9 million barrels per day. At its peak ten years earlier, oil production was 3.3 million barrels per day, and until 2016 it had been steady at 2.6–2.8 million barrels per day. The most recent figures from September 2019 showed Venezuelan oil production only at 640,000 barrels per day (Waine, 2019a). PDVSA's heavy financing of social programs has come at the expense of its own investment. Its dependence on debt, particularly from Chinese investors, to finance exploration and development sets off alarm bells, since it is borrowing against future oil revenue (Hellinger, 2017: 71–72). A similar course was taken by the first Pérez government (1974–1979), which mortgaged its future rents and catalyzed Venezuela's debt crisis of the 1980s and the neoliberal adjustment program of the 1990s (Ellner, 2008: 79).

The August 2017 sanctions had the effect of prohibiting PDVSA from borrowing in the U.S. financial market, but the 2019 sanctions specifically targeted PDVSA's ability to export and upgrade its heavy crude. These sanctions forbid PDVSA from business transactions with any U.S. entity. In order to export Venezuela's heavy crude, diluents are needed to upgrade the crude or blend for export. Prior to the 2019 sanctions, PDVSA had been reliant on importing light distillates, particularly the diluent naphtha, from the United States in order to upgrade its heavy crude (Waine, 2019b). Since the United States stopped exporting diluents to Venezuela, Venezuela has been unable to obtain adequate supplies of diluents to maintain production of higher-valued types of crude (Waine, 2019c). Although PDVSA has increased imports of diluents from other oil companies such as Russia's Rosneft, China's CNPC, India's Reliance Industries, and Spain's Repsol, PDVSA has had to convert some of its operations, such as the Orinoco upgraders, to simple blending facilities, which produce a less valuable crude. As a result of the 2019 sanctions, PDVSA has been limited to producing lower-valued blends of crude, which has reduced oil production levels and cash access through oil sales, especially since the United States was its largest cash buyer. Moreover, refineries specializing in Venezuelan crude are based in the United States, such as CITGO, a subsidiary of PDVSA, which was prevented from repatriating profits and was subsequently seized from the Venezuelan government. The five U.S. oil companies that are in joint ventures with PDVSA—Chevron, Halliburton, Schlumberger, Baker Hughes (a GE company) and Weatherford International—were at first exempted from the sanctions.

Resource Sovereignty and Oil Dependence

A key characteristic of Pink Tide governments such as Venezuela's has been greater state control over resource profits, particularly in minerals. Previous neoliberal models of extractivism that encouraged privatization of mineral sectors were characterized by a more dominant role for private actors in developing countries. Why has Venezuela been unable to move beyond its historical dependence on oil despite greater government control over the distribution of oil profits and seemingly more equitable bilateral agreements with China?

Oil revenue redistribution in Venezuela has extended beyond social programs to investments in nonresource sectors of the economy. Significant attempts were made to reorganize the domestic economy through small-to-medium-sized enterprises in agriculture and other nonresource sectors (see Piñeiro Harnecker, 2009). Bilateral agreements between Caracas and Beijing are qualitatively different from agreements with U.S. and European governments in that they are state-to-state rather than private-sector-to-private-sector. They have also involved technology transfer in satellite engineering, military technology, mobile phones, household appliances, and transport. In the development of the Simón Bolívar satellite, ninety Venezuelan specialists worked closely with Chinese developers (Barbosa, 2008). The government's joint venture with Yutong Bus has established an assembly plant in Yaracuy state aimed at producing 3,500 buses per year (Xinhua, 2015). These early projects were all completed. Although the terms of trade are unfavorable and there are many barriers to Venezuela's entry into the world's oligopolistic industrial market, China has supported Venezuela with its infant industries by helping it diversify its nonresource export portfolio. In addition, the Sino-Venezuelan relationship differs diplomatically from Venezuela's relationship with the U.S. and European governments. In 2006, when PDVSA stopped producing Orimulsion, a specialty fuel for which China had specifically designed two power plants, the response was a strongly worded but private criticism (Ellis, 2014: 199). China respects Venezuelan sovereignty as the United States and Europe rarely have.

Nevertheless, as discussed above, the Chávez era saw increased dependence on oil rather than diversification of nonresource exports. The value of its oil exports increased from US$32.8 billion in 2004 to US$71.7 billion in 2014, peaking in 2012 at US$93.6 billion. This rise parallels the increase in the involvement of mixed companies and the MJC and JF. One explanation for Venezuela's increased dependence on oil despite high oil prices during the Chávez era draws from the earlier discussion concerning oligopolistic competition in the industrial sector (Halevi, 2016: 197; Sylos-Labini, 1962: 119, 152, 168). Given that oil, a primary good, is a key input in industrial production, price rises increase the prices of industrial goods. Therefore, when oil prices were elevated, prices for industrial products also rose; Venezuela's terms of trade did not necessarily improve with higher oil prices. The historical overvaluation of Venezuelan currency due to oil exports has meant that the nonresource export sector has not been able to compete with cheaper imports.

Because of the monetary effect of the "Dutch Disease" on the nonresource export sector and despite the Venezuelan government's efforts to ameliorate the effect, these sectors remain extremely reliant on government funds to survive (Lander, 2014: 5–6). This is reflected in the promotion of small-to-medium-sized enterprises and workers' cooperatives in agriculture and other nonresource sectors, which often depend heavily on the government in all phases of the economic cycle (Piñeiro Harnecker, 2009; Azzellini, 2012). This dependence is also seen in the many regional integration projects that many left-wing Latin American and Caribbean governments have initiated (Girvan, 2008; Jácome, 2011; SELA, 2015). In theory, oil extraction transformed into capital would easily transfer from one sector to another, but this assumption rests on unclear distinctions between the short run and the long run and on a level playing field and does not take asymmetries in technical knowledge and economies of scale into account.

The notion that factors are easily transferable across sectors is based on neoclassical assumptions of a level playing field in a world of perfect competition (see Sraffa, 1926), but the world oil industry is rife with asymmetries and oligopolistic in its market structure. Of its three parts—upstream, downstream, and exchange (Palazuelos, 2012: 125)—the Venezuelan government controls only the first, which involves extraction and the supply of oil for export. The downstream (transport, refining, chemical transformation) and exchange (selling and buying) stages are controlled by top transnational corporations such as the CNPC, Sinopec, Royal Dutch Shell, and Exxon Mobil. The organization of these transnationals links almost all phases of the supply chain, and this strengthens the barriers to entry and allows the transnationals to set prices.

Although structural economic factors hold Venezuela back from diversifying, domestic institutional factors are also important. As discussed earlier, the formation of the Venezuelan state coincided with significant intervention from international oil companies that produced a state much more apt at negotiating contracts with transnationals than at presiding over complex tax systems and managing resources (Karl, 2007: 263). The embeddedness of oil in the formation of the Venezuelan state has also meant that oil is taken for granted in Venezuela. It is the assumption that underlies all political demands across the political spectrum (Coronil, 1997: 91, 94). Competing political demands aside, since the discovery of oil the emphasis has consistently been on maximizing oil income through the state rather than pursuing revenue by other means such as taxes. Increasing participation in decision making at the local institutional level (see Azzellini, 2017) has not extended to decisions about the oil industry, the core of the Venezuelan economy. More equitable distribution of oil profits is important, but the decision making for that distribution remains centralized. While the explosion in local self-organization through the *misiones*, communal councils, communes, and social enterprises has helped create a sense of collective capacity after the breakdown of the social fabric during the late 1980s and 1990s (Edgardo Lander, cited in Uval, 2017), it has not been matched by participation in decision making in oil and other sectors of the Venezuelan economy. As at previous moments when oil prices have been low or when the oil industry was sabotaged in 2002–2003, the danger of relying on imports of basic consumption goods such as food has been very much exposed.

Some commentators have pointed to the initial problem of "unconditional" loans, such as Venezuelan intermediaries more interested in pocketing loan money than in ensuring the completion of projects with Chinese contractors complicit in this dubious use of sovereign debt (Ferchen, 2018; Kaplan, 2016; Kaplan and Penfold, 2019). The picture that these commentators have painted is one of lender-trap diplomacy in which poor decision making on the part of the Venezuelan government has ensnared China in Venezuela's long-term economic pain. This picture absolves the Chinese government and private sector from responsibility and accountability in not delivering on projects. One could also draw parallels with the lending of recycled petrodollars by the U.S. financial sector that precipitated the Latin American debt crisis; lenders have a degree of responsibility for the outcomes of their lending decisions. The Chinese government has indicated that it is not willing to be a lender of last resort for Venezuela, but its policy of "nonintervention" may be ill-advised. Economic instability giving rise to an opposition government would also not be a good return on China's investments in Venezuela.

South-South cooperation or a rearticulation of dependent geopolitical relationships should not be considered mutually exclusive. The behaviors of the Chinese state and private companies are intertwined. Chinese government actors have given development advice to the Venezuelan government on infrastructure projects based on the ethos of South-South cooperation and issued "unconditional" loans to finance this development. The state-state agreements for technology transfer and investment in development reflect South-South cooperation. At the same time, the motivation behind this financing is part of the long-term pursuit of increasing market participation of the Chinese banking sector and expansion into the global energy sector. Private Chinese companies' on-selling of Venezuelan oil, labor relations, bribery of Venezuelan intermediaries to secure contracts, and abandonment of projects reflect short-term profit-maximizing behavior. This behavior has many similarities with the way private sectors from developed countries have long conducted business in underdeveloped states.

Conclusion

China's economic influence has not replaced that of the United States in Venezuela, but China has definitely become integrated into Venezuela's political economy. Dependency on oil has been reinforced in the Sino-Venezuelan relationship, but attempts to promote infant industries in the nonresource sectors during the initial period of Sino-Venezuelan relationship appear to be more than just lip service to the "social debt." Despite significant problems with Venezuelan monetary policy and economic planning, Venezuela's relationship with China on a state-state level includes important elements of cooperation, albeit with many problems. The Sino-Venezuelan relationship is contradictorily characterized by both cooperation and dependence.

The early oil-for-loan agreements promoted cooperation and stability for both China and Venezuela. For China they guaranteed price certainty in the purchase of oil, while for Venezuela they involved finance for important investments in the industrial sector. Unlike the private-sector-oriented and short-term outlook of previous IMF agreements, the Sino-Venezuelan relationship is a 20-year development plan that includes infrastructure needs as well as technology transfer. In contrast to the overt intervention of the United States, the Sino-Venezuelan diplomatic relationship is more subdued. This is reflected in the case of China's politely objecting to but ultimately accepting Venezuela's decision to cease production of Orimulsion, a type of fuel for which China had especially designed two power plants. The Sino-Venezuela diplomatic and trade relationship also has been crucial in helping Venezuela survive U.S. sanctions.

At the same time, the trade relationship in which Venezuela imports high-valued industrial Chinese goods while China imports the highly volatile-priced primary commodity of oil from Venezuela reflects a relationship of dependence with "Chinese characteristics." This reinforces many of the long-term structural problems that Venezuela has long faced. The relationship between PDVSA and Chinese oil companies and the manner in which Chinese companies carry out Venezuelan government contracts reflect the wider shift of the Asian country's participation in the global economy, in which Chinese companies are now key players alongside U.S. and European capital.

Beyond some small-scale success stories in the communal sector, massive redistribution of oil rents to social development has not led to long-term successes in nonresource sectors such as manufacturing and agriculture. Disproportionate dependence on oil and borrowing to finance imports such as basic foods persists. With their impact on oil income and borrowing capacity, the U.S. sanctions have further exposed the vulnerability of this strategy.

An institutional structure that specializes in managing oil income needs to be questioned. Nation-states with diversified economies typically extract taxes from the population and direct resources toward long-term sustainable development, something that successive Venezuelan governments have been unable to achieve. The current Venezuelan government has repeated the mistakes of previous governments by mortgaging future oil revenue. The Venezuelan economy will continue to be susceptible to the vagaries of the world oil market unless the political structure that treats oil as a given rather than a finite resource is modified.

Notes

1. This chapter is a revised version of an article coauthored with Rodrigo Acuña and published in 2019 in *Latin American Perspectives* (46 [2]: 126–140). I thank Stuart Rosewarne, Jack Clancey, and Steve Ellner for comments on this manuscript.
2. "Sow the oil" (*sembrar el petróleo*) is a phrase coined by the Venezuelan intellectual Arturo Uslar Pietri (1936), who argued that oil export revenues should be reinvested in productive sectors such as agriculture.
3. The previous ruling establishment was known as the Pact of Punto Fijo. Initially three political parties agreed to a power-sharing arrangement in 1958 after the fall of the dictator Marcos Pérez Jiménez. The key aim of the pact was to exclude political actors such as the Communist Party that had helped to overthrow the dictator.
4. When many of the supply contracts between China and Venezuela were first established in 2007 through the JF, the price of oil per barrel was well above US$100 (it peaked at US$146 per barrel in 2008).
5. The arrangements between China and Venezuela are best characterized as derivative contracts such as futures and call options. Derivatives are financial instruments used to offset risk in an environment of uncertainty and volatility. A futures contract is an agreement to buy or sell an asset at an agreed-upon price today with delivery and payment at a future agreed-upon time. A call option contract is an agreement in which the buyer has the right but not the obligation to buy a commodity at the given market price within a specific time period.

References

Acosta, Alberto

2009 *La maldición de la abundancia*. Quito: Producciones Digitales Abya Yala.

2011 "Extractivismo y neoextractivismo: dos caras de la misma maldición," in M. Lang and D. Mokrani (eds.), *Más allá del desarrollo*. Quito: Editorial El Conejo.

Aporrea

2016 "Trabajadores piden a empresa china 'CITIC Construction' que contrate personal venezolano." December 13. https://www.aporrea.org/trabajadores/n301527.html.

AVEX (Asociación Venezolana de Exportadores)
2016 "El comercio con China." *Avex.com*. September 21. http://www.avex.com.ve/index.php/blog/192-el-comercio-con-china.
Azzellini, Dario
2012 *La construcción de los dos lados: Poder constituido y poder constituyente en Venezuela*. Vol. 2. Caracas: Fundación Editorial El Perro y la Rana.
2017 "Class struggle in the Bolivarian process: workers' control and workers' councils." *Latin American Perspectives* 44 (1): 126–139.
Barbosa, Rui C.
2008 "China launch VENESAT-1—debut bird for Venezuela." *NASA Spaceflight.com*. October 29. http://www.nasaspaceflight.com/2008/10/china-launch-venesat/.
BBC Mundo
2016 "Por qué China invierte una fortuna en Venezuela a pesar de la crisis económica." March 3. http://www.bbc.com/mundo/ noticias/2016/03/160302_venezuela_china_inversiones_ deuda_ab.
BCV (Banco Central de Venezuela)
2015 "Información estadística: indicadores: exportaciones e importaciones de bienes y servicios según sectores." http://www.bcv.org.ve/c2/ indicadores.asp.
Berwick, Angus
2019 "How a Chinese venture in Venezuela made millions while locals grew hungry." *Reuters*. May 7. https://www.reuters.com/investigates/special-report/venezuela-china-food/.
Buitrago, Deisy
2014 "Asia overtakes US as top destination for Venezuela oil—PDVSA." *Reuters*. April 10.
CCTV
2015 "Ferrocarril Tinaco-Anaco, ejemplo de colaboración chino-venezolana." *CCTV.com. Español*. January 8.
CITIC Limited
2014 "Annual report." http://www.citic.com/Managed/ Resources/docs/FinancialReports/ENG/ar2014e.pdf.
2017 "Annual report." https://www.citic.com/uploadfile/2018/0420/20180420052934291.pdf.
2018 "Annual report." https://www.citic.com/uploadfile/2019/0418/20190418044301701.pdf.
Corden, W. Max
1984 "Booming sector and Dutch Disease economics: survey and consolidation." *Oxford Economics Papers* 36: 359–380.
Coronil, Fernando
1997 *The Magical State: Nature, Money, and Modernity in Venezuela*. London: University of Chicago Press.
CREC (Chinese Railway Engineering Corporation)
2018 "The high-speed rail project in Northern Venezuela." China Railway Group Limited. http://www.crecg.com/english/2745/2808/49275/index.html.

Crooks, Nathan, and Daniel Cancel
2012 "Chávez misses $10 billion a month curbing oil spending: energy." *Bloomberg News.* February 16.
Eaton, Collin, and Luc Cohen
2019 "Explainer: US sanctions and Venezuela's trade and oil industry partners." *Reuters.* August 15. https://www.reuters.com/article/us-venezuela-politics-crude-sanctions-ex-idUSKCN1V420P.
EIA (Energy Information Administration)
2017 "US imports from Venezuela of crude oil." https://www.eia.gov/dnav/pet/hist/LeafHandler.ashx?n=PET&s= MCRIMUSVE2&f=A.
Ellis, R. Evan
2014 *China on the Ground in Latin America: Challenges for the Chinese and Impacts on the Region.* New York: Palgrave Macmillan.
Ellner, Steve
2008 *Rethinking Venezuelan Politics: Class, Conflict, and the Chávez Phenomenon.* London: Lynne Rienner Publishers.
Ferchen, Matt
2018 "China-Venezuela relations: a perfect storm." *ReVista: Harvard Review of Latin America.* September 24. https://revista.drclas.harvard.edu/book/china-venezuela-relations.
Girvan, Norman
2008 "ALBA, Petrocaribe, Caricom: issues in a new dynamic." *Norman Girvan: Caribbean Political Economy.* http://www.normangirvan.info/ wp-content/uploads/2009/03/alba-petrocaribe-and-caricom.pdf.
Golinger, Eva
2005 *The Chávez Code: Cracking US Intervention in Venezuela.* Havana: Editorial José Martí.
Goodman, James, and David Whitworth
2008 "The minerals boom and Australia's 'resource curse.'" *Journal of Australian Political Economy* 61: 201–219.
Gudynas, Edgardo
2010 "Si eres tan progresista ¿porqué destruyes la naturaleza? Neoextractivismo, izquierda y alternativas." *Ecuador Debate* 79: 61–81.
Guo, Shuqing
2010 "Fertile ground." *South China Morning Post.* January 22.
Halevi, Joseph
2016 "Paolo Sylos-Labini's contribution to modern economics theory," pp. 284–306 in G. Harcourt, Peter Kriesler, Joseph Halevi, and John Neville (eds.), *Post-Keynesian Essays from Down Under,* Vol. 3, *Essays on Ethics, Social Justice and Economics.* London: Palgrave Macmillan.
Hellinger, Daniel
2017 "Oil and the Chávez legacy." *Latin American Perspectives* 44 (1): 54–77.
Jacobs, Justin
2014a "Venezuela woes hit China's Petro-King." *Petroleum Economist.* June 19.

2014b "China gives Venezuela a break on oil-for-loan repayment." *Petroleum Economist*. October 24.
2017 "Venezuela crunch time." *Petroleum Economist*. November 17.
2018a "Venezuela's oil exports to the US fading fast." *Petroleum Economist*. January 29.
2018b "Venezuela's unprecedented supply collapse." *Petroleum Economist*. March 29.

Jácome, Francine
2011 "Petrocaribe: the current phase of Venezuela's oil diplomacy in the Caribbean." Friedrich Ebert Stiftung Programa de Cooperación en Seguridad Regional, Policy Paper 40. http://library.fes.de/pdf-files/bueros/la-seguridad/08723.pdf.

Kaplan, Stephen B.
2016 "Banking unconditionality: the political economy of Chinese finance in Latin America." *Review of International Political Economy* 23: 643–676.

Kaplan, Stephen B., and Michael Penfold
2019 *China-Venezuela Economic Relations: Hedging Venezuelan Bets with Chinese Characteristics*. Washington, DC: Latin American Program, Woodrow Wilson International Center for Scholars.

Karl, Terry Lyn
2007 "Ensuring fairness: the case for a transparent fiscal social contract," pp. 256–285 in M. Humphreys, J. D. Sachs, and J. E. Stiglitz (eds.), *Escaping the Resource Curse*. New York: Columbia University Press.

Koerner, Lucas
2017 "Venezuela and China sign new $2.7 billion development deal." *Venezuelanalysis.com*. February. https://venezuelanalysis.com/ news/12931.

Lander, Edgardo
2014 "Venezuela: ¿crisis terminal del modelo petrolerorentista?" *Rebelión.org*. September. http://www.rebelion.org/docs/ 191388.pdf.

Luces Rondón, Danela
2011 "Paralizaron construcción del tramo Tinaco-Anaco." *El Tiempo*. August 23.
2014a "Por segunda vez este año paralizaron obra ferrovaria." *El Tiempo*. September 30.
2014b "Construcción del tramo ferroviario en Anaco se mantiene con 20 obreros." *El Tiempo*. November 23.

Mather, Steve
2006 "Venezuela signs more deals with China." *Venezuelanalysis.com*. August 23. http://venezuelanalysis.com/ news/1905.

Ministry of Foreign Affairs of the People's Republic of China
2014 "Xi Jinping holds talks with President Nicolás Maduro of Venezuela: two heads of state announce to promote China-Venezuela relations to comprehensive strategic partnership." July 21. http://www.fmprc.gov.cn/mfa_ eng/wjb_663304/zzjg_663340/ldmzs_664952/gjlb_664956/3538_ 665158/3540_665162/t1177107.shtml.

Niu, Haibin
2018 "A strategic analysis of Chinese infrastructure projects in Latin America and the Caribbean," pp. 180–193 in Enrique Dussel Peters, Ariel C. Armony, and Shoujun Cui (eds.), *Building Development for a New Era: China's Infrastructure*

Projects in Latin America and the Caribbean. Mexico City: Red Académica de América Latina y el Caribe sobre China.
Palazuelos, Enrique
2012 "Modelos de oligopolio en la industria petrolera: las 'siete hermanas' *versus* la OPEP." *Revista de Historia Industrial* 48: 119–153.
Paz, Gonzalo Sebastián
2013 "China and Venezuela: oil, technology and socialism," in A. Hearn and José Luis León-Manríquez (eds.), *China Engages Latin America: Tracing the Trajectory.* London: Lynne Rienner Publishers.
PDVSA (Petróleos de Venezuela S.A.)
2009 "Informe de gestión anual 2009." http://www.pdvsa.com/interface.sp/database/fichero/ free/5889/1049.pdf.
2011 "Informe de gestión anual 2011." http://www.pdvsa.com.
2014 "Estados financieros consolidados." http://www.pdvsa.com.
2016 "Estados financieros consolidados." http://www.pdvsa.com.
Petroleum Economist
2015 "Venezuela borrows $5bn more." September 30.
Piñeiro Harnecker, Camila
2009 "Workplace democracy and social consciousness: a study of Venezuelan cooperatives." *Science and Society* 73: 309–339.
Prebisch, Raúl
1951 *Problemas teóricos y prácticos del crecimiento económico.* Santiago: ECLAC.
Riutort, Matías
1999 "El costo de erradicar la pobreza," pp. 15–26 in L. Ugalde, et al. (eds.), *Pobreza: Un mal posible de superar.* Resumenes de los documentos del Proyecto Pobreza, Vol. 1. Caracas: Universidad Católica Andrés Bello.
Rodríguez, Dulce María
2013 "Trabajadores chinos laboran hasta 14 horas diarias en la Misión Vivienda." *El Universal.* January 9.
Sachs, Jeffrey
2007 "How to handle the macroeconomics of oil wealth," pp. 173–193 in M. Humphreys, J. D. Sachs, and J. E. Stiglitz (eds.), *Escaping the Resource Curse.* New York: Columbia University Press.
Sanderson, Henry, and Michael Forsythe
2012 *China's Superbank: Debt, Oil and Influence—How China Development Bank Is Rewriting the Rules of Finance.* Singapore: Wiley.
SELA (Sistema Económico Latinamericano y del Caribe)
2015 "Evolution of the PETROCARIBE Energy Cooperation Agreement." Permanent Secretariat, Caracas, Venezuela, June, SP/Di No. 6-15. http://www.sela.org/media/1950653/evolution-of- petrocaribe.pdf.
Singer, Hans
1950 "The distribution of gains between investing and borrowing countries." *American Economic Review* 40: 473–521.
Sraffa, Piero
1926 "The laws of return under competitive conditions." *Economic Journal* 36 (144): 535–550.

Sun, Hongbo
2015 "The Sino-Venezuelan oil cooperation model: actors and relationships," pp. 167–182 in Enrique Dussel Peters and Ariel C. Armoney (eds.), *Beyond Raw Materials: Who Are the Actors in the Latin America and Caribbean–China Relationship?* Buenos Aires, Mexico City, and Pittsburgh: Nueva Sociedad/Friedrich-Ebert-Stiftung/Red Académica de América Latina y el Caribe sobre China/University of Pittsburgh Center of Latin American Studies.
Svampa, Maristella
2011 "Extractivisimo neodesarrollista y movimientos sociales. ¿Un giro ecoterritorial hacia nuevas alternativas?" pp. 185–218 in M. Lang and D. Mokrani (eds.), *Más allá del desarrollo*. Quito: Editorial El Conejo.
Sylos-Labini, Paolo
1962 *Oligopoly and Technical Progress*. Cambridge: Harvard University Press.
Tinker Salas, Miguel
2009 *The Enduring Legacy: Oil, Culture, and Society in Venezuela*. Durham, NC: Duke University Press.
Tovar, Ernesto J.
2011a "PDVSA desatendió pagos al Fisco por presión del Fondo Chino." *El Universal*. November 11.
2011b "Plantean elevar envíos de crudo en pago al Fondo Chino." *El Universal*. November 23.
Uslar Pietri, Arturo
1936 "Sembrar el petróleo." *Ahora*. July 14.
Uval, Natalia
2017 "Entrevista con Edgardo Lander: sociólogo venezolano cuestiona la 'solidaridad incondicional' de la izquierda latinoamericana con el chavismo." *La Diaria*. March 26.
VTELCA (Venezolana de Comunicaciones, C.A.)
2017 "Sobre nosotros." http://www.vtelca.gob.ve/? page_id=3.
Waine, Charles
2019a "China spurns Venezuelan exports." *Petroleum Economist*. October 19.
2019b "Sanctions squeeze Venezuela's heavy crude output." *Petroleum Economist*. July 18.
2019c "US sanctions debilitate Venezuela oil output." *Petroleum Economist*, June 17.
Weisbrot, Mark and Jeffrey Sachs
2019 "Economic sanctions as collective punishment: the case of Venezuela." *Research Paper*. April. Washington, DC: Center for Economic and Policy Research. https://cepr.net/images/stories/reports/venezuela-sanctions-2019-04.pdf.
Xinhua
2015 "China's technology transfer boosts Venezuela's production capacity." September 11. http://news.xinhuanet.com/english/2015-09/12/c_ 134618299.htm.
Yu, Mei
2013 "State ownership and firm performance: empirical evidence from Chinese listed companies." *China Journal of Accounting Research* 6: 75–87.

II

THE PINK TIDE COUNTRIES

More than fine lines of distinction separated Pink Tide governments and those of the rest of the continent. Most important, their anti-neoliberalism went far beyond discourse; neoliberal policies had a pronounced impact on economic and social fronts. One of the salient features of Pink Tide governments was their resource nationalism, as expressed in the assertion of greater control of extractivist industries, in some cases through nationalization, and in the tax regimes they implemented. In the area of the territorial rights of local communities, including indigenous ones, environmental protection, and policy toward protest movements, the differences were less pronounced but become evident in comparisons with conservative and especially right-wing governments. The chapters in the following part as well as throughout the book shed light on these relative differences across the region.

In the opening chapter, Luis Angosto-Ferrández attempts to explain the extended popularity of Pink Tide presidents when compared with that of leaders who followed their exit from power, as demonstrated at the polls (in the case of Argentina) and on the streets (in the case of Bolivia). In examining this phenomenon, Angosto-Ferrández analyzes the nationalist component of resource nationalism. He cites various scholarly studies that show the relationship between foreign investments in extractive industries and strong nationalistic sentiment. He notes that the "critics of resource nationalism pay scant attention" to the way in which foreign ownership of natural resources helps "shape the political subjectivities of many Latin Americans." The detractors of Pink Tide governments on both the right and the left who write on extractivism focus on government, while overlooking the full scope of popular attitudes and political culture. Nationalism also needs to be considered in that the responsibility for environmental contamination in the South largely falls on the consuming nations of the North. "This crucial factor in the local interpretations of the transnational dimensions of extractivism," according to Angosto-Ferrández, is "overlooked by critics of Pink Tide governments and resource nationalism."

In the empirical part of the chapter, Angosto-Ferrández shows how territoriality intersects with economics in the case of the Pemon people in Venezuela's Gran Sabana. In addition to working as artisanal miners, Pemones are owners and occupy managerial positions in some small-scale mining ventures, while Pemon communities issue licenses for mining operations. These cases of participation help explain why "significant fractions of the indigenous population have actively supported Pink Tide governments and the principles of resource nationalism."

In their chapter, María J. Paz and Juan Ramírez-Cendrero examine the impact of foreign direct investment strategy, as incorporated in the National Development Plan of 2006, on Bolivia's hydrocarbons industry. In doing so they hope to "clarify the debate on the characterization of ... [Pink Tide] governments: neo-extractivism (as their critics describe it) vs. resource nationalism." They conclude that policies contributed to the fulfillment of some of the government's developmental goals but also had serious limitations and that, if anything, dependence on the global economy actually increased. On the one hand, hydrocarbons policy promoted incipient joint ventures, forced companies to reduce the importation of petroleum derivatives, and ensured "that the state would determine the destination of production." Resource nationalism also translated into "a fiscally more demanding framework that has altered the distribution of oil revenues in favor of the Bolivian state." On the other hand, the government failed to establish required levels of investment, the replenishment of reserves and production linkages and to achieve gas industrialization.

Darcy Tetreault's chapter on the current Mexican President Andrés Manuel López Obrador also highlights both anti-neoliberal advances in the area of extractivism and basic shortcomings including a failure to modify the grip of global capitalism. On the positive side are measures to assert greater national control of the petroleum industry through the strengthening of the state oil company Pemex, progress in the construction of a major refinery, and the elimination of practices in the industry that were conducive to corruption. Tetreault also discusses in detail the "reconfiguration of . . . relations between the state and unionized workers in extractive sectors." The government investigated the corrupt dealings of the longtime leader of the oil workers' movement, who had gone along with neoliberal reforms, and in the process helped pressure him to resign. At the same time, the governing party established close ties with the head of the metalworkers' union who had strongly resisted neoliberal-inspired modifications of labor legislation—a relationship that fit well with López Obrador's anti-neoliberal discourse. López Obrador has, however, failed to reverse the neoliberal-inspired policies he inherited. Even though he opposes fracking, the practice continues unabated, and he has also refrained from improving the terms of the existing taxes and royalties applied to mining and petroleum companies. These and other policies and inactions speak "to a strong inclination toward continuity during the first 18 months of . . . [his] presidency with regard to the neoliberal logic that persists at the root of Mexico's extractive policies."

In her chapter, Teresa Velásquez demonstrates the importance of indigenous narratives, particularly the concept "water is life," in reaching the urban population, previously unconcerned with peasant problems. This appeal was "critical in building political coalitions" that were instrumental in "framing national debates over [President Rafael] Correa's proposed water law [and] challenging his plans to . . . expand extractive industries." Velásquez examines the "progressive extractivism" of Correa and his movement as reflected in the 2014 water law, which she analyzes in depth. The law exemplified the resource nationalism embodied by Correa in that it assigned the state the key role in the formulation of national water policy. The law had features supported by the protest movement, including "indigenous collective rights to participate, manage, and protect water sources" and the requirement of informed consultation of communities for projects involving the flow of water. In addition, it conferred on indigenous groups the right to manage water "in collective and traditional form" and recognized their "fiscal and administrative autonomy." Although the indigenous and antimining movements had "significantly shaped" the legislation, they also criticized it for failing "to place any limits on mining in headwaters and watersheds." Furthermore, the state water authority was allowed to "grant water permits for mining projects in sensitive watersheds." Not surprisingly, the law's ambiguities generated tensions within progressive extractivism.

In the section titled "From Progressive to Neoliberal Extractivism," the marked contrast between Correa's policies and those of his neoliberal successor Lenín Moreno becomes evident. Moreno renounced resource nationalism, eliminating the 70 percent windfall tax and reducing royalties from 5–8 percent to 3–8 percent. Velásquez notes that his neoliberal policies and his promotion of mining promised to undo previous gains including the indigenous consultation rights for water use stipulated in the 2014 law.

Amalia Leguizamón asks why the soybean industry enjoys such widespread approval among Argentines in spite of its negative environmental and social impact. She responds by analyzing the hegemonic discourse in the nation, which exalts the "domination of man over nature in the pursuit of economic growth." She points to the way this "hegemonic masculinity" was expressed in the interviews she conducted in the soybean-producing region of the Pampas. In spite of the risks posed to children by the agrochemicals used in the cultivation of genetically modified crops, many of the male interviewees defended the investments of the biotech company Monsanto on grounds that they generated employment. In contrast, she quotes a member of one of the two women-based movements in the region whose activities she describes: "You give them bread, I give them life!"

In highlighting this gender contrast, Leguizamón points out that Argentina's Pink Tide President Cristina Fernández de Kirchner combined the two strands. She shows how Fernández, "a charismatic leader . . . masterfully alternat[ed] between embodying femininity and a maternalistic ethics of care and adopting a paternalistic attitude" rooted in traditional Peronism. During her presidency and that of her predecessor and husband Néstor Kirchner, resource nationalism manifested itself in the form of a 30–35 percent tax on soybean exports whose revenue was used for social programs for the popular sectors. In contrast, her successor Mauricio Macri favored "large agribusinesses by reducing agricultural export taxes and by modifying seed and rural labor laws."

4

Reframing Resource Nationalism

Social Forces and the Politics of Extractivism in Latin America's Pink Tide

Luis Fernando Angosto-Ferrández

ONE ASPECT OF THE POLITICS of extractivism that is often neglected in academic debates on this topic is why resource nationalism receives mass support as the engine of development projects in Latin American countries. That support facilitates the contingent crystallization of interclass alliances and political blocs involving political elites and native capitalists but also workers, indigenous groups, and, in general, fractions of the subaltern classes. In supporting resource nationalism, members of these groups pursue different goals, but all of them find in this governmental orientation the potential for (at least partial) realization of those goals. In this chapter I will attempt to explain this situation. The discussion aims to overcome the limitations that an analytical focus on governments imposes on the study of resource nationalism in twenty-first-century Latin America. That focus rests on a tacit conceptualization of governments as autonomous subjects that, in their interventions in the politics of extractivism, merely pursue self-serving corporatist interests. It distracts attention from the analysis of the social forces that, beyond governments, demand and support the implementation of political agendas based on resource nationalism.

The same constraining approach has conditioned the assessment of Latin America's Pink Tide among analysts of the most diverse ideological inclinations. Thus rightist critics have presented the Pink Tide and particularly its more transformative currents as a doomed-to-fail movement of state-centric populist governments (e.g., Castañeda and Morales, 2008). The support bases of these governments, when not ignored, are presented as victims of governmental deceit, or as irrational, or merely as political clients instead of being recognized as conscious subjects. In turn, some leftist analysts present the Pink Tide as a failed process of social transformation in which governments did not follow the orientations of social movements and thus ended up playing the tune of national and international capital. From this perspective there are no social movements supporting resource nationalism.

These assessments have never provided convincing explanations of why governments driven by resource nationalist principles have received sustained mass support in the past two decades, notwithstanding opposition from economic elites and fractions of the popular classes. This chapter argues that this is because of both the focus on governments as autonomous subjects (detached from supporting social forces) and two complementary weaknesses: a misunderstanding of the way the transnational dimensions of extractivism inform the political choices of many Latin Americans and a mechanical association of conflicts around extractive projects, especially in indigenous territories, with opposition to extractivism *tout court*. The latter tendency misrepresents disputes over extractive rights or the conditions under which extractivism is to be regulated, a point I will analyze on the basis of an ethnographically informed examination of mining in the Gran Sabana, Venezuela.

The first part of the chapter engages debates on resource nationalism in relation to Latin America's Pink Tide. Discussions of the former have come to be inextricably linked to assessments of the latter (Farthing and Fabricant, 2018; Veltmeyer, 2012; see also Ellner's introduction to this volume), and against this background I will underscore the necessity of critically revisiting some of the premises that have generally pervaded and constrained those discussions and assessments. I contend that the political assessments of the Pink Tide have been conditioned by the same analytical preconceptions that set boundaries to debates on resource nationalism. Specifically, I will argue that advocates of what I will call the thesis that "the Pink Tide is over" have been misled in their assessments of continental politics by their marked misunderstanding of the social forces that sustain and support Pink Tide governmental orientations.

I do not intend to minimize the relevance of some critical perspectives on the model of accumulation that Pink Tide governments have reinforced through their approach to extractivist politics. Questions of power, rights, dispossession, exploitation, and environmental sustainability are central to the analysis of resource nationalism. But it is precisely in relation to these questions that this chapter seeks to provide insight into the reasons why extractivism mobilizes mass support when it is bound to principles of resource nationalism. Overlooking this support hinders the possibility of finding viable solutions to the problems with which extractivism is associated—problems of poverty, social injustice, and inequality as well as problems of environmental sustainability.

The Thesis that the Pink Tide Is Over: Premises and Limitations

As 2019 dawned, the thesis that Latin America's Pink Tide is a vanished movement had few opponents (Gold and Zagato, 2020; González, 2019). The factual pillars that sustained that thesis were seemingly robust: since 2015, rightist forces had secured a succession of electoral victories in several Latin American countries. Analysts diverged in the interpretation of the factors that had led to that scenario (see overview in Ellner, 2019a: 4–11), but for those who supported the thesis the interpretative corollary was unquestionable: that those right-wing victories had changed the orientation of governance in the continent, removing any shades of red from it.

However, the thesis was grounded in questionable premises, and in that respect it is unsurprising that it has lost adherents over the past year. From the outset, its advocates failed to recognize and characterize the social forces that sustain and support Pink Tide governmental orientations. They minimized or ignored the mass support that these policy orientations received—orientations that were made possible through the adoption of resource nationalist principles. Electoral support was sustained over time and remarkably strong even when it did not amount to absolute majorities. Several Pink Tide governments completed successive terms backed by significant majorities, while the electoral victories of rightist candidates were obtained by very narrow margins. Beyond elections, expressions of support have included mass mobilizations in support of sovereignty, against parliamentary coups, and against neoliberal governments. These were already evident in 2015 but became even more prominent during 2019.

Proponents of the Pink-Tide-is-Over thesis (PTIO thesis, from now on) never granted much importance to evidence that countered their contentions. For instance, Venezuela and Bolivia, countries that remained identified with the more radical currents of the Pink Tide, were still in 2019 led by governments with post-neoliberal orientations and committed to supporting the structures of regional integration that had become another distinctive trait of the Pink Tide (Muhr, 2012). But for advocates of the thesis those cases did not amount to much. Bolivia could be presented as an exception and, furthermore, lacked the financial muscle and the international projection that Venezuela had enjoyed under the governments of Hugo Chávez at the peak of the Pink Tide. In addition, a variety of political commentators, particularly from conservative outlets, predicted a defeat of Evo Morales in the presidential elections due later in the year (Ruiz de Arcaute, 2019; Latinamericanpost, 2018; Infobae, 2018). In short, Bolivia could soon lose its status of exception and therefore, in the view of its advocates, the PTIO thesis would be reinforced.

As for Venezuela, its profound economic crisis was used as evidence for the idea. By 2019 the country was an easy target for critics of post-neoliberal economic orientations. Maduro's government could not flag the positive indicators of socioeconomic development that had previously illustrated the success of Pink Tide orientations. In addition, Maduro's support base seemed to be weakening—an appreciation that was widespread even among commentators who nonetheless identified the self-proclaimed "interim" presidency of Juan Guaidó (launched in those days) as part of a United States–supported plan to destabilize Maduro's government and facilitate an international blockade of it (Buxton, 2019; Hetland, 2019).

Beyond the cases of Bolivia and Venezuela, the PTIO thesis proved impermeable to other sources of evidence that weakened its validity. The turbid circumstances under which some rightist candidates had won elections were never taken into account when it came to testing the substance of the thesis (the background of Bolsonaro's victory in Brazil was one instance [Goldstein, 2019]). The instability of the governments that implanted orthodox neoliberal agendas after defeating left-leaning candidates seemed not to affect the acceptance of the thesis, either. Macri's government in Argentina illustrates this case: it was incapable of gaining popular support or economic stabilization, as the negotiations with the International Monetary Fund in 2018 came to demonstrate (Natanson, 2018).

However, as 2019 went on, the PTIO thesis seemed to generate fewer adherents or at least less firm ones. Halfway through the year it became more common to hear commentators referring to Latin America as "a continent in dispute" (Katz, 2019)—a concept launched in previous years (Serrano Mancilla, 2015) but disregarded by supporters of the thesis. The conceptual shift that took place during 2019 was an indirect recognition that the certification of the Pink Tide as defunct might have been a precipitous act.

A succession of political events obliged commentators to reconsider their assessment of the political scenario in the continent (Baird, 2019). In October, Alberto Fernández won the Argentine presidential election at the head of a left-leaning platform (Frente de Todos) strongly associated with the legacy of Pink Tide governments—indeed, Cristina Fernández de Kirchner was a key figure in the formula that facilitated the victory of the Frente de Todos candidate. Elsewhere, rightist governments faced the results of their sustained failure to combine economic growth with social inclusion. Furious protests exploded in Chile, bringing Piñera's government, an active promoter of an anti–Pink Tide agenda through both rhetoric and foreign policy, to the verge of collapse (Morán Faúndes, 2019). In Colombia, a national strike revealed the depth of accumulated discontent with governments that had shown an incapacity to reduce marked inequality levels even under favorable macroeconomic conditions—gross domestic product growth of 3.7 percent between 2010 and 2018 and a four-point decline of the Gini coefficient in this same period (from 54.7 to 50.4 [Banco Mundial, 2018]). President Iván Duque, openly supportive of a United States–backed international agenda in the continent (including the sanctions on Venezuela [Council on Foreign Relations, 2019]), had to backtrack on some of his proposals for neoliberal economic reform, among them a pension reform that incidentally replicated key aspects of the "Chilean model," with privately owned funds administering the system.

Finally, the 2019 presidential election in Bolivia provided yet another instance of a political phenomenon that had been granted little importance by proponents of the thesis that the Pink Tide is over: rightist forces unable to defeat consolidated leftist candidates at the ballot box pave their way to government through parliamentary maneuvers (often called "parliamentary coups"), "lawfare" strategies, and/or direct military interventions. Seizing power for these forces seems to depend on neutralizing electorally legitimized leftist leaders. The case of Morales in 2019 epitomized this phenomenon: he won the election but was eventually forced to leave the country by an elite-led rebellion backed by commanding sectors of the army. It replicated the cases of other Pink Tide leftist leaders who were prevented from completing their terms or from competing in the electoral arena.

In Brazil, Lula da Silva's controversial conviction for corruption prevented him from competing electorally with the rightist Bolsonaro, who furthermore emerged as a national figure only in a scenario of institutional crisis marked by the ousting of President Dilma Rousseff (like Lula a leader of Partido dos Trabalhadores) through a questionable parliamentary impeachment in 2016 (Antunes et al., 2019: 97–99). In Paraguay, Fernando Lugo had been subjected to a similar process four years earlier (ominously, Lugo's impeachment was in its day labeled a "coup" by Rousseff, among other Latin American leaders [*La Nación*, 2012]). The Honduran President Manuel Zelaya (2006–2009) was also ousted from office through a military-backed coup, cutting short a term that included some pro-poor policies and sought to incorporate the country into the new Latin American regionalism that emerged with the Pink Tide (Ruhl, 2010: 98–100). Most recently (April 2020), amid increasing signs that he could return to play a direct active role in the Ecuadorian political arena, Rafael Correa, president for ten years (2007–2017), was convicted of corruption after a controversial trial that would ban him from holding political office for more than two decades (Schützhofer, 2020).

In sum, 2019 provided instances of three types of evidence that weaken the thesis that the Pink Tide is over: electoral victories of pro-leftist candidates associated with the Pink Tide kept occurring (e.g., Argentina, Bolivia); right-wing politicians reached government by sidestepping direct electoral competition with qualified leftist counterparts (e.g., Bolivia); and mass extrainstitutional collective action took place on the streets of countries with right-leaning governments, mobilizing demands for socioeconomic enfranchisement (e.g., Chile, Colombia). These diverse types of evidence are interconnected by a common factor: they all reveal the existence of mass social forces that, channeled through different streams of collective action (electoral politics, extrainstitutional mobilization), support the governmental orientations that characterize the Pink Tide and oppose neoliberal governance. This evidence revealed the inadequacy of the PTIO thesis's premises, which were always impervious to the signs of the social forces that Pink Tide governmental orientations helped to crystallize, with resource nationalism as one of their drivers.

The next section elaborates further on the political drivers for these social forces, showing how the transnational dimensions of extractivism inform the political choices of many Latin Americans. In doing so, it reveals key weaknesses in analyses of twenty-first century extractivism that fail to recognize why this governmental orientation receives such sustained support throughout the continent,

Local Readings of the (Transnational) Politics of Extractivism

Critics of resource nationalism pay scant attention to the transnational dimensions of extractivism as factors that shape the political subjectivities of many Latin Americans. These writers devote little or no effort to examining the motivations driving the support that members of different social groups provide to resource nationalism, and this erodes their capacity to develop adequate explanations for that support.

Most analysts are quick to acknowledge the transnational dimensions of extractivism, but not all of them grasp the political implications of these dimensions. This acknowledgment of transnationalism is unsurprising, since extractivism generates easily identifiable transnational interconnections. For instance, capital flows are indispensable. The scale and technological complexity of extractive operations make them dependent on intensive capital investment, and for extractive ventures in Latin America that capital is (at the very least) partly "foreign"—provided by corporations and agents with fiscal addresses in countries other than the "host" country (where the extraction takes place). Underscoring the transnational dimensions of extractivism, the participation of foreign capital in Latin American extractive projects has increased significantly over the past few decades, also revealing the "reprimarization" of many national economies (Veltmeyer, 2016: 775–777).

But these transnational dimensions are also identifiable in other flows that extractivism generates, such as flows of material resources. Some of these flows are measurable. For example, scholars register and compare the amounts of minerals extracted in Latin American countries and exported to other world destinations. This flow illustrates the "unequal ecological exchange" that pervades globalization (Foster and Holleman, 2014): countries in regions like Latin America provide "nature" that guarantees the metabolism of capital and the material sustenance of countries in regions of the core of the world system. This flow has increased remarkably in recent decades, underlining the transnational implications of Latin American extractivism (measured in millions of tons, mineral exports multiplied by two between 2000 and 2016 [Bárcena, 2018: 29]).

The transnational character of extractivism is also revealed by the flows of labor that it articulates. Historically, the incorporation of foreign labor was characteristic of some extractive industries in Latin American countries, a result of managerial tactics aimed at exerting tighter control over workers and filling in occasional labor shortages. Foreign workers often occupied the less skilled and worse-remunerated jobs as well as some of the intermediate positions in the occupational hierarchies of these industries. This hierarchical pattern of labor distribution was well illustrated in the early stages of the oil industry in countries like Venezuela, for instance, when Chinese, Afro-Caribbean, and Mexican workers provided a significant amount of the required labor (Tinker Salas, 2003: 155–156, 2009: viii, 136–137).

At present, the lower and middle echelons of the occupational hierarchy in these industries, and even some high-ranking managerial positions, are more commonly occupied by "native" labor (workers of the host country). This is the outcome of political struggle, for union movements pushed for it in pursuit of improved labor conditions and enhanced bargaining power, on occasion supported by nationalist governments that renegotiated the participation of foreign corporations in these industries (Lucena, 2007: 90–96). Nevertheless, today as in the past (91–92), some echelons of the occupational hierarchy of this industry remain occupied by foreign labor: in the foreign capital-holder corporations participating in these industries, all or most of the commanding managerial staff is foreign. In sum, to this day flows of labor, along with the flows of capital and natural resources, reinforce the transnational dimensions of extractivism.

These transnational dimensions have political implications that are not always taken into account in studies of extractivism in Latin America. For instance, studies that use the nation-state as the unit of analysis cannot provide insight into the ways in which the transnational dimensions of extractivism shape nation-state politics. The same is true of studies that, while adopting a transnational unit of study, approach the examination of extractivism through disembodied methods of analysis. For example, this is the case in studies whose empirical grounding includes measurable outcomes of the extractivist process (e.g., Russi et al., 2008) but no exploration of how that process and those outcomes are interpreted by different social groups in the countries in which resource extraction takes place. It is also the case in some studies framed by world-system theory that, underestimating the importance of the balance of social forces in specific national formations or the ideological orientations of different governments, contend that states that do not fully break with capitalism necessarily operate in the interest of capital (e.g., Petras and Veltmeyer, 2007: 372). In sum, various studies of extractivism sidestep the discussion of how the transnational dimensions of extractivism inform the political outlooks (and the electoral choices) of many Latin Americans. Overlooking this discussion impedes the understanding of why resource nationalism receives mass support in Latin America, a shortcoming this section of the chapter seeks to correct.

Though currently played down, this aspect of the politics of extractivism has previously been underscored by influential studies of Latin American politics. June Nash (1993) in *We Eat the Mines and the Mines Eat Us* was critical of analyses of the working class in underdeveloped countries like Bolivia that underestimated workers' capacity to understand and respond to the conditions under which they lived. Nash showed that Bolivian workers recognized the national and international dynamics influencing their lives, conditioned by their structural position as members of a class opposed to managerial elites in their own country and by their position as members of a dependent society subject to varying degrees of domination by members of developed countries. Furthermore, she contended that, in comparative perspective, Bolivian miners demonstrated a better understanding of the international dynamics of capitalism than their counterparts in the United States (see also Bergquist, 1986).

There is ample evidence that local readings of the expressions of uneven development and the global divisions of labor continue to inform the political views and electoral preferences of many people in Latin American countries. And, as in Nash's study, extractivism is still today a central focus of the processes and experiences that underpin this phenomenon. For instance, the flows of labor I have referred to constitute a source of relevant experience for many Latin Americans. Among workers in extractive industries, the occupational hierarchies that maintain foreign managers at the summit of the social pyramid in the workplace are expressions of a structure of power that mirrors international divisions of labor: Latin American countries provide natural resources and labor, and, along with capital, developed countries provide technological equipment and managers. But, beyond the experiences of workers directly situated in these occupational hierarchies, the power structures articulated by extractive industries have impacted much broader aspects of national culture and society in Latin American countries, obviously influencing their politics.

Tinker Salas's (2009) study of the Venezuelan oil industry provides rich grounding for an understanding of the reach of those influences, unveiling how the managerial plans and policies of foreign oil corporations operating in the country (ranging from segregated housing of employees to ethnically determined occupational hierarchies) contributed to recasting and often deepening preexisting class and racial cleavages in the country. As shaped by foreign corporations, the development of the oil industry was conducive to the generation of middle classes identified with the interests of the managerial elites, but also to exacerbating anti-imperialist (and even anti-immigrant) sentiment in other sectors of Venezuelan society. That sentiment is key to understanding why sovereignty has been a driving goal of progressive social forces in Venezuela and in other Latin American countries. In the Venezuelan case, left-leaning actors have promoted ideals of sovereignty and national independence in relation to the management of the oil industry since this industry took off. These ideals, sometimes shaped by the idioms of anti-imperialism, were also from its inception identifiable drivers of Chávez's Bolivarian movement (Ellner, 2014: 262–266; Raby, 2006: 145–146), a movement that, once in government, soon established nationalist interventions in the oil industry as one of its political landmarks (Hellinger, 2016: 64–66). Comparable conceptualizations of sovereignty, shaped by anti-imperialist sentiments, feed into the nationalist vein that, with different degrees of intensity, has characterized the orientation of Venezuelan and other Pink Tide governments in their reading of international relations. Indeed, the supranational organizations that these governments fostered at the peak of the movement, which gave expression to the so-called new Latin American regionalism, explicitly introduced notions of anti-imperialism and sovereignty as prominent discursive ingredients of political mobilization (Angosto-Ferrández, 2013: 5–6). These conceptualizations of sovereignty and anti-imperialism are of course connected with the transnational dimensions of extractivism and, through their influence on electoral behavior in Latin American countries, contribute to explaining why governments associated with resource nationalism have received strong, sustained electoral support.

The maintenance of a clear-cut division between national and international spheres in the discussion of Latin American politics (including its electoral politics) constitutes an analytical obstacle when it comes to assessing the support of the Pink Tide governments. This point has been treated in relation to the analysis of Venezuelan politics in studies showing that Venezuelans in general do not dissociate their personal political preferences and opinions from readings of a supranational scenario (Ellner, 2014: 262–266; Angosto-Ferrández, 2013: 3–4). In the view of many Venezuelans, the boundaries between national and international politics are blurry, and this view is also an identifiable ingredient in politics and electoral politics in particular.

Politicians of all orientations constantly acknowledge and refer to Venezuela's role in a supranational scenario. References to geopolitical conditions have been common in public declarations of governmental agents in Venezuela. For instance, from 2003 on, and particularly after being subjected to the 2002 coup and perceiving increased hostility from the Bush administration, Chávez made frequent reference to "imperialism" with regard to the role of the United States in regional and global geopolitics (Ellner, 2014: 262–263). Appeals to supranational political conditions have also been common among representatives of the opposition: a fundamental ingredient in the discursive repertoire of the opposition leader Juan Guaidó is his reference to the support of the international community for his position. Beyond rhetoric, his self-proclamation as president was granted recognition by more than fifty foreign governments, and this support brought with it a number of United States–led economic sanctions against Maduro's government, some of them targeting the operations of the Venezuelan oil industry (Weisbrot and Sachs, 2019: 299–311), the pillar of resource nationalism in the country. These and other international sanctions on Venezuelan governments generate immediate reactions within the country, with supporters of the government, or merely supporters of Venezuelan sovereignty, mobilizing through different avenues, from mass rallies to collections of signatures to social media "hashtagging."

The lack of attention to these transnational aspects among some neo-extractivism writers is well illustrated by the categories they use in attempting to explain why many Latin Americans support the principles of resource nationalism. For instance, they suggest that notions of "ownership of enormous ecological riches that must be intensively used" pervade an "old South American culture" (Gudynas, 2012: 135) or that an "eldoradista" (El Dorado-like) vision influenced by colonial ideologies of access to wealth still permeates "even indigenous communities and certain social organizations" (Svampa, 2013: 43). These categories, which highlight cultural aspects of ideological formation, are used to explain the disregard of supporters of resource nationalism for the negative aspects of extractivism (such as economic reprimarization, environmental degradation, and sustainability). They are problematic, however, because they underestimate or overlook key political ingredients of the mass support that resource nationalism receives. These political ingredients include nationalistic interpretations of the transnational dimensions of extractivism and the unequal distributions of wealth that it generates. For the popular classes, whose socioeconomic enfranchisement has been historically fragile in most Latin American nations, access to the rents derived from extraction is totally dependent on governmental mediations in relation to specific taxation regimes (politically determined conditions on extractive operations that result in rent generation) and in relation to the implementation of redistributive policies that can transform part of the rents captured by governments into access to services and/or economic transfers. This access to rents and services is at the core of popular support for and demand for resource nationalist orientations in government.

There is, however, an additional, crucial factor in the local interpretations of the transnational dimensions of extractivism that must be considered and is also overlooked by critics of Pink Tide governments and resource nationalism—the negative ecological impacts of extractivism. For many Latin Americans, the transnational frame of analysis I have described underpins a particular political reading of the (differential) degrees of responsibility that extractivism generates as a practice with (unquestionable) negative environmental impacts. Extractivism involves not only the countries in which it takes place and those of the providers of capital and labor, but also any country whose citizens consume goods and services for whose production and circulation resources extracted from Latin America have been used. These countries are materially dependent on resources extracted elsewhere (Angosto-Ferrández, 2015: 211–213). Thus the responsibility for the negative impacts of extractivism can also be transnationally distributed rather than placed on the Latin American governments and the populations that support them. Why should these governments be made solely responsible for a phenomenon that is spurred by other governments and the social forces that support them, particularly when the latter show no sign of effectively trying to reduce their consumption of resources extracted elsewhere?

This is the transnational background that shapes the political views of many Latin Americans. Most important, it contributes to explaining why there is mass support for Latin American governments that, under the principles of resource nationalism, have intervened in the politics of extractivism to alleviate the socioeconomic disenfranchisement of large sectors of their populations. Environmental degradation is indeed an urgent problem, but it is unethical to try to persuade the poorer populations of poorer nations that it is they who must start the shift toward sustainability. Setting aside questions of inequality, the concept of sustainability appears to many Latin Americans a goal whose achievement does not depend on the sacrifices that abandoning resource nationalism would impose upon them.

Resource Nationalism, Indigenous Rights, and Disputes over Extractivist Rights

Pink Tide leaders such as Chávez, Morales, and Correa appealed to indigenous rights as they campaigned to reach government. Those appeals contributed to mobilizing support for their political movements, and indigenous rights ended up occupying a prominent position in the constitutions later approved. Indeed, the constitutions of Venezuela (1999), Ecuador (2008), and Bolivia (2009) included elaborate sets of differentiated rights for the indigenous population and were informed by principles of indigenous autonomy. In the Bolivian and Ecuadorian cases, those principles underpinned the constitutional declaration of plurinationality as the political foundation of the state (Lupien, 2011).

Some scholars have argued, however, that the governments of those leaders and others in the orbit of the Pink Tide fell short of materializing indigenous rights and particularly rights related to territorial autonomies (see Ellner's introduction to this volume). This argument is often grounded in the fact that government-fostered development projects affecting indigenous territories have frequently produced significant debate, including opposition from indigenous groups (e.g., McNeish, 2013; Anthias, 2018). This opposition has generated debate on the relations between indigenous movements and Pink Tide governments (Lalander, 2014; Becker, 2013) that has in turn given rise to some generalizations about those relations, often presented as conflictive and even as antagonistic. Yet broad generalizations about the relations between indigenous movements and Pink Tide governments create obstacles to the analysis of resource nationalism, which continues to generate support among important sectors of the indigenous populations. They also fail to explain convincingly why sectors of these populations participate directly in extractive industry.

I have elsewhere demonstrated, through a focus on the Venezuelan case, that significant fractions of the indigenous population have actively supported Pink Tide governments and the principles of resource nationalism (Angosto-Ferrández, 2015, 2018). The development of a state-supporting indigenous movement was key to facilitating an unprecedented level of enfranchisement for the indigenous population. Members of this indigenous movement undertake collective action through institutional avenues that include electoral and party politics, but also through their involvement in the implementation of government-fostered social programs (including health and education programs). They also participate in other forms of extrainstitutional mobilization, developing synergies with diverse foci of activism and organizations that, while generally associated with Chavismo, do not preclude criticism of government agencies. This situation destabilizes the aforementioned generalizations about the antagonistic relations between indigenous movements and Pink Tide governments.

At the same time, some sectors of the indigenous population are directly involved in extractivism, participating as workers in extractive industries and in some cases also as owners and/or managers of small-scale extractive ventures. Here I will focus on this latter case through an examination of mining in Venezuela's Gran Sabana,[1] but this form of indigenous participation in extraction is also identifiable in other areas of the continent. Some introductory commentary is in order to avoid misguided representations of sectors of the indigenous population as "less environmentalist" than others or as failing, as Alcida Ramos put it (1994), to match the "hyper-real" model that features an essentialist association of indigenous people with environmental conservation (for a discussion of artisanal miners elsewhere in the continent, see Toledo Orozco's chapter in this volume).

When mining in indigenous territories is capital-intensive, its realization entails dispossession and displacement of the indigenous population. This population, which generally lacks capital, is immediately excluded from the possibility of controlling extraction and, if it opposes extraction, is often violently dispossessed of land and resources through extraeconomic means. In these cases, opposition to extractivism has sometimes been read as an expression of the "environmentalism of the poor" (Martínez-Alier, 2002) even when it is not accompanied by demands for environmental protection: the defense of local community's own means of sustenance is inextricably linked to such protection. However, when extraction is not capital-intensive, the same concern with local community sustenance spurs direct indigenous participation in extraction. In these cases, ownership of or managing control over extractive ventures occurs (for example, in gold and diamond mines in certain areas of the continent). Conflicts over extractivism in indigenous territories are common in any of those scenarios, but the configuration of and the demands at stake in them vary. In some cases, conflict results from local opposition to extractive projects, in others from disputes over extractive rights or the conditions under which extractivism is to be regulated.

Mining in the Gran Sabana

The Gran Sabana is a vast region of southern Venezuela that is traditional Pemon territory. The majority of settlements in the region are still indigenous communities. Territorial regulation of the region is complex in normative terms (Martens, 2011) and includes overlapping sets of conservationist legislation, zones under military administration and some indigenous land titles. The region contains important reserves of minerals such as gold and diamonds, and mining has taken place there at different scales for well over a century. Though environmental and other regulations prohibit extraction, illegal mining continues in various parts of the region, undertaken by Venezuelans from other parts of the country, by foreigners (Brazilians, Colombians and Guyanese primarily), and by members of the local Pemon population.

Gold and diamonds can be extracted with relatively simple and cheap equipment through so-called artisanal methods. Partly because of this and through active organization, Pemon miners have been able to gain control of shares of the mining business in and near some of their communities as owners and managers of small-scale ventures or as de facto license providers for other miners. This control has been fought for and is precarious. In many Pemon communities, including those not directly involved in mining, the perception of encroachment and fear of land and resource dispossession associated with the flows of nonindigenous miners is constant.

Conflicts over extraction in the Gran Sabana are not new, but they are intensifying. Here I will focus on conflicts over extractive rights. I do not suggest that mining is supported by all of the region's population, but I do contend that this focus is important because it sheds light on aspects of extractivism that continue to be neglected in debates over resource nationalism and extractivism and because mining in the Gran Sabana is developing significantly and deserves renewed attention.

Disputes over Extractivism Rights

Here are the words of a Pemon man from the Ikabarú area, to this day an important mining spot in the Gran Sabana, recorded in the early 1990s by Colchester and Watson (1995: 23):

> They forbade us from mining because they say that mining destroys the river and destroys the forest. We left the mines alone. But now who can explain why [foreigners] went into the Abismo, the great forest, with much more destructive machines than our mining pans? Why do they take Indians out of the mines, Venezuelan Indians? Why, after excluding the Indians, do they permit foreigners to exploit that which they forbid us?

Let us compare these words with those of a Pemon woman from the Urimán area (another mining hotspot in the region) two decades later, directed face-to-face to a high-ranking National Guard officer (Angosto-Ferrández, 2015: 227):

> This land is ours, and you are not going to take it away from us. What do you want, to give it to the Chinese, the Russians, for them to come and damage the land of the Pemon? [Now that you are in our community lands], if we want to take you hostage we will do so, because here we Pemon Indians are in charge.

Rather than being part of a protest against mining, this woman's appeals to land ownership and foreign appropriation of the land were part of the protests undertaken after the National Guard had suspended flights to Urimán in effort to halt illegal mining in the area. Many in Urimán live off mining, and their food and other supplies largely depend on air transport (river and land communications are extremely complicated). Without those flights, living conditions deteriorate rapidly for the inhabitants of that area, and mining is also severely affected.

These quotations illustrate a sentiment that has intensified among sectors of the Pemon population in the past two decades. The sentiment both reflects concerns over the threat of dispossession of land and resources and informs a demand for extractive rights. Pemon miners conceptualize these rights as an extension of indigenous land rights. By contrasting the two quotations we can also gain insight into a parallel phenomenon: in demanding extractive rights the Pemon have become far more belligerent. When the woman from Urimán warned the National Guard officer that her people could take him hostage, she was not merely speaking hypothetically but referring to something that had occurred several times in recent years. Hostage taking is one expression of conflict over extractivism in the Gran Sabana that has disputes over extractive rights at its core.

Because of these disputes over extractive rights, some Pemon groups involved in mining have established armed guards to supervise mining and defend extractive rights. This is in response to groups disputing those rights, including nonindigenous armed organizations (generally called *sindicatos*) that have de facto control over and regulate extraction in parts of the region. These latter groups have pressured mining spots in the Gran Sabana more and more intensely in recent years. The decline of other sectors of the Venezuelan economy since 2013, aggravated by the international sanctions imposed upon the country by the United States and some of its international allies, has converged with sustained strong prices of minerals such as gold and diamonds. In this scenario, the government has launched a vast scheme to promote mineral extraction around the so-called Orinoco Mining Arc (Angosto-Ferrández, 2019a), but also, and independently, many Venezuelans have arrived in areas like the Gran Sabana where artisanal mining takes place. This augmented flow of people in search of jobs associated with mining (ranging from miners to traders to the most diverse service providers) has exacerbated what was already intense competition over access to and control of mineral extraction. Episodes of violence associated with mining disputes have been recurrent in this period.[2]

The belligerent defense of extractive rights on the part of Pemon miners is also a response to the (illegal) rent-capture imposed on artisanal miners by some sectors of the military. There have been recurrent denunciations of extortion of miners by military personnel in exchange for informally granted permission to mine and/or for the circulation of goods and people. These denunciations have set the stage for instances in which Pemon have taken military personnel hostage. Kidnappings have taken place after state security forces implemented operations against illegal mining (Angosto-Ferrández, 2019b).

In sum, mining in the Gran Sabana is a case of direct indigenous participation in extractive practices and also of disputes over extractive rights. The local indigenous population demands these rights as part of its territorial rights in opposition to the rights that the state, nonindigenous miners, and corrupt sectors of the security forces may claim. This situation destabilizes the mechanical association of conflict over extractivism in indigenous territories as opposition to extractivism itself (Picq, 2014), but it also recasts the debate about extractive rights, with the issue of who holds them coming to the fore. It is also important to shed light on the reason why people take up mining, which goes beyond El-Dorado-type motivation. Poverty, fear of proletarianization, and lack of reliable economic alternatives are the key factors.

Why Pemon People Undertake Mining

I will now turn to an ethnographically informed explanation as to why people participate in mining, with a focus on communities whose inhabitants engage in mining only temporarily as a source of cash. In those communities, families avail themselves of access to land and other common-pool resources that enable them to produce some of the food they consume (Angosto-Ferrández, 2006, 2013, 2016). The capacity to produce food autonomously is highly appreciated and often explicitly contrasted with the hardships that people experience when they have to travel to criollo towns for some reason (e.g., for bureaucratic processes, visits to medical centers, shopping). Normally, people have very little cash or none at all when traveling and are generally detached from networks of kin that might provide support. "Enduring hunger" is an expression that features prominently in recollections of these travels. It captures real experiences of hunger but also refers to the hardships associated with leaving one's community. In one's own community, as some Pemon put it, "one can always at least have some food at hand."

This appreciation of autonomous food production goes in tandem with constant concern about its limitations. Access to protein is very limited, and agricultural production is always exposed to potential shortages due to poor harvests. In fact, when cash is available people buy commercial foods such as canned fish, rice, corn flour, or pasta even when this may involve significant travel (shops are available only in some Pemon communities or in the municipal capital, Santa Elena).

Beyond food, people in these communities of course need cash to buy all other necessary commercial goods (from clothing to basic inputs for production), and cash is very difficult to obtain. For instance, in a community like Tuauken (200 inhabitants), where I have conducted most of my fieldwork in the Gran Sabana, no one has guaranteed income except the schoolteachers (who receive their salaries through the public educational system). The rest of the families in the community have to resort to a variety of activities to obtain cash. Some sell occasional agricultural surplus in neighboring communities, but this activity is burdensome for the seller (who has to personally carry the produce) and generates only small amounts of cash. In peak tourist seasons, many people also travel to nearby communities that attract visitors, where they sell handicrafts or do petty jobs while staying with relatives. These are temporary activities, subject to fluctuations (varying numbers of tourist visitors, varying amounts of agricultural surplus), and do not generate large amounts of cash either. Leaving these options aside, waged work is the only alternative, and it involves migrating outside the community and often outside the Gran Sabana. This labor migration is not taken lightly, often being recalled as a time of personal degradation and deep crisis. Not surprisingly, many of those who migrate return after a period of time, expressing a preference for life in their communities.

This is the scenario in which mining appears as an option to obtain cash and potentially in larger amounts than can be got through activities like the ones described above. Moreover, mining can in some cases be undertaken without leaving the Gran Sabana and thus without fully severing ties with preexisting social networks. The Pemon who travel to mines near other indigenous communities in the region generally do so with the support of networks of kin, a factor that mitigates the alienation that underpins the association of labor migration with personal crisis. Many of those who engage in mining in these communities would not do so if they found stable alternatives. Even for those who undertake it temporarily and in sites where they have networks of kin, mining involves detachment from local community and family. Moreover, mining is hazardous, and it is increasingly exposed to violent competition. This combination of factors and the ways in which they are experienced by some Pemon people can be illustrated with story that I present in the following paragraphs.

When I first met Ovidio (a pseudonym), in 2004, he was in his twenties and living in Tuauken with his parents and his unmarried siblings. He had completed secondary schooling in a nearby mission center, but after that he returned to his community, where he helped with the preparation and maintenance of family gardens. He was notably active in the search for cash (more than some of his younger siblings), selling bananas, plantains, or cassava bread in nearby communities when he could and working throughout the year on simple handicrafts that he tried to sell in tourist seasons in Chinak Meru Falls, where he has relatives. He had done some mining in the past, near Ikabarú, where in-laws of his older brother worked the mines, but he had returned to Tuauken after a few months of work and did not go into the mines again in several years.

In 2009 he married into a family from a nearby community, San Luis, and was soon expecting a baby. After living there for a few months he decided to return to the mines temporarily. On this visit, his leg was broken in a landslide, and it took months for him to recover during which he could not work. I met him shortly after he had recovered mobility, and he was very contented with a teaching job in his new community, where they had added a position to the existing school—something that was happening in several indigenous communities in the region as a result of the expansion of education promoted by the government.

Ovidio's story illustrates some of the factors that lead people in Pemon communities to engage in mining as a source of cash and provides insight into a parallel phenomenon that helps explain the sustained electoral support for the Bolivarian governments in these communities over the past two decades. This support has partly to do with the redistributive policies that those governments have implemented, ranging from educational *misiones* to credit through the communal councils and the Banco de la Mujer to direct investment in infrastructure. These schemes have not fully succeeded in producing structural transformations that could consolidate sustainable development for the population of the region, but they have been backed electorally. Study of electoral behavior in the region indicates that political opinion there is primarily informed by assessments of performance in the provision of social services and material assistance (Angosto-Ferrández, 2012) and by principles of "descriptive representation" and the ethnic ascription of the candidates in relation to voters. Bolivarian candidates in national, regional, and municipal elections in the Gran Sabana have consistently received majority support, often above national averages.

Closing Remarks

As a major pillar of the Pink Tide, resource nationalism has received mass support in Latin America over the past two decades, and I have provided arguments that help to explain why this is the case. Misunderstanding of that support and of the reasons for it characterizes the analyses of some writers who participate in the debates on extractivism in Latin America. Such misrepresentation results from the theoretical choices that analysts make in approaching these debates, which often lead to failing to examine the social forces that support (and demand) resource nationalism as a framework for socioeconomic development. I have argued that the political assessment of the Pink Tide, particularly among advocates of the "it is over" thesis, has been conditioned by comparable limitations. In essence, a focus on governments as autonomous agents of policy implementation has led to a misunderstanding of the widespread social support for Pink Tide governmental orientations among the popular classes.

Furthermore, I have shown why the transnational dimensions of extractivism are key to developing an adequate understanding of the support for resource nationalism. As a result of colonial history but also of current geopolitical conditions, many Latin Americans interpret these dimensions in overtly political terms, as an engine of sovereignty claims. There continues to be among them a strong vein of nationalistic feeling shaped by opposition to multinational control of resource extraction. Additionally, the transnational dimensions of extractivism are interpreted by many Latin Americans in relation to the responsibilities generated by the negative impacts of extractivism, suggesting that wealthy countries that consume resources extracted from Latin America should bear the brunt of the burden of the scaling back of extractive industries. In this way the reduction would occur without condemning large proportions of the populations of the continent to continued socioeconomic disenfranchisement.

I have also underscored the importance of analyzing the reasons that lead the indigenous population to participate in extractivism in their territories. I argue that their participation is rooted in concerns over the poverty and proletarianization to which they are exposed. This phenomenon, which destabilizes generalizations about indigenous movement opposition to extractivism, is an invitation to reframe current debates on this economic practice, bringing to the fore the question of who should legitimately possess extractive rights, under what regulatory conditions, and why.

Notes

1. I started field research in the Gran Sabana in 2003 and lived in the region while conducting fieldwork in 2014. Between 2006 and 2011 I undertook several shorter periods of field research every year while based in Venezuela. Between 2012 and 2016 I completed six more weeks of fieldwork there.

2. This is illustrated by a recent event in the Ikabarú area, where eight people died (Tal Cual Digital, 2019), but this was far from an isolated case. Several Pemon people have been murdered in the past few years in disputes associated with mining, and just a few months earlier there were allegations that five people from the community of San Luis del Morichal had been murdered (Fe y Alegría, 2018).

References

Angosto-Ferrández, Luis Fernando

2012 "Participación y representación indígena en los procesos electorales venezolanos." *América Latina Hoy*, no. 60: 153–182.

2013 "Democracy, revolution, and geopolitics: Venezuela and the international politics of discontent," pp. 1–12 in Luis Angosto-Ferrández (ed.), *Democracy, Revolution, and Geopolitics in Latin America: Venezuela and the International Politics of Discontent*. New York: Routledge.

2015 *Venezuela Reframed: Bolivarianism, Indigenous Peoples, and Socialisms of the 21st Century*. London: Zed Books.
2016 "Natural value: rent-capture and the commodification of a waterfall in Gran Sabana, Venezuela" pp. 112–131 in Luis Angosto-Ferrandez and Geir Henning Presterudstuen (eds.), *Anthropologies of Value: Cultures of Accumulation Across the Global North and South*. London: Pluto Press.2017 "Indigenous peoples, social movements, and the legacy of Hugo Chávez's governments." *Latin American Perspectives* 44 (1): 180–198.
2019a "Neoextractivism and class formation: lessons from the Orinoco Mining Arc Project in Venezuela." *Latin American Perspectives* 46 (1): 190–211.
2019b "The battle of the 'lost world' in Venezuela's Gran Sabana." *NACLA .org*. April 22. https://nacla.org/news/2019/04/22/battle-%E2%80%9C-lost-world %E2%80%9D-venezuela%E2%80%99s-gran-sabana.
Anthias, P.
2018 "Indigenous peoples and the new extraction: from territorial rights to hydrocarbon citizenship in the Bolivian Chaco." *Latin American Perspectives* 45 (5): 136–153.
Antunes, R., M. A. Santana, and L. Praun
2019 "Chronicle of a defeat foretold: the PT administrations from compromise to the coup." *Latin American Perspectives* 46 (1): 85–104.
Baird, Vanessa
2019 "Is the 'pink tide' returning to Latin America?" https://newint.org/features /2019/10/30/pink-tide-returning-latin-america.
Banco Mundial
2018 "Índice Gini—Colombia." *Bancomundial.org*. https://datos.bancomundial .org/indicador/SI.POV.GINI?locations=CO.
Bárcena, Alicia
2018 "Estado de la situación de la minería en América Latina y el Caribe: desafíos y oportunidades para un desarrollo más sostenible." *CEPAL.org*. November 19. https://www.cepal.org/sites/default/files/presentation/files/181119-final_final_ corta-giz_revisada_alicia_barcena_ministros_mineria_limarev.pdf.
Becker, Marc
2013 "The stormy relations between Rafael Correa and social movements in Ecuador." *Latin American Perspectives* 40 (3): 43–62.
Bergquist, Charles
1986 *Labor in Latin America: Comparative Essays on Chile, Argentina, Venezuela and Colombia*. Stanford, CA: Stanford University Press.
Buxton, Julia
2019 "The missteps of Venezuela's opposition—again." *NACLA Report on the Americas* 51 (2): 130–133.
Castañeda, Jorge G., and Marco A. Morales
2008 *Leftovers: Tales of the Latin American Left*. New York: Routledge.
Colchester, M., and F. Watson
1995 *Venezuela: Violations of Indigenous Rights (Report to the International Labour Office on the Observation of ILO Convention 107)*. Chadlington, UK: Forest Peoples Programme.

Council on Foreign Relations
2019 "A conversation with President Iván Duque of Colombia." *Cfr.org*. September 27. https://www.cfr.org/event/conversation-president-ivan-duque-colombia.
Ellner, Steve
2014 *El fenómeno Chávez: Sus orígenes y su impacto hasta 2013*. Caracas: Celarg.
2019a "Pink-tide governments: pragmatic and populist responses to challenges from the right." *Latin American Perspectives* 46 (1): 4–22.
2019b "Class strategies in Chavista Venezuela: pragmatic and populist policies in a broader context." *Latin American Perspectives* 46 (1): 167–189.
Farthing, Linda, and Nicole Fabricant
2018 "*Open Veins* revisited: charting the social, economic, and political contours of the new extractivism in Latin America." *Latin American Perspectives* 45 (5): 4–17.
Fe y Alegria
2018 "Reportan 5 asesinatos de pemones por grupos armados en Bolívar." https://www.aporrea.org/ddhh/n326134.html.
Foster, John Bellamy, and Hanna Holleman
2014 "The theory of unequal ecological exchange: a Marx-Odum dialectic." *Journal of Peasant Studies* 41 (2): 199–233.
Gold, Marina, and Alessandro Zagato (eds.)
2020 *After the Pink Tide: Corporate State Formation and New Egalitarianisms in Latin America*. New York: Berghahn Books.
Goldstein, A. A.
2019 "The new far-right in Brazil and the construction of a right-wing order." *Latin American Perspectives* 46 (4): 245–262.
Gonzalez, Mike
2019 *The Ebb of the Pink Tide: The Decline of the Left in Latin America*. London: Pluto Press.
Gudynas, Eduardo
2012 "Estado compensador y nuevos extractivismos: las ambivalencias del progresismo sudamericano." *Nueva Sociedad*, no. 237: 128–146.
Hellinger, Daniel
2017 "Oil and the Chávez Legacy." *Latin American Perspectives* 44 (1): 54–77.
Hetland, Gabriel
2019 "Venezuela's deadly blackout highlights the need for a negotiated resolution of the crisis." *Thenation.com*. March 13. https://www.thenation.com/article/archive/venezuela-blackout-us-sanctions-maduro/.
Infobae
2018 "Evo Morales podría ser derrotado en las elecciones de 2019, según una encuesta." *Infobae.com*. July 31. https://www.infobae.com/america/america-latina/2018/07/31/evo-morales-podria-ser-derrotado-en-las-elecciones-de-2019-segun-una-encuesta/.
Katz, Claudio
2019 "Los protagonistas de la disputa en América Latina." *Cadtm.org*. November 21. https://www.cadtm.org/Los-protagonistas-de-la-disputa-en-America-Latina.

La Nación
2012 "Argentina 'no convalidará el golpe en Paraguay' mientras que Brasil sugirió que quedaría fuera de la Unasur y el Mercosur." *Lanacion.com.ar*. June 23. https://www.lanacion.com.ar/el-mundo/unasur-y-mercosur-tomaria-medidas-severas-ante-la-remocion-de-lugo-nid1484357.
Lalander, Rickard
2014 "Rights of nature and the indigenous peoples in Bolivia and Ecuador: a straitjacket for progressive development politics?" *Revista Iberoamericana de Estudios de Desarrollo* 3 (2): 148–173.
Latinamericanpost
2018 "Bolivia: Carlos Mesa could end the government of Evo Morales." *Latinamericanpost.com*. October 15. https://latinamericanpost.com/23904-bolivia-carlos-mesa-could-end-the-government-of-evo-morales.
Lucena, Héctor
2007 *El movimiento obrero petrolero: Proceso de formación y desarrollo*. Caracas: Catalá/El Centauro.
Lupien, Pascal
2011 "The incorporation of indigenous concepts of plurinationality into the new constitutions of Ecuador and Bolivia." *Democratization* 18: 774–796.Marens
McNeish, J. A.
2013 "Extraction, protests and indigeneity in Bolivia: the TIPNIS effect." *Latin American and Caribbean Ethnic Studies* 8 (2): 221–242.
Martens, Raquel
2011 "La demarcación del habitat y tierras de comunidades y pueblos indígenas del estado Bolívar, entre el desarrollo nacional y la identidad cultural." *Boletín Antropológico* 82: 132–162.
Martínez Alier, Joan
2002 *The Environmentalism of the Poor: A Study of Ecological Conflicts and Valuation*. Cheltenham: Edward Elgar.
Mendonça, M. L., and F. T. Pitta
2018 "International financial capital and the Brazilian land market." *Latin American Perspectives* 45 (5): 88–101.
Morán Faúndes, José M.
2019 "Chile despertó: el modelo chileno, la matriz de la desigualdad y la protesta de 2019." *Crítica y Resistencias* 9: 54–69.
Muhr, Thomas
2012 "(Re)constructing popular power in our America: Venezuela and the regionalisation of 'revolutionary democracy' in the ALBA–TCP space." *Third World Quarterly* 33: 225–241.
Nash, June C.
1993 *We Eat the Mines and the Mines Eat Us: Dependency and Exploitation in Bolivian Tin Mines*. New York: Columbia University Press.
Natanson, José
2018 "Mauricio Macri en su ratonera: el fin de la utopía gradualista." *Nueva Sociedad*, no. 276: 24–33.

Petras, James, and Henry Veltmeyer
2007 "The 'development state' in Latin America: whose development, whose state?" *Journal of Peasant Studies* 34 (3–4): 371–407.
Picq, Manuela
2014 "Self-determination as anti-extractivism: how indigenous resistance challenges world politics," pp. 26–33 in Marc Woons (ed.), *Restoring Indigenous Self-Determination: Theoretical and Practical Approaches*. Bristol: E-International Relations.
Raby, Diana
2006 *Democracy and Revolution: Latin America and Socialism Today*. London: Pluto Press.
Ramos, A. R.
1994 "The hyperreal Indian." *Critique of Anthropology* 14 (2): 153–171.
Ruhl, J. Mark
2010 "Trouble in Central America: Honduras unravels." *Journal of Democracy* 21 (2): 93–107.
Ruiz de Arcaute, Miguel
2019 "Desgaste, corrupción y autoritarismo: por qué Evo Morales podría perder las elecciones en Bolivia." https://www.abc.es/internacional/abci-desgaste-corrupcion-y-autoritarismo-morales-podria-perder-elecciones-bolivia-201906010209_noticia.html?ref=https%3A%2F%2Fwww.google.com%2F.
Russi, D., A. C. Gonzalez-Martinez, J. Silva-Macher, S. Giljurn, J. Martinez-Alier, and M. C. Vallejo
2008 "Materials flows in Latin America: a comparative analysis of Chile, Ecuador, and Peru, 1980–2000." *Journal of Industrial Ecology* 12: 704–720.
Schützhofer, Timm Benjamin
2020 "In Ecuador, lawfare marches on despite coronavirus." *NACLA.org*. April 27. https://nacla.org/news/2020/04/28/ecuador-lawfare-marches-despite-coronavirus.
Serrano Mancilla, Alfredo
2015 *América Latina en Disputa*. Caracas: El Perro y la Rana.
Svampa, M. N.
2013 "Consenso de los commodities y lenguajes de valoración en América Latina." *Nueva Sociedad*, no. 244: 30–46.
Tal Cual Digital
2019 "Hallan cuerpos de hermanos asesinados en masacre en mina de Ikabarú." *Talcualdigital.com*. November 25. https://talcualdigital.com/fiscalia-registra-6-muertos-en-masacre-de-pemones-en-ikarabu/.
Tinker Salas, Miguel
2003 "Races and cultures in the Venezuelan oil fields," pp. 143–164 in Vincent Peloso (ed.), *Work, Protest, and Identity in Twentieth-century Latin America*. Wilmington, DE: Scholarly Resources.
2009 *The Enduring Legacy: Oil, Culture, and Society in Venezuela*. Durham, NC: Duke University Press.

Veltmeyer, Henry
2012 "The natural resource dynamics of postneoliberalism in Latin America: new developmentalism or extractivist imperialism?" *Studies in Political Economy* 90 (1): 57–85.
2016 "Extractive capital, the state, and the resistance in Latin America." *Sociology and Anthropology* 4: 774–784.
Weisbrot, Mark, and J. Sachs
2019 "Punishing civilians: U.S. sanctions on Venezuela." *Challenge* 62 (5): 299–321.

5

Extractivism and Resource Nationalism in Bolivia

Foreign Direct Investment Policy and Development under Evo Morales

María J. Paz and Juan M. Ramírez-Cendrero

Foreign direct investment inflows are of crucial importance given the absence of national investments that is typical of the developing world. The 1980s and 1990s were characterized by an increase in foreign direct investment inflows into developing economies. These inflows were stimulated by, among other factors, favorable neoliberal policies, which were considered to contribute significantly to economic development. However, since the beginning of the twenty-first century there has been a proliferation of academic literature questioning the effects of foreign direct investment inflows, and this has led to a rethinking of the role of corresponding policies (Gallagher and Chudnovsky, 2010; Lall and Narula, 2004; UNCTAD, 2003). As a result of these assessments, various governments in Latin America have substantially modified their foreign direct investment policies in the natural-resources sector, in some cases nationalizing companies that had been privatized over the previous two decades. Among these governments, that of Bolivia is considered a pioneer and stands out for the apparent radicalism of the measures taken.

This chapter attempts to answer two questions: What were the changes in foreign direct investment policy with regard to oil and gas following the rise to power of Evo Morales, and did they help achieve the Morales government's development goals? Our analysis is designed to contribute to the current debate on the role of foreign direct investment policy in development. As suggested by Rugraff et al. (2009: 47–48), this requires case studies as a complement to econometric analyses, which have failed to provide a universal answer. Although our results cannot be fully extrapolated to other economies, they may help identify the scope and limits of some of the current changes in foreign direct investment policy in the extractive sectors.[1]

Our choice of the oil and gas industry in Bolivia is justified by several considerations. First is the importance of the extractive sectors in the "new" development strategies. The National Development Plan, formulated in 2006, is a good example. According to the plan, the extractive sectors are central as the core of structural change throughout the economy (the new productive matrix) and as revenue generators; therefore, what happens in this sector largely determines the outcome of the development strategy as a whole. As a result, the scope of our conclusions transcends the purely sectorial, because their implications for development strategy will be crucial. Second, these sectors have clear limitations associated with the excessive presence of such investment. Third, at least a priori, nationalization would seem to be a radical shift toward the recovery of policy space for national governments in developing economies. Fourth, in recent years some writers (Webber, 2011) have called for closer analysis of the policies of the Movimiento al Socialismo (Movement toward Socialism—MAS), and in fact many specialists have noted a gradual distancing of the economic policy of the Bolivian government from the MAS's basic principles (Estermann, 2012).

This chapter seeks to provide a specific analysis of changes in foreign direct investment policy in the hydrocarbons sector from the perspective of the government's development goals. This allows us to contribute to the debate raised in this book's introduction about the characterization of Pink Tide governments such as that of Morales. In fact, the analysis of foreign direct investment policies adopted in the oil and gas industry by Pink Tide leaders is a key element that helps to clarify the debate on the characterization of those governments: neo-extractivism (as its critics describe it) vs. resource nationalism. The proposed analysis of foreign direct investment policies in the framework of the National Development Plan sheds light on both the distancing from the Washington Consensus and the limitations derived from the renewed role of the extractive sector, taking into account Bolivia's social, political, and geographical particularities.

To address our objective, we begin by discussing the influence of foreign direct investment policy on economic development. We also attempt to identify the key aspects that should inform foreign direct investment policy for the oil and gas industry. In the third section we present the main features of the Bolivian National Development Plan. Finally, after describing the Bolivian pattern of development, we evaluate whether the changes in policy were conducive to the achievement of the development goals outlined in that plan and then we will synthesize our main conclusions.

Foreign Direct Investment Policy and Development

A review of the economic literature about the effects of foreign direct investment on developing economies allows us to reject the automatism of this relationship (both in favor and against) advocated for decades (Moran et al., 2005; Rugraff et al., 2009: 29–55; UNCTAD, 2003). Since the late 1990s, a consensus has emerged regarding the contradictory and heterogeneous nature of the effects of foreign direct investment inflows (Dunning, 1994; Jenkins, 1989; Shaikh, 2009).[2] In our opinion, deterministic approaches should be rejected. As Weeks (2009) points out, they have in common that they depend on a static view of competition, with the implication that transnational corporations transfer their competitive advantages when they invest in other countries. When capitalist competition is understood dynamically, it is apparent that the effects of foreign investment and the transfer of competitive advantages depend on the (competitive) context in which the investment takes place. How this occurs in each economy will be influenced by endogenous and exogenous factors (sectorial specialization, number of local enterprises, national and international regulatory frameworks, and investment modality).

This approach is shared in part by the literature on "absorptive capability," which focuses on endogenous factors. These studies hold that the effects of foreign direct investment depend fundamentally on the capability of host economies to enhance the transfer of transnational corporations' competitive advantage (Lall and Narula, 2004). In any case, the attractiveness of an economy—particularly a developing one—may lie precisely in its lack of "development" (for example, the limited protection of labor rights and the environment). Thus, at any given time, the development goals of a government may not coincide with the objectives of transnational corporations—a divergence that becomes crucial when it affects key elements of a development strategy. This may be the case with some developing economies (including that of Bolivia) seeking to transform their primary-export model by industrializing their natural resources while the goal of the transnational corporations remains fundamentally extractive.

Three factors that affect the impacts of foreign direct investment on host economies are the strategies of transnational corporations, the structural economic configuration of the host economy, and foreign direct investment policy. These factors are not independent of each other: the transnational corporations' strategies are conditioned by the economy, by the recipient sector, and by the political and institutional frameworks, and the design of the latter may be linked to the objectives and strategies of foreign capital. To determine the influence of these variables we must take as a starting point the economic configuration of the developing economy. Despite the increasing diversity of these economies, certain common traits persist that will act in many cases as an initial (structural) obstacle determining the types of foreign direct investment inflows and their effects. Disarticulation between foreign and national capital, for example, hinders technology transfer and the development of links with local firms. This means that the inflow of foreign direct investment can help to strengthen external integration rather than transforming the production model. This risk is much greater if, as in the case of Bolivia, the foreign direct investment inflows are essentially in the extractive sectors, in which the generation of backward and forward linkages is more complicated.

From the point of view of developing economies and bearing in mind these structural obstacles, policy turns out to be a key variable in influencing the impacts of foreign direct investment (see Rugraff et al., 2009: 2–4; UNCTAD, 2012). Clearly, policy is not the only determinant of impacts, but it is the one that governments can control and therefore conditions the other two. This concept is critical because it allows us to show the importance of foreign direct investment policy while recognizing its limits. Certain measures can generate unexpected effects depending on the structural constraints of economies or the strategies of transnational corporations.

The relevance of government policy as a determinant of the effects of foreign direct investment has gained importance in the literature since the end of the 1990s in a context increasingly marked by the rejection of neoliberalism in many developing countries and the attempt to recover autonomy in the design of development strategies. Not surprisingly, a number of governments have implemented changes in foreign direct investment policy. According to the UNCTAD, since 2000 there has been an increase in the number of regulatory changes less favorable to foreign direct investment, although they remain a minority. Thus, while in 2000, 6 out of every 100 changes were less favorable to foreign direct investment, by 2010 this figure was 32, the turnaround being especially remarkable after 2003. The less favorable investment measures affect a wide variety of issues (UNCTAD, 2012: 75–92), but the majority have occurred in the extractive sector, especially in Africa and Latin America. The type of change varies from one country to another, but we can highlight the following: higher taxes and royalties, renegotiation of contracts with foreign operators, and nationalization of private companies. They all involved reversing trends that were dominant during the 1990s.

According to the UNCTAD (2012: 79), three factors have led to regulation less favorable to foreign capital: the high prices of commodities, greater state interventionism, and dissatisfaction with the performance of foreign companies. Furthermore, the extractive sectors have become a key element of the new economic strategies adopted by some developing countries motivated by rises in commodities prices and by unsuccessful attempts to imitate the Asian industrialization model (which prioritizes exports to achieve developmental goals).

We believe that foreign direct investment policy should depend on the articulation of three variables: the objectives of development policy, the demands and strategies of the transnational corporations, and the locational advantage of the host country. The first of these variables highlights the mistake of attempting to standardize foreign direct investment policy. No single concept of development is possible (Escobar, 2005; Payne and Phillips, 2010; Rist, 2002), and so there can be no single foreign direct investment policy favorable to development. In any case, there must be coordination between foreign direct investment policy and development policy so that the two work hand in hand (Ríos and O'Donovan, 2006). This coordination and functionality will be especially important in sectors considered strategic for development policy such as the oil and gas industry in Bolivia.

It is difficult to establish an effective practice that fits all countries. Experience shows that the type of contract (concession, production sharing, or service) is not as important as its specific content, which may vary even within the same contract type (Likosky, 2009). What is relevant is that each contract contains the mechanisms necessary to guarantee that sector performance follows the channels established in the development strategy. This will require that contracts cover investment requirements, a rate of exploitation that ensures adequate replenishment of reserves at the rate consumed, environmental policy, and mechanisms for stimulating backward and forward linkages, thus enhancing value-added activities.

Second, from a fiscal perspective, foreign direct investment policy should ensure oil revenue sharing between the state and the transnational corporations, guaranteeing the rights and needs of the country while making activity viable for the transnational corporations. Although the distribution of oil revenue is a key factor, its role in a development strategy should be limited to discouraging rent seeking. The rise in commodity prices may increase the bargaining power of some states. However, from a fiscal point of view, it is necessary not only to balance the distribution of oil revenues between states and transnational corporations but also to ensure that the use of oil revenues is consistent with the state's development goals. Some countries, among them Bolivia, have focused on the first of these issues, but without concurrent progress in the second there is a risk of exacerbating rent seeking.

Changes in Policy for the Oil and Gas Industry: The MAS Development Pattern

In the field of development policy, the new proposals generated in recent years have been largely a result of varying assessments of neoliberalism. These views (those of the World Bank, the Barcelona Development Agenda, and the Porto Alegre Manifesto) have one thing in common—they go beyond neoliberalism (Williamson, 2003; Yusuf, 2009).

In Latin America, responses to neoliberalism have consolidated around the convergence of social movements and a heterodox academic tradition long marginalized in the debate on economic policy. Some elements of these responses include the following: the claim of basic needs as the axis of economic policy, the overcoming of a Western notion of development that excludes indigenous populations, the claim of nature as a subject of development rather than a mere production input, and the recovery of national control over natural resources (Escobar, 2005). This scenario has shaped proposals such as those of Rafael Correa in Ecuador, Evo Morales in Bolivia, and (with some peculiarities) Hugo Chávez in Venezuela. Despite this commonality, the MAS victory and the policies subsequently implemented were a response to features of the Bolivian situation that differed from those of other countries in the region. The relevance of these characteristics challenges the "commodities consensus" thesis which tends to overemphasize uniformity between Pink Tide and other governments (Ellner, 2020: 45–50).

Among the events that defined the Bolivian situation was the gas war–the social mobilization against plans by the transnational corporations to export Bolivian gas to the United States and Mexico that caused the fall of the Sánchez de Lozada government in October 2003–and the victory of the MAS in December 2005. Therefore, gas nationalization and the changes in foreign direct investment policy are important not only in an economic sense (particularly with regard to the National Development Plan) but also in a political one.

In addition, the MAS, as a political instrument, has always been characterized by its strong indigenous-peasant identity and the heterogeneity of the social movements that it brings together. However, the influence of these two features on the definition and implementation of a Bolivian development strategy remained controversial, particularly because the indigenous-peasant identity that was a clear determinant of electoral victories was subsequently challenged by conflicts between the government and various indigenous organizations. Although an analysis of these conflicts is beyond the scope of this chapter, it is worth pointing out that indigenous people and peasants have always distanced themselves from traditional left parties, to the point that "socialism" is conceived more as a recovery of the reciprocal relations still in force in the indigenous communities than as a reference to any tradition with Marxist or social democratic roots (Stefanoni, 2005: 32). This explains why the government did not pursue a total break from the transnational corporations but instead attempted to modify its regulatory framework in the direction of greater state control (resource nationalism) as an alternative to neoliberalism. This intention was summarized in Evo Morales's famous phrase "We want partners, not bosses." The heterogeneity of the social movements and interests that the MAS brought together was such that, according to some writers, we are unlikely to find in it any commonality of interests beyond the overcoming of colonialism, the traditional relegation of indigenous peoples to second-class citizenship (Rossel, 2009: 26). This heterogeneity also hindered the development of a more coherent and radical developmental strategy.

The National Development Plan's own background reflects these circumstances. The fall of Sánchez de Lozada opened spaces for negotiation between the different social sectors and the state under President Carlos Mesa Gisbert. This period was also the prelude to the constituent assembly, in which the country sought to redress long-standing grievances, and this was reflected in the character of the new constitution (Gosálvez and Dulon, 2010). An alternative view of development was identified that included acknowledgment of the link between social and cultural issues, popular participation as the fundamental instrument in the definition of processes and activities, and the objective of a Bolivia that would be both productive (overcoming the primary-export model) and united in solidarity (eradicating poverty). The victory of the MAS meant the rise to government of the emerging social movements that drove that view. Thus one of the first measures taken by Evo Morales was his presentation on June 16, 2006 of the Plan Nacional de Desarrollo "Bolivia Digna, Soberana, Productiva y Democrática," the predecessor of the National Development Plan adopted on September 12, 2007.[3]

The MAS development strategy was reflected in the National Development Plan. Among its objectives, two were critical: "to contribute to the country's transformation, dismantle the development model derived from colonialism and neoliberalism, and change the primary-export development pattern" and "to promote . . . the construction of a pattern of diversified and integrated development" (Article 5). The core of the MAS development strategy emanated from these two objectives, responding to a development pattern characterized by the building of a stronger, more autonomous diversified and integrated production model requiring a new productive matrix and a less dependent economy.[4] The strategy for productive transformation sought to configure a new productive matrix in the Bolivian economy in which three groups of sectors articulate:

1. Strategic sectors: surplus-generating hydrocarbons, mining, electrical power, and environmental resources. These sectors are capital-intensive, and the state must participate through robust public companies in producing, controlling, and distributing the surplus. The performance of private capital must be restricted by state regulation.
2. Sectors that generate employment and income: agriculture, manufacturing, tourism, and housing. These are labor-intensive activities that contribute to balanced development and the social sector by creating a dense and cohesive productive fabric.
3. Transversal sectors: infrastructure (transport and telecommunications) and support for production services (financial and technological). These sectors must be promoted by the state.

The strategy for creating a less dependent economy was based on an analysis of trade liberalization policies and investment, given that it was the neoliberal-style opening previously experienced in Bolivia that had consolidated its dependent position in the world economy. With regard to foreign investment, the National Development Plan indicated that policy in this area had not been "focused on the development of a productive matrix based on the processing and export of goods with higher value added" (Article 5.3.2). From this diagnosis, the plan proposed to replace the primary-export pattern with a more diversified one that generated value added, restored the importance of the domestic market, and diversified foreign markets. Furthermore, it called for a new treatment of foreign investment that was "equitable" vis-à-vis domestic private capital and public investment.

In sum, the new pattern of Bolivian development sought an international economic relaunch based on participation in different ways in the various markets and an industrialization strategy based on the processing of natural resources (such as that of Norway, Australia, or New Zealand) as opposed to alternatives such as the Asian model, with manufacturing to evolve from the technologically simple to the more complex (Molero and Paz, 2012). In these strategies, the state was regarded as the "promoter and protagonist of national development," implying productive and commercial participation in the strategic sectors, encouragement of the activity of the other productive sectors (generators of income and employment), promotion of improved productivity, expansion of the domestic market, the engineering of a better position in the international market; and the establishment of a new regulatory legal framework for foreign investment to boost technology transfer, employment, and preference for the use of local raw materials and services.

The pattern of development advanced by the MAS assigned a central role to the state and to hydrocarbons, and it advocated crowding the transnational corporations out of the center of economic activity in that sector. It also sought to overcome the export orientation (unprocessed goods) and to prioritize the domestic supply of increasingly elaborate products. However, the role of oil as a strategic industry retained elements of continuity with the traditional primary-export model; this is why some writers describe these strategies, in which some of the negative aspects of traditional extractivism persist, as "neo-extractive" (Acosta, 2011; Acosta and Brand, 2017). Indeed, overcoming the primary-export model requires the industrialization of the hydrocarbon industry itself against other, more traditional methods of industrialization from manufacturing activities. In addition, the government's characterizing of the hydrocarbons sector as a generator of surplus reinforces its extractive nature, since this key objective may conflict with other objectives of the energy sector such as efficiency, energy diversification, management of sustainable environmental impacts, and universal supply. These two considerations do not, however, make the MAS development pattern continuous with those of previous governments but point to certain structural obstacles (economic, social, political) that will condition its content and results.

Changes in Foreign Direct Investment Policy under Morales

The hydrocarbons strategy in force in Bolivia from 1996 to 2005[5] included neoliberal-style policies to attract foreign investment in business units of the national oil company, Yacimientos Petrolíferos Fiscales Bolivianos (YPFB). These policies, which included tax incentives, limited YPFB's powers of oversight and the administration of contracts and were based on a contractual model that was typically concessionary in the phases of exploration and exploitation, giving private enterprise full responsibility and risk. Thus hydrocarbons policy incorporated explicit measures to encourage inflows of foreign investment. The inclusion of transnational corporations became a priority given that YPFB was reduced to administrative tasks, without local business facilities; only the transnationals could manage the complex activities of the sector.

To compare the Morales government with what went before, we will have to answer three questions: (1) During the Morales presidency, did the transnational corporations assume specific, well-defined commitments? (2) Did the changes in taxation increase the state-controlled surplus? (3) Did the relationship between domestic enterprises and transnational corporations change? In other words, did the state assume a greater role in productive activities?[6]

Contracts and commitments. According to the 1996 Hydrocarbons Law, exploration for and exploitation of oil and gas in Bolivia took place only through risk-sharing contracts between private companies and YPFB. The contracts included the right to explore, exploit, and market the oil produced except for the amount needed to satisfy YPFB's gas export obligations (mainly to Brazil). The companies also agreed to minimum investment commitments amounting to US$2.2 billion over the period 1997–2003 (Campodónico, 2004). Investments in exploration and development in that period amounted to US$2.7 billion (Molero et al., 2011).

In 2006 the nature of the contracts changed substantially, and the requirements imposed on transnational corporations changed to a degree. Currently there are two types of contracts: migration and service. The migration contracts[7] were signed in October 2006 by the foreign companies operating in Bolivia at the time in acceptance of the new conditions arising from the nationalization decree. Most of them (36 of the 43) involved exploitation of fields already discovered by the companies themselves in areas where they were already operating. Under these contracts the companies agreed to sell all their hydrocarbons production to YPFB. The service contracts were for exploration and exploitation of fields reserved to YPFB under joint ventures, and they were still little developed. In 2012 there were fifty-six areas reserved for YPFB, and for four of them there were contracts between YPFB and the Bolivian company Gas to Liquid International. Twelve areas were to be explored by Petroandina, a joint venture of YPFB and the Venezuelan national oil company, Petróleos de Venezuela S.A.

In the case of the service contracts, when exploration was successful joint ventures were formed between the company and YPFB in which they became responsible for the operation and development of the field and assumed the obligations and rights of the contract. The service contracts lack key aspects with regard to local content and technology transfer, and the National Hydrocarbons Agency and the Ministry of Hydrocarbons and Energy have little authority to verify compliance with investment commitments. Whereas under the migration contracts the transnational corporation maintains effective control of the activity in the pits, the joint venture in the framework of the service contracts allows YPFB to participate in the operations and develop its productive and technological capacities. The development of these capacities was a major challenge for YPFB in its effort to become an autonomous operator capable of increasing production for the domestic market and the industrialization of natural resources, both objectives of the MAS development strategy.

Taxation and state-controlled surplus. The transnational corporations present in Bolivia now operate within a fiscally more demanding framework that has altered the distribution of oil revenues in favor of the Bolivian state. The 1996 law stipulated that transnational corporations would pay 18 percent of the value of production in royalties, in addition to the tax on company profits. Under the current rules the state retains 50 percent of the value of production through two

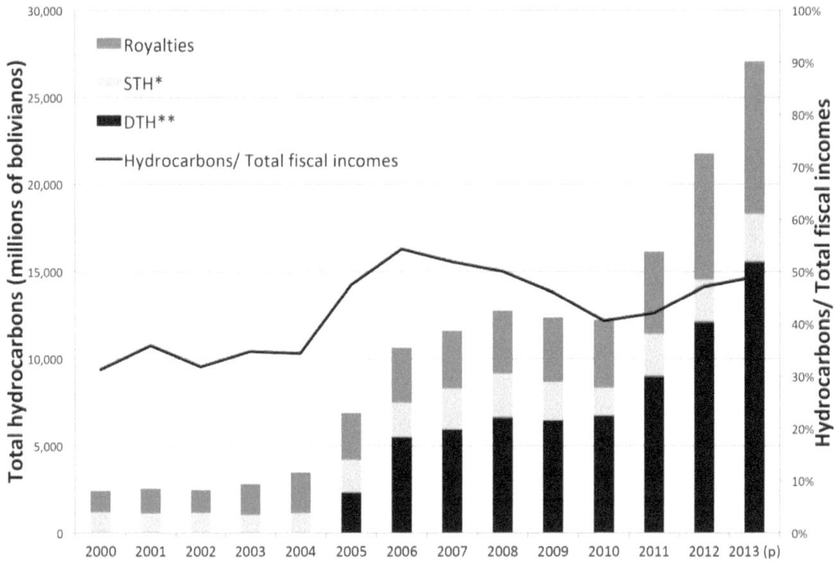

FIGURE 5.1
Bolivian fiscal incomes of the hydrocarbons sector, 2000–2013. * special tax on hydrocarbons. ** direct tax on hydrocarbons. *Source:* Based on UDAPE statistics and data from the Ministry of Economics and Finance, 2013.

instruments, a direct tax and royalties. The direct tax is applied in the first stage of marketing and amounts to 32 percent of the value of production.

These changes in hydrocarbons fiscal regulation, together with the increase in production and international oil prices, increased the government's intake of oil and gas revenues and made it more dependent on those revenues. In 2013, almost 50 percent of the nation's tax revenue came from the hydrocarbon sector (figure 5.1).

However, this achievement of the development plan's objectives must be qualified in two ways. First, in the absence of comprehensive tax reform, oil and gas incomes became a significantly larger share of total tax revenues, generating greater dependence on hydrocarbon production and international prices. Moreover, the use of oil revenues (see table 5.1) was marked by the decentralization of the state during the neoliberal period, favoring a large share for oil-producing departments and municipalities and thus accentuating regional inequalities. The government of Evo Morales tried to correct this imbalance but at the expense of central government revenues, which were already characterized by a small share. Much of the new direct tax revenue was assigned to social policies

To be less dependent on oil revenues, Bolivia required a more demanding tax system, and detailed criteria for the distribution and use of state oil

TABLE 5.1
Distribution of Government Take in the Oil and Gas Sector

	%
Royalties	18
Producer regional departments	11
National Treasury	6
National compensatory royalties	1
Direct tax on hydrocarbons	32
Regional departments	3.2
Municipalities	9.8
Universities	1.8
Indigenous fund	0.5
National development fund	0.6
Renta Dignidad	8.7
National Treasury	7.4

Source: Chávez (2013: 7)

revenues needed to be established. The distribution of oil revenues to the departments and to the Treasury was regulated by several decrees. All of these regulations had the potential to facilitate greater protection of the most vulnerable social groups, as in the case of the Renta Dignidad (a monthly payment for those over sixty years of age), but no instrument that might have guaranteed a balance between expenses and savings was put in place. Furthermore, the fragmented distribution of oil revenues hindered centralized use for large or ambitious projects (Ramírez-Cendrero, 2014).

The state and transnational corporations. Just as the Morales government established new contracts for transnational corporations and changed the tax system, it also provided for the participation of YPFB in all hydrocarbons activities. Indeed, it called for the expansion of YPFB, refinancing its operations and awarding it majority ownership of the oil companies that had been privatized. The nationalization decree was explicit in its intention to "nationalize the country's hydrocarbon resources whereby the state recovers the ownership, possession, and total and absolute control of these resources" (Article 1). Specifically, YPFB was proclaimed an entity that "takes over marketing, defining the conditions, volumes, and prices both for the domestic market and for export and industrialization" (Article 2); also, there was to be a "nationalization of the stock necessary for YPFB to control over 50 percent of the companies Chaco S.A., Andina S.A., Transredes, Petrobras Bolivia Refinación, and Compañía Logística de Hidrocarburos de Bolivia S.A" (Article 7). In sum, "the state takes control and direction of the production, transportation, refining, storage, distribution, marketing, and industrialization of hydrocarbons" (Article 5) and "recovers its full participation in the entire oil production chain" (Article 6). The 1996 Act had excluded YPFB from exploration, production, refining, distribution, and commercialization of hydrocarbons, reserving those activities to private domestic or foreign companies that signed the corresponding contracts or acceded to administrative concessions. The private companies had performed all the activities of the sector while the state played only a supervisory role. Thus until 2006 transnational corporations had access to a sector in which they operated with little oversight, only weak commitments to other investors, and limited taxation. Subsequently, the fiscal requirements of transnational corporations increased substantially while the Bolivian state, through YPFB, not only supervised but participated in all hydrocarbons activities. This is most clearly reflected in the near-monopoly of YPFB downstream. Meanwhile, however, the investor requirements of transnational corporations remained limited.

The foreign direct investment policy established in connection with the hydrocarbon nationalization of 2006 also led to changes in the functioning of the sector. First, transnational corporations operating in the industry were required to present plans to develop fields, deliver all production to YPFB, and enter into joint ventures with YPFB. In this case, there were no strict commitments regarding the amounts invested. Second, the tax requirements increased significantly, thus reducing the share of the transnational corporations in oil revenues to the benefit of YPFB. Finally, the role of the Bolivian state was greater, since it participated in the upstream and virtually monopolized the downstream by acting as the sole marketer. At the same time, YPFB certified production and conducted supervision and control. The transnational corporations reduced their participation in areas where YPFB operated, but they continued to dominate exploitation and had effective control of extraction (despite the obligation to supply all production to YPFB). This fact in particular indicates one of the greatest difficulties faced by the state in increasing its role in strategic sectors as required by the National Development Plan. Because of limited state capacity, the exploratory activities launched in fields under exploration had to be conducted by joint ventures between YPFB and the transnational corporations.

Foreign Direct Investment Policy and Development Objectives

We noted at the beginning of our analysis that a foreign direct investment policy favorable to development must be consistent with development strategies. The basic principle is the recognition of the sovereign right of each country to establish the conditions under which foreign firms operate. Our analysis has highlighted that the MAS's development pattern sought profound changes in the economic configuration of Bolivia reflected in two strategies: productive transformation to achieve a diversified, integrated, and sustainable productive model and the creation of a less dependent economy that abandoned the primary-export model. In these strategies, the Bolivian state was assigned the role of promoter of national development including control of the production and marketing of hydrocarbons and other strategic sectors.

The following sheds light on the degree to which the changes in foreign direct investment policy in the hydrocarbons sector were consistent with development strategies and the role assigned by the National Development Plan to the Bolivian state:

1. The transnational corporation with a contract had no specific investment commitments beyond those around development projects in the fields involved. This affected both the amount invested and the activities conducted. Since 2006, exploration activities declined even as the production rate grew. This imbalance between exploration and exploitation was taken into account in the contracts signed after 2011. With the new contracts, the beneficiary companies were obliged to undertake exploration that—if successful—would lead to the establishment of joint ventures with YPFB. This requirement was designed to ensure production and to replenish reserves. Without exploration, the rate of exploitation of the fields could not have been maintained. This is why after 2010 YPFB was granted a greater role in investment activity through a change in the modality of the contracts. The YPFB Investment Plan of 2012–2016 nevertheless allotted only US$1.3 billion to exploration as opposed to US$2.9 billion for the development and exploitation of existing fields (YPFB Logistics, 2012). This approach raises questions about the sector's ability to have maintained its strategic course.

In addition, subsequent government measures regarding the activity of transnational corporations were even less likely to stimulate exploration. Presidential Decree 1202 (April 2012) provided a "unique incentive applicable to oil production" to "promote exploration and reduce the import of derivatives." The decree granted transnational corporations a traditional demand but without requiring further exploration in return. Until the issuance of the decree, oil companies delivered their production to refineries at a price of US$27.11 per barrel of liquid hydrocarbon. That price net of royalties, taxes, and transportation costs, allowed firms to obtain US$10.29 per barrel, a figure that ensured a profit. The new decree guaranteed a price of US$30 per barrel. In this context, a better option for promoting exploration and increasing the volume of oil produced would have been to create incentives for exploration in new areas. In reality, the government measure involved accepting the requirement that the transnational corporations obtain within the country the same returns they would receive selling oil on the international market.

2. The effective control of upstream operations remained in the hands of the transnational corporations. The contracts of 2006 did not change that

situation. The changes effectuated in 2011 were intended to give YPFB basic control of operations through the formation of joint ventures. Without such control, YPFB would have encountered considerable difficulty in performing its supervisory role in addition to its functions as an operator upstream and its near-monopoly downstream. Several years after the signing of contracts for 2006 that included plans for field development, the state was unable to certify whether that activity had been undertaken.

3. The state's share in the oil revenue increased very significantly, with a minimum take of 50 percent. Certain calculations (Carvajal, 2012) estimate that state participation in oil revenues in the period 2006–2011 reached 70.7 percent but with large swings from year to year, resulting in US$12.4 billion in total revenues. Furthermore, a mechanism was set in place to channel oil revenue into multiple recipients (universities, the national police, the army, assistance funds to social sectors). Nevertheless, despite ample resources, the sector fell short in another of its strategic functions—the use of resources to promote industrialization.

4. A key aspect of the productive transformation strategy and an objective embraced by the Bolivian government was the industrialization of gas, but it remains locked in place. At the same time, gas export commitments to Brazil and Argentina are an obstacle to industrialization, sending abroad raw material that should be transformed internally. While the state decided the destination of oil and gas production, it dealt with them as traditional primary exports, contrary to the provisions of the National Development Plan and to the pattern of development proclaimed by the Bolivian government.

5. Instruments were not established for boosting production linkages between hydrocarbons activity and other industries.

Conclusions

The changes in Bolivian foreign direct investment policy had contradictory results for the hydrocarbons sector. On the one hand, the changes failed to ensure ongoing investment, the promotion of exploration to permit the replenishing of depleted reserves, a guarantee of YPFB's effective participation in the control of operations, or the generation of production linkages. Furthermore, the government failed to make progress in gas industrialization. On the other hand, the Morales government achieved significant gains in the state's control of oil revenues and ensured that the state would determine the destination of production. We conclude with some thoughts about foreign direct investment policy and its importance to development vis-à-vis the Bolivian experience in an attempt to answer our key research question:

whether nationalization and foreign direct investment policy have promoted development.

As we have noted, foreign direct investment policy toward hydrocarbons was not fully consistent with Bolivia's development strategy in that it failed to provide sufficient mechanisms for achieving such objectives as increasing investments. In addition, investments remained ultimately dependent on the global strategies of transnational corporations more than on regulatory mechanisms (as shown by the decline in transnational corporation investments in Bolivia after 1999).

Although some significant changes in foreign direct investment policies impacted the hydrocarbons sector, not enough progress was made in the consolidation of the National Development Plan's two central strategies: productive transformation and transformation of Bolivia's position in the world economy. On the contrary, the hydrocarbons sector appeared to be moving toward the consolidation of the traditional extractive pattern, although with alterations to the proportion of oil revenue sharing between the state and the transnational corporations due to higher tax rates and the revival of an YPFB that acts both as operator and as auditor. The changes in the types of contracts entered into since 2011 could contribute to progress toward the goals set out in the National Development Plan. Particularly important was the possibility of the achievement of coherence between foreign direct investment policy in the hydrocarbons sector and other areas of policy (industrial, energy, and fiscal) to reduce the dependence of the Bolivian economy upon the extractive industries.

Despite the limits to the scope of the policies promoted by the Morales government, we consider that they were an effective alternative to neoliberalism. The first measures of the de facto government of Jeanine Añez, implemented after the coup d'état in November 2019, are revealing of the differences that a reintroduction of a clearly neoliberal program implies. Decisions such as the liberalization of agricultural exports, restricted during the MAS governments to give priority to the internal market, contained in Decree 4139 of January 22, 2020, have been promoted by the agroindustry of Santa Cruz, the department that represents the fief of the traditional exporting oligarchy. What government emerges in 2020 will determine whether the turn toward neoliberal policies is consolidated.

Notes

1. This chapter is a revised version of an article published in *Latin American Perspectives* in 2018 (45 [5]: 18–34).

2. In fact, even writers close to a Marxist approach, traditionally the strongest critics of foreign direct investment and transnational corporations, argue that the exploitation

of workers or the extraction of surplus by foreign capital may be accompanied by the development of the productive forces through technology transfer or contribution to gross fixed capital formation (Shaikh, 2009: 85–96). Elsewhere, writers who have traditionally defended the contributions of foreign direct investment to development recognize that they will not be positive unless policies and institutions are in place that are conducive to a transfer of competitive advantage to the host economy (Dunning, 1994).

3. During 2006 and 2007, numerous workshops and meetings were held with the participation of academics, indigenous leaders, farmers, and businessmen in which important aspects of the plan were discussed and modified (Déniz et al., 2011).

4. According to the plan, "changing the primary export pattern is, therefore, a necessary condition for overturning inequality and the exclusion of the indigenous population, urban and rural, and to eradicate poverty" (p. 6).

5. The current oil law (Act 3058) of 2005 established the powers of YPFB and introduced a direct tax on hydrocarbons and new types of contracts.

6. Most of the data used in this section was obtained from the Ministry of Economics and Finance (2013) and YPFB (2012).

7. In 2006, 44 migration contracts were signed, but one was returned (by Petrobras) in 2008.

References

Acosta, Alberto

2011 "Extractivismo y neoextractivismo: dos caras de la misma maldición," pp. 17–33 in Grupo Permanente de Trabajo sobre Alternativas al Desarrollo, *Más allá del desarrollo*. Quito: Abya Yala/Fundación Rosa Luxemburgo.

Acosta, Alberto, and Ulrich Brand

2017 *Salidas del laberinto capitalista: Decrecimiento y postextractivismo*. Barcelona: Icaria Antrazyt.

Campodónico, Humberto

2004 *Reformas e inversión en la industria de hidrocarburos de América Latina*. Santiago: CEPAL.

Carvajal, Roberto

2012 "Adiós al 82%: El Estado Plurinacional redujo su participación en el negocio de los hidrocarburos." http://www.bolpress.com/art.php?Cod+201290903.

Chávez, Gonzalo

2013 *Ingresos fiscales por explotación de hidrocarburos en Bolivia*. IFB-PB-199. Washington, DC: Inter-American Development Bank.

Déniz, José, Omar de León, and Antonio Palazuelos

2011 *Nuevas estratégicas económicas en América Latina*. Madrid: Los Libros de la Catarata.

Dunning, John

1994 "Re-evaluating the benefits of foreign direct investment." *Transnational Corporations* 3 (1): 23–51.

Ellner, Steve
2020 "Has the Pink Tide cycle come to an end? Will it have a long-lasting impact?" pp. 39–58 in Steve Ellner (ed.), *Latin America's Pink Tide: Breakthroughs and Shortcomings*. Lanham, MD: Rowman and Littlefield.
Escobar, Arturo
2005 "El 'postdesarrollo' como concepto y práctica social," pp. 17–33 in Daniel Mato (ed.), *Políticas de economía, ambiente y sociedad en tiempos de globalización*. Caracas: Universidad Central de Venezuela.
Estermann, Josef
2012 "Crisis civilizatoria y vivir bien: una crítica filosófica del modelo capitalista desde el allin kawsay/suma qamaña andina." *Polis* 11 (33): 1–18.
Gallagher, Kevin, and Daniel Chudnovsky
2010 *Rethinking Foreign Investment for Sustainable Development: Lessons from Latin America*. London and New York: Anthem Press.
Gosálvez, Gonzalo, and Jorge Dulon
2010 *Descolonización en Bolivia: Cuatro ejes para emprender el cambio*. La Paz: Vicepresidencia del Estado Plurinacional de Bolivia/Fundación Boliviana para la Democracia Multipartidaria.
Jenkins, Rhys
1989 *Transnational Corporations and Uneven Development: The Internationalization of Capital and the Third World*. London and New York: Methuen.
Lall, Sanjaya, and Rajneesh Narula
2004 "Foreign direct investment and its role in economic development: do we need a new agenda?" *European Journal of Development Research* 16: 447–464.
Likosky, Michael
2009 "Contracting and regulatory issues in the oil and gas and metallic minerals industries." *Transnational Corporations* 18 (1): 1–42.
Ministry of Economics and Finance
2013 "Boletín de ingresos tributaries." http://www.economiayfinanzas.gob.bo/index.php?opcion=com_contenido&ver=contenido&id=3328&id_item=670&seccion=269&categoria=1561.
Molero, Ricardo, and María J. Paz
2012 "Development strategy of the MAS in Bolivia: characterization and initial results." *Development and Change* 43: 531–556.
Molero, Ricardo, María J. Paz, and Juan M. Ramírez-Cendrero
2011 "Les hydrocarbures dans le processus de transformation bolivien: nacionalisation et capital étranger (2006–2009)." *Revue Tiers Monde* 208 (4): 139–158.
Moran, Theodore H., Edward M. Graham, and Magnus Blömstrom
2005 *Does Foreign Direct Investment Promote Development?* Washington, DC: Institute for International Economics, Center for Global Development.
Payne, Anthony, and Nicola Phillips
2010 *Development*. Cambridge: Polity Press.
Ramírez-Cendrero, Juan M.
2014 "Has Bolivia's 2006–12 gas policy been useful to combat the resource curse?" *Resources Policy* 41: 113–123.

Ríos Morales, Ruth, and David O'Donovan
2006 "¿Pueden los países de América Latina y el Caribe emular el modelo irlandés para atraer inversión extranjera directa?" *Revista de la CEPAL* 88: 51–70.
Rist, Gilbert
2002 *Desarrollo: Historia de una creencia occidental.* Madrid: Los Libros de la Catarata.
Rossel, Pablo
2009 "El proyecto de Evo Morales más allá de 2010." *Nueva Sociedad,* no. 21: 23–32.
Rugraff, Eric, Diego Sánchez-Ancochea, and Andy Sumner (ed.)
2009 *Transnational Corporations and Development Policy: Critical Perspectives.* London: Palgrave Macmillan.
Shaikh, Anwar
2009 *Teorías del comercio internacional.* Madrid: Maia.
Stefanoni, Pablo
2005 *El nacionalismo indígena como identidad política: La emergencia del MAS-IPSP (1985–2003).* Buenos Aires: CLACSO.
UNCTAD (United Nations Conference on Trade and Development)
2003 *FDI Policies for Development: National and International Perspectives.* Geneva: United Nations.
2012 *Towards a New Generation of Investment Policies.* Geneva: United Nations.
Webber, Jeffrey
2011 *From Rebellion to Reform in Bolivia.* Chicago: Haymarket Books.
Weeks, John
2009 *Teoría de la competencia en los neoclásicos y en Marx.* Madrid: Maia.
Williamson, John
2003 "From reform agenda to damaged brand name." *Finance and Development* 40 (3): 10–13.
YPFB (Yacimiento Petrolíferos Fiscales Bolivianos)
2012 *Boletín estadístico.* La Paz: YPFB.
YPFB Logistics
2012 *Plan Estratégico Empresaria 2012–2016.* La Paz: YPFB.
Yusuf, Shahid
2009 *Development Economics through the Decades.* Washington, DC: World Bank.

6

Extractive Policies in Mexico at the Outset of López Obrador's Presidency

Darcy Tetreault

ANDRÉS MANUEL LÓPEZ OBRADOR (AMLO) became president of Mexico on December 1, 2018, five months after having won a decisive electoral victory that gave him over half of the popular vote. The Movimiento Regeneración Nacional (National Movement of Regeneration—MORENA), the political party he had created just four years earlier, secured a majority in both the Chamber of Deputies and the Senate. This, combined with polls suggesting a high approval rating during the first months of his presidency, has given AMLO the political power to make sweeping changes to the policies and institutions put in place by neoliberal governments since the 1980s. To be sure, his progressive project for transforming Mexican society "involves not just putting a human face on the same old neoliberal policies but eradicating the entire neoliberal logic at its roots" (Ackerman, 2020: 325). Accordingly, this chapter seeks to examine what his government has done to eradicate the logic of neoliberalism with regard to extractive policy and the mediation of related social environmental conflicts.

The chapter is organized into six sections. The first briefly reviews debates regarding neo-extractivism in relation to Latin America's Pink Tide in electoral politics. The second investigates AMLO's policies vis-à-vis the ownership of subterranean resources and private-sector participation in extractive activities. The third describes the mechanisms in place to capture and redistribute resource rents. The fourth examines environmental regulation and the government's mediation of social environmental conflicts; the fifth analyzes reforms in the state's relation with labor in extractive industries. The final section provides an assessment of the changes and continuities that AMLO's government has brought to Mexico's extractive policies during its first eighteen months, observing a tendency toward the persistence of neoliberal logic.

Neo-Extractivism Versus Classical Extractivism

Gudynas (2010) uses the term "neo-extractivism" to refer to a policy-orientation trend among Pink Tide governments toward imposing greater control on extractive industries. The general aim of this progressive orientation is to garner for the state a greater share of the resource rents generated by extracting raw materials and selling them on the world market and to use these resource rents to finance social policies for working-class and marginalized sectors of the population. For the governments that formed the first wave of the Pink Tide during the first decade of the new millennium, this was achieved in a variety of ways, from increasing royalties and taxes on private firms to strengthening state-owned enterprises and nationalizing strategic sectors of the primary economy.

This progressive policy agenda is contrasted by some writers with a model of "classical extractivism" associated with neoliberalism and the Washington Consensus (for example, Gudynas, 2010; Petras and Veltmeyer, 2014). Until recently, Mexico was considered an example of classical extractivism (Petras and Veltmeyer, 2014), especially because of the country's mining policies during the boom years of the first decade of the twenty-first century, when private and foreign mining companies paid no royalties and only a token fee for mining concessions (ASF, 2011). I have argued elsewhere that the royalties and rent-redistribution mechanisms introduced by Enrique Peña Nieto's government in 2013 for mining and hydrocarbons exploitation represent steps toward "new" or "neo"-extractivism (Tetreault, 2020). These steps were paradoxically taken in tandem with the energy reform to further open the sector to private and foreign investment.

What neo-extractivism and classical extractivism have in common is a general orientation toward increasing the rates of extraction of minerals, metals, and hydrocarbons. This is at the core of what Svampa (2015) refers to as the commodities consensus. It highlights that, irrespective of the way resource rents are distributed, a rapidly expanding extractive frontier defies calls from the scientific community to leave most remaining hydrocarbons in the ground in order to avert catastrophic climate change; it condones toxic mega-mining in the name of development, and it leads to social environmental conflicts with the rural and indigenous communities directly affected.

Of course, this is not to say that there are no important differences between conservative and progressive governments, including possible differences in the mediation of social environmental conflicts. Indeed, as Ellner says in the introduction to this book, the commodities consensus is not an all-encompassing economic doctrine like the Washington Consensus: "Important policies related to extractivism differentiate not only Pink Tide governments from conservative ones but also governments within both categories." Using this as a working hypothesis, this chapter seeks to investigate the policies related to extractivism that differentiate AMLO's government from its predecessors and to identify what has remained the same.

Ownership and Private-Sector Participation

Article 27 of the Mexican Constitution establishes that subsoil resources belong to the nation and that the federal government has the faculty to grant concessions to private firms to exploit them. This article was modified in December of 2013 to allow for greater private and foreign investment in upstream activities in the petroleum sector, thereby putting a definitive end to the monopoly held by Pemex, the state-owned oil and gas company that was created shortly after the sector was nationalized in 1938.

Since becoming president, López Obrador has ended the bidding process for granting contracts to private firms for exploration and exploitation either alone or in association with Pemex. At the same time, he has committed to honoring the terms of the 111 contracts that were established with private oil and gas companies during the three auctioning rounds that took place between 2014 and 2018. In addition, he has created integrated contracts for exploration and extractive services to give private and foreign capital new opportunities to participate in upstream activities, remunerating them in dollars per unit of hydrocarbon extracted.

In AMLO's discourse and development strategy, Pemex is meant to serve as a lever of development. Accordingly, he has taken several measures to strengthen the state-owned company, including (1) changes to the hydrocarbons income law reducing the taxes paid by Pemex from 65 percent of its total income to 54 percent; (2) negotiating in May 2019 for a US$8 billion loan-financing agreement between Pemex and JPMorgan Chase, HSBC Holdings PLC, and the Mizuho Financial Group, Inc. (which incidentally was not enough to prevent Fitch Ratings from downgrading Pemex's debt to junk status the next month); (3) injecting US$5 billion into Pemex in September 2019 to meet payments on a total debt of more than US$106 billion in 2019; and (4) actions to combat the theft of hydrocarbons, which according to official statistics reduced the amount stolen from 20.4 billion barrels in 2018 to 5.1 billion barrels in 2019. All of this is in line with Pemex's 2019–2023 business plan, whose first three strategic objectives are to strengthen the company's financial position, to accelerate the incorporation of reserves, and to increase hydrocarbons exploitation.

Another strategic objective is to increase the country's refining capacity and thereby reduce its dependence on the United States, from which more than three-quarters of the gasoline consumed in Mexico was imported in 2018. This is to be done by revamping the country's six existing refineries, which were estimated to be operating at only 40 percent of capacity when López Obrador became president, and by building a new refinery at the port of Dos Bocas, in the state of Tabasco. The new refinery, one of AMLO's flagship megaprojects, is meant to help the country reach a higher level of energy self-sufficiency, to create jobs, and to stimulate economic growth. It is highly controversial for a number of reasons, including environmental ones. It has been estimated that the refinery will emit 2.16 million tons of carbon dioxide annually into the atmosphere. Also, it is being built in a low-lying coastal area that is expected to be increasingly prone to flooding as climate change advances.

Initially, AMLO tried to auction off the project in its entirety to four foreign companies that were invited to submit bids: Bechtel-Techint, Worley Parsons-Jacobs, Technip, and KBR. However, since none of these companies submitted a proposal that fit within the project's budget of US$8 billion and/or the time frame of completing construction by the end of 2022, AMLO announced in May 2019 that his government would go ahead with the project under the direction of the Ministry of Energy and Pemex. The refinery's infrastructure was then divided into five "packages" for the purposes of a second bidding process in which select private firms were invited to participate. In this way, six firms were awarded contracts to initiate the construction of the new refinery in July 2019: Kellogg Brown & Root, ICA Fluor, Samsung Engineering, Fluor Enterprises, Constructora Hostotipaquillo, and Asociados Constructores DBNR.

Turning now to mining, it is important to note that, unlike the petroleum sector, Mexico's mining sector was never nationalized. Private firms have always dominated mining activity in Mexico, in spite of workers' struggles to nationalize the industry during the twentieth century. Legislation passed in 1961 increased national control over the sector by stipulating that all mining companies in Mexico had to be at least 51 percent Mexican-owned. Further changes were made to the mining law in 1976 to increase state ownership, especially in companies extracting minerals and metals considered to be strategic for feeding the industrialization process, including copper, iron ore, and coal. However, all of this was jettisoned in the wake of the 1980s debt crisis and as part of the neoliberal restructuring of the country's economy along the lines of privatization, free trade, deregulation, and labor flexibility.

During the first years of Carlos Salinas's presidential term (1988–1994), parastatal mining companies were sold cheaply and in a nontransparent manner to politically well-connected Mexican businessmen (Delgado Wise and del Pozo Mendoza, 2005). Then, with the passage of a new mining law in 1992, the sector was completely opened to foreign investment, the duration of mining concessions was doubled to fifty years and made renewable thereafter, and mining was given priority over any other productive use of the land. Between 1994 and 2018, the federal government granted 45,537 mining concessions to the private sector, covering an area of approximately 105 million hectares, more than half of the country's territory.[1] The indigenous communities directly impacted were not informed of these concessions (López Bárcenas, 2017), much less invited to participate in processes of free, prior, and informed consent in accordance with Convention 169 of the International Labour Organization (which Mexico had ratified in 1990).

Because of the way the privatization process played out and has been consolidated, Mexican companies still own over half of the mines operating in the country (Pérez Jiménez, 2018: 51). At the same time, foreign capital, especially Canadian mining firms in search of precious metals, has taken the lead in exploration. Of the sixty-five mining projects that were under construction in 2017, 60 percent belong to Canadian firms, 10 percent to U.S. firms, and 20 percent to Mexican ones (Pérez Jiménez, 2018: 49).

On the campaign trail in early 2018, AMLO stated that one of the ways that he would respond to the aggressive economic policies of the Trump administration would be to invite Canadian mining companies to invest more in Mexico. This came as a disappointing surprise to the people and community-based organizations struggling against mega-mining projects in Mexico, including some with which AMLO had declared solidarity in previous years, such as the Frente Amplio Opositor a Minera San Xavier in San Luis Potosí.

Since becoming president, AMLO has given mixed signals regarding mining policy. On the one hand, he stated in August of 2019 that his government would not issue any more mining concessions. On the other, the post of undersecretary of mining went to Francisco Quiroga, who had served in the Ministry of the Economy during the late 1990s and early 2000s before becoming an executive for three large mining companies (Grupo Villacero, ArcelorMittal, and C & F International). More important, AMLO's government has so far failed to make changes to the existing mining law or to the environmental laws that were introduced to govern extractive activities during the neoliberal era.

Mechanisms to Capture and Redistribute Resource Rents

One of the reasons Mexico's mining policies were until recently considered representative of "classical" extractivism is that mining companies did not have to pay royalties; they paid only a token fee for concessions and very low effective taxes. The cost of concessions started at just over 5 pesos per hectare during the first two years and increased to 111 pesos per hectare after ten years. Mexico's Chief Audit Office (ASF, 2011: 4) calculated that between 2005 and 2010, when international prices for minerals and metals were soaring, the fees paid by mining companies operating in Mexico amounted to only 1.2 percent of their gross earnings.

Enrique Peña Nieto's government promised to introduce royalties on mining activities as part of the "Pact for Mexico," a negotiated agreement signed on January 23, 2013, by the leaders of the country's three most important political parties at the time, essentially to apply neoliberal structural reforms to the energy sector and education. This initiative took the form of changes to the Federal Law of Rights in December of that year to introduce royalties equal to 7.5 percent of the net income declared by mining companies plus 0.5 percent on the sale of precious metals, coming into effect at the beginning of 2014. In addition, 77.5 percent of the resources derived from these royalties were to be channeled to the Fund for the Sustainable Regional Development of Mining States and Municipalities and 20 percent to the Ministry of Finance and Public Credit, with the remaining 2.5 percent assigned to operating expenses.

The mining fund was meant to finance social development projects in mining regions in order to compensate local populations for the ecological damage and social disruption caused by toxic mega-mining. The 2013 changes to the Federal Law of Rights established that 62.5 percent of the fund's resources would be delivered to municipalities where mining activities are concentrated, with the remaining 37.5 percent going to the corresponding state governments. These resources were earmarked for financing projects in the areas of public transport, water and sewer systems, solid waste management, roads, schools, and electricity. However, as documented by Fundar (2018), during Enrique Peña Nieto's presidency the mining fund was administered with an appalling lack of transparency and accountability at all levels of government.

In May 2019, AMLO announced that he was going to centralize the fund's resources in the hands of the federal government, cutting out transfers to state and municipal governments. A group of governors and municipal presidents in mining regions opposed this measure and unsuccessfully appealed to the country's Supreme Court. On December 12, 2019, the Federal Law of Rights was again modified, with 85 percent of the mining fund's resources to go to the Ministry of Education, 10 percent to the federal government to develop infrastructure, and 5 percent to the Ministry of the Economy to strengthen the administration of the mining sector. At the same time, the mechanisms for concentrating the mining fund's resources on social spending in mining regions were eliminated. In Fundar's (2019: 2) assessment, these modifications did not bring "transparency or certainty regarding allocation criteria, nor mechanisms to foster participation."

As for the petroleum sector, the system currently in place in Mexico for capturing and distributing rents was established by changes made to Articles 25, 27, and 28 of the Mexican Constitution in December of 2013 and by corresponding modifications made to multiple laws the following year. At the center of this rent-redistribution system is the Mexican Petroleum Fund for Stabilization and Development, a public trust created to "receive, administer, and distribute the income derived from assignments and contracts" (Article 28)—the former referring to the areas assigned to Pemex and the latter to the contracts established with private oil and gas firms, alone or in association with Pemex. Oil and gas firms in Mexico pay multiple fees and royalties depending on the type of contract, the phase of a field's development, and the prices of oil and gas. In 2019 the fund distributed a sum of 431.9 billion pesos, equal to about US$22.4 billion and representing 1.7 percent of Mexico's gross domestic product (GDP) that year.

The petroleum fund distributes these resources to five subfunds and to the federal Treasury in an order of priority established in Article 16, which puts in first place the Budget Revenue Stabilization Fund to cover shortfalls in paying for the federal government's planned expenditures. Article 16 states that the fund must deliver the equivalent of 4.7 percent of GDP to the subfunds and the federal Treasury before channeling any additional resources to long-term savings. However, because of the decline of oil prices that coincided with the fund's creation, it has not transferred anything close to that amount in any single year; the most was in 2018, when the total transfers represented 2.4 percent of GDP.

Besides the aforementioned fees and royalties, Pemex and the private oil and gas firms operating in Mexico pay two taxes: income tax on earnings from petroleum exploitation, with a number of allowable deductions, and the tax on hydrocarbons exploration and extractive activities, which is based on the surface area under contract or assigned to Pemex. The latter goes to the Fund for Hydrocarbon-producing States and Municipalities, which channels the distribution of its resources to the states and municipalities where petroleum activity is concentrated. The states that receive these resources must redistribute 20 percent to the municipalities within their jurisdictions that are most impacted by oil and gas exploration and extraction. Like the mining fund in its original design, the fund for states and municipalities is meant to compensate the local population for the environmental and social impacts of extractive activity by financing the same types of social development projects as the mining fund.

Environmental Policy and Conflicts

The environmental laws and agencies that regulate extractive activities in Mexico were constructed during the neoliberal era, beginning with the landmark proclamation of the General Law of Ecological Balance and Environmental Protection on January 28, 1988. This law was modified forty-one times between 1996 and 2018. AMLO's government has not to date made any changes to it.

One front of resistance that has gained organizational strength in the wake of the 2013 energy reform is the opposition to hydraulic fracturing (fracking). The Mexican Alliance against Fracking was created the same year as the energy reform as a collective of more than forty community and civil-society organizations from across the country seeking to prohibit fracking in defense of water and territory. AMLO has repeatedly promised to ban fracking, a pledge that to date has not been translated into law. At the same time, his government's budgets for Pemex in 2019 and 2020 included millions of dollars for fracking projects. As Hernández Ibarzábal and Bonilla (2020: 4) observe, "The inconsistencies between the president's commitment to ban fracking, the exploration plans approved by the National Hydrocarbons Commission (CNH), and the USD220 million that will be invested by Pemex in shale oil and gas projects in 2020 indicate that the development of unconventional resources is likely to continue."

Perhaps the most significant change made to Mexico's environmental policy by AMLO's government has been the cutting of the budget and staff of the Ministry of the Environment and Natural Resources. The ministry's budget in 2019 was 21 percent less than in 2018 and less than half of what it was in 2015, and in 2020 further cuts were made. Madrid Ramírez (2020: 7–8) reports that since AMLO became president all of the ministry's state-level delegates and 30 percent of the administrative staff have been laid off and not replaced. In her words, this amounts to the "institutional dismantling of the environmental sector" (2020: 1).

AMLO originally put at the head of the Ministry of Environment and Natural Resources Josefa González Blanco, a niece of former president Carlos Salinas with direct family ties to a number of high-ranking officials in Enrique Peña Nieto's government. Her credentials, based mostly on her work with nongovernmental organizations in Chiapas dedicated to the conservation of exotic wild species, were questionable, to say the least. In any case, she was forced to resign less than six months into the job because of a scandal that erupted when she had a commercial flight in Mexicali delayed forty minutes on May 24, 2019, so that she would not miss it. Shortly thereafter, Victor Toledo became the new head of the ministry, bringing a major change in its leadership profile as a renowned researcher who has published much on social environmental conflicts and in the fields of ethnobiology and agroecology. He petitioned to increase the ministry's budget for 2020, but to no avail.

A group of researchers under his direction at the Morelia campus of the National Autonomous University of Mexico compiled an inventory of 560 social environmental conflicts in Mexico between 2012 and 2017. Of these, 173 revolved around mining, 86 around water, and 74 around energy, the three most numerous categories.[2] These conflicts typically involve campesinos and indigenous groups struggling to defend their territories, healthy living environments, traditional livelihoods, and culture (Tetreault et al., 2018). To be sure, not all local struggles reject extractive projects per se; some are predominantly oriented to securing greater economic benefits for the local population, pressuring extractive firms to fulfill promises, and/or reducing environmental destruction.

In any case, the people who participate in organized resistance to extractive projects in Mexico have been subject to various forms of repression from all levels of government. The Mexican Center of Environmental Rights (CEMDA, 2020) registered 499 "attacks" on them between 2012 and 2019, including threats (175), physical aggression (84), criminalization of protest (82), intimidation (70), and murder (68). In this inventory, 29 percent of the attacks were related to energy projects and 15 percent to mining projects, the two most numerous categories. The same report found that the Mexican government, on one level or another (municipal, state, or federal), could be linked to 39 percent of the attacks recorded during this eight-year period and 40.5 percent of the thirty-nine attacks carried out in 2019, the first full year of AMLO's presidency. While the number of attacks occurring in 2019 was lower than in any year since 2012, it is worrisome that murders made up 38.5 percent of them.

As these figures suggest, AMLO's government has brought some changes to the way in which the state mediates social environmental conflicts in Mexico. One significant positive change is that he has so far followed through on his promise not to use police or military forces to repress protests. At the same time, his deriding of the people involved in these struggles has created a hostile environment for them.

A case in point is the murder of Samir Flores Soberanes, an indigenous leader of the resistance to a thermoelectric plant in the state of Morelos that threatens the water supply and safety of numerous smallholder farming communities. AMLO had labeled those who opposed the completion of this project "left-wing radicals, who for me are only conservatives." He announced that the decision whether to go ahead with it would be made through "popular consultation," an exercise that he and his supporters had carried out on two previous occasions. The consultation was designed to include large urban centers that stood to gain from the thermoelectric plant's operation through lower energy costs, thereby diluting the vote of the directly affected rural communities and violating the right of indigenous people to free, prior, and informed consent.

Flores Soberanes was shot dead outside of his home on February 20, 2019, just three days before the popular consultation was scheduled to take place. AMLO insisted on going ahead with it anyway; the impacted communities refused to take part, and the results were, as expected, a majority of votes in favor of completing the project and operating the plant. Over a year later, however, the plant in Morelos remains paralyzed because of legal action by organized groups in the affected communities. Meanwhile, no one has been brought to justice for the murder of Flores Soberanes, who is just one of eighteen defenders of land, territory, and the environment who were murdered with impunity in Mexico during the first year of López Obrador's presidency (Velázquez Hernández, 2020).

Extractive Labor, Unions, and the State

In the model of resource nationalism promoted by the Mexican state during the post–World War II period, unionized labor was integrated into a tripartite corporativist system of negotiation between the state, labor, and capital. Workers in each sector of the economy were organized into local chapters of unions with national reach, characterized by centralized top-down political control in the hands of union bosses, many of whom remained in power for decades. Until neoliberal structural reforms were introduced, this corporatist system served to mediate the interests of the working class and those of capital in a development project oriented toward fostering industrialization and high economic growth rates and based on a Fordist model that included social policies for workers and their families. In this context, miners and Pemex workers with permanent contracts earned relatively high salaries and attractive social security benefits. Miners were represented by the National Union for Mine, Metallurgical, and Similar Workers of the Mexican Republic, created in 1934, and petroleum workers by the Union for Petroleum Workers of the Mexican Republic, created a year later.

In the late 1940s and early 1950s, the executive branch of the federal government intervened to replace militant national-level union leaders with more subservient ones. This political arrangement became known in Mexico as a *charrazo*, a term that alludes to "the demobilization of workers, the total absence of democracy within unions, and a lack of respect for the statutes of their organizations" (Alonso and López, 1986: 73). Accordingly, the political bosses who gained control of the unions thereafter have been referred to as *charros*,[3] the most famous and long-lasting in the petroleum sector being

Joaquín Hernández Galicia, nicknamed "La Quina." La Quina became the general secretary of the petroleum workers' union in 1961 and controlled the union either directly or through proxies until he was incarcerated by President Carlos Salinas in 1989.

Carlos Romero Deschamps, the leader of the union from June 1993 until October 2019, had served as La Quina's chauffeur and apparently played the role of Judas in handing him over to the military forces sent by Salinas (Pérez, 2017: 138–140). Over the years, Romero Deschamps has been at the center of a number of corruption scandals, including "Pemexgate" in 2000, when he helped to siphon off US$53 million from Pemex to finance the campaign of the Partido Revolucionario Institucional's presidential candidate that year, Francisco Labastida Ochoa. In 2012 images of his daughter's extravagant lifestyle were taken from her Facebook page and circulated widely in multiple media. For over two decades dissident movements within the petroleum workers' union have denounced him for corruption and illicit personal enrichment and struggled to democratize the union (Herrera Montelongo, 2003), so far without success.

Romero Deschamps went along with the 2013 energy reform, which led to massive layoffs and cuts in pension benefits for Pemex workers. Between 2013 and 2018, 29,956 Pemex employees lost their jobs (Pemex, 2019: 12). In November 2015 he agreed to a new collective agreement for the petroleum workers that increased the retirement age from 55 to 60 years for employees with less than fifteen years of service and introduced a defined contribution plan for new employees while maintaining privileges and perks for union leaders. The last collective agreement for the union that he signed, in March 2020, included a salary increase of 3.37 percent and benefit increases amounting to 1.80 percent for workers and an 80 percent reduction in commission payments and in traveling expenses for union leaders. By the time this agreement was signed, renewed calls for investigating Romero Deschamps on accusations of corruption had grown to a clamor. AMLO's government eventually announced that an investigation was under way. Faced with mounting pressure, he resigned in October 2019, leaving behind a power vacuum that has yet to be filled.

Manuel Limón Hernández, the union's home secretary and Romero Deschamps's righthand man, has become the interim leader, but he and his cohorts are facing attacks on multiple fronts. Three of the most visible dissident currents are the National Movement for Petroleum Transformation, led by María Lourdes Cruz Díaz, the National Petroleum Front, led by Sergio Morales Quintana, and the Movement of Active Oil Workers in Evolution for a New Mexico, led by Miguel Arturo Flores Contreras. In addition, a rival union has emerged under the leadership of Yolanda Morales Izquierdo called Petromex, which was given legitimacy by AMLO's government through registration in March 2019. AMLO has publicly declared that Pemex workers will choose their union representatives through a free, direct, and secret vote in accordance with Article 245 of the Federal Labor Law of May 1, 2019.

In the mining sector, Napoléon Gómez Sada became the general secretary of the miners' union in 1961 and remained in the post until his death in 2001, shortly after which his son Napoleón Gómez Urrutia took over, maintaining this position until the time of this writing. This father-to-son handover of leadership coincided with the beginning of the twelve-year period in which the probusiness National Action Party controlled the executive branch of the federal government under the presidencies of Vicente Fox and then Felipe Calderón. During these years the miners' union began to fragment under pressure from a series of political attacks orchestrated by the federal government and big Mexican mining capital (León Salazar, 2017).

Fox's administration pushed for changes to the labor law in the direction of greater labor flexibility and more prerogatives for capital. Gómez Urrutia not only resisted these changes but also aggressively negotiated salary increases for miners in a context of rising international mineral and metal prices. The federal government responded by attempting to oust him from his position. The stakes rose in the immediate aftermath of the explosion that killed sixty-five miners in the Pasta de Conchos underground coal mine in Coahuila on February 19, 2016. The mine belonged to Germán Larrea, the owner of Grupo México. Gómez Urrutia accused both the company and the federal government of "industrial homicide" stemming from negligence. In response, Fox's government accused the union leader of embezzling union funds and issued a warrant for his arrest. Gómez Urrutia fled to Canada, where he received political asylum and citizenship, carrying on as leader of the union from abroad and taking advantage of his time in exile to forge political ties with big unions in Canada and the United States.

During the twelve years that Gómez Urrutia spent in Canada, the correlation of political forces in Mexico allowed for dissident movements within the miners' union to break from the executive committee in order to establish more cooperative and flexible relations with mining companies (León Salazar, 2017). In addition, new so-called white unions, with leaders subordinate to the interests of private firms, emerged. Under these conditions, while formally employed workers for large metal-mining companies achieved wage increases and job opportunities during the boom years between 2005 and 2013, mining labor became more flexible through subcontracting and temporary contracts (Casado Izquierdo and Sánchez Salazar, 2019; León Salazar, 2017). The latter trend was formalized by changes made to Mexico's Federal Labor Law in 2012 that not only legalized types of outsourcing but also introduced flexible labor contracts for probationary and training periods.

Since AMLO became president, there has been a profound shift in the political relations between the federal government and the miners' union. Symbolically, this is best illustrated by AMLO's announcement in 2019 that his government would attempt to rescue the bodies of sixty-three miners who died in the Pasta de Conchos mine in 2006. Institutionally, the new political relations are reflected in the inclusion of Gómez Urrutia in the federal government. He was elected senator by means of proportional representation, based on the votes cast for MORENA. He is also president of the Senate's Labor and Social Welfare Committee and in early 2019 became president of the newly created International Confederation of Workers, which brings together more than 150 unions from diverse sectors of the Mexican economy. Under his political influence, the miners' union has negotiated significant wage increases for workers at the El Coronel mine in Zacatecas and for workers at the port of Lázaro Cárdenas in Michoacán and it has won back at least one collective contract in Coahuila.

To be sure, this reconfiguration of political relations between the federal government and labor has gone beyond the mining and petroleum sectors. To begin with, it has manifested itself in modifications of the labor law in May 2019, among them the recognition of the labor rights of outsourced, domestic, and agricultural workers and the requirement that unions be more democratic and transparent. Gómez Urrutia has since led a legislative initiative to strengthen the regulation of outsourcing. On the other hand, one modification of the labor law consolidated an initiative of Enrique Peña Nieto's government to eliminate the conciliation and arbitration boards that had served to resolve labor conflicts. Luevano Bustamante (2019: 150) sees this as "the end of tripartism in labor justice, rather than the conclusion of a cycle, it is another stage in the dismantling of Mexican social rights."

Conclusions

AMLO's government has brought some important changes to Mexico's extractive policies. These include the various measures taken to strengthen Pemex—the building of a new refinery and the revamping of existing ones to add value to crude oil and to achieve higher levels of energy self-sufficiency. AMLO has canceled bidding rounds to transfer oil and gas fields to the private sector and put an end to granting new concessions in the mining sector. Moreover, his government has made legal reforms to better protect the rights of subcontracted workers and to push for greater union democracy and transparency. In addition, an important distinguishing feature from past governments is its non-employment of the police or the military to repress protest. Nevertheless, AMLO's deriding of people who have organized to defend their land and territory from the socio-environmental impacts of extractive projects has contributed to perpetuating a climate of insecurity for these people, who continue to be attacked and murdered, mostly with impunity.

As part of the reconfiguration of political relations between the state and unionized workers in extractive sectors of the economy, AMLO's government has incorporated and empowered one long-standing union boss (Gómez Urrutia), in the mining sector, where union representation is fragmented and contested, while bringing about the fall of another (Romero Deschamps), in the petroleum sector, where intensified struggles have emerged among multiple groups for the leadership of Pemex workers. One important difference between Gómez Urrutia and Romero Deschamps is that the former strongly resisted neoliberal reforms to the labor law and was persecuted for it by previous governments. Thus, AMLO's embracing of Gómez Urrutia fits well with his anti-neoliberal discourse. Another difference is that Gómez Urrutia has strong political ties to big unions in the United States and Canada, making him a useful political ally for the AMLO government in international negotiations. Romero Deschamps, by contrast, is more unequivocally guilty of corruption and illicit personal enrichment in the eyes of the general public. Because of this, his downfall was necessary to give legitimacy to AMLO's anticorruption crusade. In addition, given the strategic importance assigned to the petroleum sector in AMLO's development strategy, it is convenient for him that the petroleum workers' union is in disarray, since this weakens its ability to negotiate or possibly resist his initiatives.

With regard to environmental policy, two positive signals stand out: AMLO's promise not to use fracking to extract hydrocarbons and his appointment of Victor Toledo to head the Ministry of the Environment and Natural Resources. However, the continuation of fracking in practice, the cutting of the ministry's budget and administrative staff, and the maintenance of environmental laws put in place during the neoliberal era combine to eclipse these positive signals and to establish an institutional orientation of relegating environmental concerns to a second level of importance. This is confirmed by the explicit objective of accelerating the rate of extracting hydrocarbons through government subsidies to Pemex and by not changing laws that give priority to petroleum and mining activities.

As far as resource rents go, AMLO's government has failed to modify the taxes and royalties paid by privately owned mining and petroleum companies. Instead, AMLO has promised to honor the terms of the contracts that were established before he became president. Further, he has eliminated the mechanisms for channeling the mining fund's resources to social spending in mining regions and he has created new opportunities for private-sector participation in petroleum exploitation. He has also encouraged the expansion of mining, which is completely dominated by the private sector, in part by appointing a former executive of big mining as undersecretary of the mining ministry. All of this speaks to a strong inclination toward continuity during the first eighteen months of AMLO's presidency with regard to the neoliberal logic that persists at the root of Mexico's extractive policies.

Notes

1. There are many contradictory figures regarding the area granted to private companies through mining concessions in Mexico. This figure was calculated from information presented by the executive branch of the Mexican federal government in December 2019 (https://www.gob.mx/presidencia/prensa/que-sea-un-dia-de-solidaridad-y-fraternidad-con-los-que-sufren-expresa-presidente-en-visperas-de-navidad) and cross-checked with information presented by Nuñez Rodríguez (2016: 45–48).

2. https://www.mexicoambiental.com/investigadores-de-la-unam-revelan-mas-de-500-conflictos-ambientales-en-mexico-y-construye-mapa-que-los-georeferencia-y-categoriza/.

3. In Mexico, *charro* refers to horsemen in elaborate traditional dress. It was incorporated into the union lexicon in 1948 when president Miguel Alemán, faced with a call by various labor leaders to carry out a nation-wide strike, used police force to install as leader of the National Railroad Workers' Union Jesús Díaz de León, whose nickname was "El Charro" because of his traditional horse riding.

References

Ackerman, J. M.

2020 "The last surfer to hit the beach: Mexico and the 'Pink Tide,'" pp. 319–342 in S. Ellner (ed.), *Latin America's Pink Tide, European Integration and the Post–Cold War World*. Lanham, MD: Rowman and Littlefield.

Alonso, A., and R. López

1986 *El sindicato de trabajadores petroleros y sus relaciones con PEMEX y el estado 1970–1985*. Mexico City: Colegio de México.

ASF (Auditoría Superior de la Federación)

2011 "Informe del resultado de la fiscalización superior de la cuenta pública 2010." http://www.asf.gob.mx/Trans/Informes/IR2010i/Grupos/Desarrollo_Economico/2010_0809_a.pdf.

Casado Izquierdo, J. M, and M. T. Sánchez Salazar

2019 "Los mineros en el México neoliberal." *Investigaciones Geográficas* 98: 1–20.

CEMDA (Centro Mexicano de Derecho Ambiental)

2020 *Informe sobre la situación de las personas defensoras de los derechos humanos ambientales*. Mexico City: CEMDA.

Delgado Wise, R., and R. del Pozo Mendoza
2005 "Mexicanization, privatization, and large mining capital in Mexico." *Latin American Perspectives* 32 (4): 65–86.
Fundar
2017 "La agenda de la sociedad civil frente a las industrias extractivas en México." https://fundar.org.mx/la-agenda-de-la-sociedad-civil-frente-a-las-industrias-extractivas-en-mexico/.
2018 "Las actividades extractivas en México: minería e hidrocarburos hacia el fin del sexenio, anuario 2017." http://fundar.org.mx/mexico/pdf/AnuarioExtractivas2017.pdf.
2019 "Fondo Minero: preocupaciones y propuestas." https://fundar.org.mx/wp-content/uploads/2019/11/Fondo-Minero_Posicionamiento_Nov04.pdf.
Gudynas, E.
2010 "El nuevo extractivismo del siglo XXI: diez tesis sobre el extractivismo bajo el progresismo sudamericano actual." *Revista Memoria* 242/243: 12–17, 24–30.
Hernández Ibarzábal, J. A., and D. Bonilla
2020 "Examining Mexico's energy policy under the 4T." *The Extractive Industries and Society*. https://doi.org/10.1016/j.exis.2020.03.002.
Herrera Montelongo, J.
2003 "Entrevista: La lucha por la democracia en el sindicato petrolero." *Política y Cultura* 19: 239–253.
León Salazar, C.
2017 "La fragmentación del sindicalismo minero-metalúrgico: entre la persecución a Gómez Urrutia y las estrategias corporativas de cambio organizacional." *El Cotidiano* 201: 107–118.
López Bárcenas, F.
2017 *La vida o el mineral: Los cuarto ciclos del despojo minero en México*. Mexico City: Akal.
Luevano Bustamante, G.
2019 "¿A dónde va el derecho del trabajo mexicano?" *Revista Direitos Humanos & Sociedade* 2 (1): 150–167.
Madrid Ramírez, L.
2020 *El desmantelamiento institucional del sector ambiental: Un balazo en el pie*. Mexico City: CCMSS.
Nuñez Rodríguez, V.
2016 *Minería mexicana en el capitalismo del siglo XXI*. Mexico City: Itaca.
Pemex
2019a *Anuario estadístico 2018*. Mexico City: Pemex.
2019b *Plan de negocios de petroleros mexicanos y sus empresas productivas subsidiarias 2019–2023*. Mexico City: Pemex.
Pérez, A. L.
2017 *PEMEX RIP: Vida y asesinato de la principal empresa mexicana*. Mexico City: Grijalbo.

Pérez Jiménez, S.
2018 "Análisis cartográfico de la expansión del extractivismo minero en México." *Revista de Geografía Espacios* 16 (8): 39–72.
Petras, J., and H. Veltmeyer (eds.)
2014 *Extractive Imperialism in the Americas: Capitalism's New Frontier.* Leiden and Boston: Brill.
Svampa, M.
2015 "The 'commodities consensus' and valuation languages in Latin America." *Alternautas* 2 (1): 45–59.
Tetreault, D.
2020 "The new extractivism in Mexico: rent redistribution and resistance to mining and petroleum activities." *World Development* 126: 1–10.
Tetreault, D., C. McCulligh, and C. Lucio (eds.)
2018 *Social Environmental Conflicts in Mexico: Resistance to Dispossession and Alternatives from Below.* London and New York: Palgrave Macmillan.
Velázquez Hernández, L.
2020 "La defensa del ambiente en México, ¿cuestión de vida o muerte?" *Diálogos Ambientales* 1 (1): 41–46.

7

Tracing the Political Life of Kimsacocha

Conflicts over Water and Mining in Ecuador's Southern Andes

Teresa A. Velásquez

Kimsacocha is the Pachamama. She nourishes us, she sustains us. . . . If the miners take out the gold, it's like taking out a liver or a kidney.

—Rosita Chuñir, Victoria del Portete, Ecuador, 2009

In the past decade, the emergence of an ideologically heterogeneous group of progressive governments has signaled a new era in Latin American state making. Critical of the Washington Consensus, post-neoliberal governments tend to protect national markets, expand investment in social sectors, and promote the values of "social well-being, fraternity, and social solidarity" (Ellner, 2012: 106). Led by Rafael Correa, the Ecuadorian "Citizens' Revolution" coincided with a decrease in poverty, increased literacy, and overall economic growth (Becker, 2013). Notwithstanding the social gains made under Correa's administration, the national indigenous movement remained divided over its support for it. Some indigenous organizations challenged what they perceived to be the exclusion of the resource rights of many farmers. The political tensions are representative of the challenges that post-neoliberal governments faced in the region as they tried to maintain political legitimacy while carrying out century-old extractivist policies (Galeano, 1973). This chapter focuses on conflicts over state-backed projects in Ecuador in which farmers, with the help of the national indigenous movement, have mounted significant opposition to mining.[1]

In the Andean parishes of Victoria del Portete and Tarqui, family farmers perceived a disjuncture between the administration's language of social inclusion and state support for mineral extraction. The 2008 constitution produced by Correa's party, Alianza País, in response to the demands of indigenous and environmental organizations established Ecuador as a plurinational and intercultural country,[2] incorporated *sumak kawsay* (life in plentitude) as an alternative notion of development to balance environmental sustainability with growth, and granted Mother Earth (Pachamama) the right to "maintain and regenerate cycles of life, structure, functions, and evolutionary processes" (República del Ecuador, 2008: Article 71). While these articles appeared to challenge the commodification of nature under neoliberalism, the constitution also allowed the state to exploit nonrenewable resources in environmentally protected areas if such projects were declared to be "of national interest" (República del Ecuador, 2008: Article 407). Eduardo Gudynas (2009: 188) critically refers to this development strategy as "progressive extractivism." He observes the tendency of progressive governments to "maintain a style of development based on the appropriation of Nature" in which the state "plays an active role and gains a greater legitimacy through the redistribution of some of the profits generated by such extractivism."

This chapter follows dairy farmers as they challenged a proposed water law that would allow for mineral extraction in communal watersheds, strategically reappropriating and transforming the Andean epistemologies incorporated into the constitution as a new language of protest against state-financed and multinational-financed mineral projects. The proposed law aimed to centralize water resources so as to overcome the sharp inequalities in access to water that had historically plagued the country (see Acosta and Martínez, 2010). It also opened up the possibility of mineral extraction in fragile and sensitive wetlands, including rural watersheds. Given the state's concomitant efforts to expand mineral extraction, farmers feared that the law would enable the state to distribute water to multinational mining companies that would then monopolize or harm their communally managed water supplies. Farmers affiliated with a communal water board that provides more than 1,500 families with drinking and irrigation water, alongside Catholic priests, environmentalists, and urban allies, mobilized alternative understandings of nature to challenge the law. They framed their communally managed watershed, known as Kimsacocha, as the embodiment of the Pachamama, a life-giving entity that sustains the farming families living 6,000 feet below the Kimsacocha headwaters. This chapter asks whether the Andean cosmologies recognized by the constitution can be transformed into an effective language of protest against state plans for mineral extraction.

Farmers appropriated Andean cosmologies, with uneven outcomes, as a way to navigate the perceived contradictions in Correa's post-neoliberal agenda by attempting to set an ethical limit to progressive extractivism. These cosmologies were part of an essentialized language of indigeneity that helped farmers broaden their coalition against the water law to include indigenous communities that were not affected by mining but similarly concerned about the privatization of water under the bill. The strategic use of Andean cosmologies created an ethnically plural movement in defense of life. Referencing the imagery of death and destruction that accompanies industrial mining activity, this framing was consistent with the expression of resource struggles in Guatemala, Argentina, and Peru as struggles over life itself (Nelson, 2013; Zibechi, 2012). Through the performance of public rituals in the Kimsacocha watershed, the farmers and their allies redefined it as the embodiment of the Pachamama, which brings life, and therefore as off-limits to mineral extraction. While the vocabulary of the Pachamama helped the farmers intervene in public debates over the water law, the state's appropriation of the language in a revised law instantiated piecemeal sustainable conservation initiatives that were compatible with industrial mining activity.

Indigeneity, the State, and Social Movements

"Indigeneity" can refer to "a process; a series of encounters; a structure of power; a set of relations; [and] a matter of becoming" (de la Cadena and Starn, 2007: 11). It has been invoked by groups to make claims to citizenship, rights, and social inclusion based on the constitutional recognition of the collective rights of indigenous people (Sieder, 2002; Van Cott, 2000). Indigeneity also intersects with an internationally recognized language of rights (Warren and Jackson, 2002) even as it enhances divisions among leaders and the grassroots communities they claim to represent (Canessa, 2006; Shah, 2010). Indigeneity is imbricated with a new form of governmentality in which the neoliberal state and international financial institutions have incorporated some of the demands of indigenous people without fully coming to terms with their petitions for collective resource rights, particularly in cases where such demands will "violate the integrity of the productive regime" (Hale, 2005: 18). Conflicts over resources deepened in the 2000s, and indigeneity emerged as a discourse through which class-based popular demands for meaningful social change were articulated and ultimately set the stage for the election of post-neoliberal governments in the region (Postero, 2007a).

Post-neoliberal governments in Ecuador and Bolivia—where the Law of Mother Earth and Integral Development for Living Well was approved in 2012—integrated Andean cosmologies into their governing frameworks, and the latest round of multicultural reforms is said to have laid the groundwork for a decolonial political and economic project (Radcliffe, 2012). In anthropology the ontological turn has drawn attention to the "multiplicity of forms of existence in concrete practices" (Holbraad et al., 2014) and the ways in which "arrangements [of existents] . . . maintain their apparent unity and reproduce this apparent unity over time" (Povinelli, 2014). In Ecuador, state recognition of Pachamama rights was initially interpreted as a challenge to the Eurocentric or modern constitutional framework. As an "earth-being" in the public sphere, the Pachamama reorganizes the hegemonic arrangements of human and nonhuman entities (de la Cadena, 2010). Arturo Escobar (2010: 39) describes the recognition of Pachamama rights as an "epistemic-political event that disrupts the modern political space because it occurs outside such space, as a challenge to liberalism, capitalism, and the State." The presence of "earth-beings" in Ecuadorian and Bolivian legal frameworks questions Cartesian models of progress and development based on the separation of humans from nature and serves as a springboard for a radical rethinking of development (Gudynas, 2011).

Recent scholarship in Ecuador shows the limits of Andean cosmologies as a state practice. Sarah Radcliffe (2012) argues that state implementation of sumak kawsay as a transformative discourse is seriously limited because state documents neither create the foundations for a truly intercultural society nor contemplate the redistribution of land and other resources for indigenous communities. Carmen Martínez Novo (2014: 108) reaches a similar conclusion, arguing that the Correa regime "is appropriating indigenous symbols and demands, but is not recognizing indigenous people as actors" and instead constructs them as "obedient subjects" who must toe the government line to receive any material benefits. She observes a reversal of the gains made under neoliberal multicultural reforms. Erin Fitz-Henry (2012: 266) shows that Pachamama rights have been deployed in largely symbolic ways compatible with market-oriented conservation practices while simultaneously justifying "further expropriations of Indigenous, poor, and Afro-Ecuadorian communities."

Through ethnographic research, this chapter extends critical studies of the multicultural reforms as they unfold in the context of mining conflicts. I examine Andean cosmologies as a form of knowledge practice that simultaneously strengthens—even as it challenges—post-neoliberal state formation. Mining conflicts expanded and intensified under neoliberal and post-neoliberal regimes (Bebbington, 2009). Corporate knowledge practices are well documented in the literature on mining (Himely, 2014; Kirsch, 2014; Li, 2009), but less is understood about the kinds of knowledge systems that activists mobilize and their effects (Osterweil, 2013). Andean knowledge systems are celebrated as the basis for a kind of oppositional politics that connects human and nonhuman entities in life projects that challenge extractive industry (Escobar, 2008; Blaser, 2010). In this chapter, I conceptualize Andean cosmologies as part of a "language of contention" in which the state establishes the terms in which people express their collective demands (Roseberry, 1994). Andean cosmologies enabled farmers to expand their political coalition into an ethnically plural movement in defense of life and symbolically transform the Kimsacocha watershed into the Pachamama, whose rights were protected by the constitution. Thus antimining activism was based on global discourses of indigeneity that ironed out complexities and internal differences regarding "local" views of nature for the creation of an antimining movement rooted in environmental politics (see critiques from McNeish, 2013; Ramos, 2012). At the same time, when farmers' demands for Pachamama rights were acknowledged by the state, Andean cosmologies became the discursive basis through which the state promoted watershed conservation along with mineral extraction. In effect, Andean cosmologies are part of state governing frameworks that shape both the terrain of political opposition and the future of sustainable mineral extraction in Ecuador even as farmers oppose such development projects.

This chapter is organized as follows. First, I show that multinational and state actors have defined the highland landscape as a lucrative mineral deposit with the potential to finance social welfare programs. Second, I show how farmers mobilized the metaphor "water is life" as a way to expand their allies and redefine the Kimsacocha watershed as the embodiment of the Pachamama. Third, I show how the state redeployed the language of the Pachamama in ways that fundamentally undermined the claims of the coalition. Research for this chapter was carried out over the course of nearly thirty months of sustained ethnographic research between January 2008 and May 2010. I conducted participant observation with antimining activists, attended community meetings and workshops, rallies, and marches, conducted interviews with farmers, priests, and urban activists, and collected additional data through the internet, newspaper resources, and nongovernmental organizations involved in the protest movement.

Quimsacocha as a Mining Project

Quimsacocha was originally the name of a multinational mining project and not the name attributed to the highland watersheds by the dairy farmers themselves. The Toronto-based IAMGOLD Corporation named its project Quimsacocha shortly after securing 12,000 hectares of mineral concessions in a highland wetlands area that coincides with a nationally protected forest. The toponym "Quimsacocha" is Quechua for "three lakes." IAMGOLD secured its concessions on the heels of the passage of a neoliberal mining law in 2001 that opened protected areas to prospecting and extraction and introduced an environmental framework for the nascent mining sector. Companies were required to prepare an environmental impact assessment for exploratory work, and state environmental monitoring agencies were established.

Opposition to the Quimsacocha project began shortly after the company made its environmental impact assessment available. Partly to fulfill its obligations under the law and partly as a form of corporate social responsibility, IAMGOLD invited communal water board leaders to a meeting where consultants explained that high-valued mineral deposits overlapped with community watersheds. IAMGOLD identified approximately 3.3 million ounces of gold and additional deposits of silver, copper, and molybdenum in the effluents of the Irquis River from which several communal systems draw water. A citizens' group made up of irrigation users was the first to organize peasants in the rural parishes of Victoria del Portete and Tarqui, located just outside of Cuenca, Ecuador's third-largest city. The movement gained momentum in 2006 and 2007 with the formation of the National Coordinating Committee in Defense of Life and Sovereignty and the participation of the Victoria-Tarqui communal water board—the largest drinking-water board in the two parishes. Communal water boards are influential in community politics, often representing their members in second- and third-tier organizations. Many farmers supported the movement out of fear that IAMGOLD's project would adversely affect water quality and quantity.

Testimonies I gathered from dairy farmers expressed a sense of betrayal when they found Correa supporting IAMGOLD's Quimsacocha project. Farmers recall that during his campaign for the presidency he had promised to safeguard water supplies. In 2007, shortly after a 5,000-person-strong protest had rocked the southern highlands, the president and the minister of energy and mines, Alberto Acosta, engaged community water board leaders in a dialogue about the fate of IAMGOLD's concessions. At the request of the authorities, water board leaders presented evidence that IAMGOLD had violated three different bodies of law to secure its concessions. Expecting that the government would therefore withdraw the concessions, farmers were surprised when it required IAMGOLD to set aside only a small part of its concession for conservation and ultimately left the project intact (see Moore and Velasquez, 2013). In December 2007 Correa told the press, "We wanted to avoid this at first, but if there are $100 billion [in minerals in the ground], then we will have to permit open-pit mining" (Soto, 2007). He said that the profits could be used to finance social development projects for Ecuadorians and put an end to poverty (*El Comercio*, December 3, 2007). Only a month after the new constitution was ratified in 2008, the Correa administration announced a new mining law that would promote and regulate mineral extraction. The law increased government control over extraction and guaranteed the state a majority of the profits from mining activities. Activists estimated that, including additional taxes in royalty payments and special and corporate taxes levied against companies such as IAMGOLD, the law would result in at least 75 percent profit sharing (Zorrilla, 2008). Farmers in Victoria del Portete scrambled to oppose the law, which allowed the expropriation of lands and watersheds slated for mineral extraction without community consent. While they staged marches, road blockades, and even a hunger strike, they were unable to stop or meaningfully change it. First, they were unable to develop a nationwide coalition against it. In several organizational meetings I attended in late 2008, social and environmental groups remained divided over the political timing and the scope and framing of the demands. The Confederación de Nacionalidades Indígenas del Ecuador (Confederation of Indigenous Nationalities of Ecuador—CONAIE) did not mobilize its base communities until late January 2009, after the law had been passed. Secondly, Correa succeeded in discursively tying the country's future to industrial mining. An editorial in a Cuenca newspaper titled "Absurd Savagery" called for the "authorities to use an iron fist against the abuse and prepotency of the [antimining] protesters, who should be more concerned with producing more for the economic benefit of the country" (*El Mercurio,* January 10, 2009).

The Water Law

On August 26, 2009, Correa sent the National Assembly a draft of a new water bill that was framed as a way to recover sovereignty and increase social equity. The preface identified the status quo as "unequal access and distribution, distortion in the management of irrigation water, and lack of participation of water users." To address these problems, the proposed law declared water a public good and a human right, guaranteed a minimum amount of water to every Ecuadorian citizen, prohibited the privatization of water (the hallmark of neoliberal governance), and strengthened public institutions in anticipation of their better management and protection of water resources.

A heterogeneous group of dairy farmers quickly emerged as a vociferous critic of the proposal for opening up highland watersheds to mineral extraction. Carlos Pérez Guartambel, a lawyer and president of the Tarqui-Victoria communal drinking water system and the Unión de Sistemas Comunitarios de Agua del Azuay (Union of Community Water Systems of Azuay—UNAGUA), became a spokesperson for the group. UNAGUA produced a pamphlet for distribution to farmers in consciousness-raising workshops and water board meetings pointing out that the law contained "authorizations for the economic use of water for mining activities" and that, although it prohibited mining in headwaters, there was an exception for mining that was declared "of national interest." IAMGOLD's Quimsacocha project was repeatedly identified in the press as one of the four largest and most advanced mining projects under consideration. Members of communal water systems feared that the state would use the exception to turn their watershed into a gold mine. Carlos Pérez Guartambel urged water users to defend Kimsacocha as a "space of life" and, as such, a no-mining zone.

Pérez Guartambel formed an alliance with the highland indigenous organization ECUARUNARI and with the CONAIE. While many of ECUARUNARI's member communities and organizations were not directly affected by mining, they were affected by the monopolization of water resources by private companies. The proposed water law prohibited privatization of water sources, but it did not require the state to review its water concessions to private firms, essentially leaving water in the hands of the large agribusinesses, bottled-water companies, and cut-flower producers that dominated it in the central and northern highlands. Leaving inequalities over water access in the highlands virtually intact would render Correa's socialist framing of the law a hollow promise. The UNAGUA, the CONAIE, and ECUARUNARI agreed that water law reform was desperately needed, but they did not view their own political and economic interests as compatible with Correa's vision of a centralized state.

Water Is Life

The metaphor of water as life framed popular marches in opposition to the proposed water law and helped create a cohesive protest narrative that brought the diverse members of the coalition together under an alternative understanding of water. On September 11, 2009, two weeks before the National Assembly was scheduled to debate the law, as many as 6,000 protesters flooded Cuenca's central park to stop the law. Many held placards that read "El agua no se vende, se defiende" (Water is not to be sold but defended). A microphone amplified voices of dissent from Correa's efforts to centralize water resources. One indigenous woman who addressed the crowd articulated the metaphor of water as life: "The state wants to be the owner of water. Water should be communitarian because it is life. Indigenous people and campesinos give life. We women have the use and rights to water because water is the blood of our life. Water flows through our veins; without water, there is no life. Without [agricultural] production, there is no life." She drew on gendered imagery to conceptualize the right to water as a complex web of interdependence that makes life possible. By comparing water to blood she materialized the interdependence of indigenous people and peasants with water and also of city dwellers with peasants and indigenous people, suggesting that water was a central force in sustaining agrarian and urban life. She argued that water should be managed by groups rather than individual, state, or private interests.

Metaphors, as understood by Lakoff and Johnson (1980: 4), reflect cultural values that "structure how we perceive, how we think, and what we do." By suggesting that water was a living and life-producing entity, farmers argued that mining threatened the right of humans and nonhumans to exist. "Water Is Life" helped coalition leaders articulate a complex set of political and economic demands in Andean terms. Most immediately, the coalition demanded that the National Assembly shelve the water law pending further consultation with peasant and indigenous organizations. It demanded that a revised draft law include the establishment of a plurinational water council to be made up of elected officials and representatives of indigenous, Afro-descendant, and peasant organizations to decide national water policy, community management of local watersheds and rivers, autonomy for communal water boards, and the prohibition of mining in critical water zones. It argued that the inclusion of voices from indigenous and popular movements would democratize water policy in the country, leading to a more equitable distribution of water and greater support for small and mid-scale agricultural activity.

The coalition's long-term demand was that the government move away from extractive industries as the main form of development and draw upon Andean values to promote sustainable development. In a letter written to the National Assembly in March 2010, the water board leaders and the CONAIE declared themselves united. Pérez Guartambel read the letter aloud during a rally, stating that they aimed to "construct an economically and socially sustainable development model based on the principles of the *ayni*, of reciprocity . . . to guarantee respect between brothers and sisters and, above all, nature." He continued: "We propose a commitment to struggle against the capitalist, extractivist neoliberal model." Ultimately, they "demand[ed] that all laws passed by the National Assembly recognize the rights of nature and water" (field recording, March 3, 2010).

Discursive links between water and life are not new in the Andean region. Scholars have pointed out that in the Andes water is imbued with life-giving powers and that pre-Hispanic societies traced their origins to sacred mountains lakes, springs, rivers, and other bodies of water (Gelles, 2000). When faced with the privatization of municipal water systems, leaders of the well-publicized Bolivian water war turned "water is life" into a protest slogan. Farmers' claims to water were based on customary law (*usos y costumbres*), and reciprocity and collective governance of water were "primordial" Andean values (Albro, 2005) that challenged its commodification. The language of indigeneity as it is mobilized for political uses in Bolivia and Ecuador is akin to what Nancy Postero (2007b: 4) calls "Andean utopias"—a historically situated discourse of indigeneity in which actors strategically deploy "elements of traditional narratives and myths . . . to produce consensus about the kinds and forms of change that are appropriate and possible." Because strategic mobilization of Andean cosmologies can be used to "articulate projects for social justice beyond exclusive notions of ethnic identity" (de la Cadena and Starn, 2007: 11), the issue is not so much about affirming an indigenous cultural identity as about articulating a political position against the commodification of water and the democratization of water policy.

Farmers in this case turned to Andean cosmologies as a "political discourse for what needs to be reclaimed, reinvented, and reimagined" (Fabricant, 2012: 4) in the Citizens' Revolution. They and their allies strategically deployed alternative notions of nature as a way to stop the commodification of their water supplies and advance a struggle for collective rights recognized in international and national legislation but not implemented by the Correa regime. In 2007 farmers in Victoria del Portete and Tarqui filed a petition for recognition of the collective rights to consultation guaranteed under the 1998 constitution and International Labour Organization Convention 169 without success. In 2008 the National Constituent Assembly issued the Mining Mandate, in which mining concessions granted without community consultation were to revert to the state, but the Correa administration never implemented this part of the mandate; instead it temporarily halted IAMGOLD activities until the new mining law was passed in 2009. When the farmers were unable to develop an effective language of opposition to mining that attracted broad support, they turned to Andean cosmologies to defend their watersheds. Framing water struggles in terms of Andean values such as water as a living entity and reciprocity is part of what Perreault (2008: 846–847) calls the "cultural politics of livelihood," in which meaning and materiality meet to reconfigure power relations and democratize water governance.

The coalition initiated and shaped public debate over the legitimacy of Correa's proposed water law. In response to the demonstrations, the National Assembly members revised the proposed legislation to recognize the rights of various collectivities including rights to water. A revised draft law circulated in November 2009 defined the Pachamama as a rights-bearing entity whose waters were life-sustaining. It recognized the rights of Pachamama as the source of life, whose waters had the right to be conserved, holistically managed, and repaired if contaminated (República del Ecuador, n.d.). It added a new chapter on the collective rights of communities and nationalities to manage, conserve, protect, be consulted, and participate in decisions regarding water use according to their own worldviews and to maintain, strengthen, and recover their spiritual, cultural, and ancestral knowledge and practices with regard to water. Moreover, it adopted the CONAIE's proposal of the creation of a plurinational water council to formulate and carry out national water policy. Article 73, which had authorized companies to use water for mining, was replaced with Article 104, "No water will be authorized for use in the exploitation of mining within 2,500 feet of ecosystems associated with hydrological cycles that influence water sources." Article 74, problematic because it allowed for mining in headwaters if declared of national interest, was replaced by Article 105, "Authorization for . . . mining exploitation will not be granted within the areas of influence of water sources."

Pérez Guartambel considered these significant advances but not enough: "We need to be two steps ahead, not just one" (interview, Cuenca, November 14, 2009). In late November 2009 he convened an UNAGUA meeting in which he shared his skepticism about the law, pointing out that Article 105 did not declare the highlands free of mining. The dispute over language and framing was important, he said. Declaring Kimsacocha a no-mining zone was not guaranteed. "We have to protect everything, the entire highlands, not just part of it." Whereas the law assumed that mining was an industry whose impacts could be managed and contained, he viewed Kimsacocha as a system that could be affected whether mining occurred in water sources or 2,500 meters away. The UNAGUA rejected the new draft law for proposing piecemeal conservation as a way of appeasing critics of mining.

Kimsacocha: From a Mining Project to the Pachamama

The UNAGUA pursued a two-pronged strategy: deepening political coordination with the CONAIE and ECUARUNARI and mobilizing a diverse local coalition. In December 2009, the indigenous movement—with the support of the UNAGUA—engaged in high-level dialogues with the Correa administration. Meanwhile, the UNAGUA and its regional allies used the slogan "Water Is Life'" as a way to transform Quimsacocha from a mining project into the Pachamama and thus to protect the watershed from mining. Catholic priests played a crucial role in this reframing.

On December 12, 2009, dairy farmers, journalists, environmentalists, and international supporters gathered around Father Samuel, who was about to begin an outdoor mass at Kimsacocha. Women filled plastic bottles with lake water and placed them in a circle for blessing. Father Samuel's homily drew from the Beatitudes and invoked the group as an ethical community defending life itself:

> Jesus says, "Blessed are the poor," because you the poor value this space, this place as a sacred place, as the temple of God. A rich man comes here

> and looks around and thinks, "There is a great opportunity to make money." By contrast, when a poor man comes to this place, he says "God is here." Instead of making calculations, he says, "We have to defend this, because this is the source of life, of living water and free water that we all want."

Father Samuel's invocation of a mineral-rich watershed as a sacred place rather than a commodity, as a place that invites contemplation rather than calculation, articulated a politics of life as the linchpin of an antiextractivist movement. Water as a living, sacred entity brought together the farmers and the progressive wing of the Catholic Church. Father Samuel practiced what he called "eco-liberation theology," which he described as a "reflection of [Catholic] teachings about the entire planet" (interview, Cuenca, March 15, 2010). He was the coordinator of the social pastoral office of the Cuenca diocese and worked with poor communities for structural transformation. He organized popular education workshops in the Freire tradition in which he distributed some of his writings on water conflicts. In one of his unpublished essays he attributed social inequality and ecological problems to capitalist resource extraction. He found a solution to such problems in the convergence of Catholic and Andean traditions, whereby "water is considered sacred" (interview, Cuenca, December 12, 2009). The emphasis on Andean or indigenous values as a solution to modern problems is part of a longer tradition of liberation theology in Ecuador. In the 1960s, Salesian priests promoted intercultural theology, holding that indigenous people "naturally" held anticapitalist values that needed to be developed and molded (Martínez, 2013).

Priests have played an active role in shaping the language and practices of Andean worldviews in Ecuador. It was Father Lucio, a Salesian priest, who first suggested turning Quimsacocha into a sanctuary. "I told Carlos, 'We need to build a beautiful sanctuary here. . . . If we build one they won't mine here'" (interview, Cuenca, July 24, 2013). After the December 12 mass led by Father Samuel, the farmers built an outdoor sanctuary. A group of men poured concrete into the shape of a *chakana*—an Andean cross—in anticipation of the arrival of the newly minted Virgin of the Waters of Kimsacocha. Dairy farmers and their allies appropriated the name of IAMGOLD's mining project and "indigenized" its spelling by replacing the Q with a K. (According to early records of antimining activism in the region, activists once referred to the watershed as Sombrederas.) Some months later the group held another lakeside mass to bless the stone statue representing the Virgin of the Waters of Kimsacocha. Activists increasingly linked Kimsacocha with the Pachamama in political speeches, rallies, and everyday talk. Don Ismael is representative of the transformation. In a conversation about mining he told me, "Kimsacocha is the Mother Earth. Just like the veins that we have in our body, so does the

Pachamama. Instead of blood, her [veins] are filled with water. Kimsacocha is her body" (interview, Cuenca, July 30, 2013).

The movement in defense of life made important political gains. First, the coalition made Kimsacocha matter to an urban audience that had generally dismissed peasant concerns during the public debates over the mining law. Journalists attended the lakeside performances and the community trips to Kimsacocha, and favorable media coverage increased. *El Tiempo*, Cuenca's second-most-important regional newspaper, dedicated a full-page article with seven pictures to Kimsacocha. The article began "Preservation. It is impossible not to be filled with admiration before one of the most sublime scenes of Azuay nature" (*El Tiempo*, November 29, 2009). The article echoed the idea of Kimsacocha as a site of "life": "The presence of small trout that feed on the algae . . . on the edge of lake is life in its purest state." At the same time that the nation was discussing the water law, a serious drought was affecting water supplies and causing massive energy shortages. Urban audiences viewed the preservation of Kimsacocha as a solution to climate change and the security of a future water supply. The language of "life" brought together unlikely actors whose political agendas were not always in line with each other. Eco-politics is often founded on the premise that "native peoples' views of nature . . . are consistent with Western conservation principles," although such principles are often at odds with demands for community resource autonomy (Conklin and Graham, 1995: 695). This was the beginning of a critical turning point in local antimining politics. The argument that large-scale mining companies would bring in new technology to safeguard watersheds eroded (Moore and Velásquez, 2013), and campesinos' struggle to defend life was later shared by many Cuencanos.

Secondly, the coalition won an ambivalent victory. After a heated national debate over the water law that included publicly aired debates between movement leaders and state officials, radio commercials, and fiery street protests, the National Assembly shelved the water law debate on the basis of a lack of consultation over the law. The movement had successfully mobilized the argument that the Constitution of 2008 required prelegislative consultation with the communities affected by the law. In a communication circulated by e-mail on May 17, 2010, Marlon Santi, then CONAIE president, celebrated the decision as a victory: "In spite of a media campaign full of lies . . . gifts, projects, and intense disinformation from the Correa government, we have won this battle." According to the National Assembly's Commission for Food Sovereignty, the legislative body reportedly consulted more than 1,600 organizations and held public forums in every province of the country in the following years. Yet, the process was marred by accusations that the Assembly members were not operating in good faith.

The final draft of the water law passed in 2014 illustrates the tensions within progressive extractivism. The law upheld the precepts of resource nationalism: it centralized national water policy in the hands of the state and strategically incorporated aspects of a plurinational political platform while allowing for mineral extraction in critical watersheds. Similar to the previous draft that was revised in response to protests, the official bill recognized indigenous collective rights to participate, manage, and protect water sources, including the right to "free, prior, informed, and obligatory consultation before legislative decisions or state authorized use of water that flows through their lands and territories." The law did not guarantee the same rights with regard to watersheds that might be earmarked for extraction but did not flow directly through their territories. It did uphold the role of community water systems and of *pueblos* and nationalities to manage water in "collective and traditional form" and recognized their "fiscal and administrative autonomy"—an important point that would later be disputed in its implementation. Moreover, it incorporated indigenous demands for an intercultural and plurinational water council, but, as the indigenous leader Lourdes Tiban pointed out, the council was included simply as an "adornment" without any teeth, subsumed under the Secretariat of Water. After participating in numerous forums and speaking before the National Assembly, Carlos, the ECUARUNARI president, believed that they had been taken for a ride (*nos tomaron el pelo*).

Although the protest movement had significantly shaped the water law, the indigenous and antimining movement continued to be critical of it because it failed to place any limits on mining in headwaters and watersheds. The articles pertaining to the prohibition of mining within 2,500 meters of watersheds disappeared from it. Although it incorporated recognition of "the rights of Nature or Pachamama to the conservation of water properties that support all forms of life," it allowed the state water authority to grant water permits for mining projects in sensitive watersheds. It attempted to reconcile the seeming contradictions between mining and conservation by requiring the mining companies to return treated water to the original channel without affecting water for domestic use.

From Progressive to Neoliberal Extractivism

The election of a new president brought an end to indigenous worldviews such as sumak kawsay as a nationalist state project. In 2017, President Lenín Moreno became a successor to Rafael Correa's Citizens' Revolution but did an about-face by implementing neoliberal reforms. In 2018 his government passed the Productive Development Law to attract private investment through tax reforms.[3] In 2019 it acquired a controversial US$4.2 billion loan from the International Monetary Fund and a US$500 million loan from the World Bank and promoted the adoption of macroeconomic reforms that harked back to the 1990s and early 2000s, when unpopular reforms had spurred the wave of anti-neoliberal protest that former president Correa had ridden to electoral power in 2007. The loans were part of a joint effort of multilateral lending institutions to increase the efficiency of public spending and promote structural reforms to remove barriers to private sector development.[4] Collectively, the reforms dismantled Correa's Citizens' Revolution through a series of decrees and regulations reducing and/or eliminating subsidies in fuel, gas, and electricity, modifying and increasing taxes on working populations and small businesses, reducing corporate taxes, shrinking the public sector by eliminating or fusing public institutions, and including an international arbitration clause in large contracts.[5]

The acceleration of mineral extraction and the adoption of neoliberal structural adjustment policies will likely eliminate any of the movement's limited gains, including the recognition of indigenous consultation rights to water use and authorization in the 2014 water law. In March 2019 Yaku (formerly known as Carlos) Pérez Guartambel and the community water boards of Girón spearheaded a popular referendum to protect the "hydrological system of Kimsacocha" from mining activities.[6] Less than a month after rural residents voted overwhelmingly against mining in Kimsacocha, the government unveiled a new national mining policy to promote foreign investment and growth in the mining sector. It included anticipated mining revenues in its projection of GDP gains in the IMF negotiations and since the passage of the Productive Development Law in 2018 has made successive reforms to the mining sector (*El Universo,* 2019). It reformed the mining tax system by eliminating the 70 percent windfall tax and reducing the royalty scale from 5–8 percent to 3–8 percent (*Mining Journal,* 2019a). Moreover, reforms to the public sector prompted the merging of the Secretariat of Water with the Ministry of the Environment—a move that some activists fear will only fast-track the water permitting process for mining in sensitive areas (interview, Cuenca, August 28, 2019). New multilateral loan commitments are looking to the mining sector as a way to reduce the national deficit as oil prices have collapsed in connection with the COVID-19 pandemic, creating even greater pressure to develop controversial projects such as the one in Kimsacocha. The Ministry of Nonrenewable Resources has taken its case to the Constitutional Court in an effort to stop a referendum against mining in the province of Azuay that would potentially block the Quimsacocha project (now owned by Canadian-based INV Metals and renamed the Loma Larga project) as well as the controversial nearby Rio Blanco project owned by the Chinese investment firm Junefield. Even after an 11-day anti-neoliberal popular strike shook the country, the vice minister of mines announced that mining projects would not stop simply because people living in the areas opposed mining (YouTube, 2020).

Progressive and neoliberal extractivism in Ecuador have both pursued mining as a model of development but in divergent ways. The discourses and practices of the Citizens' Revolution that framed mining as a national good to meet the objectives of sumak kawsay *(buen vivir)* have disappeared from the neoliberal national mining policy under President Moreno, which makes no mention of sumak kawsay or buen vivir. Modification of Article 3 of the mining law has replaced "National mining policy will promote . . . social participation and buen vivir" with "It is declared as the policy of the state to attract and promote investment . . . to foment foreign exchange earnings."[7] Moreover, the government announced plans to liquidate Ecuador Estratégico, a public company that channeled anticipated mining revenues into schools, housing projects, and water infrastructure for mining communities—a cornerstone of Correa's Citizens' Revolution. While many of the environmental defenders I worked with rejected Ecuador Estratégico investment as another buy-off intended to divide communities, it was also without a doubt a key piece of governance that allowed Correa to pursue controversial mineral projects while criminalizing antimining activism with some measure of local support. His Citizens' Revolution created new forms of citizenship and inclusion through the material benefits of extractive rents and in ways that connected the "emotive ideals of development and nationalism" with the historical constructions of the "will to improve" creating support among indigenous and campesino farmers at sites of oil and mineral extraction (Van Teijlingen, 2016: 903; Lu et al., 2017). Without the promise to "do things differently" or to reinvest in social welfare programs, it is likely that neoliberal plans will confront robust opposition with continued use of violent repression such as the world witnessed during the protests of October 2019.

Conclusion

This chapter has examined the ways in which farmers in highland Ecuador and the state have appropriated, mobilized, and resignified Andean epistemologies in the context of growing conflicts over mineral extraction and water rights legislation. Changes to resource use regimes became flashpoints of contention in which the direction of Ecuador's Citizens' Revolution was hotly disputed by variously positioned left-leaning groups, some favoring a nationalist development strategy based on the extraction of nonrenewable resources and some rejecting that strategy. These tensions were stoked by constitutional recognition of the Pachamama as a subject of rights and the simultaneous promotion of progressive extractivism as a way of challenging the hegemony of neoliberal rule.

Constitutional frameworks for legislating Andean cosmologies became the discursive terrain through which farmers pursued their claims, with contradictory outcomes. Farmers drew upon ontological differences recognized in the constitution to suggest that mineral extraction violated a form of collective rights that included humans' and nonhuman entities' right to life. As a global political discourse, Andean epistemologies are based on essentialized constructions of indigeneity that underscore harmonious human-environment interactions, reciprocity, and democratic equality. These constructions were critical in building political coalitions. The malleability of indigeneity enabled farmers to ground their struggles for water and life in claims to disputed territories as sacred embodiments of the Pachamama. The staging and performance of spiritual rituals that venerated the Kimsacocha watershed as a sacred entity were intended to create "zones of exception" (Ong, 2007)—places where the incursion of commodity-driven logics was ethically limited and replaced by an alternative notion of governance recognizing water as a living system that included (rather than excluded) people. The coalition succeeded in framing national debates over Correa's proposed water law, challenging his plans to deepen and expand extractive industries across the Andes and the lowland Amazon, and materialized an ethnically diverse movement for the defense of life powered by the participation of the country's most important indigenous organizations.

The shift in political and economic framework in the country from progressive to neoliberal extractivism poses new challenges for social movements. The narrative framework employed by antimining activists based upon buen vivir and Pachamama may or may not be as effective in future activism considering that such discourses and practices have disappeared from mining policy. This means that new reforms to the mining sector will likely limit any state-led investments in strategic communities, thus changing the social conditions under which mining occurs and potentially sparking more opposition to mining as social investment wanes.

New mining concessions have also galvanized municipal and provincial support for protecting rural and urban watersheds. Prior to leaving power, President Correa's administration granted INV Metals 30,000 hectares of mineral concessions overlapping with protected areas and city watersheds north of Kimsacocha. While city water officials had quietly sided with the Canadian mining companies, they have become public critics of mining in upland watersheds. Inspired by the defense-of-life movement, urban middle-class residents are articulating their own political project to defend life. Efforts to protect urban watersheds have prompted the formation of new activist groups and the passage of municipal council resolutions against mining in headwaters and inspired local political candidates—even those who were allies of the Correa administration—to become "defenders of life." As a former municipal council member told me, "It is now politically incorrect to be in favor of mining" (interview, Cuenca, August 28, 2019). Illustrative of this shift in public opinion, Pérez Guartambel became the first indigenous leader to be elected prefect of Azuay in May of 2019 on a platform of defending the watersheds from mining projects—a significant feat in an area where racism and strong anti-indigenous sentiment is pervasive (Mancero Acosta, 2012; Velásquez, 2017). For the more immediate future, the challenges will be bringing together urban and rural activism and securing and implementing referendums against mining at the county and provincial levels.

Notes

1. This is a revised version of an article that appeared in *Latin American Perspectives* in 2018 (45 [5]: 154–169). The manuscript benefited from suggestions from Emily Billo, Marc Becker, Nicole Fabricant, and an anonymous reviewer. Fieldwork was funded by a fellowship from the Inter-American Foundation and a National Science Foundation doctoral dissertation grant. The Latin American Faculty of Social Sciences in Quito also provided support.

2. Carmen Martínez Novo (2014: 113) defines "plurinationalism" as "territorial autonomy, redistribution of resources, and recognition of indigenous representation," while "interculturalism" is associated with "the right to be diverse, antidiscrimination measures, and inclusion in the nation."

3. See "Ley para Fomento Productivo, Atracción de Inversiones, Generación Empleo," in *Registro Oficial*, no. 309, August 21, 2018, and summary of changes in http://www.fundacionmicrofinanzasbbva.org/revistaprogreso/ley-fomento-productivo/#:~:text=El%20pasado%2021%20de%20agosto,y%20lograr%20una%20estabilidad%20fiscal.

4. The lending institutions included the World Bank, the IMF, the Inter-American Development Bank, the Corporación Andino de Fomento, and the Latin American Reserve Fund. The World Bank also provided Ecuador with a US$6 million loan in May 2020 during the COVID-19 pandemic to continue private-sector growth and development.

5. See IMF (2019) and, for a summary of the IMF austerity reforms, Rogatyuk (2020).

6. Following the referendum, INV announced that it would relocate the planned mining plant outside of Girón (*Mining Journal*, 2019b).

7. Changes in the mining law were introduced in December 2018 by Moreno's Productive Development Law.

References

Acosta, Alberto, and Esperanza Martínez
2010 *Agua: Un derecho fundamental*. Quito: Abya-Yala.

Albro, Robert
2005 "The water is ours, ¡*carajo*! Deep citizenship in Bolivia's water war," pp. 249–271 in June Nash (ed.), *Social Movements: An Anthropological Reader*. Oxford: Blackwell.

Bebbington, Anthony
2009 "The new extraction: rewriting the political ecologies of the Andes?" *NACLA Report on the Americas*, September/October, 12–20.

Becker, Marc
2013 "The stormy relations between Rafael Correa and social movements." *Latin American Perspectives* 40 (3): 43–62.

Blaser, Mario
2010 *Storytelling Globalization from the Chaco and Beyond*. Durham, NC: Duke University Press.

Canessa, Andrew
2006 "*Todos somos indígenas*: towards a new language of national political identity." *Bulletin of Latin American Research* 25 (2): 241–263.

Conklin, Beth, and Laura Graham
1995 "The shifting middle ground: Amazonian Indians and eco-politics." *American Anthropologist* 97: 695–710.

de la Cadena, Marisol
2010 "Indigenous cosmopolitics in the Andes: conceptual reflections beyond 'politics.'" *Cultural Anthropology* 25: 334–370.

de la Cadena, Marisol, and Orin Starn
2007 "Introduction," pp. 1–30 in Marisol de la Cadena and Orin Starn (eds.), *Indigenous Experience Today*. Oxford: Berg.

Ellner, Steve
2012 "The distinguishing features of Latin America's new left power: the Chávez, Morales, and Correa governments." *Latin American Perspectives* 39 (1): 96–114.

El Universo
2019 "Ingresos mineros, parte del Acuerdo con el FMI." April 24. https://www.eluniverso.com/noticias/2019/04/24/nota/7299563/ingresos-mineros-parte-acuerdo-fmi.

Escobar, Arturo
2008 *Territories of Difference: Place, Movements, Life*, Redes. Durham, NC: Duke University Press.
2010 "Latin America at a crossroads: alternative modernizations, post-neoliberalism, or post-development?" *Cultural Studies* 24 (1): 1–65.

Fabricant, Nicole
2012 "Symbols in motion: katari as traveling image in landless Movement politics in Bolivia." *Latin American and Caribbean Ethnic Studies* 7 (1): 1–29.

Fitz-Henry, Erin

2012 "The natural contract: from Lévi-Strauss to the Ecuadorian Constitutional Court." *Oceania* 82: 264–277.

Galeano, Eduardo

1973 *Open Veins of Latin America: Five Centuries of the Pillage of a Continent.* New York: Monthly Review Press.

Gelles, Paul

2000 *Water and Power in Highland Peru: The Cultural Politics of Irrigation and Development.* New Brunswick, NJ: Rutgers University Press.

Gudynas, Eduardo

2009 "Diez tesis urgentes sobre el extractivismo bajo el progresismo sudamericano actual," pp. 187–225 in Jürgen Schuldt et al. (eds.), *Extractivismo, política y sociedad.* Quito: CAAP/CLAES.

2011 "Buen vivir: today's tomorrow." *Development* 54: 441–447.

Hale, Charles R.

2005 "Neoliberal multiculturalism: the remaking of cultural rights and racial dominance in Central America." *PoLAR: Political and Legal Anthropology Review* 28 (1): 10–28.

Himely, Mathew

2014 "Monitoring the impacts of extraction: science and participation in the governance of mining in Peru." *Environment and Planning* 46: 1069–1087.

Holbraad, Martin, Morten Axel Pedersen, and Eduardo Viveiros de Castro

2014 "The politics of ontology, anthropological positions: Field sites—theorizing the contemporary." *Cultural Anthropology Online.* January 13. http://culanth.org/fieldsights/462-the-politics-of-ontology-anthropological-positions.

IMF (International Monetary Fund)

2019 *Second and Third Reviews under the Extended Fund Facility Arrangement and Request for Nonobservance and Modifications of Performance Criteria—Press Release and Staff Report.* Country Report 19/375. Washington, DC: International Monetary Fund.

Kirsch, Stuart

2014 *Mining Capitalism: The Relationship between Corporations and Their Critics.* Oakland: University of California Press.

Lakoff, George, and Mark Johnson

1980 *Metaphors We Live By.* Chicago: University of Chicago Press.

Li, Fabiana

2009 "Documenting accountability: environmental impact assessment in a Peruvian mining project." *Political and Legal Anthropology Review* 32 (2): 218–236.

Lu, Flora, Gabriela Valdivia, and Néstor L. Silva

2017 *Oil, Revolution, and Indigenous Citizenship in Ecuadorian Amazonia.* New York: Palgrave Macmillan US.

Mancero Acosta, Mónica

2012 *Nobles y cholas: raza, género, y clase en Cuenca 1995–2005.* Quito: Facultad Latinoamericana de Ciencias Sociales Ecuador.

Martínez Novo, Carmen

2013 "Struggles for the meaning of 'indigenous' within inculturation theology in Ecuador," in Marc Becker (ed.), *Indigenous and Afro-Ecuadorians Facing the Twenty-first Century.* Newcastle, UK: Cambridge Scholars Publishing.

2014 "Managing diversity in postneoliberal Ecuador." *Journal of Latin American and Caribbean Anthropology* 19 (1): 103–125.

McNeish, John-Andrew

2013 "Extraction, protest, and indigeneity in Bolivia: The TIPNIS effect." *Latin American and Caribbean Ethnic Studies* 8 (2): 241–242.

Mining Journal

2019a "Ecuador eases tax burden on miners." February 8. https://www.mining-journal.com/politics/news/1356116/ecuador-eases-tax-burden-on-miners.

2019b "Giron says no to mining: Loma Larga to relocate plant." March 26. https://www.mining-journal.com/gold-and-silver-news/news/1359564/giron-says-no-to-mining-loma-larga-to-relocate-plant.

Moore, Jennifer, and Teresa Velásquez

2013 "Water for gold: confronting state and corporate mining discourses in Azuay, Ecuador," pp. 119–148 in Anthony Bebbington and Jeffrey Bury (eds.), *Subterranean Struggles: New Dynamics of Mining, Oil, and Gas in Latin America.* Austin: University of Texas Press.

Nelson, Diane M.

2013 "'Yes to Life = No to Mining': counting as biotechnology in life (Ltd) Guatemala." *The Scholar and the Feminist Online Journal* 11 (3).

Ong, Aihwa

2007 "Neoliberalism as mobile technology." *Transactions of the Institute for British Geography* 32 (1): 1–7.

Osterweil, Michal

2013 "Rethinking public anthropology through epistemic politics and theoretical practice." *Cultural Anthropology* 28: 598–620.

Perreault, Thomas

2008 "Custom and contradiction: rural water governance and the politics of *usos y costumbres* in Bolivia's irrigators' movement." *Annals of the Association of American Geography* 98: 834–854.

Postero, Nancy

2007a *Now We Are citizens: Indigenous Politics in Post-Multicultural Bolivia.* Stanford, CA: Stanford University Press.

2007b "Andean utopias in Evo Morales's Bolivia." *Latin American and Caribbean Ethnic Studies* 2 (1): 1–28.

Povinelli, Elizabeth

2014 "Geoontologies of the otherwise: field sites—theorizing the contemporary." *Cultural Anthropology Online.* January 13. http://www.culanth.org/fieldsights/465-geontologies-of-the-otherwise.

Radcliffe, Sarah

2012 "Development for the postneoliberal Era? *Sumak kawsay,* living well, and the limits to decolonization in Ecuador." *Geoforum* 43: 240–249.

Ramos, Alcida

2012 "The politics of perspectivism." *Annual Review of Anthropology* 41: 481–494.

República del Ecuador

n.d. *Ley orgánica de recursos de hídricos, uso y aprovechamiento del agua* [draft]. Quito: República del Ecuador.

Rogatyuk, Denis

2020 "Ecuador's government is persecuting the man who doubled health care spending." *Jacobin*. April 19. https://www.jacobinmag.com/2020/04/ecuador-lenin-moreno-coronavirus-rafael-correa-health-care.

Roseberry, William

1994 "Hegemony and the language of contention," pp. 355–366 in Gilbert M. Joseph and Daniel Nugent (eds.), *Everyday Forms of State Formation: Revolution and the Negotiation of Rule in Modern Mexico*. Durham, NC: Duke University Press.

Shah, Alpa

2010 *In the Shadows of the State: Indigenous Politics, Environmentalism, and Insurgency in Jharkand India*. Durham, NC: Duke University Press.

Sieder, Rachel

2002 *Multiculturalism in Latin America: Indigenous Rights, Diversity, and Democracy*. New York: Palgrave Macmillan.

Soto, Alonso

2007 "Ecuador permitirá minería a cielo abierto si recibe beneficios." *Reuters América Latina*. December 1. http://lta.reuters.com/article/idLTAN01352504 20071201.

Van Cott, Donna

2000 *The Friendly Liquidation of the Past: The Politics of Diversity in Latin America*. Pittsburgh: University of Pittsburgh Press.

Van Teijlingen, Karolien

2016 "The 'will to improve' at the mining frontier: neo-extractivism, development and governmentality in the Ecuadorian Amazon." *The Extractive Industries and Society* 3: 902–911.

Velásquez, Teresa A.

2017 "Enacting refusals: mestiza women's anti-mining activism in Andean Ecuador." *Latin American and Caribbean Ethnic Studies* 12 (3): 250–272.

Warren, Kay B., and Jean E. Jackson

2002 *Indigenous Movements, Self-Representation, and the State in Latin America*. Austin: University of Texas Press.

YouTube

2020 "Enrique Gallegos-Anda, Viceministro de Minas, expuso los lineamientos que marcarán su gestión." https://youtu.be/5hnLUDsnMxc.

Zibechi, Raúl

2012 "Latin America: a new cycle of struggles." *NACLA Report on the Americas* 45 (2): 37–49.

Zorrilla, Carlos

2008 "Ecuador's constitution and mining." *Upside Down World*. August 13. http://upsidedownworld.org/news-briefs/news-briefs-news-briefs/ecuadors-constitution-and-mining/.

8

The Gendered Dimensions of Soybean Extractivism in Argentina

Amalia Leguizamón

THE POLITICAL ECONOMY OF THE environment in Latin America takes the form of extractivism. From a sociological perspective, this drives dynamics surrounding the control of natural resources that sustain life, the social and ecological consequences of those decisions, and the distribution of the resulting costs and benefits across society (Rudel et al., 2011). Natural-resource extraction for export—particularly of minerals, oil, and cash crops—has historically been central to Latin America's socioeconomic development. The logic of extractivism is that of a "treadmill of production" that, as it becomes more intensive, causes social and environmental decline (Schnaiberg and Gould, 1994). Leftist leaders elected in several Latin American countries around the turn of the twenty-first century have aimed to reduce the social inequalities resulting from neoliberal policies by redistributing the profits gained through extractivism. Yet, the paradigm of extraction—centered on control and domination of nature via technological innovation aimed at bringing efficiency, modernization, and economic growth—has continued, and with it have its negative social and ecological consequences (Gudynas, 2009).

Argentina has been at the forefront of neoliberal extractivism in Latin America (Giarracca and Teubal, 2013). No region in the country has escaped the treadmill of extraction: open-pit mining in the western Andes, hydraulic fracturing for shale gas and oil in southern Patagonia, and large-scale monocultures of genetically modified soy in the central Pampas and northern Chaco. Soybeans are the "golden egg" of the Argentine model, the key accumulation strategy for socioeconomic development under the country's neoliberal and post-neoliberal governments (Leguizamón, 2014). Argentina is the third-largest global grower and exporter of soybeans, which cover half of the country's arable land and represent a third of total exports. The "soy boom" has fostered economic growth and, through taxes on exports, a reduction in poverty and inequality. However, it has also had negative social and environmental consequences, including health risks from agrochemical spraying and violent displacements of peasant populations whose land is expropriated. Critics emphasize the power imbalances this model creates, because soy exports disproportionately benefit the elite (Gras and Hernández, 2014) while the powerless bear a disproportionate share of the costs (Leguizamón, 2016a).

This chapter highlights gender as a key determinant of the unequal distribution of social and environmental risks and benefits under resource extractivism (Bell and Braun, 2010; Krauss, 1993). In a seminal piece, Risman (2004) argued that gender should be understood as a structuring force of social inequality just like politics and the economy. Following her lead in conceptualizing gender as a social structure, I explore the gendered dimensions of large-scale soy production in Argentina. This approach sheds light on the complex social processes that create environmental injustice (both social inequality and environmental degradation), as well as on its gendered resistances and the opportunities for transformation.[1]

Gender intersects with other structures of inequality, such as race, class, and ethnicity, to create multiple vectors of oppression and domination (Collins, 1990; Lugones, 2010). The socio-environmental movements that have emerged around the world to protest environmental injustice reflect this intersectionality: poor indigenous peoples are often at the forefront of these struggles (Martínez Alier, 2014; Toledo et al., 2015). Moreover, women typically make up the majority of and are the leaders of such movements. For example, women are leading protests against mining in the Americas, from Appalachia to the Andes (Bell, 2013; Jenkins, 2015). In looking at extractivism as a gendered structure, I do not consider gender the primary form of domination. Much of the literature on environmental justice, particularly in the United States, debates the relative impacts of various forms of domination (consider the emphasis on race in the environmental racism literature). Critics argue that a more fruitful approach for academic inquiry and activism is to analyze how different structures of inequality operate synergistically to exacerbate power and powerlessness (Gould et al., 2008; Pellow 2018). Exploring the synergies of power increases our analytical ability, a prerequisite for applying social theory to social change.[2]

This chapter draws on archival and secondary research and on in-depth interviews with rural and peri-urban inhabitants of the Pampas region.[3] To identify how and why environmental injustice occurs, I analyze resource extractivism along three structural dimensions: institutional, individual,

TABLE 8.1
Gendered Dimensions of Resource Extractivism in Argentina's Soy Model

	DIMENSIONS OF THE GENDER STRUCTURE		
	Institutional	*Individual*	*Interactional*
SOCIAL PROCESSES	*(1) Distribution of resources* (M) Control over natural resources and technological innovation	*(3) Identity work* (F) Collective identity of socio-environmental movements = motherhood, protectors of health and life	*(4) Cognitive Bias* Concern over health and environmental risks of agrochemical spraying (M) No risk, best practice (F) Main grievance
	(2) Ideology (M) Techno-science: Modernization = development		*(5) Status Expectations* (M) Producers, breadwinners, experts (F) Caretakers, housewives *(6) State Paternalism* (M) "Father knows best" (M) "Father provides"

Note: Adapted from Risman (2004: 437). This table is not exhaustive of all causal mechanisms, but lists only those analyzed in this chapter. (M) = Male-dominated and associated with bio-hegemonic masculinity; (F) = Female-dominated and associated with emphasized femininity

and interactional (table 8.1). Following Risman (2004), I identify six causal mechanisms that serve either to produce and reproduce inequality and injustice (the status quo) or to challenge it. This framework is similar to power structure research in political and economic sociology but looks specifically at gender relations (Connell and Messerschmidt, 2005). I focus on gendered actors and their identities, the gendered discourses they deploy, and the gendered institutions and organizations they belong to.

First, I describe the political economy of soybean production in Argentina. Against this background I focus on the male-dominated institutions with the power to control natural resources and technological innovation: agribusiness corporations and the state. These institutions promote the adoption of the technological package of genetically modified seeds using an ideology based on the promise of increased growth, productivity, and profits. At the individual level, social structures constrain actions but also create opportunities for social change. In this section I look at the two most visible and successful movements against the soy model, the Grupo de Madres de Barrio Ituzaingó Anexo (hereafter Mothers of Ituzaingó) and the Asamblea Malvinas Lucha por la Vida (hereafter the AMLV). Both are women-led movements organized around concerns over the risks to children's health posed by agrochemical exposure. I then address the gendered interactions that create and maintain dominance and inequality in Argentina's soy boom. I follow gender scholars who argue that it is critical to analyze masculinity and femininity as complementary relationships that serve to legitimate a structure of gendered inequality and domination (Connell and Messerschmidt, 2005; Schippers, 2007).

Scholars have argued that extractive economies exacerbate gender inequalities (Bell and Braun, 2010; Fabricant and Gustafson, 2014). Yet there has been little analysis of how unequal gender relations operate in agro-export contexts of South America (Ferro, 2013; Oliveira and Hecht, 2016) or how gender shapes the patterns of adoption and impact of genetically modified crops (Rauchecker and Chan, 2016; Schnurr, 2017). This chapter theorizes and analyzes the gendered nature of the political economy and its resistances by exploring how and why gendered actors, practices, and institutions of resource extractivism produce and reproduce dominance and inequality, power, and injustice in Argentina's soy agro-industry.

Resource Extractivism in Argentina: Large-Scale Soy Production for Export

Argentina's development has historically relied on the extraction and exportation of natural resources and, in particular, on capitalist agrarian production. In the late nineteenth and early twentieth centuries, the Pampas became the center of the first agro-export boom, positioning the nation as "the granary of the world" (Leguizamón, 2020). In the late twentieth century, the extractivist model turned from wheat and beef to nontraditional commodities in a global context of high commodity prices and demand, leading to a boom in soybean production.

The neoliberal restructuring promoted by the Menem administration in the 1990s provided the most conducive institutional context for the adoption and expansion of genetically modified soybeans (Leguizamón, 2014). Transgenic soybean seeds were first planted in 1996; since then, soybean production has grown steadily, breaking records year on year. The expansion of large-scale soy production hinges on the adoption of a technological package combining genetically modified soybean seeds with agrochemical spraying and no-till machinery. Genetically modified soybean seeds are herbicide-tolerant, meaning that farmers can seed directly without tilling to control weeds. Instead, they spray glyphosate-based herbicide, which kills weeds but not the genetically modified plants. Profitability is a key motivation for agricultural producers to plant soy and adopt no-till farming (Trigo, 2011). The technological package offers farmers higher profits through increased scale and reduced costs (for labor and agrochemicals in particular).

While neoliberal reform opened the doors to soybean extractivism, it was under the Kirchner administrations that the model flourished. Néstor

Kirchner and Cristina Fernández de Kirchner ran Argentina's presidency for twelve years. Néstor was elected president in 2003. Fernández, his wife, succeeded him in 2007 and was reelected for a second term (2012–2015). (Néstor Kirchner died in 2010.) The Kirchners were part of the Pink Tide of leftist leaders that swept Latin America in the early twenty-first century. Pink Tide leaders directed their countries toward resource nationalism, continuing the reliance on extraction and exportation of natural resources for socioeconomic development but with a key difference: the government regained control over the profits of extractivism with the goal of social redistribution to benefit the poor (see Ellner's introduction to this book). Under the Kirchner administrations, soybean exports were taxed at rates of 30 to 35 percent. These taxes funded a wide variety of social and infrastructure development programs, helping to legitimize the model and build popular support.

The bust of the global commodity boom in the mid-2010s showed the limits of resource nationalism. Despite unprecedented economic growth, the Kirchners failed to break dependency; with dwindling foreign currency reserves came recession, inflation, and a reversal of progressive redistribution policies (Thwaites Rey and Orovitz Sanmartino, 2020). It was in this context of a weak economy and intense social polarization that Mauricio Macri rose to power in December 2015; his was the first center-right coalition ever to win power in Argentina and the first non-Peronista president to complete his term (Anria and Vommaro, 2020).

Macri was elected with broad support from the agro-export sector, since he promised to incentivize agricultural production and gradually reduce export taxes—a major source of contention between soybean producers and the Kirchners. Macri's administration promoted the interests of large agribusinesses by reducing agricultural export taxes and by modifying seed and rural labor laws—changes that had a negative impact on rural workers and smallholder peasants (Isidro and Forlani, 2019). Macri was unable to stabilize the economy, however, and in December 2019 he turned the presidency over to the newly elected center-left Peronista candidates: Alberto Fernández and Cristina Fernández de Kirchner. One of the first executive measures Alberto Fernández took was to raise soybean export taxes to 30 percent, showing a clear intent to return to the resource nationalism of former progressive governments.

While through the decades soybean extractivism has brought great economic benefits, it has also had numerous negative social and ecological consequences: deforestation, violent displacement of peasant and indigenous families from their land, and increased health risks due to agrochemical spraying, which have triggered socio-environmental protest movements (Cáceres, 2015). In the Pampas, these movements consist of "citizen assemblies" organized in defense of health and life following the spread of agrochemical-induced illnesses in their communities (Leguizamón, 2016a). To protect their children's health, women have put their bodies on the line to lead these protests (Aranda, 2015).

The Institutional Domain: Bio-Hegemonic Masculinity and Genetically Modified Soy

A puzzling aspect of Argentina's soy model is the widespread, enthusiastic support it receives despite the social and environmental harm it creates. Newell (2009) coined the term "bio-hegemony" to explain how the corporate and state elite (the actors that adopt, promote, and benefit from genetic-modification biotechnology) are able to silence potential dissent and project soy extractivism as universally desirable and beneficial for society. He shows how support for biotechnology as a key accumulation strategy for Argentina has been secured through material, institutional, and discursive means.

Efforts to create bio-hegemony are relentless in the Global South and have become a major topic for scholars interested in the political economy of the environment and development (Schurman, 2017). An aspect not fully explored in this literature, however, is how structured gendered dimensions embedded in bio-hegemony legitimate extractivism as the domination of man over nature in the pursuit of economic growth. Various material and discursive practices aim to produce and reproduce the subordination of nature to man, feminine to masculine, and women to men—what Connell and Messerschmidt (2005) term "hegemonic masculinity." At the institutional level two social processes produce and reproduce environmental injustice by recreating gender inequality: distribution of resources and ideology. As Connell and Messerschmidt (2005) argue, these gender hierarchies are social constructions; they are not immutable but rather contextual, historical, and thus subject to change.

Controlling the distribution of material resources is a primary structural mechanism through which power is secured. From the standpoint of the political economy of the environment, the key question is which actors have the power to "control the institutions and organizations that produce and regulate the flows of material resources that sustain people" (Rudel et al., 2011: 222). Newell (2009) demonstrates that in Argentina agribusiness corporations and the state are allied in a pro-biotech bloc with the material and legal power to control natural resources and guide technological innovation, including by establishing regulations that foster adoption of genetically modified seeds and classify glyphosate as not harmful to human health.

An analogous follow-up question from a gender relations perspective would be how these institutions and organizations are gendered and how they reproduce gendered inequalities (Kimmel, 2013). Politics and the economic world—the "public sphere"—are traditionally men's places. Not surprisingly, men occupy almost all the executive positions in government and in the largest agribusinesses operating in Argentina. In government, with the exceptions of Cristina Fernández de Kirchner, Felisa Miceli (minister of the economy 2005–2007), Gabriela Michetti (vice president 2015–2019), and María Eugenia Vidal (governor of Buenos Aires 2015–2019), since the neoliberal turn in the 1990s all executive positions important to biotechnology have been filled by men (a very consistent pattern since the agro-export model was established in the late 1800s).[4]

While the women in government, particularly Cristina Fernández, have repeatedly highlighted the exceptionality of their position as female leaders in male-dominated institutions, gender scholars concur that women in positions of power are required to behave more according to the gendered (masculine) standards of the offices they hold than to their gendered (female) identities (Kimmel, 2013). A charismatic leader, Fernández has masterfully played with this tension, alternating between embodying femininity and a maternalistic ethics of care and adopting a paternalistic attitude characteristic of many heads of state. In a famous speech she declared herself the "mother of all Argentines" while also asserting that her leadership position was akin to that of Juan Domingo Perón, an emblem of paternalist politics (*Clarín*, March 27, 2014).

Among the top 17 corporations operating across the Argentine soybean value chain—from seed and agrochemical inputs (e.g., Monsanto, Nidera) through processing and trading (e.g., Cargill, Bunge) to soybean production (e.g., Los Grobo, El Tejar, Cresud)—only seven of the top eighty-one executive positions are occupied by women.[5] Los Grobo, one of the largest agribusinesses in Argentina and South America, is an interesting exception. After their father stepped down from the family business, Gustavo Grobocopatel became president and his two sisters assumed two of the remaining three leadership positions. Concerned over the lack of gender diversity in leadership positions and the barriers women face in reaching the executive level, Andrea Grobocopatel, director and vice president of Los Grobo, started the Fundación Liderazgos y Organizaciones Responsables to promote the development of professional and business women. In an interview with *La Nación* (April 30, 2016) she acknowledged that gender quotas in leadership positions are necessary because men and women have different motivations: "The engine that drives women to act is their emotional life." Therefore, she continued, women reach different decisions; in particular, because women "are much more careful when taking decisions that impact people," she said, highlighting themes typically associated with feminine identity and expectations.

Gender roles at the production level of soy show an intensification of historical patterns of gender inequity and inequality in the region (Ferro, 2013). During the nineteenth century, European migrants settled in the Pampas and established a type of capitalist agriculture based on large-scale production for export. Known as *chacareros, gringos,* and *colonos* —a type closer to American farmers than to campesinos—they organized labor across traditional European gender lines, with men (husband/father and adult sons) responsible for the commercial farming and women for managing the home. Women did farm work when extra hands were needed, but with the introduction of mechanization in the late 1950s they were no longer needed and "completely disappeared from commercial agrarian production" (Stølen, 2004: 70, my translation). While women have equal rights to own land under Argentine inheritance laws, indirect mechanisms exclude them from control of agricultural production. In practice, males in the family tend to take over the farm while women migrate to cities to marry, study, or work (Ferro, 2013). The introduction of the technological package of genetically modified soy (which requires highly skilled labor) and the entry of financial investors into commodity production have exacerbated unequal gender patterns, leaving men in charge of agricultural production in the Pampas (Ferro, 2013; Stølen, 2015). The Pampas model of family-run entrepreneurial agriculture for export is rapidly transitioning into investment pool agribusinesses (known as *pools de siembra*).[6] The Pampas-style agro-export model has also subordinated subaltern peasant and indigenous communities and agro-ecological production systems oriented to the domestic market (Ferro, 2013).

Perhaps if women were to assume positions of power in agricultural production, its priorities would gradually shift toward a feminine ethics of care, but for now the few women in CEO positions have to compete as representatives of shareholders and therefore must reproduce bio-hegemony in order to stay in power.[7] Grobocopatel, known as the "King of Soy," is one of the main promoters of the agrarian "revolution" that has transformed Argentine agricultural production through constant technological innovation and expansion of the promise of genetically modified seeds to "feed the world" (Leguizamón, 2016b). At present, the mandate of soybean extractivism reflects the gendered identity of the men who control it: a rational-technical (masculine) mentality of domination and control of nature via scientific and technological innovation with the goal of increasing productivity and profits.

Ideology is a second mechanism that creates and, more significant, legitimates gendered inequality (Risman, 2004). Gramsci's (1972) concept of hegemony refers to the way ruling classes seek to maintain power by creating legitimacy. To maintain the status quo, it is crucial that the subordinated classes come to accept their situation. The greatest power comes when consensus is created around social hierarchies, whether of class, race, or gender. Thus, Gramsci emphasizes the significance of having power to manipulate cultural and symbolic practices to create consent. Newell (2009) shows that the pro-biotech bloc in Argentina has been able to promote bio-hegemony because it wields material and legal but also discursive power, especially through control of the mainstream media. Further, the hegemonic discourse of the soy model is based on the belief that constant technological innovation will bring progress and development for the country (Gras and Hernández, 2016).

In equating genetically modified soy with modernization, development, and progress, bio-hegemony follows the logic of techno-science (Barri and Wahren, 2013)—the Western belief that the fastest and widest possible control and appropriation of nature via scientific and technological innovation will unquestionably increase human well-being (Shiva, 1991). Feminist scholars have long denounced techno-science as a masculine logic that reproduces gender hierarchies (Harding, 2006). Lugones (2010: 745) argues that the "instrumental modern concept of nature central to capitalism" is closely tied to the modern dichotomous and hierarchical concept of gender. The desire to control a feminized and racialized nature is the epistemic and ontological premise of capitalist modernity.

Thus, paraphrasing Newell (2009) and Connell and Messerschmidt (2005), the male-dominated institutions that promote and benefit from soybean extractivism in Argentina deploy bio-hegemonic masculinity—the material, institutional, and discursive practices that create and maintain patriarchal control, which, under neoliberal capitalism, has assumed this particular extractive form against women and nature with the adoption of biotechnology. Oppression also works by excluding feminized subjects from the realm of power struggles. As de la Cadena (2010) argues, Gramsci's hegemony at work is not specific to politics (as pertaining to the way those in power curb or eliminate conflict) but also determines who is worthy of participating in the political sphere. Male-led and male-dominated institutions often exclude women from power in a democracy. The handful of women that may gain positions of power is more likely to reproduce bio-hegemonic masculinity than to address inequality.

As Gramsci implied, however, the need to create consent exists because underneath hegemony there is always the possibility of dissent. Hegemonic masculinities and femininities are contextual and historical and thus open to challenge and change, as women-led socio-environmental movements in Argentina illustrate.

Identity Work: Mothers Organize for Health and Life

The Mothers of Ituzaingó and the AMLV are two of the most important movements in the country against large-scale soy production. The sites of struggle for these organizations are, respectively, the neighborhood of Ituzaingó

Anexo and the town of Malvinas Argentinas. Located 20 miles apart, these are working-class enclaves in the industrial belt surrounding Córdoba, the capital of Córdoba province. Córdoba province has the second-largest economy in the country, relying primarily on agro-industry and car manufacturing, and is the second-largest grower of genetically modified soybeans in the Pampas region. Córdoba city, in the heart of the province, is the second-largest urban center in Argentina. Its economy is diversified across services and manufacturing, with the surrounding areas dominated by soy farms. Many residents in the industrial suburbs of Córdoba city are regularly exposed to toxins from industrial facilities (e.g., car factories, bioethanol plants) and agrochemical spraying from neighboring farms.

Across South America, the use of glyphosate-based herbicides has increased dramatically with the expansion of herbicide-resistant genetically modified soy monocultures (Catacora-Vargas et al., 2012). The emergence of glyphosate-resistant weeds has prompted farmers to apply greater volumes of glyphosate combined with more toxic agrochemicals, such as 2,4-D, dicamba, and endosulfan (Binimelis et al., 2009). In 2016, agrochemical and fertilizer use in Argentina rose by 50 percent from the previous year, reaching 3.9 million tons (Infocampo, 2017). In 2014, 88,000 tons of glyphosate were sprayed over 20 million hectares of genetically modified soy (Benbrook, 2016). Within Argentina, physicians have documented increased rates of miscarriages and congenital birth defects among mothers with a history of direct exposure to pesticides (REDUAS, 2010). Moreover, the costs of pesticide drift (the unintentional diffusion and potential negative effects of agrochemical spraying) are disproportionately borne by the poor, farmworkers, peasant and indigenous families, women, and children (Harrison, 2011; Lapegna, 2016).

The Mothers of Ituzaingó were among the first to organize against agrochemical spraying in Argentina and have since become a model for other groups organizing against it (GRR, 2006; REDUAS, 2017). The group formed in early 2002, when thirteen working-class women with no formal organizing experience united to examine why so many family and community members, young and old, were sick and dying. They knew that the water was polluted, probably by the local car factory or the electric power plant. They wondered if the crop dusters spraying agrochemicals over the soy fields down the street—fields where children played—were also to blame, observing that people commonly suffered from headaches, coughing, and skin rashes after spraying. With marches and picketing, they pressured the authorities to test the water and run blood studies. The results confirmed their suspicions: there were higher than average residues of agrochemical and industrial pollutants in the water and in their bodies. They mapped more than 200 cases of cancer, respiratory and skin diseases, miscarriages, and birth defects in a neighborhood of 5,000 (Carrizo and Berger, 2009). In 2012, in alliance with academics and scientists, they won a historic lawsuit against a soy producer and a crop duster for willful environmental pollution, the first of its kind in Latin America (Arancibia, 2013). More than fifteen years into their struggle, they continue demanding that authorities provide the promised medical treatment to those affected in their neighborhood, which was long ago declared a health emergency.

According to the 2010 census, Malvinas is the poorest city in the province; of its 12,187 inhabitants, 25.7 percent are unable to fulfill their basic needs, two-thirds are unemployed or underemployed, and 70.4 percent have no health insurance. Local doctors have identified among its residents a host of illnesses characteristic of pesticide drift: lung disease, dermatitis, tumors, cancers, congenital malformations in children, and the highest rate of miscarriages in the country (22 per 100) (Ruderman et al., 2013). Yet, in Malvinas, as in most soy towns in Argentina, residents did not identify agrochemical pollution as a grievance worth mobilizing for—until Monsanto arrived in town. In June 2012 President Fernández announced Monsanto's plans to build Latin America's second-largest genetically modified seed factory in Malvinas. Less than half a mile from the public school, the factory would have had 240 silos operating day and night, potentially spewing toxic fumes into the community. Concerned about their children's health, a coalition of neighbors organized as the AMLV in mid-2012 to halt the construction of the plant pending environmental impact assessments. Under the rallying cry "A Spring without Monsanto," protesters blockaded the road to the construction site in September 2013, eventually creating a permanent occupation that effectively halted Monsanto's construction plans for over three years. In early 2017, Monsanto sold its land and left town (*La Voz del Interior*, April 23, 2017). The struggle of the AMLV is a symbolic David-over-Goliath story told among the many anti-Monsanto movements around the world (Sitrin, 2015).

The Mothers of Ituzaingó and the AMLV, like socio-environmental movements worldwide, are mostly composed of and led by women. Their main motivation for protesting the soy industry is concern for the health of community members, children in particular, echoing global calls to protect health and life against the social and environmental hazards of large development projects (Bell, 2013; Jenkins, 2015; Martínez Alier, 2014; Toledo et al., 2015). Health concerns are a common grievance among victims of agrochemical spraying, whether they mobilize or not (Lapegna, 2016; Leguizamón, 2020). In interviews, activists singled out their identity as women, as mothers and grandmothers, as a major catalyst for mobilization, referring to women's "instinct" to protect their children. In their understanding, when their children are sick, it is mothers' "duty" to protect them.

"Why women only?" I asked the Mothers when I interviewed them in August 2015. "I don't know why," one replied,

> but it's always the women. When you watch the news about a community claim, who is the one talking? A woman. Always. I've been paying attention now, when there is a claim, even if so small as a demand for a light bulb, it is a woman who is at the lead. Not to mention a child, the death of a child. It's always women. Women are more able to express what is going on, what the needs are. Men . . . yes, they are able to speak up, but women have something more special. Something special!

A second activist continued the thought: "It's because of being a mother! The woman is mother, nurse, teacher, doctor . . . everything! Because when you have a child, you know before the doctor if he is running a fever, what's hurting, what's going on with him." These experiences reflect how women, so often at the heart of communities struck by the poverty and precarious consequences of neoliberal restructuring, have become central actors in the struggles for social and environmental justice in Latin America and across the Global South. Subaltern women, excluded from traditional sources of privilege and power and usually presented as poor victims, are leading revolts from below in a marked feminization of resistance (Motta, 2013; Motta and Seppälä, 2016).

At the individual level, identity work is a third mechanism that shapes and transforms gendered social structures that may superficially appear static. Poor and working-class women activists of Ituzaingó and Malvinas Argentinas have created a shared identity around motherhood that allows them to challenge the existing paternalistic structure. Motherhood catalyzes opposition to genetically modified soy around themes traditionally associated with women's expectations and identities. This is not simply identity-based politics or narrow protection of the private but rather a challenge to private-public dichotomies through a politicization of motherhood (Mason-Deese, 2016; Motta and Seppälä, 2016). For the Mothers of Ituzaingó, choosing to identify themselves as "mothers" is clearly a political act (Carrizo and Berger, 2009; Torrado, 2016). It is a direct reference to the Mothers of the Plaza de Mayo, their "role models," as they told me, whom they also resemble in their protest performances.[8] Most important, identifying themselves as mothers gives them both legitimacy and protection from those who may want to question (or silence) their activism; in their words, "No one can tell you, 'Who authorized you [to protest]?!' The fact of being a mother already authorizes you to speak up. No one can question you, if my son is sick, if I want to denounce [what happened to] him, [or] take him wherever I want" (quoted in Carrizo and Berger, 2009: 241, my translation).

Womanhood and motherhood thus become catalysts and justifications for activism. Women activists defend their right to protect their children and, by extension, the community and the environment (see Bell, 2013). As a female

AMLV leader told me, "[We have to understand that] environmentalism is not a romanticism but a common good. It is a matter of survival." The struggle for health and life is a struggle for clean water, clean air, access to health care, safe jobs—in short, for social and environmental justice.

By politicizing the personal, women activists challenge traditional divisions between public and private spheres. Previously excluded from political debates, feminized and poor subjects take center stage as political actors who challenge extractivism and the macro-structures of power by promoting an ethics of care for family, community, and environment. Womanhood, motherhood, family, and community thereby become a "terrain of resistance" (Motta, 2013: 44). By raising awareness of the health hazards of transgenic agriculture and demanding that protection of health and life take precedence over production, growth, and profitability, women activists are challenging bio-hegemonic masculinity. Gendered interactions within the political economy of soybean extractivism can shed further light on the relationship between male and female actors.

Gendered Interactions

The third dimension that structures gender inequality is gender-based cultural expectations attached to men's and women's interactions (see table 8.1). Gendered interactions are "the means by which status differences shape expectations and the ways in which in-group and out-group membership influence behavior" (Risman, 2004: 436). Certain interactional-level social processes help to explain why the logic and actors for and against extractivism are divided along gender lines, recreating gendered outcomes and environmental injustice: a cognitive bias in relation to the perceived risks of agrochemical spraying, different statuses and role expectations for men ("producers," "breadwinners," "experts") versus women ("caretakers," "mothers," "housewives"), and state paternalism that legitimates extractivism on a national level.

A salient finding of my interviews with people who lived or worked on or near large farms and thus were at greater risk of pesticide drift was that women were far more likely than men to express concerns over potential health hazards. Men were more likely to be skeptical of possible risks and to describe agrochemical spraying (especially glyphosate) as harmless. This gendered cognitive bias cut across class: male rural workers were more likely to support agrochemical use, while the middle- and upper-class wives of soybean producers were more likely to question its safety (see Leguizamón, 2020).

Cognitive bias is the result of different status expectations for men and women (Risman, 2004). In line with traditional gender roles, the soybean producers I interviewed defined themselves as "producers" and "experts." They identified the benefits of large-scale farming in bio-hegemonic masculine terms: increasing efficiency and profits and creating jobs. Most female rural inhabitants I interviewed, whether or not they benefited directly from agro-industrial production, embraced the traditional female role of caretaker. While motherhood is an identity shared by poor and working-class women who do not benefit directly from the soy model and who organized against it, even women who do benefit, either directly (household income comes from farming) or indirectly (their husbands work in agriculture or are business owners who benefit from prosperity in rural towns), often expressed concern about the potential health risks of agrochemical use, in particular for their children, family members, and neighbors.

Gender scholars use the concept of "emphasized femininity" in opposition to hegemonic masculinity to refer to the practices women engage in to construct gender inequality in interaction with men, as wives, daughters, etc. (Connell and Messerschmidt, 2005; Schippers, 2007). This concept focuses on the interplay between masculinities and femininities and especially on the ways in which women *comply* with the gender hierarchy. This type of femininity thus highlights the ways in which women accept and reproduce patriarchal subordination. By deploying motherhood and their duty as caregivers to legitimate their right to protest against agrochemical spraying, women activists place themselves in a bind: they challenge bio-hegemonic masculinity by performing emphasized femininity. In other words, by embracing motherhood women fulfill their role expectations, but by questioning and protesting the status quo they challenge them. Hence, they break from traditional gender roles by conforming to them—potentially a reason their efforts have so far been insufficient to transform the gendered structure of extractivism.

Men continue to demonstrate masculinity by wielding power over women through stereotypical gendered interactions. For example, the Mothers of Ituzaingó recalled gendered insults such as being called "crazy" and "irrational." At meetings with male public health officials, they were reprimanded for questioning "expert" authority and called "uneducated housewives" (Carrizo and Berger, 2009: 243). In Malvinas Argentinas, the protests against the Monsanto plant pitted neighbors against each other. Many male residents supported construction on the basis of the promise of much-needed jobs and countered female activists by citing their role as breadwinners for their families. A female AMLV leader said that she often replied to those men, "You give them bread, I give them life!" This legitimized her activism but reinforced stereotypical gendered roles.

The final important mechanism reproducing environmental injustice in Argentine soy production is state paternalism. The state has projected a "father knows best" attitude by passing laws and regulations that promote the transgenic soy model without input from civil society, beginning with the approval of genetically modified seeds for commercial use in 1996 (Verbitsky, 2009). A main grievance of AMLV activists is that Monsanto received approval to start construction without the required prior consent from the community (the issue of community consent is dealt with in Ellner's introduction and the chapter by Bebbington, Fash, and Rogan). In general, and at all levels, the government has established itself as the expert authority that determines risk, demanding trust and acquiescence from the population (Leguizamón, 2020). Most significant in this regard, government agencies continue to classify glyphosate-based herbicides as harmless if used according to best practices.

Paternalism of the "father provides" type became more prevalent under the Kirchner administrations through their emphasis on directing the profits of extractivism to government antipoverty interventions. During these administrations, the 30–35 percent federal tax on soy exports funded a series of social welfare programs, such as Plan de Jefes y Jefas de Hogar (Plan for Male and Female-Headed Households), Plan Familias (Families Plan), and Asignación Universal por Hijo (Universal Child Allowance). While no one doubts the importance of these programs in a context of high poverty and unemployment, critics argue that they did nothing to promote paid employment. Instead, they served to reinforce women's traditional gender roles as housewives and mothers (Lopreite, 2015). In general, cash transfer programs, compared with social programs focusing on income and job creation, reinforce citizens' dependency on the state. Paternalism is at the core of the collective memory of the Peronista-style politics that were revived under the Kirchners (see Auyero, 1999). Redistribution legitimates the gendered structure of soybean extractivism while increasing dependency on the state, which, in turn, fosters acquiescence and discourages mobilization.

Conclusion

Gender is a key structuring force of environmental injustice and its resistances in soybean-based resource extractivism in Argentina. In this chapter I have explored certain institutional, individual, and interactional social processes in order to conceptualize and analyze the gendered (and classed) nature of the political economy and forms of resistance to it.

The male-led and male-dominated institutions that control natural resources and technological innovation produce and reproduce bio-hegemonic masculinity. Political and economic elites have garnered public consent for soybean extractivism based on a rational-technical mentality of domination and control over women and nature. While touted as promising modernization and development, genetically modified crops (and, one could argue, technological innovation to facilitate extractivism in general) actually become a tool of power that promotes acquiescence and consent in the face of environmental injustice by subordinating and exploiting feminized (and racialized) subjects and nature.

Poor and working-class women, traditionally excluded from the political realm, have taken center stage to challenge bio-hegemonic masculinity. Women activists in Ituzaingó and Malvinas Argentinas have politicized motherhood, challenging the traditional divisions between public and private spheres. By organizing to demand an ethics of care for family, community, and the environment, women activists challenge the capitalist political economy and patriarchy.

Deploying motherhood traps women activists in a contradiction, however. They challenge bio-hegemonic masculinity by performing emphasized femininity —recreating hierarchical gender relations. Political and economic elites respond with traditional gendered insults and practices to silence and discipline them. There is an inherently gendered dimension to political-economic relations, but because of its hierarchical nature it constrains even as it drives resistance.

In the twenty-five years since genetically modified seeds were first adopted in Argentina, the soy model has created economic growth but also extensive social and ecological harm. The costs and benefits of the model have been very unequally distributed, increasing profits for elites by pushing the externalized costs of production downstream and downwind into poor and working-class communities and over the lives and territories of indigenous peoples. Gendered, classed, and racial analyses of the political economy and its resistance are urgently needed. Only by understanding the multiple axes of domination and inequality at play in resource extractivism can we identify opportunities to rethink and enact socio-environmental relations that prioritize care over profits, life over a political economy of destruction.

Notes

1. This chapter is a revised version of an article that appeared in *Latin American Perspectives* in 2019 (46 [2]: 199–216).

2. My analysis focuses on gender and, at times, the way it intersects with class to create injustice and mobilization. Because there is no substantial indigenous-peasant population in the region of study, the Pampas, I have not looked at the nuances of Argentines' race/ethnic hierarchies in depth. For information on the way indigenous-peasant people resist and accommodate to genetically modified soybean production in northern Argentina, see Lapegna (2016).

3. The Pampas, where more than 80 percent of Argentina's soybeans are grown, has historically been Argentina's agro-export region. It encompasses the provinces of Buenos Aires, La Pampa, Córdoba, Santa Fe, and Entre Ríos. Interviews took place in 2011–2012 and 2015. I conducted forty-five interviews with rural workers, small, medium-sized, and large soy producers, rural contractors, agribusinesses employees and CEOs, members of the Grupo de Madres de Barrio Ituzaingó Anexo and Asamblea Malvinas Lucha por la Vida, researchers of the Consejo Nacional de Investigaciones Científicas y Técnicas, and rural inhabitants who do not profit directly from soy production. Interviews quoted with members of the two women's organizations took place in August 2015.

4. The presidency, the vice presidency, the governorships of provinces in the Pampas region, the ministers of agro-industry (until 2009 of agriculture) and the economy, and, in 2016, the leaders of the agencies responsible for regulating biotechnology, the Servicio Nacional de Sanidad y Calidad Agroalimentaria, the Instituto Nacional de Tecnología Agropecuaria, and the Comisión Nacional Asesora de Biotecnología Agropecuaria.

5. The top seventeen agribusinesses are from Regunaga (2010). Executives' names are from Dow Jones Factiva (accessed July 19–20, 2016).

6. Los Grobo is a good example of the transition of a European immigrant family farm to a nonfamily agribusiness trading in the global financial market (see Leguizamón, 2016b).

7. A feminine ethics of care emphasizes context, unequal power relations, and affect. Recent scholarship calls for applying this ethics of care to the appraisal and regulation of agricultural biotechnology (see Preston and Wickson, 2016).

8. On the nineteenth of every month, the Mothers of Ituzaingó, their allies, and their sick children and family members march in Córdoba's courthouse square with their mouths covered by surgical masks, evoking the Mothers of the Plaza de Mayo with their headscarves.

References

Anria, Santiago, and Gabriel Vommaro
2020 "En Argentina, un 'giro a la derecha' que no fue y el improbable regreso del Peronismo de centro-izquierda." *Más Poder Local* 40: 6–10.

Arancibia, Florencia
2013 "Challenging the bioeconomy: the dynamics of collective action in Argentina." *Technology in Society* 35 (2): 79–92.

Aranda, Darío
2015 *Tierra arrasada: Petróleo, soja, pasteras y megaminería*. Buenos Aires: Editorial Sudamericana.

Auyero, Javier
1999 "Re-membering Peronism: an ethnographic account of the relational character of political memory." *Qualitative Sociology* 22: 331–351.

Barri, Fernando, and Juan Wahren
2013 "El modelo del 'agronegocio' en la Argentina: el paradigma cientifista-tecnológico," pp. 73–96 in Norma Giarracca and Miguel Teubal (eds.), *Actividades*

extractivas en expansión: ¿Reprimarización de la economía argentina? Buenos Aires: Antropofagia.

Bell, Shannon

2013 *Our Roots Run Deep as Ironweed: Appalachian Women and the Fight for Environmental Justice.* Urbana: University of Illinois Press.

Bell, Shannon, and Yvonne Braun

2010 "Coal, identity, and the gendering of environmental justice activism in central Appalachia." *Gender and Society* 24: 794–813.

Benbrook, Charles

2016 "Trends in glyphosate herbicide use in the United States and globally." *Environmental Sciences Europe* 28 (3). DOI: 10.1186/s12302-016-0070-0.

Binimelis, R., W. Pengue, and I. Monterroso

2009 "'Transgenic treadmill': responses to the emergence and spread of glyphosate-resistant Johnsongrass in Argentina." *Geoforum* 40: 623–633.

Cáceres, Daniel

2015 "Accumulation by dispossession and socio-environmental conflicts caused by the expansion of agribusiness in Argentina." *Journal of Agrarian Change* 15 (1): 116–147.

Carrizo, Cecilia, and Mauricio Berger

2009 *Estado incivil y ciudadanos sin estado: Paradojas del ejercicio de derechos en cuestiones ambientales.* Unquillo, Córdoba: Narvaja Editor.

Catacora-Vargas, G., P. Galeano, S. Agapito-Tenfen, D. Aranda, T. Palau, and R. Nodari

2012 *Soybean Production in the Southern Cone of the Americas: Update on Land and Pesticide Use.* Cochabamba, Bolivia: Virmegraf.

Collins, Patricia Hill

1990 *Black Feminist Thought: Knowledge, Consciousness, and the Politics of Empowerment.* New York: Routledge.

Connell, R. W., and James Messerschmidt

2005 "Hegemonic masculinity: rethinking the concept." *Gender and Society* 19: 829–859.

de la Cadena, Marisol

2010 "Indigenous cosmopolitics in the Andes: conceptual reflections beyond 'politics.'" *Cultural Anthropology* 25: 334–370.

Fabricant, Nicole, and Bret Gustafson

2014 "Moving beyond the extractivism debate, imagining new social economies." *NACLA Report on the Americas* 47 (4): 40–45.

Ferro, Silvia

2013 *Género y propiedad rural: República Argentina.* 2d edition. Buenos Aires: MAGyP.

Giarracca, Norma, and Miguel Teubal (eds.)

2013 *Actividades extractivas en expansión: ¿Reprimarización de la economía argentina?* Buenos Aires: Antropofagia.

Gould, Kenneth A., David N. Pellow, and Allan Schnaiberg

2008 *The Treadmill of Production: Injustice and Unsustainability in the Global Economy.* Boulder: Paradigm.

Gramsci, Antonio
1972 *Selections from the Prison Notebooks.* New York: International.
Gras, Carla, and Valeria Hernández
2014 "Agribusiness and large-scale farming: capitalist globalisation in Argentine agriculture." *Canadian Journal of Development Studies* 35: 339–357.
2016 "Hegemony, technological innovation, and corporate identities: 50 years of agricultural revolutions in Argentina." *Journal of Agrarian Change* 16: 675–683.
GRR (Grupo de Reflexión Rural)
2006 "Pueblos fumigados: informe sobre la problemática del uso de plaguicidas en las principales provincias sojeras de la Argentina." http://www.grupodereflexionrural.com/trabajos/Plaguicidas%20en%20la%20Argentina.pdf.
Gudynas, Eduardo
2009 "Diez tesis urgentes sobre el nuevo extractivismo," pp. 187–225 in Jürgen Schuldt (ed.), *Extractivismo, política y sociedad.* Quito: Centro Andino de Acción Popular.
Harding, Sandra
2006 *Science and Social Inequality: Feminist and Postcolonial Issues.* Urbana: University of Illinois Press.
Harrison, Jill
2011 *Pesticide Drift and the Pursuit of Environmental Justice.* Cambridge: MIT Press.
Infocampo
2017 "El consumo de agroquímicos y fertilizantes creció 47,1% en 2016." January 13. http://www.infocampo.com.ar/el-consumo-de-agroquimicos-y-fertilizantes-crecio-471-en-2016/.
Isidro, María Eugenia, and Nicolás Forlani
2019 "Derecha y agronegocio en Argentina y Brasil: cambios y continuidades." *Universitas* 31:59–77.
Jenkins, Katy
2015 "Unearthing women's anti-mining activism in the Andes: Pachamama and the 'mad old women.'" *Antipode* 47: 442–460.
Kimmel, Michael
2013 *The Gendered Society.* New York: Oxford University Press.
Krauss, Celene
1993 "Women and toxic waste protests: race, class and gender as resources of resistance." *Qualitative Sociology* 16 (3): 247–262.
Lapegna, Pablo
2016 *Soybeans and Power: Genetically Modified Crops, Environmental Politics, and Social Movements in Argentina.* New York: Oxford University Press.
Leguizamón, Amalia
2014 "Modifying Argentina: GM soy and socio-environmental change." *Geoforum* 53: 149–160.
2016a "Environmental injustice in Argentina: struggles against genetically modified soy." *Journal of Agrarian Change* 16: 684–692.
2016b "Disappearing nature? Agribusiness, biotechnology, and distance in Argentine soybean production." *Journal of Peasant Studies* 43: 313–330.

2020 *Seeds of Power: Environmental Injustice and Genetically Modified Soybeans in Argentina.* Durham, NC: Duke University Press.
Lopreite, Debora
2015 "Gender policies in Argentina after neoliberalism: opportunities and obstacles for women's rights." *Latin American Perspectives* 42 (1): 64–73.
Lugones, María
2010 "Toward a decolonial feminism." *Hypatia* 25: 742–759.
Martínez Alier, Joan
2014 "The environmentalism of the poor." *Geoforum* 54: 239–241.
Mason-Deese, Liz
2016 "Unemployed workers′ movements and the territory of social reproduction." *Journal of Resistance Studies* 2 (2): 65–99.
Motta, Sara C.
2013 "'We are the ones we have been waiting for': the feminization of resistance in Venezuela." *Latin American Perspectives* 40 (4): 35–54.
Motta, Sara C., and Tiina Seppälä
2016 "Feminized resistances." *Journal of Resistance Studies* 2 (2): 5–32.
Newell, Peter
2009 "Bio-hegemony: the political economy of agricultural biotechnology in Argentina." *Journal of Latin American Studies* 41: 27–57.
Oliveira, Gustavo, and Susanna Hecht
2016 "Sacred groves, sacrifice zones and soy production: globalization, intensification and neo-nature in South America." *Journal of Peasant Studies* 43 (2): 251–285.
Pellow, David
2018 *What is Critical Environmental Justice?* Cambridge: Polity Press.
Preston, Christopher, and Fern Wickson
2016 "Broadening the lens for the governance of emerging technologies: care ethics and agricultural biotechnology." *Technology in Society* 45: 48–57.
Raucheker, Markus, and Jennifer Chan (eds.)
2016 *Sustentabilidad desde abajo: Luchas desde el género y la etnicidad.* Buenos Aires: CLACSO.
REDUAS (Red Universitaria de Ambiente y Salud)
2010 *Informe Primer Encuentro Nacional de Médicos de Pueblos Fumigados.* http://www.reduas.com.ar/informe-encuentro-medicos-pueblos-fumigados/.
2017 "Agronegocio, entre Barrio Ituzaingó y Barrio San Antonio." September 9. http://reduas.com.ar/agronegocio-entre-bo-ituzaingo-y-bo-san-antonio/.
Regunaga, Marcelo
2010 *Implications of the Organization of the Commodity Production and Processing Industry: The Soybean Chain in Argentina.* Washington, DC: World Bank, Latin America and the Caribbean Region.
Risman, Barbara
2004 "Gender as a social structure theory wrestling with activism." *Gender and Society* 18: 429–450.
Rudel, Thomas K., J. Timmons Roberts, and JoAnn Carmin
2011 "Political economy of the environment." *Annual Review of Sociology* 37: 221–238.

Ruderman, L., B. Cabrera Fasolis, G. Dozzo, C. Nota, and M. Avila Vazquez
2013 "Análisis de la salud colectiva ambiental de Malvinas Argentinas-Córdoba." *REDUAS*. http://www.reduas.com.ar/wp-content/uploads/downloads/2013/02/Informe-Malvinas-corregido1.pdf.
Schippers, Mimi
2007 "Recovering the feminine other: masculinity, femininity, and gender hegemony." *Theory and Society* 36 (1): 85–102.
Schnaiberg, Allan, and Kenneth Gould
1994 *Environment and Society: The Enduring Conflict*. New York: St. Martin's Press.
Schnurr, Matthew
2017 "Can genetically modified crops help the poor? Incomplete answers to a flawed question." *Canadian Journal of Development Studies* 38 (1): 125–128.
Schurman, Rachel
2017 "Building an alliance for biotechnology in Africa." *Journal of Agrarian Change* 17: 441–458.
Shiva, Vandana
1991 *The Violence of the Green Revolution: Third World Agriculture, Ecology, and Politics*. London: Zed Books.
Sitrin, Marina
2015 "If we can stop Monsanto, we can change the world." March 1. https://www.telesurtv.net.
Stølen, Kristi
2004 *La decencia de la desigualdad: Género y poder en el campo argentino*. Buenos Aires: Antropofagia.
2015 "Agricultural change in Argentina: impacts of the gene modified soybean revolution," pp. 149–161 in Arve Hansen and Ulrikke Wethal (eds.), *Emerging Economies and Challenges to Sustainability*. New York: Routledge.
Thwaites Rey, Mabel, and Jorge Orovitz Sanmartino
2020 "Kirchnerism in Latin America's anti-neoliberal cycle," pp. 137–158 in Steve Ellner (ed.), *Latin America's Pink Tide: Breakthroughs and Shortcomings*. Lanham: Rowman and Littlefield.
Toledo, Víctor, David Garrido, and Narciso Barrera-Basols
2015 "The struggle for life: socio-environmental conflicts in Mexico." *Latin American Perspectives* 42 (5): 133–147.
Torrado, Marla
2016 "Madres en contra de la soja: planeamiento, salud y resistencia en Córdoba, Argentina," pp. 169–190 in Markus Rauchecker and Jennifer Chan (eds.), *Sustentabilidad desde abajo: Luchas desde el género y la etnicidad*. Buenos Aires: CLACSO.
Trigo, Eduardo
2011 *Fifteen Years of Genetically Modified Crops in Argentine Agriculture*. Buenos Aires: ArgenBio.
Verbitsky, Horacio
2009 "Verano del '96." *Página/12*. April 26.

III

CONSERVATIVE AND RIGHT-WING GOVERNMENTS

THE RISE OF RIGHT-WING GOVERNMENTS in Latin America heightened the contrast between Pink Tide and other presidents on issues related to extractivism. Following the presidential election of Mauricio Macri in Argentina in 2015, presidents who were generally labeled rightist reached power in Chile, Colombia, Brazil, Bolivia, Honduras, and Uruguay. While the Pink Tide's embrace of resource nationalism was from the beginning a distinguishing feature, the contrast with right-wing governments was also pronounced on the issues of violation of indigenous rights, environmental destruction, repression of protest movements, and dependence on extractivism. Chapters throughout this book point to grave shortcomings of Pink Tide governments on each of these issues, but contrasts need to be highlighted.

Anthony Bebbington, Benjamin Fash, and John Rogan point to a number of factors to explain different outcomes of the efforts to limit mining in order to protect watersheds in El Salvador and Honduras. One variable was the degree of autonomy enjoyed by state officials, which depended on "the existence of Weberian work cultures within the bureaucracy." Pressure from social movements and the Church hierarchy, including a leading member of the Salvadoran branch of Opus Dei, also favored the implementation of stringent measures in the mining sector. In addition, the Salvadoran Pink Tide governments of the Farabundo Martí National Liberation Front were subject to pressure from social movements linked to its political base to honor its campaign commitment to ban mining. Finally, there was widespread acceptance even among the elite of the narrative that "water is such a critical and vulnerable resource for El Salvador that it should be controlled by the public for the public." The authors of the chapter call this conviction an expression of resource nationalism "but around water rather than mining."

In Honduras, even though there was a legacy of social resistance to the devastating effects of mining activity, extractivism was more closely tied to the accumulation strategies of the nation's political and economic elite. Bebbington and colleagues document the vacillations and ambivalence with regard to mining concerns of the Pink Tide governments in El Salvador and that of Manuel Zelaya in Honduras. At the same time, however, they contrast the positive aspects of those governments with the retreats of conservative governments, particularly the repressive one of Juan Orlando Hernández (who has been tied to drug cartels), after Zelaya's overthrow,

Zaraí Toledo Orozco focuses on a topic largely ignored by extractivism writers: the state policy toward the activity of artisanal gold miners under conservative and right-wing governments in Peru and Colombia and the progressive one of Evo Morales in Bolivia. She shows that the governments of Peru and Colombia pursued a strategy of strict regulation of small-scale mining in order to convince multinational investors of the "high levels of social control" and the "stable and investment-attractive" economies that existed in their countries. Both governments, however, came up against a context adverse to the achievement of these goals. Neoliberal reforms had weakened the state's institutional ability to assert this type of control, and in addition the strategy came into direct contradiction with the absence of the state in rural and peripheral areas. By contrast, the Morales government did not prioritize multinational investment, since the nation's constitution "recognized different forms of production" including "mining at different scales." Government strategy with regard to noncorporate mining "combined cooperation and negotiations." The most important difference among the three countries, according to Toledo Orozco, is that the Bolivian communities surrounding mining camps were less exposed to repression and nonstate violence than those of Peru and Colombia.

The chapter by Castriela Hernández Reyes contributes to our understanding of how ethnic-based resistance to extractivist projects has clashed with paradigms created by elites, especially in the case of conservative and right-wing governments. She points to the inability of Western feminism to go beyond the issue of gender discrimination by incorporating race and class into its analysis. As a corrective, she advocates for a "black/decolonial feminist theory and praxis" whose point of departure is the intersectionality of race, class, and gender. In the empirical part of the chapter, Hernández Reyes describes the way Afro-Colombian women from a gold mining community used historical symbols related to artisanal mining in their protests against the encroachment of mining corporations supported by the government. One of the biggest breakthroughs for the struggles she discusses was a 1993 law, which grew out of the 1991 Constitution, that promoted the creation of community councils in Afro-Colombian areas and required prior consultation with local communities for projects. She notes, however, that the law proved ineffective in preventing the subsequent "influx of foreign companies and the militarization of the social life of black and indigenous communities."

9

Mining Governance in El Salvador and Honduras

Lessons from Contrasting Approaches to Extractivism

Anthony Bebbington, Benjamin Fash, and John Rogan

On March 29, 2017, El Salvador passed a national law banning metal mining. Activists and nongovernmental organizations (NGOs) celebrated this as a historic, world's-first piece of legislation and the culmination of a long process of resistance and mobilization. Meanwhile, across the border in Honduras, metal-mining concessions affected large parts of the country, including watersheds that drain into El Salvador. The comparison between these two countries sheds light on the factors that made the Salvadoran legislation possible. While some factors are related to sustained social mobilization around mining, others pertain to elite ambivalence, changes in pacts among national elites, maneuvering by government technocrats, and positions assumed by the Catholic Church. These factors raise the questions how likely such changes might be in Honduras, how resilient the law is in El Salvador, and what political bases might allow for a more progressive regulation of resource extraction. At the same time, the contrast between the two countries contributes to our understanding of extractivism and resource nationalism in Latin America.

Political ecologies of large-scale extractivism have tended to fall into two broad categories. The first has primarily focused on the political economy of extraction. Whether informed by O'Connor's (1991) discussion of the contradictions between capitalism and nature, by ecological economic interpretations of the extractive economy (Martinez-Alier, 2002), or by political economy readings of an "extractive imperative" that pulls countries inexorably toward a deepening of resource extraction (Arsel et al., 2016), these studies approach resource extraction at a macroeconomic and aggregate scale and tend to emphasize the economic drivers of policy making. Discussions of the relationship between extractivism and resource nationalism also fall within this category. They reflect the role of resource extraction in national development strategies and the risk that the financing of social policy will become economically and politically dependent on continued expansion of the extractive frontier in ways that are neither environmentally nor socioeconomically sustainable (Gudynas, 2009; Svampa, 2019; Acosta, 2011).

Another body of work has focused on socio-environmental conflicts linked to resource extraction. Some studies emphasize how social movements emerge and contest particular projects; others document the social and ecological impacts of extraction on livelihoods and environments and interpret emergent contentious politics as responses to such impacts, and still others explore the everyday experience of the extractive economy as a driver of uncertainty, loss, opportunity, and dispossession (de Echave et al., 2008; Bebbington and Bury, 2013). Between these two foci (one basically macro, the other basically micro), political ecology studies have said less about the detailed politics of policy making around resource extraction (other than the politics that derive from mobilization and contention). Also, studies in these traditions tend to ascribe positions and interests to elites and to explore only in limited ways the extent to which actors within the state maneuver to take advantage of opportunities for policy innovation that might present themselves within government.

Rather than opt for one or another of these approaches, we develop a framework and an empirical analysis that draw on both of them. For this, we merge diverse literatures and lines of thinking to develop a conceptual framework which we use to describe and interpret how mining has been contested, legislated, and halted in El Salvador, and how mining has been contested, regulated, and ultimately implemented in Honduras. Methodologically the chapter draws on two research experiences not initially conceived as a comparative exercise. In El Salvador, work revolved around a series of collaborations between Bebbington, the Ministry of Environment, and the Ministry of Economy regarding stakeholder attitudes to environmental governance, the conduct of a strategic environmental assessment of the mining sector, and legislative proposals derived from that assessment. In Honduras, research involved a collaboration between Fash and Rogan, the National Autonomous University of Honduras (UNAH), Oxfam America, and Oxfam in Honduras to document the emergent geography of mining concessions in the country. The study also benefits from the fact that Fash grew up in and is a member of a Honduran community affected by mineral concessions (Copán Ruinas) and is active in community-based organizing around extractivism. These different origins for our work in the two countries make for synergies in the analysis and influence our interpretations. Insofar as we worked from positions in which individuals and organizations were trying to foster change in the face of significant structural obstacles, our accounts are inescapably tinged with a belief in agency and the capacity to promote change from within a policy-making process. Consequently, our framework places special emphasis on the internal dynamics of political settlements and boundary-spanning work, is skeptical of structural interpretations of policy and movement processes, and reflects our conviction regarding the need to recognize both the commitments and the dignity of the people involved (such as members of the state bureaucracy) and their contradictory motivations and failings.[1]

Political Settlements, Social Conflict, and the Political Ecology of Mining Policy

Capitalist Dynamics and the Subsoil

Any effort to theorize the drivers of mining policy must address the relationship between subsoil resources and the dynamics of accumulation. This begins by understanding the environment as simultaneously a means of accumulation of capital and a means for the reproduction of the conditions that make such accumulation possible. The environment's joint function applies to units of production at all scales. At the level of a rural household, land and water are central to the possibility of petty accumulation, but the continued existence of fertile land and clean, available water resources is also essential for the reproduction of the rural household as a social unit. In the mineral economy, subsoil resources and water are the primary means of accumulation; absent either of the two, no amount of finance or technology can deliver accumulation. At the same time, the reproduction of the mineral economy requires the continued reproduction of water resources. These different forms of enterprise coexist in rural areas. Thus, the water resources needed by mining are also central to accumulation and reproduction in other rural enterprises, both household and large-scale. Consequently, the enterprises need a guarantee that these resources will be reproduced over time.

Seen through this political economy lens, environmental policies are generally understood as reflections of the dual imperative to guarantee accumulation and reproduce the environmental conditions it requires. When these imperatives collide, the tendency has been to assume that policy and corporate practice will privilege accumulation (Ospina et al., 2015). The implication is that socio-environmental policy that limits mining's access to natural resources will not prosper unless mining is relatively unimportant to national models of accumulation. Conversely, policy proposals that do not affect access to resources but focus on "better" environmental management (e.g., basic environmental monitoring, technological modernization, etc.) might be expected to fare better because they do not threaten the relations of resource access (Ospina et al., 2015). Political economy readings are less useful, however, in explaining the relative influence on policy of distinct strategies of accumulation (e.g., mining or agriculture) or the details of the policy that is ultimately approved and implemented. To conceptualize the processes driving these dimensions of policy requires frameworks that delve into the specifics of the policy-making process.

Political Settlements and Subsoil Governance

The concept of political settlement "refers to the balance or distribution of power between contending social groups and social classes, on which any state is based" (di John and Putzel, 2009: 4). The concept draws attention to the extent to which governing relations are negotiated among economic and political elites. Such negotiations will tend to produce distributions of economic and political opportunity that reflect the bargaining power of these different elites (Khan, 2010). A settlement is not a broad-based consensus among social actors but an implicit or explicit agreement among actors who would otherwise have sufficient power to destabilize any settlement that excluded them. Elites who are party to the settlement manage relationships with excluded factions in such a way that these factions do not threaten it. Such relationships can be managed through the exercise of force, through discourses, through clientelism, or through modes of partial incorporation (Hickey et al., 2015).

Settlements are relatively stable arrangements. This reflects the slow-to-change nature of power structures and hegemonic ideas. Settlements do, however, change over time. Such change may be due to the arrival or increasing leverage of transnational actors with the capacity and legitimacy to affect arrangements or the emergence of actors with the capacity to challenge the existing balance of power. This capacity may be due to the value of the income streams they control, their ability to mobilize citizens, their proclivity to violence, or their ability to reframe debates and challenge ideas that have historically legitimated distributions of opportunity and power. In this sense, conflict can be a mechanism of change in the national settlement.

The value of political settlements frameworks is that they draw attention to the importance of negotiation and contention among elites as well as between elites and excluded groups in driving the policy, legislation, and norms that govern the distribution of benefits and opportunities in society. Seen through such a lens, mining policies would be expected to change when relationships of power among elites shift; when powerful elites come to the view that policy change may be in their interest; when dominant ideas in society regarding legitimate forms of development shift in ways that challenge existing settlements; when excluded actors become so strong that they are able to force themselves into the settlement, renegotiate its terms, and in the process become a new political elite; or when the leverage and/or positions assumed by critical transnational actors change (Bebbington et al., 2018). Such frameworks explain how general policies are reached but say less about their specifics: the following section discusses concepts that may help explain such details of policy change.

Agency and Change in Mining Governance

Beyond the causal influences of the dynamics of accumulation and the negotiation of political settlements, other literature suggests that forms of agency within bureaucracies have direct influence on policy design and implementation. Evans (1995) argues that key to understanding this agency is the extent to which bureaucrats and technocrats within the state apparatus are simultaneously (1) embedded in the sector that they are responsible for governing so that they adequately understand its needs and capacities and (2) sufficiently autonomous that they avoid being captured by the interests that they are ostensibly governing. Embeddedness allows for learning rather than blueprint thinking, while autonomy allows for decisions that are developmental rather than clientelistic. While officials' degree of autonomy has much to do with the broader political settlement, it also depends on the existence of Weberian work cultures within the bureaucracy that guard against capture. Embeddedness has much to do with the initiative, competence, and prior social networks of public functionaries. Such functionaries, by being able to interpret, understand, and translate between government and the sector being governed, operate in much the same ways as "boundary agents" in the literature on innovation systems (Jasanoff, 2006; Bebbington and Bury, 2009). This literature suggests that much policy design and deliberation happens through these "boundary crossings" and reciprocally embedded relationships that allow for policy learning. The crossing of such boundaries and the embedding of public functionaries can also occur when officials are pulled toward actors with whom they have historically had less contact. One mechanism for this "pulling" is through social conflict and mobilization.

Guiding Postulates

This framework leads to the following postulates. First, mining policies are heavily conditioned by accumulation dynamics. Second, mining policies are significantly fashioned by the interests and legitimating ideas associated with the dominant political settlement, some of which are related to (though not wholly determined by) the model of accumulation. Third, conflicts over mining are more likely to influence the way particular projects are governed than whether mining companies will be granted access to subsoil and water resources in the first place. Fourth, the translation of conflict into specific, legislated proposals requires the existence of public-sector and legislative actors with the predisposition to understand these demands and the capacity to turn them into politically viable policy and laws. Finally, changes in mining policy that are secured through conflict, in particular those that influence patterns of access to resources, will be sustained over time only if this conflict is accompanied by a political settlement in which mining interests are not well represented either directly or indirectly by groups whose own interests revolve around a strong mining sector.

The framework and postulates also suggest ways for thinking about extractivism and resource nationalism. Extractivism is a specific mode of accumulation led by and benefiting certain elites whose influence within the political settlement depends considerably on the relative weight of extractivism within the broader, national pattern of accumulation, as well as on those elites' investment in other nonextractivist sectors of the economy. How far extractive activities are taxed in order to finance social policy (particularly relevant under the new-extractivist model [see Gudynas, 2009; Bebbington, 2009]) also depends on the broader settlement, as well as on dominant ideas about how society and economy should be organized. In turn, resource nationalism can be understood as the idea that natural resources are of such importance to the nation that they should be subject to some form of public control (be it through taxation, ownership, protection, or some other form). The weight of extractivism in driving policy thus depends, inter alia, on the power of extractivist interests relative to other interests. *How* extractivism affects policy also depends on which ideas (resource nationalist or more neoliberal) dominate national and public thinking regarding the role that different resources should play in national development. Which ideas become dominant depends on many factors, including the arguments put forward by social movements, the media, and public intellectuals. These dominant ideas influence the room for maneuver open to bureaucrats.

El Salvador: The Long Path toward Unprecedented Policy

Postconflict Processes and the Mineral Economy

In a context of acute inequalities in access to land, a civil war from 1980 to 1992 pitted elites and conservative interests against a broad-based Marxist guerrilla force grouped under the umbrella of the Frente Farabundo Martí para la Liberación Nacional (Farabundo Martí National Liberation Front—FMLN). Following the war, the peace accord process explicitly excluded any chance of revising the market-oriented, small-state model of the economy. A new mining code was passed in 1995–1996 to foster investment, and in 1999 a new law allowed investment disputes with the state to be heard at the International Centre for Settlement of Investment Disputes (ICSID), which was part of the World Bank Group (Spalding, 2013, 2018). This was followed by a revision of the mining code further facilitating investment and reducing royalties from 4 percent to 2 percent (part of a race-to-the-bottom with Guatemala and Honduras) (Dougherty, 2011). In 2005, El Salvador signed the Central American Free Trade Agreement. These reforms were led by a series of conservative, Alianza Republicana Nacionalista (ARENA)-controlled governments with the U.S. embassy playing a critical role (Bull et al., 2015) and sought to institutionalize an open and investment-friendly postconflict economic model (Spalding, 2013). Eight international mining companies had invested in El Salvador by 2006 (Spalding, 2013), and the state had issued twenty-nine exploration licenses by 2007 (Cartagena, 2009). This investment came from international junior companies; neither large transnational enterprises nor national elites were especially invested in the sector.

Changes in the Political Settlement

While El Salvador had some history of underground mining, the economic and social significance of mining was small in comparison with that of agriculture, remittances, or other sectors. New mining exploration activities gave way to mobilization and conflict (Cartagena, 2009; Spalding, 2018; Deonandan and Dougherty, 2016). Protest movements viewed mining investment as a threat to El Salvador's fragile water resources and led to the consolidation of civil society actors that played important roles in the 2017 ban on mining—in particular the National Roundtable against Metal Mining (the "Mesa") and Oxfam America's El Salvador office.[2] In many regards, this process helped build a "resource nationalist" argument but around water rather than mining—that water is such a critical and vulnerable resource for El Salvador that it should be controlled by the public for the public. This idea, already circulating in the country, gained greater traction because of the conflict. Ultimately, the combination of conflict and arguments around water drove national discussion of mining issues, pressuring the ARENA Ministry of the Environment to suspend in 2006 all mining-related environmental impact assessment processes and placing mining-related issues on the 2008–2009 presidential campaign agenda.

The election in 2009 of an FMLN government marked a palpable shift in the balance of power among national political elites and the incorporation of previously excluded groups into policy processes. These new political elites also engaged with longer-standing business elites, largely to ensure investment for tax revenue and employment. With few exceptions, these business elites showed little interest in supporting a mining boom in El Salvador.[3] At the same time, however, they viewed the Ministry of the Environment and Natural Resources as an obstacle to investment because of its increasingly demanding environmental licensing procedures. While not supportive of international mining investors, they did not favor legislation that, by banning mining outright, might call into question the security of contracts more generally.

Mining companies' leverage within El Salvador's political settlement was therefore limited, reflecting their modest size and weak links with national elites. That said, foreign embassies also sought to exercise some influence and reduce environmental policy obstacles to mining. The very first words of the Canadian ambassador to the newly selected FMLN environment minister in 2009 were a question about his position on mining. Leaked cables subsequently indicated that the U.S. embassy viewed this minister as being antimining. Moreover, when the mining companies Pacific Rim (later Oceana Gold) and Commerce Group opened formal cases against El Salvador at the ICSID, the litigation increased their potential leverage over the government (though it undoubtedly created less sympathy for them among national elites).[4]

Processes of Policy Articulation

The shift in the national political settlement in 2009, coupled with the marginal role of mining in accumulation strategies, created political space for public officials and activists to pursue a formal change in mining policy. The FMLN government inherited the ARENA ministry's suspension of environmental impact assessment processes, along with a campaign commitment by its president, Mauricio Funes, to ban mining. Civil society organizations linked to the political base of the FMLN used that same campaign commitment to pressure the government to pass a law prohibiting mining (Achtenberg, 2011; Broad and Cavanagh, 2011). The FMLN government was therefore doubly invested in the demands of the antimining movement: its base was demanding a ban, and it had to develop a policy response to the ARENA moratorium. At the same time, however, it had to seek a response that would not weaken the government's case in the ICSID disputes with Pacific Rim and Commerce Group or alienate national economic elites (Bebbington et al., 2015; Spalding, 2018). Through this process the ministry sought to lay the technical and political basis for more stringent regulation of metal mining, deciding that its most important instrument would be the conduct of a strategic environmental assessment of the mining sector. This assessment was subcontracted to a Spanish company and overseen by an external committee of specialists (chaired by Bebbington).

The assessment involved vigorous debate on quality and rigor in the data collection process and on how to interpret the information generated. There was also external criticism from the Mesa and others who considered the process insufficiently consultative or participatory. Ultimately, the assessment concluded that while mining *could* technically play a part in El Salvador's economy, the parlous state of national water resources coupled with deficient legislation and acute capacity constraints in the government meant that the conditions for adequate regulation of mining did not exist.

The ministry used the assessment findings to develop a legislative proposal to suspend all administrative processes for mining indefinitely until adequate regulatory capacity was in place. Both the secretary of economic affairs and the lawyers representing El Salvador at the ICSID insisted that any proposal to ban mining outright, even if technically justified, would undermine the country's case. Conversely, the Mesa lobbied against the proposal and presented its own draft law banning mining. Ultimately, neither proposal progressed beyond the committee stage in the Legislative Assembly. However, the strategic environmental assessment and the proposed law did help further the argument that the acute vulnerability of El Salvador's water resources would make any encouragement of mining investment extremely ill-advised. This line of reasoning was also taken up as part of El Salvador's defense in the ICSID and was closely aligned with the one developed by the Mesa in the public sphere.

The Mesa Process

The Mesa had been building an argument against mining for some time, supported by, among others, Oxfam America, which helped run workshops on the risks of mining and developed links with other movements across the region. In some sense, the Mesa's process was the inverse of the strategic environmental assessment's in that the Mesa was embedded in communities, the Church, and the FMLN but relatively distant from government bureaucracy. Its process (just like the government's) did not create many opportunities for joint learning between public officials and activists.

After the two legal proposals sat languishing in the Legislative Assembly, in mid-2015 Mesa members reinitiated efforts to propose a law banning mining with the new FMLN government elected in 2014. The same Oxfam America program officer who had previously supported the Mesa, now working from the Human Rights Institute of the Jesuit Universidad Centroamericana, played an important role in coordinating the drafting of this proposal. In elaborating the law, the Mesa consulted widely, including with the president's office and former members of the strategic environmental assessment oversight committee. When in October 2016 the ICSID ruled in favor of the government in its dispute with Pacific Rim, room for maneuver for this policy initiative seemed to grow. Pushing it over the finishing line, however, ended up depending on the Catholic Church.

The Church and the Mining Ban

As Nadelman (2015) shows,[5] the Catholic authorities in El Salvador had been building technical, social, and theological arguments against mining since the early 2000s. Prior to the mid-2000s these were crafted by individual clerics and Church-related NGOs. In 2006 the bishop of Chalatenango (an area of mining conflict) pointed to the adverse impacts of mining on human dignity (Nadelman, 2015). Subsequently, the Salvadoran Bishops' Conference issued statements against mining, and from 2007 onwards the conservative (Opus Dei) archbishop of San Salvador, Fernando Sáenz Lacalle, took a public stance against mining. Trained as a chemical engineer, he took issue with industry claims about the possibility of clean mining in El Salvador and again raised the specter of risks to water resources. He was succeeded by another conservative, Archbishop José Luis Escobar Alas, who took a similar position and called on the government to halt mining (Nadelman, 2015).

The Catholic Church thus played a significant role and by March 2017 was organizing signature collection after Mass to petition the government for a mining ban. The group drafting the proposal for a ban was in conversation with Church leaders, who publicly took its antimining petition to the Assembly (Spalding, 2018). Shortly thereafter the Assembly approved a law prohibiting metal mining. Both FMLN and ARENA legislators voted in favor of the ban. Three of the six *consideranda* in the proposed law involved environmental concerns, one of them referring explicitly to the results of the ministry's environmental assessment.[6] According to one commentator close to both the ministry and the upper echelons of the Church, the ban demonstrated the enormous weight that the Church still has in the country. Its opposition to mining put everyone in a corner: the party members in the government, who believed that mining could play a role, and the promarket politicians, who presumably concluded that the political cost of coming out against the law would be too great—not least because the pope had also expressed concern about environmental devastation in his encyclical *Laudato Si* (Nadelman, 2015). Indeed, opposition to the Church's proposal could have been interpreted as opposition to the murdered archbishop, Óscar Romero, and by implication to Pope Francis, who beatified Romero in 2015 and declared him a saint in 2018. The political fallout of such a posture would have been severe.

A Still Unimplemented Law

By the time it was voted out of government in 2019, the FMLN administration had still not implemented the provisions of the mining ban. The Mesa sought to pressure the new government to do so: "We ask President Nayib Bukele to order the implementation of the law that prohibits metal mining. It is of the outmost importance to carry out environmental remediation processes and ensure the appropriate technical closures of mines" (*La Página*, 2019). The Mesa made particular reference to the need to implement environmental measures. The position of the new government on mining at the time of this writing in mid-2020 is not clear. That said, while the balance of power among elites has shifted, the arguments regarding the need for the state to protect water resources as a national and public priority possibly remain sufficiently strong and broad-based to limit the possibility of the government's stepping back from the law and pursuing an extractivist route toward financing government spending.

Honduras: A Short-Lived Victory in a Long-Term Cycle of Extractivism

Long Histories of Mining Interests

Honduras has a longer, more significant history of mining than El Salvador. Many of today's major cities were once mining towns where Spanish settlers oversaw operations, exploiting indigenous and black slaves. Mining has periodically waned—following independence in 1821, following World War I, and from 2004 to 2012, when antimining mobilizations culminated in a moratorium on new concessions. However, each bust has been followed by new mining policies (1876, 1998, and 2013), fostering new rounds of investment.

The 1876 mining law stimulated a push to reopen colonial mines and exploit capital from foreign (especially U.S.) and newly established Honduran banks. Mining companies were legally exempt from import and export duties, and minerals became the primary export for four decades (Euraque, 1996). The 1998 neoliberal reforms prompted a surge in Canadian investment, while after the 2013 reforms, investment also expanded from other countries. Throughout this history mining has also been an important accumulation strategy for national investors and politicians (a significant difference from the situation in El Salvador), placing mining interests squarely within the negotiation of political settlements and ideas about the economy. More recently, elite investments in energy projects have also become part of the equation.

Honduras also has a longer history of resistance to mining than El Salvador dating to sixteenth-century indigenous mobilizations (Barahona, 2009).

Oyuela (2003) argues that the 1960s saw a surge of Honduran environmentalism, with students from UNAH decrying contamination at El Mochito. This, coupled with nationwide union organizing, may help explain why the mining and hydrocarbons code of 1968 included the power to suspend mining activities through environmental impact assessments (IBP, 2007).

Neoliberalization

The Rafael Callejas administration began implementing structural adjustment in 1990 after a decade of militarized repression of social movements. In 1981 Miguel Facussé, owner of the Dinant Corporation, joined the Honduran military general and Callejas, among other military, business, media, and political elites, to form the far-right-wing Asociación para el Progreso de Honduras (APROH). The APROH advanced Facussé's vision of "sell[ing] the country to foreign investors," which the United States was quick to support (CEDOH, 2009). APROH, drug traffickers (Dudley, 2016), and unprecedented U.S. military aid helped the Honduran state oversee the assassination, disappearance, and torture of hundreds of activists from unions, campesino and environmental groups, and student and professional organizations (Alvarado, 1987; Philips, 2015).

Callejas initiated the wide-ranging privatization and deregulation of natural-resource governance, increasing social conflict around land, energy, and minerals.[7] The first mining reforms in 1991 focused on tax exemptions, while in 1995, the Carlos Reina administration nullified the requirement for environmental impact assessments during exploration. The mining sector then expanded, with the San Martín mine assigned to U.S.-based Glamis Gold in 1995. Congress debated a new mining law for several years and finally passed it weeks after Hurricane Mitch in 1998.

This 1998 law erased any distinction between exploration and exploitation, legalized open-pit cyanide mining and forced expropriation, reduced mining taxes, and established no limits on water use and no closure requirements. While some claim that it was a product of the Canadian mining lobby's holding hurricane relief hostage (Shipley, 2013; Escalera-Flexhaug, 2014), the law was also pushed—and taken advantage of—by national political and economic elites. It was passed under President Carlos Flores Facussé, nephew of Miguel Facussé. The latter's sons-in-law also benefited: one would later start Emco/Inversiones Pinares, the mining company behind the Guapinol project, which resulted in the fierce repression of environmentalists in 2019, and the other the Grupo Terra, one of the most influential energy and infrastructure investment groups in Central America. Beyond the Facussés, families behind the Honduran Banco Atlántida, Banco Ficohsa, and other financial institutions have also financed numerous mines and energy projects.

Countermovement

Conflicts at the San Martín and San Andrés gold mines sparked a movement linking mining communities and Church leaders, doctors, environmentalists, scientists, and NGOs. The movement secured a 2004 mining moratorium and a 2006 Supreme Court ruling that thirteen articles of the 1998 law violated the constitution and international agreements. The ruling was a product of networked mobilization, the dissemination of information around mining, water, and health, and relationship building with state actors in the judiciary and the bureaucracy.

Though there was ample reason to protest the 1998 law on paper, it was the vivid examples of lived hardship that fueled the movement. Only three years after Canadian Greenstone Resources Limited secured the San Andrés concession, community leaders reported respiratory diseases and skin infections, broken employment promises, expropriations, and scare tactics such as shutting off access to water (Marsh, 2001). Facing similar issues, communities around San Martín joined San Andrés activists in enlisting scientific studies on contamination (Moran, 2002) and convening a national meeting with members of fifteen communities surrounding eight mines. These actions generated international attention (Marsh, 2001). Meanwhile, research demonstrated that the El Mochito mine was discharging high levels of lead, copper, and cyanide, resulting in a lawsuit. In late 2002, the new Civic Alliance for Mining Law Reform established exchanges with organizations across Central America, including Caritas and the Research Center for Investment and Commerce in El Salvador (CIDSE, 2009).

The Church, with leaders in the liberation theology tradition, figured prominently in antimining struggles and related environmental movements. In 2004, the full Bishops' Conference of Honduras signed a "call to conscience" urging the president to abolish the mining law and lending the bishops' support to the second March for Life led by Father Tamayo of the Olancho Environmentalist Movement (Equipo Nizkor, 2004). Meanwhile, the Jesuit Father Ismael Moreno took the discursive battle further through Radio Progreso. Pressure from all these sources culminated in the de jure moratorium on mining. As the Salvadoran Church would later do, on July 26, 2004, alongside 150 representatives of communities and NGOs, Cardinal Óscar Rodriguez presented Congress with a proposal for mining law reform. In turn, President Ricardo Maduro suspended new concessions by executive decree (CIDSE, 2009). The October 2006 unanimous Supreme Court ruling that the 1998 law violated the "fundamental right to harmonic conviviality with the environment and to sustainable development" (Corte Suprema, 2006: 18–19) occurred during a brief period of stability and credibility of Honduran institutions. The networked movement that drove these breakthroughs is generally obscured in literature that states that the succeeding president, Manuel Zelaya, decreed the moratorium in the context of other progressive reforms (e.g., Shipley, 2013; Truth Commission, 2013; Philips, 2015).

In fact, the momentum did not culminate in a progressive law with staying power because both Congress and Zelaya showed a degree of support for mining and expressed ambivalence toward mining prohibitions: the political settlement had not shifted. In 2006, congressional leaders voiced intentions to advance progressive legislation, but their proposal included nothing on open-pit mining, cyanide, or the tax code (ACD, 2008). Though Zelaya ratified the moratorium in 2006, his administration wavered on policy, left existing concessions unaffected, and showed little follow-through from meetings with leftists regarding resources and territory (Anderson, 2012). His ideas regarding energy generation and off-shore drilling leaned toward resource nationalism, but this was not apparent in his approach to mining: in 2008, he removed his minister of environment, who had resisted extractivist expansion, and appointed Tomás Vaquero, who favored ties with the National Metal Mining Association (Truth Commission, 2013). Meanwhile, the Office for Mining Promotion remained open to new concessions and coordinated campaigns with mayors to pave the way for mining expansion (IBP, 2007).

While the movement had secured legislative gains and the support of some bureaucrats, the weight of extractivism in elite accumulation strategies, coupled with the influence of Canadian foreign policy, ultimately stalled more stringent regulation. In retrospect, some Civic Alliance leaders lamented having focused on reform through the state apparatus instead of through grassroots organizing (CIDSE, 2009).

A Settlement around Predatory Extractivism and the Weakening of Mobilization

The coup removing Zelaya in 2009 turned national policy from ambivalence to aggressive promotion of extractivism. Recentering neoliberal hegemony, the National Party has consolidated power on the right with support from drug traffickers and the U.S. defense budget. In this political settlement, mining has been reinvigorated with the passage of a new mining law, an executive decree creating mining reserves, and a broad suite of complementary extractivist initiatives. While the 2009 coup was driven by much more than just mining interests, these took full advantage of Zelaya's overthrow (Truth Commission, 2013). Amid the postcoup chaos, Congress and Roberto Micheletti's interim administration passed a new general water law. This enabled further privatization of water resources, which had begun with a 2007 renewable energy law. Since mines need constant supplies of electricity and water, their privatization has ensured uninterrupted mining operations at the same time that citizens regularly go without those resources.

In 2013 the Porfirio Lobo administration—with future president Juan Orlando Hernández as congressional president—passed a new mining law that closely resembled the unconstitutional 1998 law. The new law permits open-pit mining, imposes no closure requirements or limits to water use, and validates communities' rejections of projects for only three years. While it prohibits forced expropriation, its modest support for the practice of consultation is far from the principle of "free, prior, and informed consent" (Fash and Sellwood, 2017). Royalties remain low, and more than one-third of them go directly toward national security. In addition, the law paves the way for mining reserves that do not require consultation and whose financial, social, and environmental regulation is left unclear.

Hopes of progressive mining policy reform have retreated further since Hernández secured a second term following highly controversial elections in 2017. Though the Supreme Court ruled seven articles of the 2013 law unconstitutional in 2017, thus delaying the approval of new concessions, new reforms were approved in September 2019. The antimining movements have retreated so far from legislative battles that by March 2020 no critiques of the reforms had been voiced. The law fast-tracks exploration licenses, while the expansion of mining is also facilitated by severe repression by United States–backed militarization in the name of antinarcotics national security.[8] Hernández, who has been tied to drug cartels, has vastly expanded security forces and appointed military leaders to leadership positions normally held by civilians (Dudley, 2016).

Bureaucrats within the state apparatus have occasionally dissented—for example, releasing mining concession data to researchers and NGOs. Numerous groups have commissioned reports analyzing the sector, warning about the risks of mining and making the case for sweeping policy reforms. In efforts to promote transparency and debate, researchers from Clark University, Oxfam, FOSDEH, and UNAH collaborated on analysis and interactive maps that activists have used in various parts of the country (Fash et al., 2019).[9] However, the level of government bureaucratic support for such initiatives is not comparable to the situation in El Salvador since 2009.

At the same time, the constituent parts of the antimining movement have weakened. Since the coup, social movement actors who had worked together splintered over strategy, personal relationships, and electoral politics. While the San Martín mine closed, the communities surrounding the San Andrés and El Mochito mines have become divided and largely ineffective in mobilizing change. The Church has stepped away from the movement since releasing statements in favor of the coup, removing Father Tamayo, and being caught up in sexual abuse scandals with Cardinal Rodriguez at the center (Telegraph, 2013).

Honduran indigenous organizations have been strong on territorial issues but have had limited success swaying national policy. Along with mestizo environmentalist groups, they have stalled mining in important areas of the country through declarations of "mining-free" and "extractivism-free" municipalities. However, their national efforts are weakened by schisms dating to the 1990s between anticapitalist groups and those more aligned with neoliberal multiculturalism in the national indigenous confederations (Anderson, 2007, 2012; Hale, 2005). These schisms are reflected in the long-standing controversy surrounding bills that require free, prior, and informed consent for development projects on indigenous lands (Fash et al., 2019).

While Honduras preceded El Salvador in securing a mining moratorium, this was due to a strongly networked movement and a successful campaign, coupled with support from select judges and bureaucrats. It was *not* due to any significant shift in the national political settlement, a progressive government of the moment, or a change in national discourses on water security and development. This and the increased weight of mining in elite accumulation strategies rendered the moratorium vulnerable and help explain the failure to strengthen it through legislation. Since the 2009 coup, Honduras has shifted toward a predatory extractivism even cruder than that existing before the 2004 moratorium and more dangerous for activists, the assassination of Berta Cáceres being one of many killings of "environmental defenders" (Global Witness, 2016; Middledorp and Le Billon, 2019).

Conclusions: Political Ecologies of Mining Regulation

El Salvador's legislation banning mining was passed because many stars were aligned. Most important, mining is not an important part of the model of accumulation in El Salvador. Neither ARENA nor (even less so) the FMLN governments prioritized extractivism as a means of financing public-sector policy. Even though the ARENA governments offered initial investment opportunities, national economic elites were not especially convinced of the potential for mining in the country. Meanwhile national religious and many political elites were either opposed or skeptical. Transnational actors—mostly small companies—linked to mining were weak. The Canadian embassy, though it had expressed its support for mining to the minister of the environment, was less interested in El Salvador than it was in fostering an expanded mining sector in Honduras [Shipley, 2013]). Finally, over the years a combination of actors in the public, business, and civic sectors (on both the left and the right) had constructed a discourse around water that framed it as both precious and vulnerable in El Salvador, and some promoted the idea that water resources would be particularly threatened if mining investment were to occur. This discourse circulated widely and was formalized in various documents: it became a sort of "resource nationalism of water."

These alignments produced a political economy and political settlement environment that favored stringent regulation of mining and created a context in which social mobilization around such measures was more likely to be successful. Even so, mining regulation was far from guaranteed. Some senior officials in the first FMLN government worried about the signaling effect of a ban on mining, while the ICSID process also made a ban problematic. During the second FMLN government, some cabinet members suggested privately that mining might be an attractive option for a country with a profound public budget problem. In these contexts, three parallel but interacting processes unfolded to create the bases for the mining ban—one with roots in the Mesa and Oxfam America, one through the Ministry of the Environment, and one in the Church, drawing on its authority in a religiously conservative country (Nadelman, 2015). The culmination of these processes in the mining ban had much to do with the work of "boundary agents," actors who were able to foster communication and temporary alliances among state managers, bureaucrats, elected officials, and civil society actors and also able to convert a principled argument into the language of legislation.

Similar elements existed in Honduras. A strong movement around the adverse impacts of mining had helped pressure the government into passing the 2004 moratorium on mining. Indeed, the Honduran mining movement was historically stronger than in El Salvador. The Honduran Catholic Church also assumed a position on the social and environmental consequences of mining and lent its voice to the call for the 2004 moratorium. However, mining and closely linked energy projects weigh much more heavily in the accumulation strategies of Honduran elites (who have invested in both sectors, along with oil palm). Furthermore, the Canadian embassy has been consistent in its support for policy reforms that favor the expansion of mining. There is also a strong national discourse around the role of privately owned and operated mining in national development (an extractivist discourse but not a resource nationalist one). While there appeared to be a political opening for more stringent regulation of the sector during both the Maduro and Zelaya governments (and the moratorium was an indicator of this opening), efforts to pass new legislation ultimately unraveled, apparently because of the continuing strength of national elites unwilling to see their interests compromised, together with Zelaya's failure to act decisively. Notwithstanding such electoral changes, the underlying political settlement simply left too little space for reform, at the same time that national extractivist discourses on development increasingly favored mining. The sorts of "boundary agents" that were able to exploit political space in El Salvador appear to have been less prominent in Honduras. Movement actors and the Church have become substantially weaker, caught up in their own internal crises and political differences. Finally, militarization has enabled mining companies to operate and proextractivist regimes to remain in power.

This interpretation of struggles over mining policy in the two countries suggests the importance of bringing into the analysis of socio-environmental policy processes such variables as the political economy of the environment, the nature of national political settlements, dominant ideas about development strategies, and the forms of network and embeddedness that cut (or fail to cut) across the boundaries between civil society, government, legislature, and religious institutions. While capitalist dynamics and politics are central to any analysis of how the environment is governed, this is not the same as saying that the environment is governed in ways entirely at the service of capitalist interests or an interest-based politics that always devalues nature in favor of elite interests in controlling rents or access to resources. The Salvadoran experience with mining governance and even moments in the Honduran case demonstrate the potential for stringent regulation, even within the terms set by the national settlement and the national political economy.

For the analysis of political ecologies of extractivism, these two cases suggest the importance of combining examination of the effects of movements on mining policy with a finer-grained reading of elite politics, of public arguments over development ideas, and of the ways in which public officials and activists maneuver within this political and discursive context. This study also makes clear the importance of actors such as the Church that are not always accorded the attention they merit (Arellano Yanguas, 2014). At the same time, our analysis recognizes the limits on mobilization, including those that derive from internal fissures within movements. Such readings become important both for analysis and for activism as part of the crafting of viable strategies. They are also important for developing a political ecological analysis of resource extraction in Latin America. This chapter also suggests the need to strike a balance between structural analysis (based on, for instance, the penetration of multinational corporations) and agency-based analysis (based on, for instance, social movements) and, in addition to addressing the conflicts between emancipatory movements, states, and capital, to consider the shifting dynamics within bureaucracies, among elites, within movements, and within religious and other institutions. While focusing on such a diversity of factors may seem knotty, even convoluted, it may provide a fuller account of how progressive change can happen and also be undone.

Notes

1. This chapter is a revised version of an article that appeared in *Latin American Perspectives* in 2019 (46 [2]: 84–106). We acknowledge an Australian Research Council Australia Laureate Fellowship to Bebbington, a National Science Foundation Graduate Research Fellowship and Fulbright Student Research Award to Fash, and an Oxfam America grant to Rogan and Fash. We are grateful for the comments of external reviewers and colleagues on their arguments and particularly to Scott Sellwood, Herman Rosa, Andrés McKinley, colleagues in PRISMA in San Salvador, David Kaimowitz, George Redman, Sara Martínez, Maria José Chanut, Rafael Corrales, Claudia Mondragón, and colleagues at the Coalición Ambientalista de Copán. We also thank Steve Ellner, Linda Farthing, and Niki Fabricant for their guidance.
2. Bebbington is currently a director of Oxfam America, though he was not at that time.
3. These elites were interviewed at different times between July 2010 and October 2014 and came mostly from the construction, agro-industrial, and finance sectors.
4. Commerce Group's case was disqualified by the ICSID.
5. Other than one discussion with a cleric touching on this issue and some interviews, this subsection is based on secondary information.
6. Considerandum #4 notes the acute environmental vulnerability of El Salvador and the potential impacts of mining on water; #5 restates the claim that mineral exploration and exploitation affect human health, imply "severe risks" for the environment, especially water, and generate social conflict; and #6 notes the environmental assessment's conclusion that given El Salvador's vulnerability it is very unlikely that the country could guarantee environmentally and socially safe forms of mining.
7. Examples include the defeat of a dam on the Río Lempa by the Honduran Civic Council of Popular and Indigenous Organizations and the defeat of a refinery by the Honduran Black Fraternal Organization.
8. It is unclear what, if any, influence drug cartels have on mining policy, though it is evident that they have taken advantage of mining operations to launder money (*La Tribuna,* June 18, 2018) and finance campaigns for both the National and the Liberal Party (Notibomba, 2016).
9. See https://territoriosenriesgo.unah.edu.hn/ for this map.

References

ACD (Alianza Cívica para la Democrácia)
2008 *Carta de la ACD a SERNA*. Santa Rosa de Copán, Honduras: ACD.
Achtenberg, Emily
2011 "A mining ban in El Salvador?" *NACLA: Report on the Americas*. https://nacla.org/article/mining-ban-el-salvador.

Acosta, Alberto
2011 "Extractivismo y neoextractivismo: dos caras de la misma maldición," pp. 83–120 in Grupo Permanente de Trabajo sobre Alternativas al Desarrollo (ed.), *Más allá del desarrollo*. Quito: Abya Yala.
Alvarado, Elvia
1987 *Don't Be Afraid, Gringo! A Honduran Woman Speaks from the Heart.* San Francisco: Institute for Food and Development Policy.
Anderson, Mark
2007 "When Afro becomes (like) indigenous." *Journal of Latin American and Caribbean Anthropology* 12: 384–413.
2012 "Garifuna activism and the corporatist Honduran state since the 2009 coup," pp. 53–74 in J. M. Rahier (ed.), *Black Social Movements in Latin America: From Monocultural Mestizaje to Multiculturalism.* New York: Palgrave Macmillan.
Arsel, Murat, Barbara Hogenboom, and Lorenzo Pellegrini
2016 "The extractive imperative in Latin America." *The Extractive Industries and Society* 3: 880–887.
Barahona, Marvin
2009 *Pueblos indigenas, estado y memoria colectiva en Honduras.* Tegucigalpa: Editorial Guaymuras.
Bebbington, Anthony
2009 "The new extraction: rewriting the political ecology of the Andes?" *NACLA Report on the Americas* 42 (5): 12–20.
Bebbington, Anthony, Abdul-Gafaru Abdulai, Denise Humphreys Bebbington, Marja Hinfelaar, and Cynthia Sanborn
2018 *Governing Extractive Industries: Politics, Histories, Ideas.* Oxford: Oxford University Press.
Bebbington, Anthony, and Jeffrey Bury
2009 "Institutional challenges for mining and sustainability in Peru." *Proceedings of the National Academy of Sciences* 106: 17296–17301.
Bebbington, Anthony, and Jeffrey Bury (eds.)
2013 *Subterranean Struggles: New Dynamics of Mining, Oil, and Gas in Latin America.* Austin: University of Texas Press.
Bebbington, Anthony, Jeffrey Bury, Nicholas Cuba, and John Rogan
2015 "Mining, risk and climate resilience in the 'other' Pacific: Latin American lessons for the South Pacific." *Asia Pacific Viewpoint* 56 (2): 189–207.
Broad, Robin, and John Cavanagh
2011 "Like water for gold in El Salvador." *The Nation.* July 11.
Bull, Benedicte, Nelson Cuéllar, and Susan Kandel
2015 "El Salvador: the challenge to entrenched elites and the difficult road to a sustainable development model," pp. 33–50 in Benedicte Bull and Mariel Aguilar-Støen (eds.), *Environmental Politics in Latin America: Elite Dynamics, the Left Tide and Sustainable Development.* London: Routledge.
Cartagena, Rafael E.
2009 "Orígenes del movimiento de oposición a la minería metálica en El Salvador." *Estudios Centroamericanos* 64 (722): 497–501.

CEDOH (Centro de Documentación de Honduras)
2009 *Honduras: Poderes fácticos y sistema político.* 3d edition. Tegucigalpa: CEDOH.
CIDSE (Coopération Internationale pour le Développement et la Solidarité)
2009 *América Latina: Riqueza privada, pobreza pública.* Quito: CIDSE/Agencia Latinoamericana de Información.
Corte Suprema de Justicia de Honduras
2006 "Resolución de la Sala de lo Constitucional de la Corte Suprema de Justicia de Honduras en la acción de inconstitucionalidad presentada en contra de la Ley General de Minería." *Corte Suprema Sala de lo Constitucional, Tegucigalpa.* http://www.derecho-ambiental.org/Derecho/Documentacion/Honduras-Inconstitucionalidad-Ley-Mineria.html.
de Echave, J., A. Diez, L. Huber, B. Revesz, X. Ricard, and M. Tanaka
2008 *Minería y conflicto social.* Lima: Instituto de Estudios Peruanos.
Deonandan, Kalowatie, and Michael L. Dougherty (eds.)
2016 *Mining in Latin America: Critical Approaches to the New Extraction.* London: Routledge.
di John, Jonathan, and James Putzel
2009 *Political Settlements: Issues Paper.* Birmingham, UK: Governance and Social Development Resource Centre.
Dougherty, Michael L.
2011 "The global mining industry, junior firms and civil society resistance in Guatemala." *Bulletin of Latin American Research* 30: 403–418.
Dudley, Steven
2016 "Élites y crimen organizado en Honduras: Juan Ramón Matta Ballesteros." *InSight Crime.* https://es.insightcrime.org/investigaciones/elites-crimen-organizado-honduras-juan-ramon-matta-ballesteros/.
Equipo Nizkor
2004 "Conferencia Episcopal de Honduras llama a abolir legislación minera del país." June 14. http://www.derechos.org/nizkor/honduras/doc/obispos.html.
Escalera-Flexhaug, Sabrina
2014 "Canada's controversial engagement in Honduras." *Council on Hemispheric Affairs.* http://www.coha.org/canadas-controversial-engagement-in-honduras/.
Euraque, Darío A.
1996 *Reinterpreting the Banana Republic: Region and State in Honduras, 1870–1972.* Chapel Hill: University of North Carolina Press.
Evans, Peter
1995 *Embedded Autonomy: States and Industrial Transformation.* Princeton: Princeton University Press.
Fash, Benjamin, Emma C. Velásquez, Alejandro Kaffati, Javier Meza, Claudia Mondragón, José Cáceres, Rafael Corrales, Antonio Carias, Claudia Molina, and Leana Corea
2019 *Territorios en riesgo II: Minería, hidrocarburos y generación de energía eléctrica en Honduras.* Tegucigalpa: UNAH/FOSDEH/Oxfam.

Fash, Benjamin, and Scott Sellwood
2017 "The scarlet macaw in the gold mine." *Oxfam Politics of Poverty Blog.* https://politicsofpoverty.oxfamamerica.org/2017/02/the-scarlet-macaw-in-the-gold-mine/.
Global Witness
2016 "Press release: new data on the murder rate of environmental and land activists in Honduras, the highest in the world." https://www.globalwitness.org/en/press-releases/global-witness-releases-new-data-murder-rate-environmental-and-land-activists-honduras-highest-world.
Gudynas, Eduardo
2009 "Diez tesis urgentes sobre el nuevo extractivismo: contextos y demandas bajo el progresismo sudamericano actual," pp. 187–225 in J. Schuldt, A. Acosta, A. Barandiarán, A. Bebbington, M. Folchi, CEDLA-Bolivia, and E. Gudynas (eds.), *Extractivismo, política y sociedad.* Quito: Centro Andino de Acción Popular/Centro Latino Americano de Ecología Social.
Hale, Charles
2005 "Neoliberal multiculturalism: the remaking of cultural rights and racial dominance in Central America." *Political and Legal Anthropology Review* 28 (1): 10–19.
Hickey, Sam, Abdul-Garafu Abdulai, Angelo Izama, and Giles Mohan
2015 *The Politics of Governing Oil Effectively: A Comparative Study of Two New Oil-rich States in Africa.* ESID Working Paper 54. Manchester, UK: Effective States and Inclusive Development Research Centre, University of Manchester.
IBP (International Business Publications, USA)
2007 *Honduras Mineral and Mining Sector Investment and Business Guide.* Washington, DC: IBP.
Jasanoff, Sheila
2006 *States of Knowledge: The Co-Production of Science and the Social Order.* London: Routledge.
Khan, Mushtaq
2010 "Political settlements and the governance of growth-enhancing institutions." MS, SOAS, London.
La Página
2019 "Piden a Nayib Bukele ordene implementar Ley de Prohibición de la Minería Metálica." June 7.
Marsh, Michael
2001 "From Québec to Copán: globalization and the case of San Andrés Minas." http://miningwatch.ca/blog/2001/6/25/qu-bec-copan-globalization-and-case-san-andr-s-minas.
Martinez-Alier, Joan
2002 *The Environmentalism of the Poor: A Study of Ecological Conflicts and Valuation.* Cheltenham, UK: Edward Elgar.
Middeldorp, Nick, and Philippe Le Billon
2019 "Deadly environmental governance: authoritarianism, eco-populism, and the repression of environmental and land defenders." *Annals of the American Association of Geographers* 109: 324–347.

Moran, Robert

2002 *What's the Big Secret? Observations and Comments on the San Andrés Mine and Mining Regulations in Honduras.* Golden, CO: Association of Non-Governmental Organizations of Honduras/Development Commission of the Department of Copán.

Nadelman, Rachel

2015 "*Let Us Care for Everyone's Home": The Catholic Church's Role in Keeping Gold Mining out of El Salvador.* Center for Latin American and Latino Studies, American University, Working Paper Series 9. Washington, DC: American University Press.

Notibomba

2016 "Narcos confirmaron que financiaron campañas de nacionalistas y liberals." *Notibomba.* https://web.archive.org/web/20161010234624/http://notibomba.com/narcos-confirmaron-que-financiaron-campanas-de-nacionalistas-y-liberales/.

O'Connor, James

1991 "On the two contradictions of capitalism." *Capitalism, Nature, Socialism* 2 (3): 107–109.

Ospina Peralta, Pablo, Anthony Bebbington, Patric Hollenstein, Ilana Nussbaum, and Eduardo Ramírez

2015 "Extraterritorial investments, environmental crisis and collective action in Latin America." *World Development* 73: 32–43.

Oyuela, Leticia

2003 *Esplendor y miseria de la minería en Honduras.* Tegucigalpa: Editorial Guaymuras.

Shipley, Tyler

2013 "The new Canadian imperialism and the military coup in Honduras." *Latin American Perspectives* 40 (5): 44–61.

Spalding, Rose

2013 "Transnational networks and national action: El Salvador's antimining movement," pp. 23–55 in Eduardo Silva (ed.), *Transnational Activism and National Movements in Latin America: Bridging the Divide.* London: Routledge.

2018 "From the streets to the chamber: social movements and the mining ban in El Salvador." *European Review of Latin American and Caribbean Studies* 106: 49–76.

Svampa, Maristella

2019 *Neo-Extractivism in Latin America: Socio-Environmental Conflicts, the Territorial Turn, and New Political Narratives.* Cambridge: Cambridge University Press.

Telegraph

2013 "Sex abuse victims list 'dirty dozen' papal candidates." http://www.telegraph.co.uk/news/worldnews/europe/vaticancityandholysee/9914186/Sex-abuse-victims-list-dirty-dozen-papal-candidates.html.

Truth Commission

2013 "The voice of greatest authority is that of the victims." *Tegucigalpa.* https://friendshipamericas.org/sites/default/files/report_cdv_honduras_english.pdf.

10

The Other Extractivism

The Andean State and Small-Scale and Artisanal Gold Mining

Zaraí Toledo Orozco

SCHOLARS STUDYING THE IMPACT OF the last commodities boom of the 2000s in South America generally argue that this period served to consolidate the economic model based on the export of raw materials (Gudynas, 2010; Svampa, 2019). Though progressive governments played a more active role than conservative ones as regulators and allocated the increased revenue to funding of a social agenda (a strategy known as "neo-extractivism"), administrations at both ends of the ideological spectrum found consensus in making extractivism the first, if not the only, developmentalist alternative. These analyses, however, consider extractivism exclusively in its large-scale form and largely neglect other forms of extractivism such as small-scale and artisanal gold mining (hereafter AGM).[1] This activity, commonly informal, is strongly rooted in Andean countries and has steadily expanded over the past two decades. It is estimated that there are around 870,000 people working in informal mining in Peru, Colombia, and Bolivia, mainly in rural and marginalized areas (Artisanal and Small-Scale Mining Knowledge Sharing Archive, 2017). Despite the important differences in state responses and outcomes, the social, economic, and political implications of this activity are barely discussed.

Previous explanations of state strategies to regulate AGM point to state capacities, external pressure from business and environmentalist groups, and the collective capacity for political mobilization of informal miners as key factors. My comparative study addresses these issues by focusing on three countries that, while showing little variation in the above-mentioned factors, differ in important ways with regard to their policy orientations. Colombia and Peru have opted for draconian policies to deter the expansion of the activity, while Bolivia has chosen to recognize the miners and even support their activities. In contrast to the large-scale mining sector, there is no commodities consensus, no common narrative orienting the state's role and policies when it comes to the extractivism of the poor. Differences in strategies among these countries have depended on the state's understanding of small-scale extractivism and of its role vis-à-vis the social forces. These different conceptions were ultimately tied to the governments' ideological orientations.

Colombia and Peru were (and still are) examples of conservative governments that placed particular emphasis on attracting foreign investment and limiting state obligations to the general population. In order to be competitive on the market, they needed to project an image of stability, making it necessary for them to assert their monopoly of resource governance and increase social control. This imperative explains why they were lenient with regard to the environmental and social impacts of large-scale mining but merciless when these impacts originated in AGM. Their approach also prevented them from developing local knowledge about small-scale mining; instead, they tended to rely on coercion-intensive and legal strategies that often criminalized the activity and conflated different mining actors in the gold supply chain. These strategies generated high degrees of contention from communities and local authorities, increased levels of violence, and led to alliances between miners and criminal groups.

By contrast, Bolivia was a progressive government that constitutionally recognized different forms of production and different types of benefits associated with mining at different scales. The state was interested in attracting foreign investment and increasing social control, but it pursued the latter by fostering cooperation with the social forces that had a comparative organizational advantage at the local level due to their employment-generating and redistributive capacity. Thus it chose to support small-scale and artisanal miners by both enhancing their political representation and creating ad hoc institutions to support their activities. By relying on the socioeconomic networks generated by informal miners, the Bolivian state was able to gather information on the activity and reduce the number of mining conflicts. More important, by incorporating the input of miners it was able to develop legislation that accounted for the particularities of the activity and the local context. At the same time, it ended up empowering miners politically and granting them more leverage to bargain for regulatory exemptions.

This chapter attempts to contribute to the analysis of the legacy of the commodities boom in Latin America by focusing on the commonly overlooked impact of national policies on local extractive actors. The case of AGM miners provides an opportunity to understand how Andean governments responded to the networks and social formations that emerged in marginalized areas where the state had little presence and what strategies states adopted to address the gap in their control over the national territory. I argue that while conservative administrations with the state's Weberian ideals have sought to maintain the fiction of total control, the Bolivian government, which had a social and historical perspective, preferred to work with the existing social forces to extend support to local communities ordinarily beyond its reach.

The fieldwork on which this chapter is based was conducted between 2015 and 2017 in Peru, Colombia, and Bolivia, where I interviewed mining leaders, local and national authorities, and private-sector actors from the largest AGM regions, Madre de Dios in Peru, Antioquia in Colombia, and rural La Paz in Bolivia. I focus on the policies implemented under the governments of Alan García and Ollanta Humala in Peru, Álvaro Uribe and Juan Manuel Santos in Colombia, and Evo Morales in Bolivia. During this time period, gold prices significantly increased, and all three countries passed reforms to regulate AGM activities. The chapter is structured as follows: I begin by discussing the challenges of informal mining's regulation. Then I explain how, in the absence of a consensus, the state's responses to the activity have depended on understanding of the functions of the many extractivisms and discuss the strategies of each country and their outcomes. In the fourth section I use this evidence to discuss what kind of state the administrations in the three countries envisioned and what their priorities were during the commodities boom.

The Extractivism of the Poor

Though extractivism has always been part of economic strategies in Latin America, Maristella Svampa (2019) has called attention to the "commodities consensus"—the consolidation of a new economic paradigm across ideologies around the irreversible expansion of extractivism as a motor of growth. The neo-extractivist development frame emerging in the past two decades has been coupled, in the case of progressive governments, with the implementation of reforms to secure the reinvestment of the revenues in social programs. Nonetheless, proponents of the concept of neo-extractivism such as Svampa argue that, overall, both conservative and progressive administrations have relegated to second place any critical discussion of the costs of relying on extractivism (Gudynas, 2010: 7). As a result, the mineral resource wealth in most of the region has fostered the perpetuation of the export-oriented model (Svampa, 2019), an increase in conflict over resource governance (Arce, 2014:

27), and the silencing of communities' demands (Li, 2015: 71). The underlying argument from this perspective is that both ends of the political spectrum were subject to the imperatives of the commodities market and that there were no significant differences in extractive policies.

However, these assessments are often based only on the extractive activities of large-scale operations led by transnational corporations. The politics of small-scale and artisanal mining, an activity that mainly relies on intensive labor and rudimentary machinery (Veiga, 1997: 2), are often overlooked. Small-scale and artisanal mining grew exponentially hand in hand with large-scale mining operations during the last commodities boom, but it had always been present in the region as a seasonal alternative for many workers. In the Andes it became a stable occupation for rural communities in the mid-1970s after the implementation of neoliberal reforms that brought cuts in agriculture-related institutions and eliminated state mining companies (Poveda et al., 2015). Additionally, in the cases of Peru and Colombia political violence and displacement forced a large number of people to switch to informal mining (Pachas, 2011; Rettberg et al., 2018: 345). Later on, when gold prices peaked in the 2000s, AGM developed as an attractive productive activity and an opportunity for social mobility.

It is unclear how the extractivism of the poor can contribute to the neo-extractivist development paradigm, because, while its production is destined for the international market, AGM does not provide the state the revenue of large-scale mining. On the contrary, its expansion is frequently at odds with the interests of mining corporations. Moreover, policies on AGM have to strike a balance between sustainability, revenue extraction, the vulnerable economic condition of informal miners, and their contribution to local communities.

To begin with, the vast majority of gold miners are inhabitants of rural areas, indigenous descendants and mestizos, who often have not finished high school, cannot be integrated into the formal economy, and are closely linked to the agricultural world. Gold mining used to be a family activity, but as it has expanded miners have formed cooperatives or associations in which they shared expenses and split the profits. Gradually the activity has attracted foreigners from nearby regions with little or no mining experience (Pachas, 2011: 95; Sarmiento et al., 2013: 54; Poveda, 2014: 61).

With the rise in international gold prices, new forms of production coexisted within AGM. The biggest and most powerful groups in informal gold mining in the three countries work with small-scale operations—mining that combines artisanal operations with the use of dredges, pumps, backhoes, and retorts (devices for distilling mercury from gold). Though in Bolivia these groups are still called "cooperatives," in all the cases studied here small-scale miners have become profitable small businesses with hierarchical structures and informal peons. When gold prices decrease or when there is lack of capital to maintain the activity, however, collective strategies are put in place. In Madre de Dios, miners invite individuals to their deposits who contribute with either machinery or labor to extract gold from alluvial deposits for a limited time in exchange for a percentage of the earnings (Toledo Orozco, 2020). Most of the gold miners in Colombia also work independently, but recently there has been renewed interest in the gold mining population in forming associations for security and political reasons. "This has been a way for us to protect each other from the state, from the company, and from other forces," the secretary of a gold mining association in Antioquia told me (interview, Medellín, August 13, 2016). The organization of associations helps miners both increase their chances of meeting legalization requirements and mobilize for their demands.

Within the sector, the most vulnerable group is miners still relying on artisanal and ancestral methods. They are mainly Quechua and Aymara indigenous people in Peru and Bolivia and Amazonian indigenous and Afro-descendants in Colombia. Colombia is by far the country with the most artisanal gold mining presence, with activities in 44 percent of the departments (Sarmiento et al., 2013: 57). Artisanal gold miners employ *barequeo* or *mazamorreo* (hand-panning) or *zambullidero* (diving in alluvial deposits) or dig wells with hand tools.

Female miners, part of this vulnerable group, tend to have lower levels of education than male miners, mostly elementary school education, and are frequently their families' sole breadwinners and mothers of at least two children (Aranibar, Sandi, and Lafuente, 2017: 24; Orozco et al., 2017: 26; Arcos and Rivera, 2018: 235). "They ignore us because we do not own land or have the means to rent it," a Peruvian female miner told me in explaining why current legislation on small-scale and artisanal mining does not include their activity (interview, Lima, July 12, 2017). The vast majority of women work either as panners or as *pallaqueras, palliris, chatarreras,* or *cucaracheras* (rock strikers), commonly extracting the remaining ore from the mineral waste left by small-scale miners. The fact that they do not own the means of production has made access to labor rights particularly challenging in the three countries and increases the hazards of their work. In Ayacucho, Peru, small-scale miners in the process of legalizing their activities, trying to avoid accusations of labor exploitation, do not want pallaqueras nearby, and therefore female miners often end up organizing long walks far from their communities to find new waste-rock deposits. Several barequeras in Antioquia, fearing accusations of gold stealing from other miners, have to pan clandestinely in the Cauca River. On average, female miners account for 6–10 percent of the total mining population, and they make US$160–230 per month (Orozco et al., 2017: 49). Only in exceptional cases are they in positions of power. For example, in

Chocó, Colombia, women account for 26 percent of the total mining population, and their earnings are considerably higher (GOMIAM, 2015). Also, until five years ago it was a woman, Goya Casas, who controlled most of the informal gold market in the Peruvian Amazon.

The unregulated expansion of the activity generates serious socio-environmental problems. While AGM involves lower volumes of mineral than large-scale mining, the "ecological rucksack" (Gudynas, 2013)—the impacts of extraction on the quality of water and land for local communities—is high. In Peru, Colombia, and Bolivia, AGM is the main mercury polluter, contributing to deforestation and the contamination of water and aquatic species (SPDA, 2015). In just two years, AGM in the Peruvian Amazon expanded by 18,000 hectares (Amazon Conservation, 2019). This rapid expansion has been accompanied by health issues, mainly silicosis, pneumocystis pneumonia, allergies, and intoxication associated with inhaling dust and breathing toxic mercury vapor. Additionally, given the lack of implementation of safety procedures and labor exploitation, miners are often exposed to hazards such as landslides and accidents with explosives (Cordi et al., 2011: 155).

Locally, some AGM communities have been impacted by insurgent left-wing forces such as the Fuerzas Armadas Revolucionarias de Colombia–Ejército del Pueblo (Revolutionary Armed Forces of Colombia–People's Army—FARC-EP), paramilitary forces such as Bacrim, and private operators, who use AGM to launder money from drug trafficking and coca cultivation. Taking advantage of the physical isolation, these groups extort miners in Antioquia, Bolivar, Caquetá, Cauca, and Nariño. In Madre de Dios they offer financial support to mining communities and reap the benefits of the intensification of gold extraction (GIATOC, 2016: 9–10). Miners' expansion into new areas has also caused violent clashes. Land tenancy disputes with community members and displacement by miners and criminal actors have impacted Amazonian communities in Beni, northern Bolivia (SPDA, 2015: 18). In Segovia and Remedios in Antioquia, the war on drugs has pushed the labor force into AGM, also increasing the number of conflicts over access to land (Massé and Le Billon, 2018: 117).

A further problem is conflicts between large companies and informal miners around gold mining. Local communities in Tambogrande, Piura (Peru), and Malku Khota, Potosí (Bolivia) that protested large-scale extractive projects are now supporting the expansion of AGM (CEDIB, 2012; Toledo Orozco and Veiga, 2018). In Marmato, Caldas (Colombia), citizens have organized several protests demanding that the state legalize small-scale mining activity instead of giving their territories in concession to multinational mining companies (*El Tiempo*, 2019).

Informal Miners as Social Forces

The majority of AGM miners in the Andes do not possess all the legal permits to operate, but their contribution to the local economy is very important. Currently, AGM is found in 21 of the 25 regions of Peru, 12 of the 32 departments of Colombia, and 4 of the 9 departments of Bolivia. The average contribution to the regional gross domestic product of the main centers of AGM over the past two decades gives us an idea of how indispensable this activity has become: 40 percent in Madre de Dios, 20–30 percent in Antioquia, and 30 percent in La Paz, where it is the third-highest employment-generating activity (Arcos and Rivera, 2018: 36; Poveda et al., 2015). AGM in all three Andean countries has the capacity to generate high levels of employment that benefit a broad range of the local population. Gold mining communities usually become economic clusters that employ local citizens, produce wealth, generate demand for mining products, and favor the arrival in remote communities of services such as hardware stores, restaurants, bars, transportation, and phone and Internet services.

A citizen from Huepetuhe, Madre de Dios, told me: "They [the miners] do as they please most of the time, but whom should I complain to? The government that thinks everybody living here is a criminal?" (interview, Madre de Dios, July 3, 2015). Citizens of mining communities choose to negotiate their own agreements with the miners, even if these are not always fair, because of the side benefits of AGM. Depending on the capacity for organization of local communities and their ties with state authorities, local actors are able to enforce deals with AGM miners. This is more common in Bolivia than in Peru and Colombia.

For this reason, local governors and mayors have refrained from regulating AGM and instead expressed their support for it. "What the government says we should do is one thing and what we can do is another. . . . What do I have to offer to all these people working in mining?" a mayor from northwestern Antioquia asked (interview, Buriticá, August 17, 2016). In some cases, miners themselves have run for office in order to increase their power of negotiation with the authorities and to contest the mining law. "Do you see any miners legalizing their activity here? No, because the norms do not allow them to do so. I have told the president that, if we do not correct the norms, this is all in vain," said Luis Otsuka, former leader of the Federation of Miners of Madre de Dios who then became governor (Ojo Público, 2016). Like Otsuka, almost all the mayors of mining towns in Madre de Dios have challenged the state by signing petitions against the mining law, marching in the streets with the miners and allowing the free transit of fuel carriers to gold mining areas (Toledo Orozco, 2020).

In these three cases, informal gold miners have a degree of power, but their states interpret the socioeconomic role of informal mining differently and they also differ in the extent to which they recognize miners' demands.

Through the Eyes of the State

Colombia and Peru have opted for coercive policies to deter the expansion of AGM, while Bolivia has chosen to recognize the miners and even provide some support for their activities. Scholars have developed various explanations for these differences. While conventional political science analysis focuses on the capacity of a state to mobilize resources, people, and institutions in pursuit of its goals in the territory it governs (Soifer, 2015: 9), the three cases examined here all demonstrate the relative weakness of the state. Another explanatory framework focuses on the pressure exerted by environmentalist groups, the media, and large-scale mining companies, which generate different incentives for states (Dargent and Urteaga, 2016: 668). A third focus is on the impact of international agreements such as the Minamata Convention on mercury that create obligations for states to regulate AGM practices. However, pressure of this nature exists in all three countries, making these explanations inadequate to account for the differences in responses.

A strong argument is made by Baraybar and Dargent (2019) that the action (and inaction) with regard to AGM mining of Andean states is determined by the level of organization of the social actors involved. From this perspective, the Peruvian and Colombian miners' lack of strong AGM organizations allowed these states to stand back initially and then, in the face of international and domestic pressure, to implement regulation relatively easily. In Colombia, pressing security concerns also motivated increased law enforcement. In contrast, cooperative miners in Bolivia are key political actors with great capacity for mobilization and official representation in the legislative and executive branches of government. This raised the political costs of regulation, pushing the state to reject strong law enforcement. Baraybar's and Dargent's argument, however, does not fully explain why the governments in Peru and Colombia continued to implement coercive policies despite their ineffectiveness and why in Bolivia the government tried to reform the mining cooperative sector, on occasion clashing with the organized interests of informal miners. More important, it largely underestimates the level of organization, collective action, and local support for AGM in Peru and Colombia.

In Peru, when in 2011 the government of Ollanta Humala (2011–2016) issued executive decrees to fast-track legalization and instructed police to confiscate mining equipment, AGM organizations led simultaneous strikes in all the mining regions of the country. The longest strike lasted twenty-three days in Madre de Dios and had strong support from citizens and local authorities. This included the mobilization of associations of Peruvian pallaqueras. At the peak of the mobilization in 2014, 4,000 miners from five regions traveled to Congress in Lima to demand the overturning of the decrees (*El Comercio*, 2014). In Colombia, miners from Antioquia, Caldas, Cauca, and Chocó organized protests and strikes to reform the mining code, often with overwhelming support from local people (as discussed by Hernández Reyes in this volume). In 2012 the National Confederation of Miners, with more than 250,000 members, demanded that President Juan Manuel Santos stop persecuting small-scale and artisanal miners and differentiate them from criminal groups (Osorio, 2012). In 2016 and 2017 miners from Segovia and Remedios organized strikes against state attempts to close all of the informal gold mines and the state's military protection of large-scale mining companies to the detriment of local miners. The latter strike lasted forty-three days, the longest in the history of the country. Local authorities, chatarreras, campesinos, and other local workers joined the protests in caravans, while campesinos and nonprofit organizations provided goods to more than 4,000 protesters and organized 35 communal kitchens (Álvarez, 2017). Simultaneous strikes in support were led by the sons of the miners in other parts of Antioquia (*El Espectador*, 2017).

Instead of being a matter of capacities, external pressures, or the contestation capacity of gold miners, the differences in these governments' approaches to AGM can be understood by examining the state's interpretation of the purposes of extractive activities and of the role of the state vis-à-vis civil society. The perceived purposes can typically be found in a country's constitution, mining laws, and national development plans. Generally, extractivism is viewed both as an activity with high revenue returns for the state and as an activity that provides benefits to local economies such as absorbing both skilled and unskilled labor, fostering wealth redistribution, and preserving local traditions. Where extractivism is only understood through its contribution to the national economy, as is the case in Peru and Colombia, the only recognized extractivism is the large-scale operation ("recognized" in this case meaning not just legally permitted but also receiving state support, often in disregard of the problems associated with it). In Peru the 1993 Constitution established that the state would promote only large-scale mining operations and thus favored foreign investment that provided immediate revenues to the Treasury through the reduction of fiscal and environmental regulations.[2] In the context of the commodities boom of the early twenty-first century, supreme decrees enacted under Alan García's conservative government (2006–2011) specified that state support of AGM was contingent on the sector's developing a formal business structure and complying with the same legalization regulations as large-scale mining. These measures generally created bureaucratic barriers that were too costly for informal gold miners. For instance, the new rules required official environmental impact assessments that cost more than the earnings of the average miner and contracts with landowners even though communities in rural areas seldom have property titles.

This policy approach to extractivism was extended through the period of the commodities boom because of the considerable influence of large-scale corporations on national legislation (Durand, 2016: 9). From the perspective of lawmakers, AGM lacked viability as part of the country's economic development more because of its lack of economic contribution to the Treasury than because of its practices. As this kind of mining continued to expand without being legally recognized, from 2009 on the executive issued decrees designed to restrict its growth and allowed police and military operations aimed at arresting miners, burning down mining camps, confiscating machinery, and deterring the expansion of mining (Supreme Decree 012-2009). These measures became part of a strategy also followed by President Humala of the Nationalist Party to "confront the problems around illegal mining[3] with regard to environmental, criminal, administrative, and tax matters" (Supreme Decree 029-2014). At the time, there were 6,618 environmentally damaged sites in Peru attributable to large-scale mining operations. In these cases, Humala's government responded very differently, granting large companies amnesty that prevented the state from collecting some US$11 million in fines (Convoca, 2015).

Colombia's mining activities are regulated by the 2001 Mining Code (Law 685) that was part of a neoliberal reform promoted by President Andrés Pastrana, which framed extractivism as an indispensable source of revenue. The successive administrations of Álvaro Uribe and Juan Manuel Santos, both of the Social Party of National Unity coalition, have continued this policy orientation. Uribe issued a number of decrees and resolutions to ensure tax breaks, relaxation of environmental standards, and bureaucratic requirements for large-scale extractivism (Sarmiento et al., 2013: 52). These decrees were justified under the argument that extractivism "needs to be supported in order [for the country] to compete under the same conditions as other countries" (Plan Nacional de Desarrollo, 2006–2010). The successive changes in mining legislation were also influenced by corporate mining actors, who lobbied to obtain privileged access to mining concessions (sometimes to the detriment of existing artisanal miners), critical geological information and the state's military security services to protect their projects against informal gold miners and insurgent forces (Pulido, 2015: 81). During President Santos's administration alone, a total of 4.8 million hectares was granted for large-scale exploitation (Massé and Le Billon, 2018: 120).

None of these reforms addressed issues related to AGM. Although Colombia's mining code recognized a special mining regime involving indigenous people and Afro-Colombians, legal changes largely ignored this part of the code. Instead, Colombian governments eliminated the different tax regimes pegged to different scales of mining (Mining Code, art. 230). This meant that local and international actors had to comply with very similar rules and obligations, making AGM economically unfeasible. By 2015 Santos was also promoting the Integral Plan for Mining Formalization and against Criminal Mining to grant the state the power to combat small-scale mining, which was called "criminal"[4] because of its damage to the environment and its links to illicit groups. Paradoxically, serious human rights violations, threats to small-scale mining leaders, and extrajudicial executions linked to the mining company AngloGold Ashanti did not trigger the same reaction from the government (CETIM, 2014).

By contrast, in Bolivia extractivism was defined by both its economic and its social contributions. The state still aggressively promoted large-scale mining and was also influenced by corporate actors. Nevertheless, the fact that Morales and his Movimiento al Socialismo (Movement toward Socialism—MAS) advocated to a certain degree for other mining actors—state mining workers and cooperativist and artisanal miners—served to counterbalance the power of corporations (Fairfield, 2015: 224). Recognition was in great part explained by the MAS's commitment to the popular sectors. In the early 2000s MAS was able to channel their discontent over the previous neoliberal reforms and articulate popular demands around a political discourse on national sovereignty, indigenous people's rights, and redistribution, which earned it considerable support. Once in office in 2006, it aimed to transform state-society relations by modifying the terms of representation of the social movements and by enabling their participation in decision making. For much of Bolivian history miners have been a force to reckon with,[5] but Morales's government enhanced their power by institutionalizing their role as representatives of a class and as spokesmen for the labor movement (Mayorga, 2009: 57).

The Constitution of the Plurinational State of Bolivia "recognizes as productive actors industrial state mining, industrial private mining and cooperative associations" (Article 369).[6] It also states that "the state will promote and strengthen mining cooperatives so that they can contribute to the socioeconomic development of the country" (Article 370). It identifies cooperatives as organizations based on the principles of solidarity, equality, and reciprocity (Article 55). In contrast to the situation in Peru and Colombia, AGM is defined in its own terms rather than in relation to large-scale mining.

This said, relations between the state and members of the cooperatives were far from stable under the Morales presidency. Bolivian mining law is more a reflection of a state-society "precarious coalition" (Mayorga, 2009: 63) in which a state that does not have full control over the social forces (not even of those that are part of its constituency) is constantly forced to engage in negotiations with them in exchange for social and economic stability and political support. "The MAS knows that miners are part of *el pueblo* [the people], hence they cannot govern without the people that elected them. We support him [Morales], but he knows that he cannot forget about the cooperatives," said Simón Condori, the president of the Departmental Federation of Mining Cooperatives from La Paz (interview, La Paz, October 8, 2017). In fact, the 2014 mining law was designed in consultation with the miners, who, after rejecting three drafts, negotiated a law with major benefits including more working areas, financial aid, and very weak environmental regulation in exchange for paying some taxes and implementing some basic safety measures in their operations (Okada, 2016: 172).

Contention and negotiation have shaped the state's approach to AGM. Bolivia is the only Andean country that was interested in regulating AGM beyond legalization. It has worked on developing pension plans for small-scale miners (Supreme Decree 29537-2008) and passed legislation against the partnership of cooperatives with private actors, thus limiting the opportunity for foreign investors to take advantage of the tax benefits of cooperatives and begin medium-scale operations. At the same time, it failed in its attempts to reform labor relations within cooperatives after miners organized several blockades and protests in 2016. This conflict resulted in the death of a deputy minister, 100 policemen injured, and 10 miners arrested. The Morales administration responded to these acts by cutting funding to the cooperatives federation, withdrawing some mining concessions, and undertaking audits of cooperatives (*La Razón*, 2016).

State Strategies and Outcomes

The views of extractivism described above fostered different strategies, outcomes, and tradeoffs. In Peru, the failure of the regulation imposed to formalize mining activities led the state to pursue more radical tactics to regain (or, more accurately, gain) authority over mining areas. Between 2014 and 2017, 1,097 investigations of environmental damage caused by informal miners were opened, and 236 army and police raids involving the burning of mining camps, the seizure of machinery, and arrests were conducted (*La República*, 2018).

This strategy had counterproductive outcomes from the beginning. Whereas the heavy bureaucratic burden made legalization very challenging for informal miners,[7] the raids drove them to seek new clandestine deposits. This in turn led to a struggle over land that increased the violence between local communities, indigenous people, and miners. Frustrated with the legalization process and persecution, many informal gold miners turned to private investors and criminal actors for funding (Toledo Orozco, 2020). Moreover, the indiscriminate use of raids, which brought together miners (many in the process of legalization), peons, and informal workers around the mining camps, created general resentment of the state among local citizens. On several occasions, members of civil society (nongovernmental organizations and priests) and local officials asked the government to change its strategies to avoid hurting workers, families living in the mining camps, and indigenous groups (Vasquez, 2019).

Colombia's approach mirrored that of Peru: heavy bureaucratic obligations for those who wanted to legalize their activities and constant coercion to deter the expansion of informal mining. By 2014 the government had conducted police and military operations in the eight departments with the highest mining production; yet AGM continued its expansion and technological development, shifting from rudimentary implements to machinery and covering 98,000 hectares in 2019 (UNODC, 2019). Though a number of institutions have requested the government to adopt more target-oriented policies (Rettberg and Ortiz-Riomalo, 2016), the state is still insisting on carrying out these operations. Coercive policies made small-scale and artisanal miners more vulnerable to the influence of criminal forces and private actors, who kept expanding their activities into new areas far from the state's reach. Worse, in towns where the state offered military support to mining companies such as Antioquia, violence against local citizens and informal miners escalated (Massé and Le Billon, 2018).

In Bolivia, the recognition of different types of mining translated into a strategy that combined cooperation and negotiations with the miners. The state developed a series of institutions such as the Center for Cooperativist Mining Commercialization, the Administrative Mining Authority, and the National Service for Registering and Monitoring the Commercialization of Minerals and Metals to identify the key issues faced by the miners, provide them with aid and training, organize their access to mineral deposits, and help them get the best market prices for their minerals. These institutions have helped to enhance the state's familiarity with the actors involved in AGM, the different local mining practices, and the supply chain.

At the same time, given their access to political representation during the Morales administration, cooperativists were able to call the government's attention to local problems that developed beyond the reach of the state, and this was conducive to direct aid for local communities surrounding mining activities (Toledo Orozco, 2020). From the conflicts, accidents, and natural disasters impacting mining communities, the Subministry of Cooperatives—led by cooperativists—often receives direct information in real time from mining cooperatives federations (Viceministerio de Cooperativas, 2016).

Peru and Colombia's executives lack these records. As a result, with important exceptions[8] the degree of violence around AGM in Bolivia is considerably lower than in the other two countries. Moreover, Bolivia is the only country in the Andean region where the majority of the miners actually pay taxes and make information on their activities publicly available.

The tradeoff of this strategy can easily be determined. Official recognition has empowered cooperativists, who use the leverage to prevent the imposition of stronger regulatory schemes. Well aware of their capacity for mobilization, cooperativist miners have used elections and other important political moments to negotiate for benefits and exemptions, and this has generated both conflict and concessions between the MAS and the miners. The miners' power has blocked, for example, development of new laws to increase fiscal and environmental regulations on cooperatives that have now become small businesses. Likewise, it has given miners' organizations an important voice in national debates relative to other social organizations (Marston and Perreault, 2017).

Conclusion: Bridging the Historical Gap

I have shown that in all three of the cases examined, AGM has a strong capacity for collective action arising from its socioeconomic contribution to the local communities. Nevertheless, interpretations of this phenomenon and the development of state regulation of the activity varied with the state's understanding of the forms of extractivism involved and of the social forces around these activities.

The conservative twenty-first-century Latin American governments faced great pressure to fulfill the high expectations of growth associated with international investment. This required them to ensure high levels of social control in order to present their economies as stable and investment-attractive. Thus the governments in Peru and Colombia envisioned a state that followed the Weberian ideal type, monopolizing social control by ensuring its authority over any other social force and centralizing the material and ideal means of rule (Weber, 1968), specifically in the case of natural resources. However, they both inherited a context adverse to achieving these goals. At the national level, neoliberal reforms had reduced the responsibilities of state institutions. The absence of the state in rural and peripheral regions prevented them from developing contextual knowledge and experience for administering these areas. In the vacuum left by the state, contesting social forces—including the miners—emerged organically and became much better equipped than the state to address local socioeconomic needs, capture resource rents, and redistribute wealth.

Facing disparities between their goals and their capacities, the conservative administrations chose to grant as many concessions and benefits as possible to large-scale mining investment in order to ensure competitiveness. With regard to informal extractivism, their behavior was completely different. They were dismissive of the organizational reality and the accumulated knowledge of small-scale and artisanal miners and perceived this kind of mining as an impediment to national development. Choosing to simplify and homogenize reality (Scott, 1998), in addressing the social complexities of informal mining—its diverse forms of association, labor practices, and informal resource governance codes—Peru and Colombia opted for standardizing rules, procedures, and goals. Generalizations were made about the different types of AGM; ahistorical land regulation was imposed on local communities with ancestral mining traditions, and the same heavy burden was required of all mining actors seeking to legalize their activities. These governments remained unaware of or unwilling to recognize the organizations and demands of the communities around the extraction of gold. Thus, when searching for information on AGM in Peru and Colombia, researchers can access an impressive amount of data on mining—detailed information on the Treasury's losses from AGM, aerial photos on the expansion of the activity, and various metrics for assessing their environmental impact—but very little on the local actors that participate in the activity. There are no detailed state records about mining practices, the informal rules of mining communities, or the people in the gold supply chain (Damonte, 2016).

In the absence of the means to make reality intelligible and facilitate compliance (Scott, 1998), state strategies in Peru and Colombia aiming to impose social control have mostly relied on legal and coercive means. This strategy has harmed vulnerable sectors of the population while intensifying the impacts of extractive activities. The persistence of these governments in pursuing this strategy despite its failure showed that they were more interested in maintaining the fiction of their control in order to sway public opinion and foreign investors than in addressing the complexity of the issue. For example, in Madre de Dios the Humala government assigned nine times the budget for formalization and social development to the funding of raids on AGM (*La República*, 2018). The fact that large-scale mining environmental damage was not punished with the same rigor indicates that these operations had nothing to do with the environment or with the protection of communities. Ironically, the more these administrations employed coercion, the more they fostered contention from the miners, who used their local networks and the support of local authorities to limit the impact of the central state's regulation. In their protests, miners showed that the rules for legalization were inviable. This further limited the authority of the state, which appeared weak, disarticulated, and delegitimized.

By contrast, the progressive government of Evo Morales, which led a constitutional reform and in doing so changed the terms of state-society relations, envisioned a different type of state. Instead of monopolizing social control it engaged in negotiations with social forces that, despite wielding collective power, had often been excluded from the state's developmental trajectory (García Linera, 2013). The government in this sense displayed an awareness of the strong geopolitical contradictions that riddled the country (Farthing and Kohl, 2014) and what Ellner in the introduction to this volume has called "sensibilities"—reflexiveness about the consequences of persistent inequality and other challenges. The state acknowledged that it could not comply with the Weberian ideal—ensuring absolute authority over all the social forces and full domination of resource governance—or offer a viable alternative for the population working in AGM. In light of this reality, the state opted for the political incorporation of the gold miners and increasing its control, which paradoxically it shared with the existing social forces. Among the many positive aspects of this strategy are instances of state-miner cooperation. On the negative side, relying on these social forces the state could not unilaterally raise environmental standards for informal mining. Additionally, as critics have correctly observed, this strategy further deepened Bolivia's commodity-dependence (Rivera Cusicanqui, 2014).

Perhaps the most important difference between the Bolivian government and the conservative administrations of Peru and Colombia is that the Bolivian communities surrounding mining camps are less exposed to state repression and nonstate violence. They are safer, and at the same time they ultimately benefit from mining activity both directly and indirectly. A mining family in rural La Paz does not live under the constant threat of violence as do the families living in nearby mining areas in Madre de Dios or Antioquia. In Bolivia problems in most cases are negotiated or resolved within informal or formal channels. The importance of this contrast cannot be overestimated.

Notes

1. I am limiting my observations to miners who work independently or in associations or cooperatives. There are also small-scale miners working for private companies in Colombia or for the state mining company in Bolivia, but since they have a different labor regime and work under different conditions, they deserve a separate discussion.
2. In 2002, the *Ley General de Minería* (Article 4) included an article supporting small-scale and artisanal mining, but it included no precise regulations.
3. Mining is considered illegal in Peru when it takes place without a permit or in forbidden areas such as parks. The state sees informal mining as an activity that has already begun a process of legalization.

4. President Santos defined "criminal mining" as activity that financed criminal or terrorist groups.

5. On the history of miners as social forces and state contesters, see Dunkerley (1984).

6. These distinctions are framed in the Constitution (Article 306) around a broader understanding of different forms of economic organization: communitarian, state, private, and social cooperativist.

7. Fewer than 5 percent of miners were legalized by 2017.

References

Álvarez, Fernando

2017 "Paro minero en Segovia and Remedios: 43 días de intensa lucha por la dignidad en Colombia." *Pueblos* 75: 9–13.

Amazon Conservation

2019 "MAAP #96: minería aurífera alcanza máximo histórico en la Amazonía Sur Peruana." January 8. https://maaproject.org/2019/peru-mineria-2018/.

Aranibar, Ana María, Eliodoro Sandi, and Daniel Lafuente

2017 *Mujeres mineras en Bolivia: Una mirada a su realidad socioeconómica.* La Paz: Solidaridad and Cumbre del Sajama.

Arce, Moisés

2014 *Resource Extraction and Protest in Peru.* Pittsburgh: University of Pittsburgh Press.

Arcos, Ander Alonso, and Estefanía Rivera

2018 *Brechas de género en la minería:. La minería artesanal y de pequeña escala colombiana desde una perspectiva de género.* Antioquia: Alianza por la Minería Responsable.

Artisanal and Small-Scale Mining Knowledge Sharing Archive

2017 "ASM inventory." http://artisanalmining.org/Inventory/.

Baraybar, Viviana, and Eduardo Dargent

2019 *State Responses to the Gold Rush in the Andes (2004–2018): The Politics of State Action (and Inaction).* Cuaderno de Trabajo 48. Lima: PUCP.

CEDIB (Centro de Documentación e Información Bolivia)

2012 "Surgen 'agromineros' en Mallku Khota." December 5. https://cedib.org/post_type_titulares/surgen-agromineros-en-mallku-khota-los-tiempos-5-12-2012/.

CETIM (Third World Centre)

2014 "Mining and human rights violations in Colombia: the case of Anglo Gold Ashanti vs the Afri-descendant community of La Toma (Cauca)." November 11. https://www.cetim.ch/mining-and-human-rights-violations-in-colombia-the-case-of-anglo-gold-ashanti-vy-the-afri-descendant-community-of-la-toma-cauca/.

Convoca

2015 "Los S/. 30 millones que no cobró el gobierno en multas mineras." August 2. https://convoca.pe/investigacion/los-s-30-millones-que-no-cobro-el-gobierno-en-multas-mineras.

Cordi, Paul, Marcello Veiga, Ibrahim Salih, Sari Al-Saadi, Stephanie Console, Oseas García, Luis Alberto Mesa, Patricio Velásquez-López, and Monika Roeser
2011 "Mercury contamination from artisanal gold mining in Antioquia, Colombia: the world's highest per capita mercury pollution." *Science of the Total Environment* 410–411 (1): 154–160.
Dargent, Eduardo, and Madai Urteaga
2016 "State response by external pressures: the determinants of the state's strengthening to face the illegal gold mining boom in Peru (2004–2015)." *Revista de Ciencia Política* 36 (3): 255–277.
Dunkerley, James
1984 *Rebellion in the Veins: Political Struggle in Bolivia, 1952–82.* London: Verso.
Durand, Francisco
2016 *Extractive Industries and Political Capture: Effects on Institutions, Equality, and the Environment.* Lima: Oxfam.
El Comercio
2014 "Marcha de mineros ilegales: miles seguirán hoy con protestas." March 21. https://elcomercio.pe/peru/marcha-mineros-ilegales-miles-seguiran-hoy-protestas-303494.
El Espectador
2017 "Desde Medellín apoyaron paro minero en Segovia y Remedios." August 4. https://www.elespectador.com/noticias/nacional/antioquia/desde-medellin-apoyaron-paro-minero-en-segovia-y-remedios-articulo-706524.
El Tiempo
2019 "Una 'luz al final del túnel' en crisis minera de Marmato (Caldas)." May 17. https://www.eltiempo.com/colombia/otras-ciudades/una-luz-al-final-del-tunel-en-crisis-minera-de-marmato-caldas-363216.
Fairfield, Tasha
2015 *Private Wealth and Public Revenues in Latin America: Business Power and Tax Politics.* Cambridge: Cambridge University Press.
Farthing, Linda, and Benjamin Kohl
2014 *Evo's Bolivia: Continuity and Change.* Austin: University of Texas Press.
García Linera, Álvaro
2013 *Democracia, Estado, nación.* La Paz: Vicepresidencia el Estado Plurinacional.
GIATOC (Global Initiative against Transnational Organized Crime)
2016 *Organized Crime and Illegally Mined Gold in Latin America.* Geneva: GIATOC.
GOMIAM (Gold Mining in the Amazon)
2015 "Un llamado a reconsiderar la minería aurífera informal en Chocó y la Amazonía: policy brief." March 15. https://www.gomiam.org/wp-content/uploads/2014/11/Policy-Brief-GOMIAM-Colombia.pdf.
Gudynas, Eduardo
2010 "The new extractivism of the 21th century: ten urgent theses about extractivism in relation to current South American progressivism." Americas Program Report. Center for International Policy. http://postdevelopment.net/2010/02/19/new-extractivism-of-the-21st-century-10-urgent-theses/.

2013 *Extracciones, extractivismos y extrahecciones: Un marco conceptual sobre la apropriación de recursos naturales.* Montevideo: CLAES.

La Razón

2016 "El Gobierno confirma la muerte del viceministro Rodolfo Illanes a manos de cooperativistas." August 25. http://www.la-razon.com/economia/Regimen-Interior-Rodolfo-Illanes-Panduro_0_2552144857.html.

La República

2018 "Minería ilegal crece pesa a operativos." May 17. https://larepublica.pe/politica/1244619-mineria-ilegal-crece-pese-operativos-interdiccion/.

Li, Fabiana

2015 *Unearthing Conflict: Corporate Mining, Activism, and Expertise in Peru.* Durham, NC: Duke University Press.

Marston, Andrea, and Tom Perreault

2017 "Consent, coercion and *cooperativismo*: Mining cooperatives and resource regimes in Bolivia." *Environment and Planning* 49 (2): 252–272.

Massé, Frédéric, and Philippe Le Billon

2018 "Gold mining in Colombia, post-war crime and the peace agreement with the FARC." *Third World Thematics* 3 (1): 116–134.

Mayorga, Fernando

2009 *Antinomias: El azaroso camino de la reforma política.* Cochabamba: CESU-UMSS.

Ojo Público

2016 "Luis Otsuka: el gobernador minero que quiere poner en jaque a PPK." August 7. https://ojo-publico.com/Luis-Otsuka-El-gobernador-minero-que-quiere-poner-en-jaque-a-PPK.

Okada, Isamu

2016 "Evo Morales, cooperativas mineras y el difícil parto de la nueva ley minera." *Revista Decursos* 18 (34): 161–193.

Orozco, Olinda, Guadalupe Eto Chero, and Franco Arista Rivera

2017 *Pallaqueras, entre piedras y oro: Diagnóstico participativo en las regiones de Arequipa, Ayacucho y Puno.* Lima: Solidaridad.

Osorio, Camila

2012 "En el Chocó, Santos enfrenta el gran dilema: ¿podrán los mineros informales ser parte del boom minero?" *La Silla Vacía.* January 30. https://lasillavacia.com/historia/en-el-choco-santos-enfrenta-el-gran-dilema-podran-los-mineros-informales-ser-parte-del-boom.

Pachas, Víctor Hugo

2011 *Historia de una incertidumbre: Hábitat, conflicto y poder en la minería artesanal de oro en el Perú.* Lima: Earth First.

Poveda, Pablo

2014 *Formas de producción de las cooperativas mineras de Bolivia.* La Paz: CEDLA.

Poveda, Pablo, Héctor Córdova, Neyer Nogales, Alejandro Pulido, William Sacher, Lino João de Oliveira, Estefanía Daró, and Pía Marchegiani

2015 *La economía del oro: Ensayos sobre la explotación en Sudamérica.* La Paz: CEDLA.

Pulido, Alejandro
2015 "El cartel de la gran minería del oro en Colombia: ¿Amenaza a las democracias locales?" pp. 77–94 in Pablo Poveda, Héctor Córdova, Alejandro Pulido, William Sacher, Lino João de Oliveira, Estefania Daró, and Pia Marchegiani (eds.), *La economía del oro: Ensayos sobre la explotación en Sudamérica*. La Paz: CEDLA.
Rettberg, Angelika, and Juan Felipe Ortiz-Riomalo
2016 "Golden opportunity, or A new twist on the resource-conflict relationship: links between the drug trade and illegal mining in Colombia." *World Development* 84: 82–96.
Rettberg, Angelika, Ralf Leiteritz, Carlo Nasi, and Juan Diego Prieto
2018 *¿Diferentes recursos, conflictos distintos? La economía política regional del conflicto armado y la criminalidad en Colombia*. Bogotá: Universidad de los Andes.
Rivera Cusicanqui, Silvia
2014 *Mito y desarrollo en Bolivia: El giro colonial del gobierno del MAS*. La Paz: Piedra Rota/Plural.
Sarmiento, Mariana, Beatriz Giraldo, Helcias Ayala, Alexandra Uran, Cristina Soto, and Leyla Martinez
2013 "Characteristics and challenges of small-scale gold mining in Colombia," pp. 46–67 in L. Cremers, J. Kolen, and M. E. M. de Theije (eds.), *Small-Scale Gold Mining in the Amazon: The Cases of Bolivia, Brazil, Colombia, Peru and Suriname*. Amsterdam: CEDLA.
Scott, James
1998 *Seeing Like a State: How Certain Schemes to Improve the Human Condition Have Failed*. New Heaven and London: Yale University Press.
Soifer, Hillel
2015 *State Building in Latin America*. New York: Cambridge University Press.
SPDA (Sociedad Peruana de Derecho Ambiental)
2015 *Las rutas del oro ilegal: Estudios de caso en cinco países amazónicos*. Lima: SPDA.
Svampa, Maristella
2019 *Neo-Extractivism in Latin America: Socio-Environmental Conflicts, the Territorial Turn, and New Political Narratives*. New York: Cambridge University Press.
Toledo Orozco, Zaraí
2020 "(Under)Mining state authority: the politics of informal gold mining in Bolivia and Peru." Ph.D. diss., University of British Columbia.
Toledo Orozco, Zaraí, and Marcello Veiga
2018 "Locals' attitudes toward artisanal mining and large-scale mining: a case study from Tambogrande, Peru." *The Extractive Industries and Society* 5: 327–334.
UNODC (Oficina de las Naciones Unidas contra la Droga y el Delito)
2019 *Informe Colombia, explotación de oro de aluvión: Evidencias a partir de percepción remota 2018 y los hallazgos preliminares para 2019*. Bogotá: UNODC and MINERGIA.

Vasquez, Mirtha

2019 "La interdicción, ¿lucha frontal contra la minería ilegal?" February 26. https://wayka.pe/la-interdiccion-lucha-frontal-contra-la-mineria-ilegal-por-mirtha-vasquez/.

Veiga, Marcello

1997 *Introducing New Technologies for Abatement of Global Mercury Pollution in Latin America.* Río de Janeiro: UNIDO/UBC/CETEM/CNPq.

Viceministerio de Cooperativas de Bolivia

2016 *Distribución nacional de cooperativas mineras y número de asociados.* La Paz: Ministerio de Minería y Metalurgia.

Weber, Max

1968 *Economy and Society: An Outline of Interpretive Sociology.* Edited by Guenther Roth and Claus Wittich. New York: Bedminster.

11

Black Women's Struggles against Extractivism, Land Dispossession, and Marginalization in Colombia

Castriela Esther Hernández Reyes

On November 17, 2014, forty black women from the Department of Cauca (La Toma, Suarez, and Santander de Quilichao) walked 400 miles to Bogotá as the first mobilization for the Care of Life and Ancestral Territories. Shouting slogans such as "Territories and life are not sold—they are loved and defended!" and "*Bateas* yes! Backhoes no!" they denounced the illegal mining, water pollution, and loss of income created by extractivism and violence in their territories. They opposed the Colombian government's neoliberal policies promoting resource extraction and agribusiness, which have created dispossession, forced displacement, and social marginalization. They further condemned the government's failure to remove illegal backhoes and other mining equipment from their collective lands. The women demanded a guarantee of their right to work in the ancestral mining, fishing, and agriculture that provide them subsistence.

The March of the Turbans, as it was dubbed by the mass media, called attention to the impacts of mining concessions granted without prior consultation to multinational corporations and white/mestizo elites that aimed to exploit the collective lands of ethno-racial communities. It denounced the mistreatment of black people by state officials, racism, and death threats against their leaders issued by armed actors (paramilitaries). The women occupied the office of the Casa Giralda (the Ministry of the Interior and Justice in Bogotá)[1] to press for dialogue with the government. By courageously expressing their anger and pain, they called into question the officials' reference to black communities as "bad-faith disrupters" and "enemies of economic progress" (Francia Márquez, quoted in PBS's series *We Shall Remain,* December 21, 2014). Under pressure, the government agreed, on a provisional basis, to stop the mining concessions granted without consultation. It also agreed to remove the illegal backhoes and other equipment and establish a mechanism for monitoring progress on the agreement.

While neocolonial extractivism produces and reproduces material forms of exclusion, racism, inequality, and oppression, mobilizations and other forms of resistance by the subaltern are growing across Latin America (Escobar, 2008; Picq, 2014; Motta, 2011; Fabricant and Postero, 2013). What do black women's struggles contribute to an understanding of this resistance and the ways in which the neoliberal economy of extractivism upholds a racist and classist order in Colombia? I address these questions by drawing on black/decolonial feminist theory and praxis to examine the political statements issued[2] during and after the 2014 march, seeking to show how black women as political actors use their feelings, collective affections, and Afro-aesthetic politics to make their exclusion, marginalization, and resistance practices visible. I also analyze their political discourse through an interview conducted with Francia Márquez, one of the most visible leaders of the march, and data gathered from a symposium entitled "Black Women, Territory, and Peace-building in the 21st Century" that I co-organized at the University of Massachusetts, Amherst, in 2016.[3] I complement this material with secondary sources to explore the intersection between black women's struggles and their feelings in their production of distinctive political narratives and practices that contribute to an understanding of the broader dynamics of racial capitalism and the marginalization of blacks in Colombia.

As a black feminist from the Global South, I believe that black/decolonial feminist theory and praxis provide a critical perspective for scrutinizing and contesting patriarchy, colonialism, and racial capitalism. They aim at deconstructing Western feminism and problematizing hegemonic and oppressive power relations and the violence produced by the colonial/patriarchal and racialized capitalist system.

In this chapter I first contextualize black people's historical struggles and activism in Colombia. Then I offer a black/decolonial feminist analysis of black women's historicity, political subjectivities, and resistance. Black feminist epistemologies do not require black men's voices for the legitimization of their discourses and struggles. In this sense, this is not an article about what black women think of black men's ideas of their struggles or how black women's voices and resistance practices compare with black men's struggles in Colombia. My contention here is that black women as political thinkers produce oppositional and situated knowledge that disrupts Western feminism and white/mestizo hegemonic knowledge production. Third, I provide a critical analysis of the way the colonial rationalities of neoliberal extractivism are incorporated into racialized capitalism. In addition, I analyze the production of black women's political subjectivities and Afro-diasporic aesthetics, concluding that black women's aesthetics, feelings, and collective affection are means of resistance that contribute to producing alternative practices of liberation and feminist Afro-epistemologies. Black women's aesthetics, subjectivities, and emotions are driving forces of their activism, political identity, and sense of belonging to African diaspora culture. Finally, in this chapter I use quotes from a wide range of scholars and social actors to demonstrate that the line of reasoning and conceptions put forward by black/decolonial feminist writers hardly constitute a fringe theory with few adherents.

Black Activism in Colombia

While some scholars suggest that strong black social movements in Colombia emerged at the end of the twentieth century with the passage of constitutional reforms and the Black Communities Law of 1993[4] (Grueso and Arroyo, 2002; Asher, 2004; Paschel, 2016), I contend that black people's activism and their collective resistance go beyond this periodization and constitute a response to the enduring historical, political, and economic project of capitalism in which structural racism and the devaluation of black bodies interlock (Pulido, 2016).

From the sixteenth through the eighteenth century, enslaved black women and men escaped chattel slavery and built autonomous self-governing territories known as *palenques*. Palenque communities were maroon[5] areas of resistance that constituted one of the first projects of liberation from slavery and decolonization in South America and the Caribbean. These communities and the Haitian Revolution were the first attempts to produce alternative forms of "decolonial thinking" in the colonial/modern system (Maldonado-Torres, 2011). During the eighteenth and nineteenth centuries, enslaved black women in South America and the Caribbean used colonial law strategically to acquire freedom for themselves and their offspring (Hernández-Reyes, 2018). In the first half of the twentieth century, a black woman named Felicita Campos resisted dispossession by white/mestizo landowners who had ordered the eviction of black people from San Onofre, Sucre (a small town on the Colombian Caribbean). She encouraged her community to organize and defend its lands with sticks and machetes. She was imprisoned several times, and her house was burned down in retaliation (Fundación del Sinú et al., 1985). In the 1960s and 1970s, black people's political discourses expressed pride for their African origins and cultural practices and drew attention to the evilness of slavery and colonial systems. People from the African diaspora demanded civil rights and the redefinition of Afro-descendant identities (Wade, 1996). In the late 1970s, this movement was led by the black student organization Soweto.[6]

The activism of Soweto members and other blacks at the time focused on ethno-racial demands and questioned the political reductionism of the old left parties, which centered on class struggle while subordinating issues of race. At the beginning of the 1980s, Soweto became Cimarrón, a national movement for the rights of black communities, which worked in defense of Afro-Colombians' human rights and blackness. In the predominantly Afro-Colombian Department of Chocó in 1988, the Organización Barrios Populares del Chocó (Organization of Popular Neighborhoods of Chocó— OBAPO), a movement of the urban poor, began fighting for black communities' right to education, territory, health, transportation, basic services, and employment. A woman from this organization, Zulia Mena, went on to become the first black congresswoman elected after the 1991 Constitution expanded Afro-Colombians' rights. OBAPO played a prominent role in the passage of the Black Communities Law (Hernández-Reyes, 2010; Paschel, 2016).[7]

Constitutional Reform and Black Struggles in the 1990s

The 1990s were the most prominent period of mobilization of black communities in Latin America as black movements in Colombia, Ecuador, Brazil, and Guatemala gained legal recognition and protection of their collective rights and their cultural diversity as defining elements of the nation (Agudelo, 2005; Lao-Montes, 2009; Asher, 2004; Escobar, 2008, 2015; Grueso and Arroyo, 2002; Paschel, 2016). Paschel argues that in previous Colombian constitutions, legal and institutional discourses were "color-blind" and therefore black communities struggled for the recognition of Afro-Colombians as an ethnic group (Paschel, 2016). Transitory Article 55 of the 1991 Constitution recognized black people's rights and led to the formulation of the Black Communities Law (Law 70 of 1993). This law recognized communal lands and prior consultation about development and promoted the creation of black community councils. Many scholars argue that it was the most important "conquest" of the black social movement in Colombia and Latin America (Agudelo, 2005; Lao-Montes, 2009; Paschel, 2016; Valderrama, 2014), even though, as Perreault (2015) points out, its liberatory promises have far from been achieved. Law 70 has ambiguities and contradictions between local and national judicial decisions in relation to the recognition of black collective territories and rights to prior consultation. For private and multinational corporations interested in seizing black territories in Colombia, it is the main obstacle to neoliberal development agendas based on the commodification of nature and the devaluation of black bodies (Escobar, 2008, 2015; Levien, 2012; Bernasconi, 2014).

A substantial number of black grassroots organizations emerged after the enactment of Law 70. One of these organizations was the Proceso de Comunidades Negras (the Process of Black Communities—PCN), which emerged at the end of 1993 as a network of local organizations that participated in the promotion and regulation of Transitory Article 55.[8] PCN promoted the creation of black community councils, including the one in La Toma of which Francia Márquez was a spokeswoman.

La Toma: Neocolonial Extractivism, Racism, Violence, and Black People's Resistance

La Toma is a small village located in the municipality of Suarez, between the Ovejas and Cauca Rivers in northern Cauca. Black people have lived in La Toma since the early 1600s, when they were brought as captives and forced to work in gold mining under Spanish domination (Ararat et al., 2013; Escobar, 2008). Mining was the most important economic activity in the colonial system, guaranteeing the wealth of elites and colonial institutions.

Currently, La Toma consists of 1,300 households in an area of 7,000 hectares (Vélez-Torres, 2014: 69), more than 80 percent of which are Afro-Colombian. The main sources of sustenance are agriculture and artisanal gold mining.[9] Black women and men spend two to three days a week growing coffee and plantains and to a lesser extent vegetables and fruits for profit and sustenance and dedicate four to five days a week to the extraction of gold with traditional methods. The ancestral mode of mining is a traditional activity and a source of subsistence for Afro-descendant families, and it does not destroy the landscape. La Toma has limited running water (20.2 percent of households) and sewerage systems (3.5 percent of households), and even though almost 95 percent of its inhabitants have electricity they have difficulty paying their bills (Ararat et al., 2013; Vélez-Torres, 2014; Bernasconi, 2014). Because of violence, poverty, water pollution, and structural racism, many black women and men migrate to urban areas to work, largely in the informal economy, or to attend school.

Since the 1980s, La Toma's people have been fighting the racial discrimination and dispossession created by the building of the Salvajina Dam on the Cauca River. The dam has produced massive displacement, poverty, and difficulties of mobility (Ararat et al., 2013: 254). In 1998 the people of La Toma set up a community council for the collective defense of their ancestral territories and resistance to extractivism and violence (Escobar, 2015). Nevertheless, the construction of the dam and the military base above its reservoir have led to the influx of foreign companies and the militarization of the social life of black and indigenous communities. "The history of the Salvajina is embedded in the dynamics of global capitalism that in northern Cauca has managed to displace thousands of people and alter an ecosystem as old as its inhabitants, while at the same time enforcing a cycle of violence from which politicians, entrepreneurs, and multinational corporations are now generating profits" (Bernasconi, 2014: 109).

At the beginning of the 2000s, the Colombian government initiated a new cycle of granting mining licenses to multinational corporations and local enterprises. Mining corporations, with their backhoes and other mining equipment, and paramilitaries that were "nothing but an unofficial arm of the government" arrived in Cauca (Bernasconi, 2014: 140–141). Paramilitaries began to control illegal mining and drug trafficking (Vélez-Torres, 2014: 75). In April 2001 they carried out a massacre in Alta Naya, killing more than 100 people and driving 3,000 members of local black, peasant, and indigenous communities from their homes (Verdad Abierta, 2009; Vélez-Torres, 2014; Bernasconi, 2014).

Over the past two decades, Colombia's national development plans have used laws and policies ostensibly focused on increasing security to grant mining licenses to transnational corporations and members of local elites. This has increased the historical process of evacuations (Alimonda, 2011) and the devaluation of black people as the surplus of neoliberal capitalism. In 2009, for example, a local judge issued an order of eviction against "illegal" black miners from La Toma. The aim was to protect the economic interests of Héctor Sarria, a mestizo miner who in 2000 was granted a 15-year license. According to the local judicial system, La Toma was not legally recognized as a black collective territory, and therefore it could be granted for large-scale mining exploitation without prior consultation. The eviction order overlooked the fact that prior consultation is an international and national mechanism for facilitating democratic participation between ethnic communities and governments (Perreault, 2015). The judge failed to take into account the fact that La Toma was, according to the 2005 Census, more than 80 percent Afro-Colombian and therefore its residents had a fundamental right to prior consultation.

In 2010 an illegal mine, San Antonio, in Santander de Quilichao collapsed and nine Afro-Colombian miners died. Representatives of La Toma's community council Yair Ortiz Larrahondo and Francia Márquez filed a lawsuit or *tutela*[10] demanding the protection of the black community's rights, the recognition of black identity and black culture, and the right to prior consultation. In its decision, the Colombian Constitutional Court not only recognized La Toma as an area historically occupied by black people but also protected their right to prior consultation. It banned large-scale mining in ethnic territories without prior consultation and determined that black communities' rights and their territories could not be violated. Despite the decision, illegal and legal mining exploitation and violence continued and included threats to and murder of community leaders by paramilitaries belonging to the notorious Aguilas Negras (Black Eagles). This became a racist mode of regulating, controlling, and governing the social lives, bodies, and cultural practices of ethno-racial communities.

Intersectionality and Black/Decolonial Feminism

Black feminist scholars argue that black feminism as a movement emerged simultaneously with second-wave white feminism in the United States in the late 1960s to challenge "white feminist movements for playing down or ignoring economic and survival issues common to the black community, and failing to examine personal [and structural] racism" (Roth, 2003: 49). Black feminism has produced a political theorization of the everyday personal experiences of black women and revealed the "overlapping, mutually constitutive nature of oppressions of race, class, gender, and sexuality" (Roth, 2003: 47). Black feminists individually and collectively create spaces that aim at challenging racism, classism, patriarchy, sexism, and violence.

While black feminism develops an "understanding of interlocking oppressive systems" (Roth, 2003: 46–47), decolonial feminism emerged to question the absence from hegemonic feminism of an intersectional analysis of multiple forms of oppression against nonwhite women and the scholarly work led by Latin American men on coloniality and modernity. What is referred to as "hegemonic feminism," dominated by white women, has furthered the historical and theoretical exclusion of nonwhite women, ignoring the intersectionality of race, class, gender, and sexuality and the fact that women of color have been victims of both the coloniality of power and the coloniality of gender (Lugones, 2008). María Lugones (2008, 2010) introduced the concept of the "modern/colonial system of gender" to break with the binary assumption embedded in modern Western logic. An understanding of Western logic and its gendered regime entails the comprehension of gender as a racialized system of power that promotes the dehumanization and subjectification of subaltern people and "the attempt to turn the colonized into less than human beings" (Lugones, 2010: 745). According to this line of thinking, racism and patriarchy are not aberrations but rather an intricate part of the capitalist system and the existing system of domination. Decolonial feminist intellectuals argue that it is necessary to expand the modern/colonial analytical matrix of male-dominated decolonial studies to understand the way power operates in gender norms (Lugones, 2008) and the "everyday practices of racialized violence" (Fabricant and Postero, 2013: 205). Along these lines, black women and women of color have criticized Western/white feminisms and their tendency to ignore and misrepresent them.

Hazel Carby (2007) contends that white feminists have misunderstood black women's life experiences and struggles, portraying them as simply "objects of research" or "passive recipients of colonial oppression." While most "contemporary feminist theory does not begin to adequately account for the experience of black women" (Carby, 2007: 111), blacks, Asians, Latinas, and many women of color have openly "criticized Western feminism for being racist in that it is overly concerned with white, middle-class women's issues" (Collins, 2000b: 5). Thus, Western/white feminists have represented only themselves rather than all women (Carby, 2007; Collins, 2000a).

Following the knowledge production of women of color, Nelson Maldonado-Torres (2016: 17) asserts that the dominant culture and knowledge production have sought to construct subaltern women as "subjects without the capacity for autonomy and self-determination." As the March of the Turbans makes evident, black and indigenous women have in fact demonstrated that they are historically subjects of resistance in the Americas at the same time that they "simultaneously face multiple oppressions [and] are in a position to reimagine emancipatory politics, produce and embody difference, and create and experiment with new subjectivities" (Seppälä, 2016: 4).

I adopt both black feminist and decolonial feminist theories and praxis critically to examine black women's resistance and to question the invisibilization of black women as political thinkers and actors in historical nation-state formations in the Global South. Black and decolonial feminist theories and praxis emphasize that to avoid essentialism about black, indigenous, and other nonwhite women, it is necessary to capture the way they use their subjectivities politically, strategically, discursively, and textually (hooks, 1992; Crenshaw, 1991; Collins, 2000b; Lugones, 2008, 2010; May, 2015). By focusing on experience-based epistemologies of black women (Collins, 2005), black/decolonial feminism contributes to affirming black women's self-definition and self-determination, which entails the production of a situated "oppositional knowledge" (Collins, 2000b; Roth, 2003; hooks, 1992; Crenshaw, 1991).

For me as a black anthropologist and black/decolonial feminist and activist, it is imperative to avoid concealing black women's voices. Thus, a black/decolonial feminist approach and praxis disrupt the ongoing processes of misrepresentation of subaltern women's stories, subjectivities, political thinking, and knowledge production. Black feminist scholars criticize the absence of emotions from the research process, arguing that emotions are not separate from intellect, and assert that "the ethic of caring suggests that personal expressiveness, emotions, and empathy are central to the knowledge validation process" (Patricia Hill Collins, 2000b: 263; hooks, 1992; Collins, 2000b). Thus theorizing the everyday experiences of black women from a black/decolonial feminist perspective has to begin from their historical and geographical location in recording their stories and experiences of resistance.

Following bell hooks (1992), I conceptualize black women's struggles as an exercise of radical and oppositional consciousness that allows us to contest, negotiate, and challenge power relations tactically. Understanding black women's activism and its patterns of resistance (May 2015) helps us to comprehend the historical rejection of Afro-Colombian women as political thinkers within the mainstream academy. Afro-Colombian women's struggles cannot be understood through fragmented viewpoints that delink their past from their present, a defect that this study of Afro-Colombian women's protests seeks to correct. This erasure of history is often the result of hegemonic epistemological projects through which elites are portrayed as the exclusive owners of the past, leaving Others invisible in history (Scott, 2012). By situating myself spatially and politically as an insider, I seek to weave alternative discursive practices that disrupt the hegemonic epistemologies that permanently objectify subaltern people who are "outside" Western logic. Thus I aim not only to contribute to "the demand to decolonize feminism" (Seppälä, 2016: 12) but also to *ennegrecer* (darken) (Carneiro, 2001) decolonial feminism through an Afro-diasporic feminist epistemology and praxis.

Neocolonialism Extractivism and Racialized Capitalism in Colombia

After the collapse of colonialism in many African countries, the advanced capitalist nations turned toward extractivism in South America (Picq, 2014) and in Africa to maintain former colonies "under the control of the capitalist-imperialist forces composed of the developed countries in the North . . . through international trade, aid and investment policies tailored to sustain the movement of resources from the developing countries" (Bbaala, 2015: 101). Since the adoption of neoliberal economics in the late 1980s and 1990s, many Latin American governments have focused their economic agendas on extractivism and agroindustry (Pulido, 2017; Picq, 2014; Escobar, 2008). Productive regimes of mining have been based in large part on the exploitation of black and indigenous people's labor force and lives and the expropriation of their lands (Fabricant and Postero, 2013: 205).

Capitalism and neoliberalism have meant "the commodification and privatization of land and the forced expulsion of populations" (Harvey, 2007: 159). Under this logic, extractive economies "have benefitted primarily foreigners and their local partners, condemning South America's largely indigenous [and black] population . . . to live in poverty and suffer from a legacy of environmental contamination" (Kohl and Farthing, 2012: 225). At the same time, capitalism and neoliberalism as means of accumulation by dispossession have reinforced the destruction of alternative forms of production and consumption (Harvey, 2007: 159), maintaining colonial and imperial economic projects through the appropriation of assets. Far from reversing historical dependencies, recent Latin American governments have exacerbated the commodification of nature as state-sponsored extractivism is promoted as the ideal model for achieving economic growth. Neoliberal extractive projects, particularly in Colombia, have been framed by "the consolidation of a military presence in order to maintain the necessary social control—through repression and threats" (Bernasconi, 2014: 94) and the military securitization of local mining settings for the control of underground resources (Vélez-Torres, 2014: 72).

Between 2001 and 2005, the Colombian Congress passed several laws (among them Law 685/2001 and Mining Code 963/2005) that fueled the participation of foreign investors (Vélez-Torres, 2014). Mining exploitation laws established the main principles safeguarding stockholders instead of protecting ethnic communities' rights. This legislation and its implementation facilitated "accumulation by dispossession" (Harvey, 2007; Motta, 2011) as an expression of contemporary "racial capitalism," through which "the development, organization and expansion of capitalist society pursued essentially racial directions" (Robinson, 2000: 2).

According to Clayton (2016: 445), state and paramilitary violence in Colombia has played a fundamental role "in the expansion of the extractive economy over the past decades, acting as a guarantee for territorial control and allowing capital to penetrate areas of the country where previous conditions limited accumulation." As a result, a confluence of illegality, counterinsurgency, and regional marginality produces and reproduces the militarization of social life in many rural territories afflicted by armed conflict (Ramírez, 2018). The situation has further deteriorated under the current presidency of Iván Duque (2018–2022), as clearly documented in a report issued by the UN's Office of the High Commissioner of Human Rights that the government denounced as a violation of national sovereignty.

Following Clayton and Ramirez, I identify the militarization of social life in La Toma as the process through which the state uses violence to control territory, bodies, and everyday lives to guarantee foreign investment and private capital. In La Toma and other poor rural areas, "the presence of the state is overall military and oppressive" (Bernasconi, 2014: 98). The building of the Salvajina Dam and military base along with extractivism, poverty, and inequality in northern Cauca illustrate "normalizing and racializing violence" (Melamed, 2011: xi; Fabricant and Postero, 2013). They also display the logic of modernity/coloniality, which fosters expropriation and exclusion (Maldonado-Torres, 2016: 17).

Black Women's Resistance to Neocolonial Extractivism and Dispossession

Subaltern and oppressed women in Colombia have played a major role in forming movements that contest neoliberal development and neocolonialism (Seppälä, 2016: 12). The political agenda of subaltern groups is promoting "alternative forms of development and politics," rejecting "extreme forms of dispossession, poverty and inequality" (Motta, 2011: 2). During the March of the Turbans, black women carried *bateas* (wooden pans or trays) and drums to dance and sing to. Black artisanal miners have been using trays to separate gold in the mines since the colonial period. For black women miners the trays are both tools for sustenance and powerful symbols of resistance. Maldonado-Torres notes that slogans such as "*Bateas* yes! Backhoes no!" and "Fears are overcome by walking together, singing together" are decolonizing and political expressions of resistance and of understanding and loving (Maldonado-Torres, 2016: 24).

Afro-Colombian women occupied the Casa Giralda to pressure the government into negotiating their political agenda, seeking to subvert the "peaceful" space of the city. During the mobilization, black women said, "We do not want to be afraid to walk along our roads. . . . We want the backhoes out of Cauca and all the deeds granted without prior consultation repealed" (Black Women's Political Statement 3, November 2014). They took this message to public universities to talk about their struggles and received the solidarity and support of students (Black Women's Political Statements 1 and 2, November 2014). The agreement they negotiated with the government, however, has remained unfulfilled (Francia Márquez, interview, November 29, 2015). Indeed, mining grants to foreign corporations have increased. The expropriation of land for mining today can be viewed as "the continuation of the 'Doctrine of Discovery' that conceptualized the New World as 'terra nullis' or 'wastelands'" (Picq, 2014: 30) at the same time that "the processes of appropriation and access to land are racialized" (Pulido, 2017). Black women's emotional expressions expose the way black territories are viewed by the government (Black Women's Political Statement 4, November 2014):

> Today, the possibilities for Afro-descendant communities are very small because we are threatened with both bodily and cultural death! We are being threatened through the processes of dispossession furthered by the mining locomotive of President Santos, who grants concessions and mining titles to multinationals and white/mestizo elites, violating our rights to prior consultation and informed consent. We are threatened with illegal mining and its backhoes that are destroying the environment and territory that we have cared for for centuries. We are threatened by

armed groups who accuse us of opposing the development policies of the government.

This example of a gender and racial-based protest shows how black women understand the intersectional nature of the racialized commodification of land and devaluation of black bodies in Colombia. It also shows how the modernity/coloniality project is being used to foster the appropriation and representation of Others. According to Rolando Vázquez, a decolonial critique, "as a form of epistemic struggle, aims to foster spaces in which listening to what has been relegated to oblivion becomes possible" (Vázquez, 2012: 2–3).

Thousands of black women displaced by paramilitary groups and illegal mining have been forced to move to various cities and "end up living either in legal or illegal slums," losing their connection with their communities and families (Seppälä, 2016). Many become domestic workers, which often involves exploitation and commodification of their labor (Collins, 2000a).

Breaking the Silence: Black Women's Discourse and Resistance Practices

Black women miners argue that ancestral mining is an important economic activity that strengthens communal forms of living for Afro-Colombian families (Jazmin Mina, interview, quoted in PBS's *Women, War and Peace II: The War We Are Living*, 2011). Mining for black women goes beyond extracting gold in that it has come to signify solidarity and communal living. Black miners in La Toma promote "mutual aid" as a collective system through which they share and "maintain a constant social interaction among the different family groups, reinforcing ties of friendship and solidarity" (Bernasconi, 2014: 56). In 2010, when twelve backhoes and equipment arrived in La Toma to extract gold, the members of the community organized to resist. Approximately 500 members of black communities blocked the road, but in retaliation they were threatened with eviction. By the end of 2012 the government had granted more than 271 licenses for mining exploitation in northern Cauca. At one point there were at least 652 claims for licenses in the department and almost 50 percent of Cauca lands were in the hands of private investors (Centro de Estudios Interculturales, 2014). In 2013 the people of La Toma went en masse to the Oveja River and formed a human chain to stop the backhoes. On November 27, 2015, two congressmen from the leftist Polo Democrático Alternativo called a public hearing in northern Cauca to listen to the communities' demands and find out what the local authorities were doing to solve their problems. Francia Márquez (interview, November 29, 2015) described the meeting: "The public hearing brought together over 500 people including peasants, blacks, and indigenous people to oppose inequalities and structural and armed violence in our territories, demonstrating our capacity for resistance. Our meeting and our articulating a defense of the territory and the life of our communities was resistance."

While the economic model in Colombia is fostering social unrest as the result of the disruption of the sociocultural dynamics of Afro-Colombian rural communities, black women are proposing alternative ways of thinking about "development": "For us, territory is not just a material space. It is the spiritual, the cultural, and the way of producing and relating among us as black people" (Francia Márquez, interview, November 29, 2015). For black women their lands and rivers represent their parents, and they feel sad and offended when the state takes their ethnic territories away in order to benefic private interests and corporations (Bernasconi, 2014).

For black women farming, singing, and dancing make them happy and help to alleviate the exclusion they face daily (Francia Márquez, remarks at University of Massachusetts, Amherst, symposium, April 5, 2016). Emotions are central to their understanding of political actions and social life (Jasper, 1998; Flam and King, 2005; Farthing and Kohl, 2013). Jasper (1998: 414) asserts that emotions are "part of a movement's own dynamics." According to him, "It is almost impossible to imagine mobilization in the absence of strong emotions. . . . In an injustice frame, the passion for justice is fueled by anger over existing injustice." Flam (2005: 19–20) argues that emotions are "social, cultural, and political constructs that operate in micro and macro political spaces. Power and oppression at the institutional level force the production in social movements of 'subversive counter-emotions.'" Black people "are concerned about defending the territory, because without the territory they will be nobody" (E3, interview, quoted in Bernasconi, 2014: 139, 152). Black women claim that their love of life is greater than their fear of death and say, "Our ancestors first and then our mothers, fathers, sisters, and brothers have spilled a lot of blood to get these lands" (Black Women's Political Statement 4, November 2014). These powerful narratives demonstrate black people's subversive counter-emotions and their disaffection (Flam, 2005: 20). Anger is experienced "as a 'real emotion' when we are confronted with power that seriously limits our autonomy and we attribute the blame for the loss of autonomy to the power-holder" (Flam and King, 2005: 22).

This understanding of anger in connection with historical experiences of marginalization was part of the black women's protest. During the meeting between officials and black women held at the Casa Giralda, Francia Márquez expressed her anger: "We are not willing to accept the Colombian government's being the one that determines whether we are formally black communities or not. We are black communities, and the government has to recognize our rights and fulfill them. That is what we demand." In essence, love, rage, fear, and courage are not only "motivations and explanations" (Jasper, 1998: 398) in black women's struggles.

The mobilizations of black women have made legible their political and cultural traditions, thus their use of symbols such as bateas and turbans in their protests. In the process, they preserve the collective and revive the social bonds of black communities as key mechanisms. The lived experiences, struggles, and political subjectivities of black women are expressed in a material world in which a feminization of poverty is contested by "a feminization of resistance that is reconfiguring and reimagining the nature, meaning, and subjects of political resistance and social transformation" (Motta, 2013: 36). Since poverty in Latin America has been not only feminized but also racialized, a feminist theory of resistance must embrace an intersectional analysis of patriarchal regimes of power to better capture the political subjectivities and experience-based epistemologies of black women and subaltern people. Black women's resistance practices entail passion, rage, bravery, and hope as well as political efforts to achieve social and racial justice. Love is at the heart of black women's struggles and politics, intimately tied to their revolutionary visions of human freedom. Given that emotions are shared ways of life that bring together the historical and contemporary experiences of political subjects (Portwood-Stacer, 2013), expressions of love and anger through struggles are examples of the intertwining of the personal and the political in black women's activism.

Afro-Aesthetic Politics and Black Women's Activism

Under slavery, black women wore turbans to cover their heads and their braids, which mapped the roads of freedom and transported the seeds essential for the survival of the maroon communities living in the new palenques (Navarro and Rebolledo, 2017). "Protest events involve ritual practices, symbolic gestures, and shared experiences of empowering, collective effervescence which affect the move from framed emotion to action" (Flam and King, 2013: 4–5). This was the case with the March of the Turbans, which was a space for highlighting and performing the practices and gestures of African heritage and black women's aesthetics. In essence, the use of turbans was for Afro-Colombians a display of beauty. Arriving in Bogotá wearing turbans and escorted by the Maroon Guard (the group of young men that manages internal conflict and protects the community from outside threats) was a powerful symbol of black aesthetics and resistance. Wearing turbans together reflects sociability and solidarity (Navarro and Arbolledo, 2017) and symbolizes a subversive narrative counter to Western hegemonic imaginaries of beauty. It is part of the Afro-aesthetic politics that connects

Afro-Colombian women to the African diaspora's legacy around the world. Wearing turbans contributes to feminine confidence and the reimagination of political freedom.

Conclusions

Black women's struggles make visible the social costs and negative impacts of a gendered and racialized commodification of land and the devaluation of black women's bodies. This commodification is a response to a systematic destruction of collective forms of living that impacts ethno-racial communities unequally because it is combined with a historical rejection of blackness, collective rights, and the knowledge production of black people that supports the political economy of racism and the rationalities of racialized capitalism (Leong, 2013). Extractivism in the context of global capitalism is a racist mode of regulation, control, and governance of the social lives, bodies, and cultural practices of members of Colombia's ethno-racial communities. Black feminism holds that the personal is political because black women's bodies and everyday life experiences are situated in historical contexts of marginalization and exclusion and of resistance and struggle (Combahee River Collective, 2014). Black/decolonial feminism opens up new possibilities for understanding black women and subaltern people from their historical and geopolitical locations. It is a tool for rethinking the world and challenging power relations, racial capitalism, extractivism, racism, patriarchy, sexism, violence, and classism. It is a political commitment and an insurgent mode of acting, writing, thinking, and producing knowledge. It questions the legitimacy of neocolonial/modern power relations controlled by transnational corporations, state-neoliberal policies of exclusion, and racialized capitalism that promote the denaturalization of nature and the dehumanization of the Other. Black women's passion, anger, courage, love, and hope are mechanisms for producing alternative practices of liberation and feminist Afro-epistemologies providing Afro-Colombian communities with meaning and a sense of belonging to African diaspora culture.

Notes

1. This chapter is a revised version of an article that appeared in *Latin American Perspectives* in 2019 (46 [2]: 217-234). The Ministry of the Interior was emblematic because it housed the Ethnic Affairs Office and the Observatory of Racial Discrimination.
2. http://mujeresnegrascaminan.com/movilizacion/comunicados/.

3. Márquez received the 2015 National Human Rights Award and the 2018 Goldman Prize for South and Central America. Both the interview and the symposium excerpts quoted are my translations from the original Spanish.

4. Law 70 recognized Afro-Colombians as a distinct ethnic group and provided a legal foundation for the defense of Afro-Colombian territorial rights. Its purpose was "to establish mechanisms for protecting the cultural identity and rights of the black communities of Colombia as an ethnic group and to foster their economic and social development" (Chapter 1).

5. Africans who escaped slavery in the Americas and formed independent settlements and their descendants.

6. Soweto was founded by university students in Pereira (Pardo, 2008).

7. The collective work of black organizations contributed to the breakdown of the long-standing project of concealing ethno-racial diversity in the country (see Valderrama, 2014; Agudelo, 2005; Escobar, 2008; Grueso et al., 2003; Paschel, 2016; Lao-Montes, 2009).

8. Since its founding in 1993, PCN has been struggling for the defense of black collective territories, the protection and control of natural resources, and the strengthening of black culture and identity in the Pacific region.

9. For many of them mining is simply a traditional means to supply some basics, but some practice it as a means to accumulate profit (Bernasconi, 2014).

10. A juridical mechanism through which members of Colombian society demand the protection of fundamental rights that are being infringed upon by institutions or persons with a certain level of power.

References

Agudelo, Carlos E.
2005 *Retos del multiculturalismo en Colombia: Política, inclusión y exclusión de poblaciones negras.* Bogotá: La Carreta Editores/ICANH.

Alimonda, Héctor
2011 "La colonialidad de la naturaleza: una aproximación a la ecología política latinoamericana," pp. 21–58 in Héctor Alimonda (ed.), *La naturaleza colonizada: Ecología política y minería en América Latina.* Buenos Aires: CLACSO.

Ararat, Lisifrey, Eduard Mina, Axel Rojas, Ana Mara Solarte, Gildardo Vanegas, Luis Armando Vargas, and Anibal Vega
2013 *La Toma: Historias de territorio, resistencia y autonomía en la cuenca del Alto Cauca.* Bogotá: Observatorio de Territorios Etnicos-Pontificia Universidad Javeriana/Consejo Comunitario Afrodescendiente del Corregimiento de La Toma.

Asher, Kiran
2004 "Texts in context: Afro-Colombian women's activism in the Pacific lowlands of Colombia." *Feminist Review* 78: 38–55.

Bbaala, Phineas
2015 "Emerging questions on the shifting Sino-Africa relations: 'win-win' or 'win-lose'?" *Africa and Development/Afrique et Développement* 40 (3): 97–119.

Bernasconi, Attilio
2014 "Afro-descendant resistance: a strategy of territorial self-determination in Colombian northern Cauca." Master's thesis, Institute of Geosciences, University of Fribourg.
Carby, Hazel
2007 "White woman listen! Black feminism and the boundaries of sisterhood," pp. 753–774 in Ann Gray, Jan Campbell, Mark Erickson, Stuart Hanson, and Helen Wood (eds.), *CCCS Selected Working Papers*. London and New York: Routledge.
Carneiro, Sueli
2001 "Ennegrecer el feminismo." http://www.mujeresdelsur.org/portal/images/descargas/ennegrecer%20el%20feminismo_sueli%20carneiro.pdf.
Centro de Estudios Interculturales
2013 "Análisis de la posesión territorial y situaciones de tensión interétnica e intercultural en el departamento del Cauca." *Universidad Javeriana*. https://www.javerianacali.edu.co/sites/ujc/files/node/field-documents/field_document_file/analisis_posesion_territorial_-tensiones_interetnicas_e_interculturales_en_el_cauca_1.pdf.
Clayton, Richard
2016 "Might the keys to peace open the doors to extractivism? Reflections on Colombia's post-conflict extractive economy," pp. 444–470 in Fredy Cante and Hartmut Quehl (eds.), *Handbook of Research on Transitional Justice and Peace Building in Turbulent Regions*. Hershey, PA: IGI Global.
Collins, Patricia Hill
2000a "Gender, black feminism, and black political economy." *Annals of the American Academy of Political and Social Science* 568 (1): 41–53.
2000b *Black Feminist Thought: Knowledge, Consciousness, and the Politics of Empowerment*. 2d edition. New York and London: Routledge.
2005 "Black women and motherhood," pp. 149–159 in S. Hardy and C. Wiedmer (eds.), *Motherhood and Space*. New York: Palgrave Macmillan.
Combahee River Collective
2014 "A black feminist statement." *Women's Studies Quarterly* 42 (3/4): 271–280.
Crenshaw, Kimberle
1991 "Mapping the margins: intersectionality, identity politics, and violence against women of color." *Stanford Law Review* 43: 1241–1299.
Escobar, Arturo
2008 *Territories of Difference: Place, Movements, Life*, Redes. Durham, NC: Duke University Press.
2015 "Territorios de diferencia: la ontología política de los 'derechos al territorio.'" *Cuadernos de Antropología Social* 41: 25–38.
Fabricant, Nicole, and Nancy Postero
2013 "Contested bodies, contested states: performance, emotions, and new forms of regional governance in Santa Cruz, Bolivia." *Journal of Latin American and Caribbean Anthropology* 18 (2): 187–121.
Farthing, Linda, and Benjamin Kohl
2013 "Mobilizing memory: Bolivia's enduring social movements." *Social Movement Studies* 12: 361–376.

Flam, Helena
2005 "Emotions map: a research agenda," pp. 19–40 in Helena Flam and Debra King (eds.), *Emotions and Social Movements*. London and New York: Routledge.
Flam, Helena, and Debra King (eds.)
2005 *Emotions and Social Movements*. London and New York: Routledge.
Fundación del Sinú, Fundación Punta de Lanza, and Fundación Oscar Arnulfo Romero
1985 *Historia gráfica de la lucha por la tierra en la Costa Atlántica*. Monteria, Colombia: Fundación Punta de Lanza/Fundación Oscar Arnulfo Romero.
Grueso, Libia, Carlos Rosero, and Arturo Escobar
2003 "The process of black community organizing in the Southern Pacific coast region of Colombia," pp. 430–477 in M. C. Gutmann, F. V. Rodríguez, L. Stephen, and P. Zavella (eds.), *Perspectives on Las Américas: A Reader in Culture, History, and Representation*. Malden, MA: Wiley-Blackwell.
Grueso, Libia, and Leyla Andrea Arroyo
2002 "Women and the defence of place in Colombian black movement struggles." *Development* 45 (1): 60–67.
Harvey, David
2007 *A Brief History of Neoliberalism*. New York and London: Oxford University Press.
Hernández-Reyes, Castriela
2010 "Convergencias y divergencias en las agendas políticas de las organizaciones afro-colombianas Movimiento Nacional Cimarrón, Proceso de Comunidades Negras (PCN) y Conferencia Nacional de Organizaciones Afrocolombianas (CNOA)." B.A. thesis, Universidad Distrital Francisco José de Caldas.
2018 "Aproximaciones al sistema de sexo/género en la Nueva Granada en los siglos XVIII y XIX," pp. 29–75 in Aurora Vergara-Figueroa and Carmen Cosme Puntiel (eds.), *Demando mi libertad: Mujeres negras y sus estrategias de resistencia en la Nueva Granada, Venezuela y Cuba, 1700–1800*. Cali: Universidad Icesi/El Centro de Estudios Afrodiaspóricos.
hooks, bell
1992 *Black Looks: Race and Representation*. Boston: South End Press.
Jasper, James
1998 "The emotions of protest: affective and reactive emotions in and around social movements." *Sociological Forum* 13: 397–424.
Kohl, Benjamin, and Linda Farthing
2012 "Material constraints to popular imaginaries: the extractive economy and resource nationalism in Bolivia." *Political Geography* 31 (4): 225–235.
Lao-Montes, Agustin
2009 "Cartografias del campo politico afrodescendiente en América Latina." *Universitas Humanística* (Bogotá) 38 (68): 207–245.
Leong, Nancy
2013 "Racial capitalism." *Harvard Law Review* 126: 2151–2227.

Levien, Michael
2012 "The land question: special economic zones and the political economy of dispossession in India." *Journal of Peasant Studies* 39: 933–969.
Lugones, María
2008 "Colonialidad y género: hacia un feminismo descolonial," pp. 13–54 in Walter Mignolo (ed.), *Género y descolonialidad.* Buenos Aires: Ediciones del Signo.
2010 "Toward a decolonial feminism." *Hypatia* 25: 742–759.
Maldonado-Torres, Nelson
2011 "Thinking through the decolonial turn: post-continental interventions in theory, philosophy, and critique, an introduction." *Transmodernity: Journal of Peripheral Cultural Production of the Luso-Hispanic World* 1 (2).
2016 "Outline of ten theses on coloniality and decoloniality." *Frantz Fanon Foundation.* http://frantzfanonfoundation-fondationfrantzfanon. com/article2360. Html.
May, Vivian M.
2015 *Pursuing Intersectionality: Unsettling Dominant Imaginaries.* New York: Routledge.
Melamed, Jodi
2011 *Represent and Destroy: Rationalizing Violence in the New Racial Capitalism.* Minneapolis: University of Minnesota Press.
2015 "Racial capitalism." *Critical Ethnic Studies* 1 (1): 76–85.
Motta, Sara C.
2011 "Social movements and/in the postcolonial: dispossession, development and resistance in the Global South," pp. 1–31 in S. C. Motta and A. G. Nilsen (eds.), *Social Movements in the Global South.* London: Palgrave Macmillan.
2013 "'We are the ones we have been waiting for': the feminization of resistance in Venezuela." *Latin American Perspectives* 40 (4): 35–54.
Navarro, Erelis, and Angelica Rebolledo
2017 *Los turbantes y peinados Afrocolombianos: Una alternativa pedagógica.* n.p.
Pardo, Mauricio
2008 "Entre la autonomía y la institucionalización: dilemas del movimiento negro colombiano." *Journal of Latin American and Caribbean Anthropology* 7 (2): 60–84.
Paschel, Tianna S.
2016 *Becoming Black Political Subjects: Movements and Ethno-Racial Rights in Colombia and Brazil.* Princeton: Princeton University Press.
Perreault, Tom
2015 "Performing participation: mining, power, and the limits of public consultation in Bolivia." *Journal of Latin American and Caribbean Anthropology* 20: 433–451.
Picq, Manuela
2014 "Self-determination as anti-extractivism: how indigenous resistance challenges world politics," pp. 26–33 in Marc Woons (ed.), *Restoring Indigenous Self-Determination: Theoretical and Practical Approaches.* Bristol, UK: E-International Relations.

Portwood-Stacer, Laura
2013 *Lifestyle Politics and Radical Activism.* New York: Bloomsbury Publishing USA.

Pulido, Laura
2016 "Flint, environmental racism, and racial capitalism." *Capitalism, Nature, Socialism* 27 (3): 1–16.
2017 "Geographies of race and ethnicity II: Environmental racism, racial capitalism and state-sanctioned violence." *Progress in Human Geography* 41: 524–533.

Ramírez, María Clemencia
2019 "Militarism on the Colombian periphery in the context of illegality, counter-insurgency, and the postconflict." *Current Anthropology* 60 (suppl. 19): 134–147.

Robinson, Cedric J.
2000 *Black Marxism: The Making of the Black Radical Tradition.* Chapel Hill: University of North Carolina Press.

Roth, Benita
2003 "Second-wave black feminism in the African diaspora: news from new scholarship." *Agenda: Empowering Women for Gender Equity*, no. 58: 46–58.

Scott, James
2012 *Decoding Subaltern Politics: Ideology, Disguise, and Resistance in Agrarian Politics.* London: Routledge.

Seppälä, Tiina
2016 "Feminizing resistance, decolonizing solidarity: contesting neoliberal development in the Global South." *Journal of Resistance Studies* 2 (1): 12–47.

Valderrama, Carlos Alberto
2014 "Black politics of folklore: expanding the sites and forms of politics in Colombia." Master's thesis, University of Massachusetts, Amherst.

Vázquez, Rolando
2012 "Towards a decolonial critique of modernity: *buen vivir*, relationality and the task of listening." *Capital, Poverty, Development, Denktraditionen im Dialog: Studien zur Befreiung und Interkulturalität* 33: 241–252.

Vélez-Torres, Irene
2014 "Governmental extractivism in Colombia: legislation, securitization and the local settings of mining control." *Third World Thematics* 1 (2): 235–248.

Verdad Abierta
2009 "El Naya." https://verdadabierta.com/los-cuatro-dias-que-estremecieron-el-naya/.

Wade, Peter
1996 "Identidad y etnicidad," in Arturo Escobar and Álvaro Pedrosa (eds.), *Pacífico ¿desarrollo o diversidad? Estado, capital y movimientos sociales en el Pacífico Colombiano*. Bogotá: CEREC/ ECOFONDO.

Index

About the Contributors

Luis Fernando Angosto-Ferrández is a senior lecturer in anthropology, Spanish and Latin American studies at the University of Sydney. He is the author of *Venezuela Reframed* (2015), the editor of *Democracy, Revolution and Geopolitics in Latin America* (2013), and the co-editor of *The Politics of Identity in Latin American Censuses* (2016) and *Symbolism and Politics* (2020).

Anthony Bebbington is Milton P. and Alice C. Higgins Professor of Environment and Society in the Graduate School of Geography at Clark University, and professorial research fellow at the University of Manchester, UK. Recent co-authored publications include *Governing Extractive Industries: Politics, Histories, Ideas* (2018), *Subterranean Struggles: New Dynamics of Mining, Oil and Gas in Latin America* (2013), and *Mega-Projects, Contentious Action, and Policy Change in Latin America* (2018, a special issue of *European Review of Latin American and Caribbean Studies*).

Steve Ellner is a retired professor of economic history at the Universidad de Oriente and a current associate managing editor of *Latin American Perspectives*. He is author and editor of over a dozen academic books and scores of journal articles and book chapters on Latin American politics, including *Rethinking Venezuelan Politics: Class, Conflict and the Chávez Phenomenon* (2008) and (editor) *Latin America's Pink Tide: Breakthroughs and Shortcomings* (2020). He has published on the Op Ed Page of the *New York Times* and *Los Angeles Times* and is a frequent contributor to *NACLA: Report on the Americas*.

Benjamin Fash is PhD candidate at Clark University and co-founder of Bolomchon, a cultural center in Chiapas. Recent publications include *Territorios en riesgo II: Minería, generación de energía eléctrica e hidrocarburos en Honduras* (2019); "Geografías del extractivismo depredador en Honduras" in *Grandes transacciones de tierra en América Latina: sus efectos sociales y ambientales* (2019); and (co-author) "Conflicts over Extractivist Policy and the Forest Frontier in Central America," *European Review of Latin American and Caribbean Studies* (2018).

Jorge García-Arias teaches in the Department of Economics, University of Leon (Spain) and Department of Development Studies, University of London. He co-authored "Philanthrocapitalism as a Neoliberal (development agenda) Artefact," *Globalizations* (2019); "Labor supply: Towards the Construction of an Alternative Conception from post-Keynesian and Institutional Economics," *Journal of Post Keynesian Economics* (2017); and "International Financialisation and the Systemic Approach to International Financing for Development," *Global Policy* (2015).

Castriela Esther Hernández Reyes is a black activist and scholar, and a doctoral candidate of anthropology at the University of Massachusetts Amherst. She is co-author of "Interrogando la gramática racial de la blanquitud: Hacia una analítica del blanqueamiento en el orden racial colombiano (*Latin American Research Review*, 2020) and author of "Aproximaciones al sistema de sexo/género en la Nueva Granada en los siglos XVIII y XIX" in *Demando mi libertad: Mujeres negras y sus estrategias de resistencia en la Nueva Granada, Venezuela y Cuba, 1700–1800* (2018).

Amalia Leguizamón is an assistant professor in the Department of Sociology at the Stone Center for Latin American Studies at Tulane University. Her publications have appeared in the *Journal of Peasant Studies*, *Geoforum*, *Latin American Perspectives*, and the *Journal of Agrarian Change*. She is the author of *Seeds of Power: Environmental Injustice and Genetically Modified Soybeans in Argentina* (2020).

Alfredo Macías Vázquez is associate professor of economics at the University of León, Spain. He is co-author of "Between 'Neodevelopmentalism' and 'Postdevelopmentalism': Towards a Theory of a Dispersed Knowledge Economy in Ecuador," *Canadian Journal of Development Studies* (2016); "Knowledge Economy and the Commons: A Theoretical and Political Approach to Post-Neoliberal Common Governance," *Review of Radical Political Economics* (2016); and "Collective Action and Symbolic Capital in the Artisanal Fisheries: An Analysis of the Local Food Systems of reloncaví estuary (Los Lagos), Chile," *Culture and History* (2016).

Juan Carlos Monedero is full professor at the Complutense University in Madrid. He is the author of over a dozen books dealing with different political topics, including *Nuevos disfraces del Leviatán: El papel del estado en la globalización neoliberal* (2018). He is also the author of "Postdemocracy, postpolitics, and populism fresh political thinking and Podemos" in *Latin American Perspectives* (2020).

María J. Paz is currently lecturer and researcher at the Complutense University in Madrid, Spain. She is the co-author of *Alternativas al neoliberalismo en América Latina? Las políticas económicas en Venezuela, Brasil, Uruguay, Bolivia y Ecuador* (2013); *Ajuste y salario. Las consecuencias del neoliberalismo en América Latina y Estados Unidos* (2009); and *Centroamérica encendida. Reformas y transnacionales españolas en el sector eléctrico* (2005). She has published in the journals *Energy Policy*, *Development and Change*, *Public Management Review*, and *Latin American Perspectives.*

Juan M. Ramírez-Cendrero is economics professor in the Department of Applied Economy and History at Complutense University in Madrid. He has published in *Capitalism, Nature, Socialism*, *Journal of Rural Studies*, *Resources Policy*, and *Energy Policy.*

John Rogan is professor of geography at Clark University. His co-authored journal articles have appeared in *Applied Geography*, *International Journal of Applied Geospatial Research*, *ISPRS Journal of Photogrammetry and Remote Sensing*, *GIScience & Remote Sensing*, and *International Journal of Remote Sensing.*

Kyla Sankey teaches in the School of Business and Management at Queen Mary, University of London. Her research focuses on mining and natural resource extraction, development, peasant livelihoods, and social movements in Colombia and Latin America. Among her publications are two articles in *Jacobin*.

Darcy Tetreault is a professor in the Department of Development Studies at the *Universidad Autónoma de Zacatecas* in Mexico. Recent publications include "The New Extractivism in Mexico: Rent Redistribution and Resistance to Mining and Petroleum Activities," *World Development*, 2020; "Resistance to Canadian Mining Projects in Mexico: Lessons from the Lifecycle of the San Xavier Mine in San Luis Potosí," *Journal of Political Ecology*, 2019; and (co-editor) *Social Environmental Conflicts in Mexico: Resistance to Dispossession and Alternatives from Below* (2018).

Emma Miriam Yin-Hang To is a PhD candidate in the Department of Political Economy at the University of Sydney. She has taught political economy, government and international relations and sociology at the University of Sydney and Western Sydney University. She has also worked as a researcher for trade unions and NGOs in Australia.

Zaraí Toledo Orozco is a PhD candidate in political science at the University of British Columbia. Her dissertation is titled "(Under)mining State Authority: The Politics of Informal Gold Mining in Bolivia and Peru (2000–2017)." She is co-author of "Local's attitudes toward artisanal mining and large-scale mining: A case study from Tambogrande, Peru" in *The Extractive Industries and Society* (2018).

Teresa A. Velásquez is an associate professor of anthropology at California State University, San Bernardino. Her research has been published in *Latin American Perspectives*, *Latin American and Caribbean Ethnic Studies Journal*, and *Resources Policy*. She is currently writing a book about anti-mining activism titled "Pachamama politics: Defending water as life in the southern Ecuadorian Andes."

LATIN AMERICAN PERSPECTIVES IN THE CLASSROOM

Series Editor: Ronald H. Chilcote

Urban Latin America
edited by Tom Angotti
Rereading Women in Latin America and the Caribbean: The Political Economy of Gender
edited by Jennifer Abbassi and Sheryl L. Lutjens
Twentieth-Century Latin American Revolutions
by Marc Becker
Development in Theory and Practice: Latin American Perspectives
edited by Ronald H. Chilcote
Latin American Extractivism: Dependency, Resource Nationalism and Resistance in Broad Perspective
edited by Steve Ellner
Latin America's Pink Tide: Breakthroughs and Shortcomings
edited by Steve Ellner
Latin America's Radical Left: Challenges and Complexities of Political Power in the Twenty-first Century
edited by Steve Ellner
Venezuela: Hugo Chávez and the Decline of an "Exceptional Democracy"
edited by Steve Ellner and Miguel Tinker Salas
Contemporary Latin American Social and Political Thought: An Anthology
edited by Iván Márquez
Mayan Lives, Mayan Utopias: The Indigenous Peoples of Chiapas and the Zapatista Rebellion
edited by Jan Rus, Rosalva Aída Hernández, and Shannan L. Mattiace
The United States and Cuba: From Closest Enemies to Distant Friends
by Francisco López Segrera
Rethinking Latin American Social Movements: Radical Action from Below
edited by Richard Stahler-Sholk, Harry E. Vanden, and Marc Becker
Memory, Truth, and Justice in Contemporary Latin America
Edited by Roberta Villalón
Latin American Social Movements in the Twenty-first Century: Resistance, Power, and Democracy
edited by Richard Stahler-Sholk, Harry E. Vanden, and Glen David Kuecker
Transnational Latina/o Communities: Politics, Processes, and Cultures
edited by Carlos G. Vélez-Ibáñez and Anna Sampaio, with Manolo González-Estay
The Cold War and Latin American Studies
by Ronald H. Chilcote

www.ingramcontent.com/pod-product-compliance
Ingram Content Group UK Ltd.
Pitfield, Milton Keynes, MK11 3LW, UK
UKHW012036150926
475560UK00001B/36

9 781538 141557